The Monogram Checklist

The Monogram Checklist
The Films of Monogram Pictures Corporation, 1931–1952

TED OKUDA

McFarland & Company, Inc., Publishers
Jefferson, North Carolina, and London

Library of Congress Cataloguing-in-Publication Data

Okuda, Ted, 1953–
 The monogram checklist.

 Includes indexes.
 1. Monogram Pictures Corporation — Catalogs.
 2. Moving-pictures — United States — Catalogs. I. Title.
 PN1999.M6038   1987   016.79143'75   86-43089

 ISBN 0-89950-286-5 (acid-free natural paper)

Printed in the United States of America.

McFarland   Box 611   Jefferson NC 28640

For my pal Ed Watz

ACKNOWLEDGMENTS

My sincere thanks to the following individuals and organizations for their help with this project: John Aben, Val Almendarez of The National Film Information Society, Dick Andersen, Bob Andrews, Eddie Brandt's Saturday Matinee, Erwin Dumbrille, the late Carol Epstein, Film Favorites, Alex Gordon, Mike Hawks of Larry Edmunds Bookstore, Roy Kinnard, Paula Klaw and Ira Kramer of Movie Star News, Cody Morgan, James Neibaur, Jerry Ohlinger, Henry and Karen Ottinger, Gregory and Mary Revak, Stephen Sally, Joe Savage, Ralph Schiller, Veto Stasiunaitis, Maurice Terenzio, Edward Watz, Tom White, and the staff of the Margaret Herrick Library of the Academy of Motion Picture Arts and Sciences.

A special debt of gratitude to Scott MacGillivray, who reviewed the manuscript of this book and made valuable suggestions, corrections, and contributions. Thanks for the much-needed help, Scott!

TABLE OF CONTENTS

Acknowledgments   vii

Preface   xi

Historical Overview   1

Feature Films
1931	7
1932	13
1933	25
1934	36
1935	50
1936	57
1937	57
1938	64
1939	78
1940	92
1941	113
1942	133
1943	153
1944	170
1945	190
1946	206
1947	227
1948	241
1949	258
1950	273
1951	288
1952	304

Short Subjects
1933/34	321
1941	321

Table of Contents

1947   322
1950   322

Film Title Index   323
Name Index   336

PREFACE

Throughout the 1930s, 1940s and 1950s, several independent movie production companies (referred to as "poverty row" studios) turned out hundreds of "B" pictures—low-budget feature films that were specifically designed to play the bottom half of double bills. This volume focuses on the output of one of these independents: Monogram Pictures Corporation.

This book does not pretend to be an in-depth examination of B movies in general or Monogram in particular; rather, this is intended to be a handy reference guide to a body of work that is still largely overlooked, despite the current number of specialized books on film history.

In doing research for this project, my biggest headache was the contradictory data found in the industry trade journals, supposedly the "official" sources for information about studio product; it was not uncommon to find multiple running times and release dates for a single title. Given this situation, I have tried to furnish the reader with the most accurate data possible.

HISTORICAL OVERVIEW

If mentioned at all by film historians, the Monogram product is usually dismissed in a cursory manner--which is understandable, since much of their output was cheap, vulgar, inept, and ultimately forgettable. But for two decades, the studio managed to thrive by providing exhibitors with a steady supply of "bread and butter" pictures (westerns, comedies, melodramas), many produced so inexpensively that they couldn't help turning a profit. Though hardly the best of the independent film companies, Monogram still turned out quite a number of pictures that were very entertaining, if conspicuously lacking in artistic merit. More so than many other poverty row operations, Monogram specialized in "series" fare, including the extremely popular Bowery Boys and Charlie Chan films.

Monogram originated from a small independent company called Rayart Productions, formed in the summer of 1924 and named after its founder, W. Ray Johnston. Westerns, melodramas and serials were released under the Rayart banner until 1929, although the company had become Syndicate Film Exchange by 1928. When talkies arrived, Syndicate turned out five pictures under their Continental Talking Pictures label (1929-1930).

Syndicate became Monogram Pictures in 1931. Johnston, who served as president, placed Trem Carr, who had produced some of the Continental Talking Pictures releases, in charge of production.

The early Monogram releases were largely indistinguishable from what was being offered by other independents of the era (Chesterfield, Ambassador-Conn, Liberty, Mascot); the majority of the efforts were cheaply made westerns and melodramas. Several productions cut budgetary corners by relying on stock footage from other pic-

1

THE
FASTEST GROWING COMPANY
IN THE INDUSTRY

W. RAY JOHNSTON
President

TREM CARR
Executive Director

STEVE BROIDY
Sales Manager

NORTON V. RITCHEY
Foreign Sales Manager

THE good will of thousands of exhibitors throughout the world is Monogram's most prized possession. Behind this intangible asset stands a deeply-rooted policy of fair dealing, and an organization dedicated to the observance of honesty in its exhibitor relations.

Ten years of successful operation have had as their basis a continuing sales policy that has never been altered. In its essentials, it is the policy of the good neighbor; of understanding, of mutual respect and appreciation of the other man's problems. To this realistic program Monogram owes its well established and progressive position today.

To W. Ray Johnston and Trem Carr, founders of the organization, Monogram is deeply indebted. A long-range policy, instituted by them a decade ago, has guided the organization through the storms of a grave economic depression to sound financial security. Monogram's program of features has, year by year, shown a steady and mounting improvement in every department and its financial history reflects great credit on their wisdom.

With Steve Broidy at the sales helm and Norton V. Ritchey guiding the foreign distribution, every indication is present that the next decade will raise to even greater heights the standards of which we today are justly proud.

A 1942 trade ad heralding Monogram's tenth anniversary. Pictured, top to bottom: founder and president W. Ray Johnston, executive director Trem Carr, sales manager Steve Broidy and foreign sales manager Norton V. Ritchey.

tures; **Law of the Sea** (1932) and **Jungle Bride** (1933) used footage from silent features (titles unknown) for the bigger action sequences, while **The Girl from Calgary**

(1932) lifted elaborate musical numbers from **The Great Gabbo** (Sono Art-World Wide, 1930).

Monogram's most notable releases from this period include **The Thirteenth Guest** (1932), an interesting mystery-thriller starring Ginger Rogers; a series of John Wayne westerns produced by Lone Star Productions; and adaptations of classic novels: **Oliver Twist** (1933), **Black Beauty** (1933) and **Jane Eyre** (1934).

In 1935 Herbert J. Yates, owner of Consolidated Film Industries (a processing laboratory that also produced optical effects), merged with Monogram and Nat Levine's Mascot Pictures to create Republic Productions, Inc., which subsequently became Republic Pictures Corporation. (Republic also took over the independent companies Majestic Pictures and Liberty Pictures.) The Monogram label was dropped, and Republic incorporated their exchanges as distribution outlets; W. Ray Johnston and Trem Carr became corporate officials in the new company.

But a year later, friction within the Republic organization resulted in Johnston and Carr withdrawing from the operation (it has been claimed that Carr frequently clashed with Yates, who was Republic's chief stockholder). In November 1936 it was indicated in the industry trade journals that Johnston and Carr would revive Monogram. By the summer of 1937 they had succeeded in resuming operations, with Johnston again serving as president and Carr as executive director in charge of production. Adopting a more ambitious production schedule, the number of annual releases was increased to an average of 40 feature films a year, as opposed to the 20-30 a year prior to the Republic merger.

A concentrated effort was made to offer "series" pictures to exhibitors, and it was in this field that Monogram excelled. Child stars Jackie Moran and Marcia Mae Jones were paired for a series of juvenile adventures, Kane Richmond played "The Shadow," Frankie Darro starred in a series of actioners that frequently teamed him with black comedian Mantan Moreland, and Duncan Renaldo and Gilbert Roland were seen at various times as "The Cisco Kid." Raymond Walburn played "Henry Latham" in a series of family comedies. "The Teen Agers"

3

ON MONOGRAM'S 1942-43 PRODUCER ROSTER

LINDSLEY PARSONS

SAM KATZMAN

GEORGE W. WEEKS

SCOTT R. DUNLAP

EDWARD FINNEY

A. W. HACKEL

FRANKLIN and MAURICE KING

series revolved around the musical-comedy antics of its youthful stars: Freddie Stewart, June Preisser, Noel Neill, Frankie Darro and Warren Mills. Bomba the Jungle Boy was Monogram's low-rent version of Tarzan; Johnny Sheffield, who was seen as "Boy" in several of the Tarzan pictures, portrayed the adolescent vine-swinger. Comic strips were the inspiration for a few Monogram series, among them Tailspin Tommy, Maggie and Jiggs ("Bringing Up Father"), Snuffy Smith and Joe Palooka.

Boris Karloff (and later, Keye Luke) starred as "Mr. Wong," Monogram's answer to 20th Century-Fox's Charlie Chan mysteries. The Charlie Chan character eventually became the property of Monogram, with Sidney Toler and, later, Roland Winters essaying the role of the Chinese criminologist.

Westerns were a mainstay of the independents, and Monogram offered series featuring Johnny Mack Brown, Tex Ritter, Jack Randall, Tom Keene, Jimmy Wakely, Whip Wilson, The Range Busters (played in most of the entries by Ray "Crash" Corrigan, John "Dusty" King and Max "Alibi" Terhune), the Rough Riders (Buck Jones, Tim McCoy, Raymond Hatton) and The Trail Blazers (Ken Maynard, Hoot Gibson, Bob Steele).

Monogram's most durable series was their Bowery Boys comedies, which originated from another Monogram series, the East Side Kids (which, in turn, was inspired by the Dead End Kids). Whatever their monicker, these pictures provided steady employment for series regulars Leo Gorcey and Huntz Hall.

Harry Langdon, Kay Francis and Bela Lugosi were among the distinguished performers whose failing careers reduced them to appearing in cheap Monogram programmers.

In 1945 Steve Broidy, formerly the general sales manager, was elected president of Monogram, with W. Ray Johnston becoming chairman of the board. In November 1946, Allied Artists Productions, Inc., was formed as a wholly owned subsidiary of Monogram to

Opposite: Monogram's 1942/43 producer roster.

handle exclusively the production of higher-budgeted films. It was the company's intention to produce and distribute high-budget pictures under the Allied Artists banner, while their usual output of low-budget programmers would carry the Monogram label. Although Allied Artists was treated as a separate entity at first, the quality and content of the Allied output soon became similar to the Monogram product, so much so that eventually there was no real difference between the two.

But by 1953 Monogram wanted to change its image as a lowly B picture unit, so the corporate name was changed from Monogram Pictures Corporation to Allied Artists Pictures Corporation, even though they would still turn out a great deal of low-budget fare that was hardly in keeping with a company that desperately wanted more prestige.

Allied Artists would continue to produce films until the mid-1960s, at which time they moved away from actual production and concentrated on the distribution activities of their domestic sales offices and television sales subsidiary (originally christened Interstate Television Corporation in 1951, it was later called Allied Artists Television Corporation).

In the early 1970s Allied Artists again resumed film production and was responsible for efforts like **Cabaret** (1972) and **The Man Who Would Be King** (1975) before going bankrupt in the late 1970s.

On the whole, one would be hard-pressed to defend the Monogram output; most were dull, shoddy efforts produced by those whose sole interest was to obtain a fast buck. But as inept as the majority of their product was, Monogram apparently appealed to their target audiences, as they succeeded where so many other independents had failed. And even if most of their films don't deserve a second (or even a first) look, they should be acknowledged and catalogued, which is the primary reason for this book.

FEATURE FILMS

This listing covers Monogram product from 1931 up to December 1952. From the beginning of 1953 their films were released as Allied Artists Productions; although they were copyrighted by Monogram, the pictures were advertised and distributed under the Allied Artists banner. Monogram didn't legally change their corporate name to Allied Artists Pictures Corporation until November 21, 1953.

Only those films released under the Monogram Pictures banner are covered. Allied Artists releases—particularly those made prior to 1952 (such as **The Babe Ruth Story, Smart Woman, Southside 1-1000, Short Grass** and **Hiawatha**)—have not been included. Also omitted is **The Adventures of Chico** (1938), a Woodward production and release that some sources have credited to Monogram.

The films are listed in order of release; those films that were released on the same day are listed alphabetically.

1931

1. Ships of Hate (drama) Directed by John P. McCarthy. Produced by Trem Carr. Story and screenplay by Wellyn Totman.

Cast: Lloyd Hughes, Dorothy Sebastian, Charles Middleton, Lloyd Whitlock, Ted Adams, Constantine Romanoff, Gordon DeMain, Jean Mason.

A cruel sea captain (Charles Middleton) oversees a rough crew.

Running time: 63 minutes. Release date: June 15, 1931.

7

Lloyd Hughes tries to disarm Charles Middleton as Dorothy Sebastian (right) looks appropriately distressed in "Ships of Hate" (1931), Monogram Pictures' first release.

2. Dugan of the Badlands (western) Directed by Robert N. Bradbury. Produced by Trem Carr. Story and screenplay by Robert N. Bradbury.

Cast: Bill Cody, Andy Shuford, Blanche Mehaffey, Ethan Laidlaw, Julian Rivero, Earl Dwire, John Elliott.

Bill Dugan (Bill Cody) befriends an orphaned boy (Andy Shuford); the pair help a sheriff (John Elliott) bring his crooked deputy (Ethan Laidlaw) to justice.

Running time: 66 minutes. Release date: June 24, 1931.

3. Partners of the Trail (western) Directed by Wallace Fox. Produced by Trem Carr. Screenplay by George Arthur Durlam. Story by Will Beale.

Cast: Tom Tyler, Betty Mack, Reginald Sheffield,

Lafe McKee, Marguerite McWade, Horace B. Carpenter, Pat Rooney.

After a man kills his wife's lover, his prairie pal is convicted of the crime; he escapes and tries to prove his innocence.

Running time: 63 minutes. Release date: July 22, 1931.

4. Mother and Son (drama) Directed by John P. McCarthy. Produced by Trem Carr. Story and screenplay by Wellyn Totman.

Cast: Clara Kimball Young, Bruce Warren, G.D. Wood (Gordon DeMain), Mildred Golden, John Elliott.

After going broke in the stock market, Faro Lil (Clara Kimball Young) returns to her former trade—as a gambling house keeper—against the wishes of her son (Bruce Warren).

Running time: 60 minutes. Release date: August 1, 1931.

5. The Montana Kid (western) Directed by Harry Fraser. Produced by Trem Carr. Screenplay by George Arthur Durlam. Story by Harry Fraser.

Cast: Bill Cody, Doris Hill, Andy Shuford, William L. Thorne, G.D. Wood (Gordon DeMain), John Elliott, Paul Panzer.

A cowboy (Bill Cody) tries to save things for a boy (Andy Shuford) whose father (John Elliott) was shot down after being framed into signing over the deed to his ranch to a gambling saloon proprietor (William L. Thorne).

Running time: 60 min. Release date: Aug. 10, 1931.

6. The Man from Death Valley (western) Directed by Lloyd Nosler. Screenplay by George Arthur Durlam. Story by Lloyd Nosler and George Arthur Durlam.

Cast: Tom Tyler, Betty Mack, John Oscar, Si Jenks, Gino Corrado, Stanley Blystone, Hank Bell.

A cowboy (Tom Tyler) rides into town to see his girl (Betty Mack) after a long absence, only to find her engaged to the local sheriff, who is secretly in league with Mexican villains planning to rob the bank.

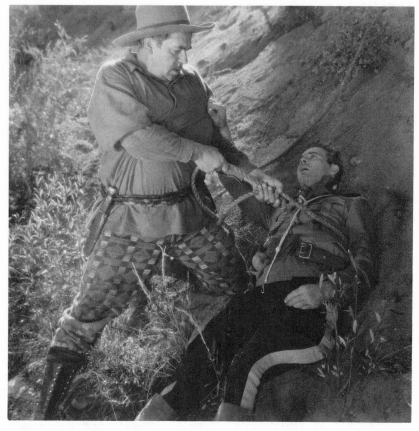

A fugitive (Noah Beery, Sr., left) saves the life of a Mountie (James Murray) in "In Line of Duty" (1931).

Running time: 62 minutes. Release date: September
9, 1931.

7. In Line of Duty (drama) Directed by Bert Glennon.
Story and screenplay by George Arthur Durlam.
Cast: Sue Carol, Noah Beery (Sr.), Francis McDonald,
James Murray, Richard Cramer, Frank Seider, Henry
Hall.
A Canadian woodsman (Noah Beery), a fugitive from
justice because of the murder of a man who wronged
him, is compelled by pity to save the life of a Royal

10

Canadian Mounted Policeman who is hunting him. The Mountie falls in love with the woodsman's daughter (Sue Carol), but despite this, intends to take the fugitive back with him.

Running time: 64 minutes. Release date: October 1, 1931.

8. Oklahoma Jim (western) Directed by Harry Fraser. Produced by Trem Carr. Screenplay by George Arthur Durlam. Story by Harry Fraser.

Cast: Bill Cody, Marion Burns, Andy Shuford, William Desmond, Si Jenks, Franklyn Farnum, John Elliott, Ed Brady, G.D. Wood (Gordon DeMain), Iron Eyes Cody, J.W. Cody, Ann Ross, Artie Ortego, White Eagle.

"Oklahoma Jim" Kirby (Bill Cody) helps a young woman (Marion Burns) save her trading post.

Running time: 53 minutes. Release date: October 10, 1931.

9. Two-Fisted Justice (western) Directed by George Arthur Durlam. Produced by Trem Carr. Story and screenplay by George Arthur Durlam.

Cast: Tom Tyler, Barbara Weeks, Bobbie Nelson, Yakima Canutt, John Elliott, G.D. Wood (Gordon DeMain), Kit Guard, William Walling, Pedro Regas, Carl DeLoue, Joe Mills, Si Jenks.

Kentucky Carson (Tom Tyler) opposes an outlaw gang threatening the postmaster (John Elliott), his daughter (Barbara Weeks) and a young boy (Bobbie Nelson) they've adopted.

Running time: 63 minutes. Release date: October 20, 1931.

10. Land of Wanted Men (western) Directed by Harry Fraser. Produced by Trem Carr. Story and screenplay by Harry Fraser.

Cast: Bill Cody, Andy Shuford, Gibson Gowland, Sheila Manners, Jack Richardson, Frank Lackteen, James Marcus.

A cowboy (Bill Cody) is made sheriff in a cattle country into which sheep have intruded.

Bill Cody (left) keeps Gibson Gowland (right) in line, while Andy Shuford and Sheila Manners look on. From "Land of Wanted Men" (1931).

Running time: 62 minutes. Release date: October 30, 1931.

11. Forgotten Women (drama) Directed by Richard Thorpe. Screenplay by Adele Buffington. Story by Wellyn Totman.

Cast: Marion Shilling, Rex Bell, Beryl Mercer, Virginia Lee Corbin, Carmelita Geraghty, Edna Murphy, Edward Earle, Jack Carlyle, Edward Kane, G.D. Wood (Gordon DeMain).

A drama set in filmland, following the triumphs and heartaches of women who try to succeed in the movie industry.

Running time: 67 minutes. Release date: December 1, 1931.

12. Galloping Thru (western) Directed by Lloyd Nosler. Produced by Trem Carr. Story and screenplay by Wellyn Totman.

Cast: Tom Tyler, Betty Mack, Al Bridge, Stanley Blystone, G.D. Wood (Gordon DeMain), John Elliott, Si Jenks, Artie Ortego.

A cowboy (Tom Tyler) arrives in town after some years of absence; after his father is murdered, he vows to avenge his death.

Running time: 58 minutes. Release date: December 5, 1931.

1932

13. Ghost City (western) Directed by Harry Fraser. Produced by Trem Carr. Screenplay by Wellyn Totman. Story by Harry Fraser.

Cast: Bill Cody, Andy Shuford, Helen Foster, Walter Miller, Kate Campbell, Charles King, Walter Shumway, Al Taylor, Jack Carlisle, Thomas Curran.

Bill Temple (Bill Cody) helps a young woman (Helen Foster) in her fight against a local badman (Walter Miller) who is trying to seize control of her mining operations.

Running time: 60 minutes. Release date: January 2, 1932.

14. Law of the Sea (drama) Directed by Otto Brower. Produced by I.E. Chadwick.

Cast: William Farnum, Rex Bell, Sally Blane, Ralph Ince, Priscilla Dean, Eve Southern, Wally Albright, Syd Saylor, Jack Clifford, Frank LaRue, Charles T. Taylor, Charles "Heine" Conklin.

A sadistic sea captain (Ralph Ince) lusts after the girlfriend (Sally Blane) of a young man (Rex Bell) whose father (William Farnum) he had blinded and cast adrift years earlier.

Running time: 61 minutes. Release date: January 20, 1932.

15. Single-Handed Sanders (western) Directed by Lloyd

Nosler. Produced by Trem Carr. Screenplay by Charles A. Post.

Cast: Tom Tyler, Margaret Norris, Robert Manning, G.D. Wood (Gordon DeMain), John Elliott, Hank Bell, Lois Bridge, Fred "Snowflake" Toones.

A blacksmith (Tom Tyler) helps ranchers fight a corrupt senator who's trying to take over a frontier town.

Running time: 61 minutes. Release date: February 10, 1932.

16. The Reckoning (drama) Directed by Harry Fraser. Screenplay by Leon Lee. Story by Dwight Cummings.

Cast: Sally Blane, James Murray, Edmund Breese, Thomas Jackson, Bryant Washburn, Pat O'Malley.

Involved in underworld activities, two young lovers (Sally Blane, James Murray) try to change their ways and go straight, but are prevented from doing so by a gang leader (Edmund Breese).

Running time: 63 minutes. Release date: February 15, 1932.

17. Police Court (drama) Directed by Louis King. Produced by I.E. Chadwick. Screenplay and dialogue by Stuart Anthony.

Cast: Henry B. Walthall, Al St. John, Leon Janney, Aileen Pringle, King Baggott, Lionel Belmore, Edmund Breese, Walter James.

A once-great stage and screen actor (Henry B. Walthall) has fallen from fame because of his alcoholism; his young son (Leon Janney) is determined to see his father "make good" again.

Running time: 63 minutes. Release date: February 20, 1932. Also known as **Fame Street.**

18. The County Fair (drama) Directed by Louis King. Produced by Trem Carr. Screenplay by Harvey Harris Gates. Story by Roy Fitzroy.

Cast: Hobart Bosworth, Marion Shilling, Ralph Ince, William Collier, Jr., Kit Guard, George Chesebro, Otto Hoffman, Arthur Millett, Thomas R. Quinn, Edward Kane, Fred "Snowflake" Toones.

Left to right: Henry B. Walthall, Edmund Breese and Leon Janney in "Police Court" (1932).

A Kentucky gentleman (Hobart Bosworth) hires a waiter (William Collier, Jr.), an ex-jockey, to train his thoroughbred race horse; a group of gamblers, however, try to prevent the horse from entering a big race.

Running time: 71 minutes. Release date: April 1, 1932.

19. The Man from New Mexico (western) Directed by John P. McCarthy. Produced by Trem Carr. Screenplay by Harry O. Hoyt. From the story "Frag Branded" by Frederick Ryter.

Cast: Tom Tyler, Caryl Lincoln, Jack Richardson, Robert Walker, Frank Ball, Lewis Sargent, John "Blackie" Whiteford, Charles "Slim" Whitaker, Lafe McKee, Frederick Ryter, Jack Long, William Nolte, C.H. "Fargo" Bussey, Lee Timm.

A detective from the Cattleman's Association (Tom Tyler) thwarts the efforts of outlaws who have kidnapped a rancher and are poisoning his stock.
Running time: 54 minutes. Release date: April 1, 1932.

20. The Midnight Patrol (mystery) Directed by Christy Cabanne. Produced by C.C. Burr. Screenplay by George Jeske. Story by Arthur Hoerl. Dialogue by C. Carrington and Barry Barriner.

Cast: Regis Toomey, Betty Bronson, Edwina Booth, Mary Nolan, Earle Foze, Robert Elliott, Mack Swain, Snub Pollard, Mischa Auer, Tod Sloan, Jim Jeffries, Ray Cooke, Eddie Kane, William Norton Bailey, Jack Mower, Barry Oliver, Wilfred Lucas, J.C. Fowler.

The efforts of a cub reporter (Regis Toomey) to make good on a murder-mystery assignment bring him fame and a fiancee (Betty Bronson) within 24 hours.
Running time: 67 minutes. Release date: April 10, 1932.

21. Vanishing Men (western) Directed by Harry Fraser. Produced by Trem Carr. Story and screenplay by Wellyn Totman.

Cast: Tom Tyler, Adele Lacy, Raymond Keane, William L. Thorne, John Elliott, Robert Manning, Charles King, James Marcus, Dick Dickinson.
Running time: 62 minutes. Release date: April 15, 1932.

22. Arm of the Law (mystery) Directed by Louis King. Produced by Trem Carr. Screenplay by Leon Lee. From the story "The Butterfly Mystery" by Arthur Hoerl. A Trojan Production.

Cast: Rex Bell, Marceline Day, Lina Basquette, Bryant Washburn, Robert Emmett O'Connor, Robert Frazer, Dorothy Revier, Dorothy Christy, Donald Keith,

Opposite: Waiter William Collier, Jr. (left, in white jacket, standing) shows concern when someone gets fresh with cigarette girl Marion Shilling in "The County Fair" (1932).

17

Larry Banthin, Gilbert Clayton, Wallace McDonald, William V. Mong, Fred "Snowflake" Toones.

A smart reporter (Rex Bell) and a detective (Robert Emmett O'Connor) investigate the murder of a cabaret star (Lina Basquette) who had been involved in a divorce scandal.

Running time: 60 minutes. Release date: April 20, 1932.

23. Mason of the Mounted (western) Directed by Harry Fraser. Produced by Trem Carr. Story and screenplay by Harry Fraser.

Cast: Bill Cody, Andy Shuford, Nancy Drexel, Jack Carlisle, Capt. Art Smith, John "Blackie" Whiteford, Nelson McDowell, James Marcus, Joe Dominguez, LeRoy Mason, Dick Dickinson, Frank Hall Crane, Jack Long, Earl Dwire, Gordon McGee.

A Northwest Mounted Policeman (Bill Cody) tracks down a murderer who is the leader of a gang of horse thieves.

Running time: 58 minutes. Release date: May 15, 1932.

24. Flames (drama) Directed by Karl Brown. Supervised by Trem Carr. Original story and screenplay by Karl Brown and I.E. Chadwick.

Cast: Johnny Mack Brown, Noel Francis, George Cooper, Marjorie Beebe, Richard Tucker, Russell Simpson, Kit Guard.

The story of a young fireman (Johnny Mack Brown) and his heroic work.

Running time: 63 minutes. Release date: May 30, 1932.

Working title: **Fatal Alarm**. Also known as **Fire Alarm**.

25. Law of the North (western) Directed by Harry Fraser. Produced by Trem Carr. Screenplay by Harry Fraser.

Cast: Bill Cody, Andy Shuford, Nadine Dore, Al St. John, William L. Thorne, Charles "Heine" Conklin, Gil Pratt, Jack Caryle, Lew Short.

A cowboy (Bill Cody), wrongfully accused of murdering

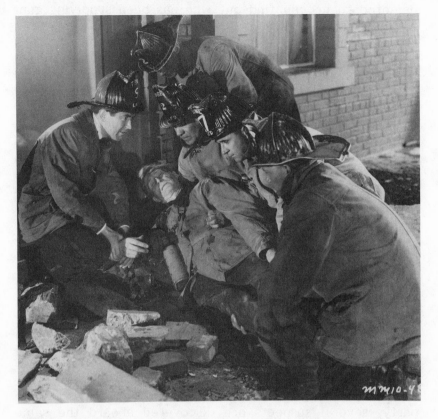

Johnny Mack Brown (left) and other firemen come to the aid of a fallen comrade in "Flames" (1932).

one of his neighbors, breaks out of jail and tries to expose a crooked judge (William L. Thorne).

Running time: 55 minutes. Release date: May 30, 1932.

26. Texas Pioneers (western) Directed by Harry Fraser. Produced by Trem Carr. Screenplay by Wellyn Totman and Harry Fraser. Story by Harry Fraser.

Cast: Bill Cody, Andy Shuford, LeRoy Mason, Sheila Manners, John Elliott, Frank Lackteen, Harry Allen, Chief Standing Bear, Iron Eyes, Ann Ross.

An army officer (Bill Cody) pretends to have been

demoted so he can find out who has been supplying guns to the Indians.
Running time: 58 min. Release date: June 18, 1932.

27. Honor of the Mounted (western) Directed by Harry Fraser. Produced by Trem Carr. Story and screenplay by Harry Fraser.

Cast: Tom Tyler, Cecilia Ryland, Francis McDonald, Charles King, Tom London, Stanley Blystone, William Dwire, Arthur Millett, Gordon Wood (Gordon DeMain), Theodore Lorch.

Suspected of murder, a Northwest Mounted Policeman (Tom Tyler) journeys to the U.S. to track down the real killer (Stanley Blystone).

Running time: 62 minutes. Release date: June 20, 1932.

28. Western Limited (mystery) Directed by Christy Cabanne. Produced by C.C. Burr. Screenplay by C.E. Roberts. Story by Evelyn Campbell.

Cast: Estelle Taylor, Edmund Burns, Lucien Prival, Gertrude Astor, Eddie Kane, James Burtis, John Vosburgh, Mahlon Hamilton, Crauford Kent, Adaline Asbury, Arthur Millett, J.L. Palmer.

After a jewel robbery at a fashionable masquerade party, several suspects are discovered aboard the same train.

Running time: 65 minutes. Release date: July 20, 1932.

29. The Girl from Calgary (musical) Directed by Phil Whitman. Produced by I.E. Chadwick. Screenplay by Lee Chadwick. Story by Leon D'Usseau. Sequences in Magnacolor.

Cast: Fifi D'Orsay, Paul Kelly, Robert Warwick, Edwin Maxwell, Astrid Allwyn, Eddie Featherstone.

A New York press agent (Paul Kelly) turns an obscure singer/rodeo performer (Fifi D'Orsay) into a big Broadway star.

Running time: 64 minutes. Release date: August 20, 1932.

Uses footage from **The Great Gabbo** (Sono Art-World Wide, 1930).

30. Klondike (drama) Directed by Phil Rosen. Produced by William T. Lackey. Story and screenplay by Tristram Tupper.

Cast: Lyle Talbot, Thelma Todd, Capt. Frank Hawks, Henry B. Walthall, Priscilla Dean, Tully Marshall, Jason Robards (Sr.), Ethel Wales, Pat O'Malley, Myrtle Stedman, George Hayes, Lafe McKee.

A doctor (Lyle Talbot) is charged with murder when a patient dies after a difficult operation. Losing his license, he embarks on a transpacific flight, but his plane is wrecked in Alaska, where new problems and romance await him.

Running time: 68 minutes. Release date: August 30, 1932.

Remade as **Klondike Fury** (Monogram, 1942).

31. The Thirteenth Guest (mystery) Directed by Albert Ray. Produced by M.H. Hoffman. Continuity by Frances Hyland. Adaptation by Arthur Hoerl. Additional dialogue by Armitage Trail. From the book by Armitage Trail.

Cast: Ginger Rogers, Lyle Talbot, J. Farrell MacDonald, James Eagles, Eddie Phillips, Erville Alderson, Crauford Kent, Frances Rich, Ethel Wales, Phillips Smalley, Paul Hurst, William Davidson, Tom London, Al Bridge, Adrienne Dore, Charles Meacham, Isobel LeMal, Robert Klein, Harry Tenbrook, John Ince, Allan Cavan, Henry Hall, Stanley J. "Tiny" Sanford, Kit Guard, Lynton Brent, Bobby Burns.

Thirteen years after her father died suddenly at a dinner party he had hosted for 13 guests, someone is trying to kill Marie Morgan (Ginger Rogers).

Running time: 68 minutes. Release date: August 30, 1932.

Released in Great Britain as **Lady Beware.**

Remade as **The Mystery of the 13th Guest** (Monogram, 1943).

32. From Broadway to Cheyenne (western) Directed

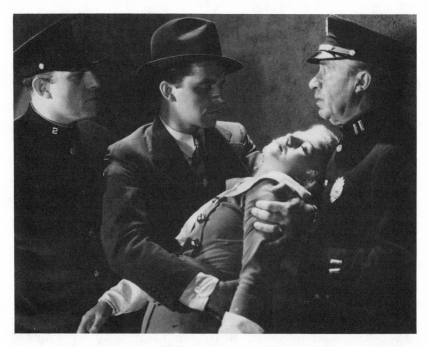

Left to right: Al Bridge, Lyle Talbot, Ginger Rogers and J. Farrell MacDonald in "The Thirteenth Guest" (1932). Because of Miss Rogers' subsequent rise to stardom, the film was kept in constant reissue throughout the 1930s.

by Harry Fraser. Produced by Trem Carr. Story and screenplay by Wellyn Totman.

Cast: Rex Bell, Marceline Day, Matthew Betz, Huntley Gordon, Roy D'Arcy, Robert Ellis, Gwen Lee, Al Bridge, Rae Daggett, John Elliott, George Hayes, Earl Dwire.

A detective (Rex Bell) thwarts a mob of Broadway gangsters trying to start a protection racket out west.

Running time: 60 minutes. Release date: September 10, 1932.

Released in Great Britain as **Broadway to Cheyenne**.

33. Guilty or Not Guilty (mystery) Directed by Al Ray. Screenplay by Frances Hyland. From the syndicated newspaper story by Arthur Hoerl.

Cast: Betty Compson, Claudia Dell, Tom Douglas, George Irving, Wheeler Oakman, Luis Alberni, Walter Percival, William Davidson, Erin LaBessoniere.

Running time: 70 minutes. Release date: October 1, 1932.

34. Hidden Valley (western) Directed by Robert N. Bradbury. Produced by Trem Carr. Story and screenplay by Wellyn Totman.

Cast: Bob Steele, Gertrude Messinger, Francis McDonald, Ray Haller, John Elliott, Arthur Millett, V.L. Barnes, Joe De LaCruz, Dick Dickinson, George Hayes, Capt. Verner L. Smith, Tom London.

A lawman (Bob Steele) uses a blimp to aid in the search over the desert for a wanted criminal.

Running time: 60 minutes. Release date: October 10, 1932.

35. The Man from Arizona (western) Directed by Harry Fraser. Produced by Trem Carr. Story and screenplay by Wellyn Totman.

Cast: Rex Bell, Charles King, Theodore Lorch, George Nash, John Elliott, Naomi Judge, Nat Carr, Les Lindsay, James Marcus, Henry Sedley, John Beck, Hank Bell, George Cooper, Bob McKenzie.

Running time: 58 minutes. Release date: October 21, 1932.

36. Young Blood (western) Directed by Phil Rosen. Produced by Trem Carr. Story and screenplay by Wellyn Totman.

Cast: Bob Steele, Helen Foster, Naomi Judge, Charles King, Henry Rocquemore, Art Mix, Hank Bell, Harry Semels, Lafe McKee, Perry Murdock, Roy Bucko.

A Robin Hood-like bandit (Bob Steele), who steals to help the poor, fights a villainous sheriff.

Running time: 59 minutes. Release date: November 5, 1932.

37. Strange Adventure (mystery) Directed by Phil Whitman. Produced by I.E. Chadwick. Screenplay by Lee

Chadwick. Story by Arthur Hoerl. Dialogue by Hampton Del Ruth.

Cast: Regis Toomey, June Clyde, Lucille LaVerne, William V. Mong, Jason Robards (Sr.), Eddie Phillips, Dwight Frye, Isabelle Vecki, Alan Roscoe, Nadine Dore, Fred "Snowflake" Toones, William J. Humphrey, Harry Myers, Eddy Chandler.

A police lieutenant (Regis Toomey) and a reporter (June Clyde) investigate the death of Silas Wayne (William V. Mong), who was murdered while reading his will to his heirs.

Running time: 60 minutes. Release date: November 20, 1932.

Also known as **Wayne Murder Case.**

38. Lucky Larrigan (western) Directed by John P. McCarthy. Produced by Trem Carr. Story and screenplay by Wellyn Totman.

Cast: Rex Bell, Helen Foster, George Chesebro, John Elliott, Stanley Blystone, Julian Rivero, G.D. Wood (Gordon DeMain), Wilfred Lucas.

A young easterner (Rex Bell) follows his girl (Helen Foster) when she heads west with her father.

Running time: 58 minutes. Release date: December 1, 1932.

39. The Fighting Champ (western) Directed by John P. McCarthy. Produced by Trem Carr. Story and screenplay by Wellyn Totman.

Cast: Bob Steele, Arletta Duncan, Charles King, Kit Guard, George Chesebro, Frank Bell, Lafe McKee, George Hayes, Henry Rocquemore.

A prizefighter (Bob Steele) finds himself out in the Wild West, where he is doped by villains prior to a big fight.

Running time: 59 minutes. Release date: December 15, 1932.

40. Self Defense (drama) Directed by Phil Rosen. Produced by William T. Lackey. Screenplay by Tristram Tupper. From "The Just Judge" by Peter B. Kyne.

Cast: Pauline Frederick, Claire Windsor, Theodore Von Eltz, Barbara Kent, Robert Elliott, Henry B. Walthall, Jameson Thomas, George Hackathorne, Willie Fung, Lafe McKee, Si Jenks, George Hayes.

Katy Devoux (Pauline Frederick) is the proprietor of a miner/lumberjack gambling house, a fact she conceals from her daughter Nona (Barbara Kent) who attends an exclusive boarding school. When a disgruntled patron gets the girl to join her mother, the dive is turned into the hotel the daughter has been led to believe it is.

Running time: 68 minutes. Release date: December 15, 1932.

Working title: **My Mother.**

41. The Diamond Trail (western) Directed by Harry Fraser. Produced by Trem Carr. Screenplay by Harry Fraser and Sherman Lowe. Story by Sherman Lowe.

Cast: Rex Bell, Frances Rich, Bud Osborne, Lloyd Whitlock, Norman Feusier, Jerry Storm, John Webb Dillon, Billy West, Larry Lamont.

Speed Morgan (Rex Bell), a New York reporter, heads west to get the story on a diamond smuggling operation.

Running time: 61 minutes. Release date: December 30, 1932.

1933

42. Jungle Bride (drama) Directed by Harry O. Hoyt and Albert Kelley. Produced by I.E. Chadwick. Story by Leah Baird.

Cast: Anita Page, Charles Starrett, Kenneth Thompson, Eddie Borden, Clarence Geldert, Gertrude Simpson, Jay Emmett, Albert Cross.

A shipwreck off the coast of Africa leaves four people stranded in the jungle: an accused murderer (Charles Starrett), a reporter (Kenneth Thompson) bringing him to justice, a woman (Anita Page) whose brother is being held for the crime and a happy-go-lucky entertainer (Eddie Borden).

Anita Page in "Jungle Bride" (1933).

Running time: 63 minutes. Release date: January 10, 1933.

43. West of Singapore (drama) Directed by Al Ray. Produced by M.H. Hoffman. Screenplay by Adele Buffington. Story by Houston Branch.

Cast: Betty Compson, Weldon Heyburn, Margaret Lindsay, Noel Madison, Thomas Douglas, Clyde Cook, Harvey Clark, Ernie Adams.

Jungle fever drives Dan Manton (Weldon Heyburn) to drink and into the arms of a fallen woman (Betty Compson), bringing sorrow to the girl (Margaret Lindsay) who loves him.

Running time: 68 minutes. Release date: January 31, 1933.

44. Oliver Twist (drama) Directed by William Cowen. Produced by I.E. Chadwick. Screenplay by Elizabeth Meehan. Based on the novel by Charles Dickens. Production supervised by Herbert Brenon.

Cast: Dickie Moore, Irving Pichel, William (Stage) Boyd, Doris Lloyd, Barbara Kent, Alec B. Francis, Lionel Belmore, George K. Arthur, George Nash, Virginia Sale, Nelson McDowell, Tempe Pigott, Harry Holman, Sonny Ray, Clyde Cook, Bobby Nelson.

Oliver Twist (Dickie Moore), a young orphan, becomes a member of a group of thieves headed by Fagin (Irving Pichel), a master pickpocket.

Running time: 80 minutes. Release date: February 28, 1933.

Charles Dickens' novel was filmed several times in the silent era, including versions in 1909, 1910, 1912, 1916 and 1922. After this Monogram production, it was remade in 1948; in 1968 as a musical titled **Oliver!**; and in 1982 as a made-for-TV version.

45. Breed of the Border (western) Directed by Robert N. Bradbury. Produced by Trem Carr. Story and screenplay by Harry O. Jones (Harry Fraser).

Cast: Bob Steele, Marion Byron, George Hayes, Ernie Adams, Wilfred Lucas, Henry Rocquemore, Fred Cavens, Robert Cord, Perry Murdock.

Speed Brent (Bob Steele), a speedcar racer, joins a gang of cattle rustlers in order to gather evidence against them.

Running time: 58 minutes. Release date: March 1, 1933.

Released in Great Britain as **Speed Brent Wins**.

46. The Phantom Broadcast (mystery) Directed by Phil Rosen. Produced by William T. Lackey. Story and screenplay by Tristram Tupper.

Cast: Ralph Forbes, Vivienne Osborne, Gail Patrick, Paul Page, Guinn "Big Boy" Williams, Arnold Gray,

Esther Ralston displays her skills as an equestrienne in "Black Beauty" (1933).

Rockcliffe Fellowes, Harland Tucker, Pauline Garon, George Nash, Mary MacLaren, Carl Miller, Althea Henley, George Hayes.

After the murder of a popular radio crooner (Arnold Gray), it is learned that he merely mouthed the singing voice of his manager-accompanist (Ralph Forbes), a twisted cripple.

Running time: 68 minutes. Release date: March 15, 1933.

Working title: **False Fronts.** Released in Great Britain as **Phantom of the Air.**

47. Black Beauty (drama) Directed by Phil Rosen. Produced by I.E. Chadwick. Screenplay by Charles Logue. From the novel by Anna Sewell.

Cast: Esther Ralston, Alexander Kirkland, Hale

Hamilton, Gavin Gordon, Don Alvarado, George Walsh, Theodore Lorch, John Larkin, Eddie Featherstone, Al Bridge, Bruce Covington.

Black Beauty, a horse, is being trained for the steeplechase upon which the fortunes of the Cameron estate depend. But when he is injured as he races for the doctor to tend his master (Alexander Kirkland), his racing days are finished before they start.

Running time: 70 minutes. Release date: April 1, 1933.

Anna Sewell's novel was filmed several times, including versions in 1946 and 1971.

48. The Gallant Fool (western) Directed by Robert N. Bradbury. Produced by Trem Carr. Screenplay by Robert N. Bradbury and Harry O. Jones (Harry Fraser). From a story by John P. McCarthy.

Cast: Bob Steele, Arletta Duncan, George Hayes, John Elliott, Theodore Lorch, Perry Murdock, George Nash, Pascale Perry.

A man (Bob Steele) accused of murder takes refuge in a small circus.

Running time: 60 minutes. Release date: May 24, 1933.

49. The Return of Casey Jones (action-drama) Directed by John P. McCarthy. Produced by I.E. Chadwick. Screenplay by John P. McCarthy and Harry O. Jones (Harry Fraser). From the "Railroad Stories" novelette by John Johns.

Cast: Charles Starrett, Ruth Hall, Robert Elliott, George Hayes, Jackie Searl, George Walsh, Margaret Sedden, G.D. Wood (Gordon DeMain), George Nash, Anne Howard.

Famed engineer Casey Jones serves as a role model for a young railroad hero (Charles Starrett).

Running time: 63 minutes. Release date: May 25, 1933.

Released in Great Britain as **Train 2419.**

50. Trailin' North (western) Directed by John P.

McCarthy. Produced by Paul Malvern. Screenplay by John Morgan. Story by Harry O. Jones (Harry Fraser).

Cast: Bob Steele, Doris Hill, George Hayes, Arthur Rankin, Fred Burns, Dick Dickinson, Norman Fensler.

A Texas Ranger (Bob Steele) journeys north to work with the Royal Canadian Mounted Police.

Running time: 57 minutes. Release date: May 1933.

51. Crashing Broadway (western) Directed by John P. McCarthy. Produced by Paul Malvern. Screenplay by Wellyn Totman.

Cast: Rex Bell, Doris Hill, Harry Bowen, George Hayes, Charles King, Louis Sargent, G.D. Wood (Gordon DeMain), Ann Howard, John "Blackie" Whiteford, Perry Murdock, Henry Rocquemore, Max Asher, Allan Lee, George Morrell, Archie Ricks, Tex Palmer.

A cowboy (Rex Bell) heads to New York to make his name as an actor.

Running time: 55 minutes. Release date: June 1, 1933.

52. The Sphinx (mystery) Directed by Phil Rosen. Supervised by Sid Rogell. Story and screenplay by Albert E. DeMond.

Cast: Lionel Atwill, Sheila Terry, Theodore Newton, Paul Hurst, Luis Alberni, Robert Ellis, Lucien Prival, Paul Fix, Lillian Leighton, George Hayes, Hooper Atchley, Wilfred Lucas.

A mute goes on the witness stand to provide alibis for his homicidal twin brother (Lionel Atwill plays both roles).

Running time: 64 min. Release date: June 1, 1933.

Remade as **The Phantom Killer** (Monogram, 1942).

53. The Fighting Texans (western) Directed by Armand Schaefer. Produced by Paul Malvern. Screenplay by Wellyn Totman and Charles Roberts. Story by Wellyn Totman.

Cast: Rex Bell, Luana Walters, Betty Mack, George Hayes, Wally Wales, Yakima Canutt, Lafe McKee, Anne Howard, Al Bridge, Frank LaRue, George Nash, Gordon DeMain.

Randolph Graves (Rex Bell), a high-pressure haberdashery salesman, is fired for arguing with a customer and gets a job selling oil stock in a nearby town; there he falls in love with the sheriff's daughter (Luana Walters) and tangles with crooked stock promoters.

Running time: 58 minutes. Release date: June 15, 1933.

Released in Great Britain as **Randy Strikes Oil.**

54. The Fugitive (western) Directed by Harry Fraser. Produced by Paul Malvern. Story and screenplay by Harry O. Jones (Harry Fraser).

Cast: Rex Bell, Cecilia Parker, George Hayes, Robert Kortman, Tom London, Gordon DeMain, Phil Dunham, Theodore Lorch, Dick Dickinson, Earl Dwire, George Nash.

A secret service man (Rex Bell) goes to jail in order to gather evidence against a crook.

Running time: 56 minutes. Release date: July 15, 1933.

55. Rainbow Ranch (western) Directed by Harry Fraser. Produced by Trem Carr. Story and screenplay by Harry O. Jones (Harry Fraser). Dialogue by Phil Dunham.

Cast: Rex Bell, Cecilia Parker, Robert Kortman, Henry Hall, George Nash, Gordon DeMain, Phil Dunham, Jerry Storm, Stanley J. "Tiny" Sanford, Van Galbert, Jackie Hoefley.

A navy boxing champ (Rex Bell) goes back to his ranch to settle the score with the man (Robert Kortman) who murdered his uncle, stole his water rights and is engaged to his girl (Cecilia Parker).

Running time: 54 min. Release date: July 25, 1933.

56. Galloping Romeo (western) Directed by Robert N. Bradbury. Produced by Trem Carr and Paul Malvern. Screenplay by Harry O Jones (Harry Fraser). Story by Robert N. Bradbury.

Cast: Bob Steele, Doris Hill, George Hayes, Frank Ball, Ernie Adams, Lafe McKee, Ed Brady, George Nash, Earl Dwire.

A couple of kind-hearted "badmen" (Bob Steele, George Hayes), who never did any real dirt, just can't seem to keep out of trouble.
Running time: 60 minutes. Release date: August 5, 1933.

57. The Avenger (drama) Directed by Edward L. Marin. Produced by Trem Carr. Screenplay by Brown Holmes. Dialogue by Tristram Tupper. Based on a novel by John Goodwin.

Cast: Ralph Forbes, Adrienne Ames, Arthur Vinton, Claude Gillingwater, Charlotte Merriam, J. Carrol Naish, Berton Churchill, Murray Kinnell, Thomas Jackson, Paul Fix, James Donlan, Leonard Carey, Boothe Howard, Wilson Benge.

A district attorney (Ralph Forbes) takes revenge on the gang of crooks who were instrumental in having him railroaded to prison.
Running time: 79 minutes. Release date: August 10, 1933.

58. The Ranger's Code (western) Directed by Robert N. Bradbury. Produced by Trem Carr and Paul Malvern. Screenplay by Harry O. Jones (Harry Fraser). Story by John T. Neville.

Cast: Bob Steele, Doris Hill, George Hayes, George Nash, Ernie Adams, Ed Brady, Hal Price, Dick Dickinson, Frank Ball.

A ranger (Bob Steele) is torn between love and duty when he has to bring in his girlfriend's brother, who is a member of an outlaw gang.
Running time: 59 minutes. Release date: August 15, 1933.

59. Skyway (comedy-drama) Directed by Lew Collins. Produced by William T. Lackey. Screenplay by Albert E. DeMond. Story by Paul B. Franklin.

Cast: Ray Walker, Kathryn Crawford, Lucien Littlefield, Tom Dugan, Arthur Vinton, Claude Gillingwater, Jed Prouty, Alice Lake, Jack Pennick, George Hayes, Jack Kennedy.

Peggy Shannon (left) and Barbara Barondess in "Devil's Mate" (1933).

A brash, hot-headed aviator (Ray Walker) takes a job at a bank for the sake of his girl (Kathryn Crawford), whose father is the bank president.
Running time: 65 minutes. Release date: August 15, 1933.

60. Devil's Mate (mystery) Directed by Phil Rosen. Produced by Ben Verschleiser. Story and screenplay by Leonard Fields and David Silverstein.
Cast: Preston Foster, Peggy Shannon, Ray Walker, Hobart Cavanaugh, Barbara Barondess, Paul Porcasi, Harold Waldridge, Jason Robards (Sr.), Bryant Washburn, Harry Holman, George Hayes, James Durkin, Gordon DeMain, Paul Fix, Sam Flint, Henry Otto, Henry Hull.
A convicted murderer (Paul Fix) sentenced to die in the electric chair is killed by a poisoned dart just

as he's about to reveal the name of the man who put him up to the crime. A police inspector (Preston Foster) and a newspaper reporter (Peggy Shannon) set out to track down the killer.

Running time: 68 minutes. Release date: August 20, 1933.

Released in Great Britain as **He Knew Too Much.**

Remade as **I Killed That Man** (Monogram, 1941).

61. Sensation Hunters (drama) Directed by Charles Vidor. Supervised by Robert Welsh. Screenplay by Paul Schofield. Story by Whitman Chambers. Dialogue by Albert E. DeMond.

Cast: Arline Judge, Preston Foster, Marion Burns, Juanita Hansen, Creighton Hale, Cyril Chadwick, Nella Walker, Harold Minjir, Finis Barton.

A young and innocent girl (Marion Burns) goes to work at a cabaret in Panama, where she's befriended by a hard-boiled member of the "joint" (Arline Judge).

Running time: 74 minutes. Release date: August 30, 1933.

62. The Sweetheart of Sigma Chi (comedy-romance) Directed by Edward L. Marin. Produced by William T. Lackey. Screenplay by Luther Reed and Albert E. DeMond. Story by George Waggner.

Cast: Mary Carlisle, Buster Crabbe, Charles Starrett, Florence Lake, Eddie Tamblyn, Sally Starr, Mary Blackford, Tom Dugan, Burr McIntosh, Major Goodsell, Grady Sutton, Purnell Pratt, Franklin Parker, Ted Fio Rito and His Orchestra.

Vivian (Mary Carlisle), a campus flirt who has collected most of the fraternity pins from the Sigma Chi members, falls for Bob North (Buster Crabbe), a strong-minded college athlete.

Running time: 76 minutes. Release date: October 1, 1933.

Remade as **Sweetheart of Sigma Chi** (Monogram, 1946).

63. Riders of Destiny (western) Directed by Robert

34

N. Bradbury. Produced by Paul Malvern. Story and screenplay by Robert N. Bradbury. A Lone Star Production.

Cast: John Wayne, Cecilia Parker, George Hayes, Forrest Taylor, Al St. John, Charles "Heine" Conklin, Earl Dwire, Lafe McKee, Horace B. Carpenter, Yakima Canutt, Hal Price, Si Jenks, "Duke."

"Singing Sandy" Saunders (John Wayne), an undercover secret service agent, thwarts a gang trying to deny ranchers of their water rights.

Running time: 58 minutes. Release date: October 10, 1933.

64. Broken Dreams (drama) Directed by Robert Vignola. Produced by Ben Verschleiser. Screenplay by Maude Fulton. Story by Olga Printzlau.

Cast: Randolph Scott, Martha Sleeper, Joseph Cawthorn, Beryl Mercer, Buster Phelps, Charlotte Merriam, Sidney Bracey, Adele St. Maur, Phyllis Lee, Martin Burton, Finis Barton, Edward LeSaint, Sam Flint.

When a doctor (Randolph Scott) remarries, there is open hostility between his son (Buster Phelps) and the stepmother (Martha Sleeper).

Running time: 68 minutes. Release date: October 20, 1933.

65. He Couldn't Take It (comedy) Directed by William Nigh. Produced by William T. Lackey. Story and screenplay by Dore Schary. Additional dialogue by George Waggner.

Cast: Ray Walker, Virginia Cherrill, George E. Stone, Stanley Fields, Dorothy Granger, Jane Darwell, Paul Porcasi, Donald Douglas, Astrid Allwyn, Franklin Parker, Jack Kennedy.

A ne'er-do-well (Ray Walker), who can never seem to hold a job any longer than it takes to get fired, becomes a process server.

Running time: 63 minutes. Release date: December 15, 1933.

Working titles: **The Process Server** and **Born Tough.**

Remade as **Here Comes Kelly** (Monogram, 1943) and **Live Wires** (Monogram, 1946).

66. The Sagebrush Trail (western) Directed by Armand Schaefer. Produced by Paul Malvern. Story and screenplay by Lindsley Parsons. A Lone Star Production.

Cast: John Wayne, Lane Chandler, Nancy Shubert, Wally Wales, Yakima Canutt, Henry Hall, William Dyer, Earl Dwire, Art Mix, Hank Bell, Charles "Slim" Whitaker, Robert Burns, Hal Price.

A cowboy (John Wayne), wrongfully accused of murder, escapes from prison and tries to find the real killer.

Running time: 58 minutes. Release date: December 15, 1933.

1934

67. 16 Fathoms Deep (action-drama) Directed by Armand Schaefer. Screenplay by A.B. Barringer and Norman Houston. Based on the American Magazine story "16 Fathoms Deep" by Eustace L. Adams.

Cast: Sally O'Neil, Creighton Chaney (Lon Chaney, Jr.), George Regas, Maurice Black, Jack Kennedy, Lloyd Ingraham, George Nash, Robert Kortman, Si Jenks, Constantine Romanoff, Richard Alexander, Russell Simpson, Philip Kieffer, Jean Gehrung, Raul Figarola.

A sponge diver (Creighton Chaney) hopes to raise enough money to buy his own boat and marry his sweetheart (Sally O'Neil); his rival (George Regas), however, tries to sabotage his plans.

Running time: 57 minutes. Release date: January 1, 1934.

Remade by Monogram in 1948.

68. The Lucky Texan (western) Directed by Robert N. Bradbury. Produced by Paul Malvern. Story and screenplay by Robert N. Bradbury. A Lone Star Production.

Cast: John Wayne, Barbara Sheldon, George Hayes, Lloyd Whitlock, Yakima Canutt, Gordon DeMain, Edward Parker, Earl Dwire, Jack Rockwell, Artie Ortego, Tex Palmer, Tex Phelps, George Morrell.

A cowboy (John Wayne) returns home to pan gold with his father's partner (George Hayes). After they strike it rich, the partner is framed for robbery and murder.

Running time: 56 minutes. Release date: January 22, 1934.

69. A Woman's Man (comedy-drama) Directed by Edward Ludwig. Produced by Ben Verschleiser. Screenplay by Frances Hyland. From the Cosmopolitan Magazine story by Adela Rogers St. John.

Cast: John Halliday, Marguerite De La Motte, Wallace Ford, Kitty Kelly, Jameson Thomas, Tom Dugan, Wallis Clark, Don Douglas, Leigh Allen, George Mayo, Harry Green, Jack Perry, Billee Van Every.

A tempestuous movie star (Marguerite De La Motte) walks out on her latest picture so she can carry on a much publicized romance with a headline-hunting prize-fighter (Wallace Ford).

Running time: 64 minutes. Release date: February 7, 1934.

70. West of the Divide (western) Directed by Robert N. Bradbury. Produced by Paul Malvern. Story and screenplay by Robert N. Bradbury. A Lone Star Production.

Cast: John Wayne, Virginia Brown Faire, George "Gabby" Hayes, Lloyd Whitlock, Yakima Canutt, Billy O'Brien, Lafe McKee, John "Blackie" Whiteford, Earl Dwire, Dick Dickinson, Tex Palmer, Artie Ortego, Horace B. Carpenter, Hal Price, Archie Ricks.

A cowboy (John Wayne) returns to the scene where his father was murdered 12 years before, seeking news of his young brother (Billy O'Brien).

Running time: 54 minutes. Release date: February 15, 1934.

71. Beggars in Ermine (drama) Directed by Phil Rosen. Produced by William T. Lackey. Screenplay and dialogue by Tristram Tupper. From the novel by Esther Lynd Day.

Cast: Lionel Atwill, Henry B. Walthall, Betty Furness, Jameson Thomas, James Bush, Astrid Allwyn, George Hayes, Stephen Gross, Lee Phelps, Clinton Lyle, Sidney DeGrey, Gayle Kaye, Myrtle Stedman, Gordon DeMain.

Left to right: George "Gabby" Hayes, John Wayne and Lloyd Whitlock in "West of the Divide" (1934), one in a series of westerns Wayne starred in for Lone Star Productions.

John Dawson (Lionel Atwill), the head of a steel mill, loses both his legs; while he's recuperating in the hospital, his wife (Betty Furness) uses the power of attorney he had given her to ruin him, and then runs off with James Marley (Jameson Thomas), one of the directors of the mill. Dawson then joins an army of beggars who roam the country; organized by him, they become a crime prevention unit in a campaign that sweeps him back to power.

Running time: 72 minutes. Release date: February 22, 1934.

72. Mystery Liner (adventure-mystery) Directed by William Nigh. Produced by Paul Malvern. Screenplay by Wellyn Totman. From the Saturday Evening Post novel "The Ghost of John Holling" by Edgar Wallace.

Cast: Noah Beery (Sr.), Astrid Allwyn, Cornelius Keefe, Gustav von Seyffertitz, Edwin Maxwell, Ralph Lewis, Boothe Howard, John Maurice Sullivan, Gordon DeMain, Zeffie Tilbury, Howard Hickman, Jerry Stewart, George Hayes, George Cleveland, Olaf Hytten, Ray Brown, George Nash.

Foreign agents try to sabotage a test of the S-505 tube, a secret device to control ocean liners, which will revolutionize warfare.

Running time: 62 minutes. Release date: March 15, 1934.

Released in Great Britain as **The Ghost of John Holling**.

73. The House of Mystery (mystery-comedy) Directed by William Nigh. Supervised by Paul Malvern. Screenplay by Albert E. DeMond. From the stage play by Adam Hull Shirk.

Cast: Ed Lowry, Verna Hillie, John Sheehan, Brandon Hurst, Liya Joy (Joyzelle), Fritzi Ridgeway, Clay Clement, George Hayes, Dale Fuller, Harry C. Bradley, Irving Bacon, Mary Foy, Samuel Godfrey, George Cleveland, Bruce Mitchell, Dick Botiller, James C. Morton.

Claimants to an old man's fortune are required to spend a week at his foreboding mansion, which is reputedly haunted by the spectre of the sacred ape of a Hindu cult.

Running time: 62 minutes. Release date: March 30, 1934. Working title: **The Ape**.

74. City Limits (comedy) Directed by William Nigh. Produced by William T. Lackey. Story and screenplay by George Waggner. From the novel by Jack Woodford (Josiah Pitts Woolfolk).

Cast: Frank Craven, Sally Blane, Ray Walker, Claude Gillingwater, James Burke, James Conlin, Jane Keckley, Henry Rocquemore, Harry Bradley, George Hayes, George Cleveland, George Nash, Fern Emmett.

A wealthy railroad president (Frank Craven), suffering

Verna Hillie is carried off by a killer ape in "The House of Mystery" (1934).

from mental and physical woes, meets two hoboes (James Burke, James Conlin) and from them learns how to really enjoy life.

Running time: 67 minutes. Release date: April 15, 1934.

Remade as **Father Steps Out** (Monogram, 1941).

75. Manhattan Love Song (comedy-drama) Directed by Leonard Fields. Supervised by Trem Carr. Screenplay by Leonard Fields and David Silverstein. From the novel by Cornell Woolrich.

Cast: Robert Armstrong, Dixie Lee, Franklin Pangborn, Nydia Westman, Helen Flint, Cecile Cunningham, Harold Walridge, Herman Bing, George Irving, Harrison Greene, Nick Copeland.

Left penniless by their financial advisor, pampered

40

socialites Jerry and Carol Stewart (Dixie Lee, Helen Flint) find it necessary to permit their unpaid chauffeur Williams (Robert Armstrong) and maid Annette (Nydia Westman) to live in their apartment in lieu of wages due.

Running time: 63 minutes. Release date: April 30, 1934.

76. Blue Steel (western) Directed by Robert N. Bradbury. Produced by Paul Malvern. Story and screenplay by Robert N. Bradbury. A Lone Star Production.

Cast: John Wayne, Eleanor Hunt, George Hayes, Edward Peil, Sr., Yakima Canutt, George Cleveland, George Nash, Lafe McKee, Hank Bell, Earl Dwire, Artie Ortego, Horace B. Carpenter, Theodore Lorch, Silver Tip Baker.

A cowboy (John Wayne) clashes with a gang of outlaws who are trying to force the entire populace of a small town to leave the gold-rich territory.

Running time: 54 minutes. Release date: May 10, 1934.

77. The Man from Utah (western) Directed by Robert N. Bradbury. Produced by Paul Malvern. Story and screenplay by Lindsley Parsons. A Lone Star Production.

Cast: John Wayne, Polly Ann Young, George Hayes, Yakima Canutt, Edward Peil, Sr., Anita Compillo, Lafe McKee, George Cleveland, Earl Dwire, Artie Ortego.

A deputy sheriff (John Wayne) goes after outlaws who are using a rodeo as their base of operations.

Running time: 55 minutes. Release date: May 15, 1934.

78. Monte Carlo Nights (adventure-mystery) Directed by William Nigh. Produced by Paul Malvern. Screenplay by Norman Houston. Suggested by the story "Numbers of Death" by E. Phillips Oppenheim.

Cast: Mary Brian, John Darrow, Kate Campbell, Robert Frazer, Yola D'Arvil, Astrid Allwyn, George Hayes, Bill Van Every, Carl Stockdale, George Cleveland.

With only one clue to go on, a man (John Darrow),

Ray Walker and Jacqueline Wells (Julie Bishop) in "The Loudspeaker" (1934).

convicted of murder, escapes from the police to search for the guilty party.
   Running time: 62 min. Release date: May 20, 1934.
   Working title: **Numbers of Monte Carlo.**

79. The Loudspeaker (comedy-drama) Directed by Joseph Santley. Produced by William T. Lackey. Screenplay by Albert E. DeMond. Original story by Ralph Spence.
   Cast: Ray Walker, Jacqueline Wells (Julie Bishop), Noel Francis, Charles Grapewin, Lorin Raker, Wilbur Mack, Spencer Charters, Sherwood Bailey, Billy Irvin, Ruth Romaine, Lawrence Wheat, Mary Carr.
   A small-town boy (Ray Walker) whose burning ambition is to become a radio star journeys to New York, where his subsequent success turns him into an insufferable egotist.

Running time: 67 minutes. Release date: June 1, 1934.
Released in Great Britain as **The Radio Star.**

80. Money Means Nothing (drama) Directed by Christy Cabanne. Produced by Ben Verschleiser. Screenplay by Frances Hyland. From the stage play "Cost of Living" by William Anthony McGuire.

Cast: Wallace Ford, Gloria Shea, Edgar Kennedy, Maidel Turner, Betty Blythe, Eddie Tamblyn, Vivian Oakland, Richard Tucker, Tenen Holtz, Ann Brody, Olaf Hytten.

A spoiled socialite (Gloria Shea) marries a penniless tire clerk (Wallace Ford) and sticks with him through adversity.

Running time: 70 minutes. Release date: June 15, 1934.

81. Randy Rides Alone (western) Directed by Harry Fraser. Produced by Paul Malvern. Story and screenplay by Lindsley Parsons. A Lone Star Production.

Cast: John Wayne, Alberta Vaughan, George Hayes, Yakima Canutt, Earl Dwire, Tex Phelps, Artie Ortego, Tex Palmer, Mack V. Wright, Herman Hack.

Randy Bowers (John Wayne) infiltrates the outlaw gang responsible for murdering the inhabitants of the Halfway House.

Running time: 54 minutes. Release date: June 15, 1934.

82. Shock (drama) Directed by Roy J. Pomeroy. Screenplay by Madeline Ruthuen. Story by Roy J. Pomeroy.

Cast: Ralph Forbes, Gwenllian Gill, Monroe Owsley, Reginald Sharland, Douglas Walton, Alex Courtney, David Jack Holt, Billy Bevan, Clyde Cook, Mary Forbes, Charles Coleman, Colin Campbell, David Dunbar, Montague Shaw, Eric Snowden, Olaf Hytten, Harry Holden.

Just after marrying an English girl (Gwenllian Gill), a British officer (Ralph Forbes) is called back to the front lines. He returns suffering from shell-shock and amnesia and fails to recognize his new spouse.

Running time: 69 minutes. Release date: July 20, 1934.

83. The Star Packer (western) Directed by Robert N. Bradbury. Produced by Paul Malvern. Story and screenplay by Robert N. Bradbury. A Lone Star Production.

Cast: John Wayne, Verna Hillie, George Hayes, Yakima Canutt, Earl Dwire, Eddie Parker, George Cleveland, Tom Lingham, Artie Ortego, Tex Palmer, Davie Aldrich, Glenn Strange, Billy Franey.

After the new sheriff is killed, U.S. Marshal John Travers (John Wayne) assumes his job and sets out to capture the notorious Shadow Gang.

Running time: 54 minutes. Release date: July 30, 1934.

Released in Great Britain as **He Wore a Star.**

84. Jane Eyre (drama) Directed by Christy Cabanne. Supervised by Ben Verschleiser. Screenplay by Adele Comandini. From the novel by Charlotte Bronte.

Cast: Virginia Bruce, Colin Clive, Beryl Mercer, Jameson Thomas, Eileen Pringle, David Torrence, Lionel Belmore, Joan Standing, Edith Fellows, Desmond Roberts, John Rogers, Clarissa Selwynne, Hylda Tyson, Gretta Gould, Claire duBrey, Ethel Griffies, Edith Kingdon, William Wagner, Olaf Hytten, William Burres, Gail Kaye, Jean Darling, Richard Quine, Anne Howard.

Jane Eyre (Virginia Bruce), a young woman raised in an orphanage, becomes a governess at the Rochester mansion, an estate shrouded in secrecy.

Running time: 70 minutes. Release date: August 15, 1934.

Charlotte Bronte's novel was filmed various times in the silent era, including versions in 1913, 1915, and 1921. After this Monogram version, it was filmed again in 1944 (20th Century-Fox) and 1971 (made-for-TV).

85. The Moonstone (mystery) Directed by Reginald Barker. Produced by Paul Malvern. Screenplay by Adele Buffington. From the novel by Wilkie Collins.

Cast: David Manners, Phyllis Barry, Gustav von

Virginia Bruce and Colin Clive in "Jane Eyre" (1934).

Seyffertitz, Jameson Thomas, Herbert Bunston, Evelyn Bostock, John Davidson, Elspeth Dudgeon, Claude King, Olaf Hytten, Charles Irwin, Fred Walton.

Shortly after a scientist's daughter (Phyllis Barry) comes into possession of the Moonstone, a famous Indian diamond, the gem is stolen.

Running time: 62 minutes. Release date: August 20, 1934.

86. Happy Landing (action-drama) Directed by Robert N. Bradbury. Supervised by Paul Malvern. Story and screenplay by Stuart Anthony.

Cast: Ray Walker, Jacqueline Wells (Julie Bishop),

William Farnum, Noah Beery (Sr.), Hyram Hoover, Morgan Conway, Warner Richmond, Donald Reed, Billy Erwin, Ruth Romaine, Eddie Fetherstone, Gertrude Simpson.

A border patrol flier (Ray Walker) is suspected of being in league with a gang of payroll thieves but proves his innocence when he thwarts an attempted robbery.

Running time: 63 minutes. Release date: September 1, 1934.

87. King Kelly of the U.S.A. (musical-comedy) Directed by Leonard Fields. Supervised by George Bertholon. Screenplay by Leonard Fields and David Silverstein. Story by George Bertholon and Howard Higgins.

Cast: Guy Robertson, Irene Ware, Edgar Kennedy, Franklin Pangborn, Joyce Compton, Fredinand Gottschalk, William von Brincken, Lorin Raker, Otis Harlan, Bodil Rosing.

A livewire showman (Guy Robertson) and his theatrical troupe journey to the bankrupt kingdom of Belgardia; there the showman falls in love with the king's daughter (Irene Ware) who is betrothed to another.

Running time: 66 minutes. Release date: September 15, 1934.

Released in Great Britain as **Irish and Proud of It.**

88. A Girl of the Limberlost (drama) Directed by Christy Cabanne. Produced by William T. Lackey. Screenplay by Adele Comandini. Based on the Gene Stratton-Porter novel.

Cast: Louise Dresser, Ralph Morgan, Marian Marsh, Henry B. Walthall, Edward Nugent, Gigi Parrish, Helen Jerome Eddy, Betty Blythe, Barbara Bedford, Robert Ellis, Tommy Bupp.

Elnora Comstock (Marian Marsh), unloved by her mother (Louise Dresser) who blames the girl for the death of the father (Robert Ellis), finds comfort with a childless neighboring couple (Ralph Morgan, Helen Jerome Eddy).

Running time: 76 minutes. Release date: October 15, 1934.

89. A Successful Failure (comedy) Directed by Arthur Lubin. Screenplay by Marion Orth. Story by Michael Kane.

Cast: William Collier, Sr., Lucile Gleason, Russell Hopton, Gloria Shea, William Janney, Jameson Thomas, George Breakston, Richard Tucker, Clarence Wilson, Francis McDonald.

An elderly newspaperman (William Collier, Sr.), driven by his thoughtless family, loses his job but finds success on radio.

Running time: 62 minutes. Release date: October 15, 1934.

90. The Trail Beyond (western) Directed by Robert N. Bradbury. Produced by Paul Malvern. Screenplay by Lindsley Parsons. From the story "The Wolf Hunters" by James Oliver Curwood. A Lone Star Production.

Cast: John Wayne, Noah Beery, Jr., Verna Hillie, Iris Lancaster, Robert Frazer, Earl Dwire, Eddie Parker, Artie Ortego, James Marcus, Reed Howes.

A lawman (John Wayne) heads for the northwest territory to find a missing girl (Verna Hillie) and a gold mine.

Running time: 55 minutes. Release date: October 22, 1934.

91. Lost in the Stratosphere (comedy-drama) Directed by Melville Brown. Produced by William T. Lackey. Screenplay by Albert E. DeMond. Story by Tristram Tupper.

Cast: William Cagney, Edward Nugent, June Collyer, Lona Andre, Edmund Breese, Frank McGlynn, Pauline Garon, Matt McHugh, Hattie McDaniel.

Two air force lieutenants (William Cagney, Edward Nugent), friendly enemies who quarrel over the same girl (June Collyer), are assigned to undertake a new stratosphere flight.

Running time: 64 minutes. Release date: November 15, 1934.

Working title: **Murder in the Stratosphere.**

92. Redhead (comedy-drama) Directed by Melville

Brown. Supervised by Mrs. Wallace (Dorothy) Reid. Screen-play by Betty Burbridge. Additional dialogue by Jesse Lasky, Jr. From the novel by Vera Brown.

Cast: Bruce Cabot, Grace Bradley, Regis Toomey, Berton Churchill, George Humbert, Rita Campagna, LeRoy Mason, Monte Carter, Jack Mack, Ed Brady, Bess Stafford, Addison Page.

A nightclub girl (Grace Bradley) weds a playboy (Bruce Cabot), expecting a sizeable payoff from her new father-in-law (Berton Churchill). But the father turns his son out into the street without a cent and private-ly promises the girl that if she can make a man of her new husband, $10,000 and a quick divorce will be hers.

Running time: 76 minutes. Release date: November 15, 1934.

Remade by Monogram in 1941.

93. Girl o' My Dreams (comedy-drama) Directed by Ray McCarey. Produced by William T. Lackey. Screenplay by George Waggner.

Cast: Mary Carlisle, Eddie Nugent, Creighton Chaney (Lon Chaney, Jr.), Arthur Lake, Sterling Holloway, Gigi Parrish, Jeanie Roberts, Tom Dugan, Lee Shumway, Beverly Crane, Betty Mae Crane, George Cleveland, Ted Dahl and His Orchestra.

A conceited college track star (Eddie Nugent), in love with a sorority queen (Mary Carlisle), has the wind knocked out of his ego when he loses an election for most popular man on campus.

Running time: 65 minutes. Release date: November 17, 1934.

94. The Lawless Frontier (western) Directed by Robert N. Bradbury. Produced by Paul Malvern. Story and screen-play by Robert N. Bradbury. A Lone Star Production.

Cast: John Wayne, Sheila Terry, George Hayes, Jack Rockwell, Buffalo Bill, Jr., Yakima Canutt, Earl Dwire, Lloyd Whitlock, G.D. Wood (Gordon DeMain), Eddie Parker, Artie Ortego, Herman Hack.

An itinerant cowboy (John Wayne) clashes with a Mexican gang trying to seize control of a gold mine owned by a young woman (Sheila Terry) and her father (George Hayes).

Running time: 54 minutes. Release date: November 22, 1934.

95. Flirting with Danger (comedy) Directed by Vin Moore. Supervised by George Bertholon. Screenplay by Albert E. DeMond. Story by George Bertholon. Additional dialogue by Norman S. Hall.

Cast: Robert Armstrong, William Cagney, Edgar Kennedy, Marion Burns, Maria Alba, William von Brincken, Gino Corrado, Ernest Hilliard, Guy Usher.

Three devil-may-care powder mixers (Robert Armstrong, William Cagney, Edgar Kennedy) are sent to work for a South American dynamite plant.

Running time: 70 minutes. Release date: December 1, 1934.

Working titles: **Dames and Dynamite** and **Reckless Romeos.**

96. Sing Sing Nights (mystery) Directed by Lewis D. Collins. Produced by Paul Malvern. Screenplay by Marion Orth. Additional dialogue by Charles Logue. Based on the novel by Harry Stephen Keeler.

Cast: Conway Tearle, Hardie Albright, Boots Mallory, Mary Doran, Ferdinand Gottschalk, Berton Churchill, Jameson Thomas, Lotus Long, Henry Kolker, Richard Tucker, George Baxter.

Three men (Hardie Albright, Jameson Thomas, George Baxter), all accused of murdering a war correspondent (Conway Tearle), are given an opportunity to tell their side of the story.

Running time: 60 minutes. Release date: December 15, 1934.

97. 'Neath the Arizona Skies (western) Directed by Harry Fraser. Produced by Paul Malvern. Story and screenplay by Burt R. Tuttle. A Lone Star Production.

Cast: John Wayne, Sheila Terry, Jay Wilsey (Buffalo Bill, Jr.), Shirley Ricketts (Shirley Jane Rickey), Earl Dwire, Weston Edwards, George Hayes, Yakima Canutt,

Jack Rockwell, Phil Keefer, Frank Hall Crane, Artie Ortego, Tex Phelps, Eddie Parker.

A cowboy (John Wayne) protects a little Indian girl (Shirley Ricketts), an oil land heiress, from murderous outlaws.

Running time: 52 minutes. Release date: December 28, 1934.

98. Million Dollar Baby (comedy-drama) Directed by Joseph Santley. Produced by Ben Verschleiser. Screenplay by Joseph Santley and John W. Krafft. Story by Joseph Santley.

Cast: Ray Walker, Arline Judge, Jimmy Fay, George E. Stone, Eddie Kane, Willard Robertson, Ralf Harolde, Lee Shumway, Edward Peil, Sr., Paul Porcasi, Wilbur Mack, Jeanette Loff, Arthur Stone, Harry Holman, The Connor Twins.

A vaudeville team (Ray Walker, Arline Judge) disguise their young son (Jimmy Fay) as a girl so they can enter him in a movie contest looking for "another Shirley Temple."

Running time: 65 minutes. Release date: December 29, 1934.

1935

99. Mysterious Mr. Wong (mystery-drama) Directed by William Nigh. Supervised by George Yohalem. Screenplay by Lew Stevenson. Additional dialogue by James Herbuveaux. Based on the novel "The Twelve Coins of Confucius" by Harry Stephen Keeler. Adapted by Nina Howatt.

Cast: Bela Lugosi, Wallace Ford, Arline Judge, Fred Warren, Lotus Long, Robert Emmett O'Connor, Edward Peil, Sr., Luke Chan, Lee Shumway, Etta Lee, Ernest F. Young, Theodore Lorch, James B. Leong, Chester Gan.

The fiendish Mr. Wong (Bela Lugosi) stops at nothing to gain possession of the 12 coins of Confucius which, according to legend, will bring him great power.

Feature Films 1935

Running time: 68 minutes. Release date: January 25, 1935.

100. Texas Terror (western) Directed by Robert N. Bradbury. Produced by Paul Malvern. Story and screenplay by Robert N. Bradbury. A Lone Star Production.

Cast: John Wayne, Lucile Browne, LeRoy Mason, George Hayes, Buffalo Bill, Jr., Bert Dillard, Yakima Canutt, Bobby Nelson, Fern Emmett, John Ince, Henry Rocquemore, Jack Duffy, Lloyd Ingraham.

When a cowboy (John Wayne) mistakenly believes he has killed his best friend by accident, he seeks solitude in the lonely life of a gold prospector.

Running time: 51 minutes. Release date: February 1, 1935.

101. Women Must Dress (drama) Directed by Reginald Barker. Produced by Mrs. Wallace (Dorothy) Reid. Story and screenplay by Dorothy Reid and Edmund Joseph.

Cast: Minna Gombell, Gavin Gordon, Hardie Albright, Lenita Lane, Suzanne Kaaren, Robert Light, Zeffie Tilbury, Allan Edwards, Paul Ellis, Gerald Young, Anne Johnson, Nell Rhoads, Madelyn Earle, Harriet deBussman, Anne Kasper, Sandra Broaux, Fay Hammar.

After her husband (Gavin Gordon) divorces her and runs off with another woman (Lenita Lane), Linda Howard (Minna Gombell) becomes a dress designer and a partner in a fashionable women's shop.

Running time: 77 minutes. Release date: February 1, 1935.

102. Tomorrow's Youth (drama) Directed by Charles Lamont. Produced by Trem Carr. Story and screenplay by Harry Sauber, Gene Whitney and Robert Meller.

Cast: Dickie Moore, John Miljan, Gloria Shea, Martha Sleeper, Jane Darwell, Franklin Pangborn, Paul Hurst, Barbara Bedford, Harry C. Bradley, Niles Welch, Edward LeSaint.

The reaction of a young boy (Dickie Moore) to his parents' divorce.

Running time: 63 minutes. Release date: Feb. 1935.

103. Rainbow Valley (western) Directed by Robert N. Bradbury. Produced by Paul Malvern. Story and screenplay by Lindsley Parsons. A Lone Star Production.

Cast: John Wayne, Lucile Browne, LeRoy Mason, George Hayes, Buffalo Bill, Jr., Bert Dillard, Lloyd Ingraham, Lafe McKee, Fern Emmett, Henry Rocquemore, Eddie Parker, Herman Hack, Frank Ellis, Art Dillard, Frank Ball.

An undercover agent (John Wayne) thwarts the plans of an outlaw gang trying to halt construction of a road that will link a small town with the county seat.

Running time: 52 minutes. Release date: March 12, 1935.

104. The Nut Farm (comedy) Directed by Melville Brown. Produced by William T. Lackey. Screenplay by George Waggner. From the play by John C. Brownell.

Cast: Wallace Ford, Florence Roberts, Oscar Apfel, Betty Alden, Bradley Page, Joan Gale, Spencer Charters, Lorin Raker, Arnold Gray, Arthur Hoyt, Syd Saylor, Stanley Blystone, John Ince, Hank Mann, Lona Andre.

Selling out his grocery store and intent upon buying a California nut farm, Bob Bent (Oscar Apfel) sees his plans go awry when his wife Helen (Betty Alden) falls for a "get-rich-through-movie-production" swindle.

Running time: 65 minutes. Release date: March 25, 1935.

105. Great God Gold (drama) Directed by Arthur Lubin. Screenplay by Norman Houston. Story by Albert J. Meserow and Elynore Dalkhart. Additional dialogue by Jefferson Parker.

Cast: Sidney Blackmer, Martha Sleeper, Regis Toomey, Gloria Shea, Edwin Maxwell, Ralf Harolde, Maria Alba, John T. Murray.

A financial reporter (Regis Toomey) and a hotel owner's daughter (Martha Sleeper) join forces to gather evidence against the leader of a crooked business racket (Sidney Blackmer).

Running time: 71 minutes. Release date: April 15, 1935.

Mary Kornman and John Wayne in "The Desert Trail" (1935).

106. The Desert Trail (western) Directed by Cullen Lewis (Lewis D. Collins). Produced by Paul Malvern. Story and screenplay by Lindsley Parsons. A Lone Star Production.

Cast: John Wayne, Mary Kornman, Paul Fix, Eddy Chandler, Carmen LaRoux, Lafe McKee, Al Ferguson, Henry Hall, Frank Ball, Artie Ortego, Lew Meehan, Wally West, Frank Brownlee, Frank Ellis, Dick Dickinson.

A cowboy (John Wayne) sets out to trap the bandit gang that held up a rodeo.

Running time: 54 minutes. Release date: April 22, 1935.

107. The Mystery Man (mystery) Directed by Ray Mc-Carey. Supervised by Trem Carr. Screenplay by John W. Krafft and Rollo Lloyd. Story by Tate Finn.

Cast: Robert Armstrong, Maxine Doyle, Henry Kolker, LeRoy Mason, James Burke, Guy Usher, James Burtis, Monte Collins, Sam Lufkin, Otto Fries, Norman Houston, Dell Henderson.

In need of funds, a newspaper reporter (Robert Armstrong) pawns a police revolver that was given to him after he cleared up a criminal case. When the gun is used in a murder, he's suspected of the killing.

Running time: 65 minutes. Release date: April 25, 1935.

Remade as **Man from Headquarters** (Monogram, 1942).

108. The Hoosier Schoolmaster (drama) Directed by Lewis D. Collins. Produced by Trem Carr. Screenplay by Charles Logue. From the novel by Edward Eggleston.

Cast: Norman Foster, Charlotte Henry, Sarah Padden, William V. Mong, Dorothy Libaire, Otis Harlan, Russell Simpson, Fred Kohler, Jr., Tommy Bupp, Wallace Reid, Jr., George Hayes, Joe Bernard.

After the Civil War, an ex-Union soldier (Norman Foster) becomes a school teacher in a small Indiana town and confronts crooked politicians who are juggling federal land grants, denying squatter-camped veterans claim to their rightful property.

Running time: 75 minutes. Release date: May 15, 1935.

Released in Great Britain as **The Schoolmaster.**

109 The Healer (drama) Directed by Reginald Barker. Screenplay by James Knox Millen and John Goodrich. From the novel by Robert Herrick.

Cast: Ralph Bellamy, Karen Morley, Mickey Rooney, Judith Allen, Robert McWade, Bruce Warren, J. Farrell MacDonald, Vessie Farrell.

A doctor (Ralph Bellamy) running a polio health farm has his head turned by a society girl (Judith Allen) and ignores his patients and his true love (Karen Morley).

Running time: 77 minutes. Release date: June 15, 1935.

Because of Mickey Rooney's subsequent success, **The Healer** was later reissued under the title **Little Pal.**

110. The Dawn Rider (western) Directed by Robert N. Bradbury. Produced by Paul Malvern. Screenplay by Robert N. Bradbury. Story by Lloyd Nosler.

Cast: John Wayne, Marion Burns, Yakima Canutt, Reed Howes, Denny Meadows (Dennis Moore), Bert Dillard, Jack Jones, Nelson McDowell, Archie Ricks, Tex Phelps, James Sheridan.

A cowboy (John Wayne) goes after the outlaws who killed his father during an express office holdup.

Running time: 57 minutes. Release date: June 20, 1935.

111. Honeymoon Limited (comedy) Directed by Arthur Lubin. Produced by Mrs. Wallace (Dorothy) Reid. Screenplay by Dorothy Reid and Betty Burbridge. Story by Vida Hurst.

Cast: Neil Hamilton, Irene Hervey, Lloyd Hughes, Russell Hicks, Lorin Raker, Joy Filmer, June Filmer, George Hayes, Henry Kolker, Gertrude Astor, Virginia Brissac, Lee Moran.

A publisher (Henry Kolker) makes a bet with a best-selling author (Neil Hamilton) that he cannot write a romantic adventure novel while making a walking trip from New York to San Francisco. During his trek, the author meets the publisher's grandchildren (Irene Hervey, Joy and June Filmer) and a pair of ex-cons (Russell Hicks, Lorin Raker) who are trying to recoup some stolen loot.

Running time: 70 minutes (previewed at 83, then cut). Release date: July 1, 1935.

112. Keeper of the Bees (drama) Directed by Christy Cabanne. Produced by William T. Lackey. Screenplay by Adele Buffington and George Waggner. From the novel by Gene Stratton-Porter.

Cast: Neil Hamilton, Betty Furness, Emma Dunn, Edith Fellows, Hobart Bosworth, Helen Jerome Eddy,

Marion Shilling, James Burtis, Barbara Bedford, Lafe McKee, George Cleveland, William Worthington, Gigi Parrish.

A war-shattered man (Neil Hamilton), believing that he is living on borrowed time, comes to an idyllic seaside village. There he becomes associated with the kindly old character Bee Master (Hobart Bosworth) and his child protegee Little Scout (Edith Fellows); through their kindness, he finds a new will to live.

Running time: 75 minutes. Release date: July 15, 1935.

Remade by Columbia Pictures in 1947.

113. Paradise Canyon (western) Directed by Carl Pierson. Produced by Paul Malvern. Screenplay by Robert Tansey and Lindsley Parsons. Story by Lindsley Parsons.

Cast: John Wayne, Marion Burns, Earle Hodgins, Yakima Canutt, Reed Howes, Perry Murdock, John Goodrich, Gino Corrado, Gordon Clifford, Tex Palmer, Herman Hack, Earl Dwire.

A government agent (John Wayne) goes after counterfeiters operating near the Mexican border.

Running time: 52 minutes. Release date: July 20, 1935.

114. Make a Million (comedy) Directed by Lewis D. Collins. Screenplay by Charles Logue. Story by Emmett Anthony.

Cast: Charles Starrett, Pauline Brooks, George E. Stone, James Burke, Guy Usher, Norman Houston, Monte Carter, Jimmy Aubrey, George Cleveland, John Elliott.

An instructor of economics (Charles Starrett), seeking a method of redistributing wealth, combines certain aspects of a chain letter with a mail-order business and, eventually, is on his way to success.

Running time: 68 minutes. Release date: July 25, 1935.

115. Cheers of the Crowd (drama) Directed by Vin Moore. Produced Trem Carr. Story and screenplay by George Waggner.

Cast: Russell Hopton, Irene Ware, Bradley Page, Harry Holman, Betty Blythe, Wade Boteler, Roberta Page, John Quillan, John H. Dilson.

A publicity expert (Russell Hopton) hires an ex-carnival character (Harry Holman) as part of a publicity stunt that draws attention to a popular show, unaware that the man is on the lam from the authorities.

Running time: 60 minutes. Release date: August 5, 1935.

1936

There were no Monogram releases in 1936 (see Historical Overview).

1937

116. The Thirteenth Man (mystery) Directed by William Nigh. Produced by Lon Young. Screenplay by John Krafft.

Cast: Weldon Heyburn, Inez Courtney, Selmer Jackson, Milburn Stone, Matty Fain, Robert Homan, Eadie Adams, Grace Durkin, Sidney D'Albrook.

A newspaper columnist (Weldon Heyburn) investigates the death of a district attorney who was killed by a type of poisoned dart used by Malay savages.

Running time: 70 minutes. Release date: June 30, 1937.

117. Blazing Barriers (adventure-drama) Directed by Aubrey Scotto. Original story and screenplay by Edwin C. Parsons.

Cast: Frank Coghlan, Jr., Florine McKinney, Edward Arnold, Jr., Irene Franklin, Guy Bates Post, Herbert Corthell, Milburn Stone, Addison Randall.

Two young city toughs (Frank Coghlan, Jr., Edward Arnold, Jr.) are sent to the Civilian Conservation Corps.

Running time: 65 minutes. Release date: July 4, 1937.

Anne Nagel and Mickey Rooney in "Hoosier Schoolboy" (1937).

118. Hoosier Schoolboy (drama) Directed by William Nigh. Produced by Ken Goldsmith. Screenplay by Robert Lee Johnson. From the novel by Edward Eggleston.

Cast: Mickey Rooney, Anne Nagel, Frank Shields, Edward Pawley, William Gould, Bradley Metcalf, Dorothy Vaughn.

A school teacher (Frank Shields) befriends a young pupil (Mickey Rooney) whose father (Edward Pawley), a shell-shocked war veteran, is the town drunk.

Running time: 62 minutes. Release date: July 7, 1937.

Reissued by Monogram in 1941 as **Forgotten Hero.**

119. Riders of the Dawn (western) Produced and directed by Robert N. Bradbury. Screenplay by Robert Emmett (Tansey).

Feature Films 1937

Cast: Jack Randall, Peggy Keyes, Warner Richmond, George Cooper, James Sheridan, Earl Dwire, Lloyd Ingraham, Ed Brady, Yakima Canutt, Steve Clark, Frank Hagney, Ella McKenzie, Ed Coxen, Chick Hannon, Tim Davis, Jim Corey, Oscar Gahan, Forrest Taylor, Tex Cooper.

A State Marshal (Jack Randall) helps rid a small western town of an outlaw gang.

Running time: 55 minutes. Release date: July 14, 1937.

120. Paradise Isle (drama) Directed by Arthur Greville. Produced by Mrs. Dorothy Reid. Screenplay by Marion Orth. From the Cosmopolitan story "The Belled Palm" by Allan Vaughan Elston.

Cast: Movita, Warren Hull, George Piltz, William Davidson, John St. Polis, Russell Simpson, Kenneth Harlan, Pierre Watkin.

On his way to Java to have a noted eye specialist operate on him, a blind artist (Warren Hull) winds up on an island shore after a shipwreck. There a native girl (Movita) nurses him back to health.

Running time: 73 minutes. Release date: July 21, 1937.

Reissued by Monogram in 1941 as **Siren of the South Seas**.

121. The Legion of Missing Men (action-adventure) Directed by Hamilton MacFadden. Produced by I.E. Chadwick. Screenplay by Sherman L. Lowe and Harry O. Hoyt. Story by Norman S. Hall.

Cast: Ralph Forbes, Ben Alexander, George Regas, Hala Linda, Jimmy Aubrey, Paul Hurst, Frank Leigh, Roy D'Arcy.

Brothers-in-arms (Ralph Forbes, Ben Alexander) join the Foreign Legion and find themselves pitted against merciless Arab killers.

Running time: 62 min. Release date: July 28, 1937.

122. The Outer Gate (drama) Directed by Ray Cannon. Produced by I.E. Chadwick. Story and screenplay by Laurie Brazee.

Cast: Ralph Morgan, Kay Linaker, Ben Alexander, Edward Acuff, Charles Brokaw.

After being imprisoned for a theft he didn't commit, a bookkeeper (Ben Alexander) is determined to get even with his boss (Ralph Morgan), the man who prosecuted him.

Running time: 62 minutes. Release date: August 4, 1937. Alternate title: **Behind Prison Bars.**

123. Shadows of the Orient (action-drama) Directed by Burt Lynwood. Produced by Larry Darmour. Screenplay by Charles Francis Royal. Original story by L.E. Heifetz.

Cast: Esther Ralston, Regis Toomey, J. Farrell Mac-Donald, Sidney Blackmer, Oscar Apfel, Eddie Featherstone, Kit Guard, Matty Fain, James B. Leong.

A young woman (Esther Ralston) inadvertently becomes involved in a plot to smuggle Chinese immigrants across the Mexican border into the United States.

Running time: 69 minutes. Release date: August 18, 1937.

124. Atlantic Flight (action-drama) Directed by William Nigh. Produced by William Berke. Story and screenplay by Scott Darling and Erna Lazarus.

Cast: Dick Merrill (holder of the World's Round-Trip Atlantic Flight Record), Paula Stone, Jack Lambie, Weldon Heyburn, Ivan Lebedeff, Milburn Stone.

A pilot (Dick Merrill) plans to compete in a national air race meet, but his efforts are hampered by a phony baron (Ivan Lebedeff).

Running time: 59 minutes. Release date: August 25, 1937.

125. God's Country and the Man (western) Produced and directed by Robert N. Bradbury. Screenplay by Robert Emmett (Tansey).

Cast: Tom Keene, Betty Compson, Charlotte Henry, Charles King, Billy Bletcher, Eddie Parker, Bob McKenzie, Merrill McCormack, James Sheridan (Sherry Tansey).

A cowboy (Tom Keene), who has an "in" with the Mounties, pursues a notorious gunman (Charles King) who is threatening a dance hall girl (Betty Compson), the owner of a gold mine.

Running time: 56 minutes. Release date: September 2, 1937.

126. Stars Over Arizona (western) Produced and directed by Robert N. Bradbury. Screenplay by Robert Emmett (Tansey) and Ernie Adams.

Cast: Jack Randall, Kathleen Elliot, Horace Murphy, Warner Richmond, Tom Herbert, Hal Price, Earl Dwire, Chick Hannon, Charles Romas, Shuma Shermatova, Jack Rockwell, Forrest Taylor, Bob McKenzie, Tex Palmer, Sherry Tansey.

A cowboy (Jack Randall) and his partner (Horace Murphy) help rid Yuba City of a bandit gang.

Running time: 62 minutes. Release date: September 22, 1937.

127. A Bride for Henry (drama) Directed by William Nigh. Produced by Dorothy (Mrs. Wallace) Reid. Screenplay by Dean Spencer. From the Liberty magazine story by Josephine Bentham.

Cast: Anne Nagel, Warren Hull, Henry Mollison, Claudia Dell, Betty Ross Clark, Harrison Greene.

After being jilted by her fiance (Henry Mollison), a rich and spoiled girl (Anne Nagel) marries a young man (Warren Hull) on the rebound.

Running time: 58 minutes. Release date: September 29, 1937.

128. Where Trails Divide (western) Produced and directed by Robert N. Bradbury. Screenplay by Robert Emmett (Tansey).

Cast: Tom Keene, Eleanor Stewart, Warner Richmond, David Sharpe, Lorraine Randall, Charles K. French, Steve Clark, Hal Price, Dick Cramer, James Sheridan (Sherry Tansey), Bud Osborne, Horace B. Carpenter, Wally West, James Mason, Forrest Taylor, Oscar Gahan.

An undercover agent (Tom Keene), posing as a lawyer, is assigned to nab a gang of stagecoach robbers.

Running time: 59 min. Release date: Oct. 13, 1937.

Kathleen Elliot and Jack Randall in "Stars Over Arizona" (1937).

129. Federal Bullets (mystery) Directed by Karl Brown. Produced by Lon Young. Screenplay by Karl Brown. Story by Maj. George F. Eliot.

Cast: Milburn Stone, Zeffie Tilbury, Terry Walker, Selmer Jackson, William Harrigan, Matty Fain, Lyle Moraine, Warner Richmond, Eddie Phillips, Betty Compson, Helen MacKeller, John Merton.

A G-man (Milburn Stone) exposes a fake philanthropic organization which is a front for a crime ring.

Running time: 61 minutes. Release date: October 30, 1937.

130. Danger Valley (western) Produced and directed by Robert N. Bradbury. Screenplay by Robert Emmett (Tansey).

Cast: Jack Randall, Lois Wilde, Charles King, Hal

Price, Frank LaRue, Chick Hannon, Earl Dwire, Jimmy Aubrey, Glenn Strange, Bud Osborne, Tex Palmer, Merrill McCormack, Oscar Gahan, Denver Dixon (Victor Adamson). A cowboy (Jack Randall) clashes with crooks who use forged papers to jump gold claims. Running time: 58 minutes. Release date: November 3, 1937.

131. The Luck of Roaring Camp (adventure) Directed by Irvin Willat. Produced by Scott R. Dunlap. Screenplay by Harvey Gates. Story by Bret Harte.

Cast: Owen Davis, Jr., Joan Woodbury, Charles Brokaw, Forrest Taylor, Bob Kortman, Charles King, Byron Foulger, Bob McKenzie, John Wallace.

A saga of the California gold rush: the arrival of a baby brings good fortune to a mining camp community. Running time: 58 minutes. Release date: November 17, 1937.

132. County Fair (drama) Directed by Howard Bretherton. Produced by E.B. Derr. Story and screenplay by John T. Neville. A Crescent Pictures Production.

Cast: John Arledge, Mary Lou Lender, J. Farrell MacDonald, Fuzzy Knight, Jimmy Butler, Harry Worth, Matty Roubert, William Hunter.

A ex-jockey (John Arledge) enters a local farm plug in the county-fair race, trying to win the prize money which will help pay off the mortgage. Running time: 72 minutes. Release date: November 24, 1937.

133. Telephone Operator (drama) Directed by Scott Pembroke. Produced by Lon Young. Screenplay by Scott Darling. Story by John Krafft.

Cast: Judith Allen, Grant Withers, Warren Hymer, Alice White, Pat Flaherty, Greta Granstedt, William Haade.

A telephone operator (Judith Allen) saves her friend's honor by her heroic action during a flood. Running time: 62 minutes. Release date: December 8, 1937.

134. Romance of the Rockies (western) Produced and directed by Robert N. Bradbury. Screenplay by Robert Emmett (Tansey).

Cast: Tom Keene, Beryl Wallace, Don Orlando, Bill Cody, Jr., Franklyn Farnum, Earl Dwire, Russell Paul, Steve Clark, Jim Corey, Tex Palmer, Jack C. Smith, John "Blackie" Whiteford, Frank Ellis.

A country doctor (Tom Keene) aids ranchers in their fight to protect their water rights.

Running time: 53 minutes. Release date: December 15, 1937.

1938

135. Boy of the Streets (drama) Directed by William Nigh. Screenplay by W. Scott Darling and Gilson Brown. Original story by Rowland Brown.

Cast: Jackie Cooper, Maureen O'Connor, Kathleen Burke, Robert Emmett O'Connor, Marjorie Main, Guy Usher, Matty Fain, George Cleveland, Gordon (Bill) Elliott, Don Latorre, Paul White.

A young boy (Jackie Cooper), growing up in the tenement-cloistered surroundings of the Bowery, struggles to find a feeling of self-worth.

Running time: 76 minutes. Release date: January 8, 1938.

136. West of Rainbow's End (western) Directed by Alan James. Produced by Maurice Conn. Screenplay by Stanley Roberts and Gennaro Rea. Story by Robert Emmett (Tansey). A Concord Production.

Cast: Tim McCoy, Kathleen Eliot, Walter McGrail, Frank LaRue, George Chang, Mary Carr, Ed Coxen, George Cooper, Bob Kortman, Jimmy Aubrey, Reed Howes, Ray Jones, Sherry Tansey.

A railroad detective (Tim McCoy) comes out of retirement to track down murderous landgrabbers who are conspiring against the railroad.

Running time: 57 minutes. Release date: January 12, 1938.

137. Saleslady (drama) Directed by Arthur Greville. Produced by Ken Goldsmith. Screenplay by Marion Orth. Based on the story "Nothing Down" by Kubec Glasman.

Cast: Anne Nagel, Weldon Heyburn, Harry Davenport, Harry Hayden, Ruth Fallows, Kenneth Harlan, Doris Rankia, John St. Polis.

A young woman (Anne Nagel), heiress to a fortune, becomes a saleslady in a department store; she marries a salesman (Weldon Heyburn) and sets up housekeeping, all the while pretending to be as poor as he is.

Running time: 65 minutes. Release date: February 2, 1938.

138. Where the West Begins (western) Directed by John P. McGowan. Produced by Maurice Conn. Screenplay by Stanley Roberts and Gennaro Rea. Story by Stanley Roberts.

Cast: Jack Randall, Luana Walters, Fuzzy Knight, Budd Buster, Arthur Housman, Dick Alexander, Ralph Peters, Joe Garcia, Kit Guard, Ray Whitley and the Six-Bar Cowboys (Ken Card and the Phelps Brothers).

A ranch foreman (Jack Randall) tries to prevent his employer (Luana Walters) from being swindled out of her land, which contains valuable sulphur deposits.

Running time: 54 minutes. Release date: February 2, 1938.

139. My Old Kentucky Home (drama) Directed by Lambert Hillyer. Produced by E.B. Derr. Original story and screenplay by John T. Neville. A Crescent Pictures Production.

Cast: Evelyn Venable, Grant Richards, Clara Blandick, Bernadene Hayes, J. Farrell MacDonald, Mildred Gorer, Margaret Marquis, Cornelius Keefe, Kitty McHugh, Raquel Davido, Paul White, The Hall Johnson Choir.

A young man from the South (Grant Richards), betrothed to a Southern girl (Evelyn Venable), becomes involved with a Northern actress (Bernadene Hayes).

Running time: 72 minutes. Release date: February 9, 1938.

140. The Painted Trail (western) Directed by Robert

Hill. Produced by Robert Tansey. Screenplay by Robert Emmett (Tansey).

Cast: Tom Keene, Eleanor Stewart, LeRoy Mason, Walter Long, Jimmy Eagles, Forrest Taylor, Harry Harvey, Ernie Adams, Bud Osborne, Glenn Strange, Frank Campeau, Bob Kortman, Dick Cramer, Tom London.

A U.S. Marshal (Tom Keene) poses as "The Pecos Kid," an outlaw, in order to infiltrate a gang of rustlers who are smuggling cattle across the border.

Running time: 50 minutes. Release date: February 23, 1938.

141. Port of Missing Girls (drama) Directed by Karl Brown. Produced by Lon Young. Original screenplay by Karl Brown.

Cast: Judith Allen, Milburn Stone, Harry Carey, Betty Compson, Matty Fain, Jane Jones, George Cleveland, William Costello, Sandra Karina, Lyle Moraine, Louis Vincent.

A San Francisco nightclub entertainer (Judith Allen) is wrongfully implicated in a gang murder; she stows away aboard a boat and heads for Shanghai, "the port of missing girls."

Running time: 65 minutes. Release date: February 23, 1938.

142. Land of Fighting Men (western) Directed by Alan James. Produced by Maurice Conn. Screenplay by Joseph O'Donnell. Original story by Stanley Roberts.

Cast: Jack Randall, Herman Brix (Bruce Bennett), Louise Stanley, Dickie Jones, Robert Burns, Wheeler Oakman, John Merton, Lane Chandler, Rex Lease, Ernie Adams, The Colorado Hillbillies.

After murdering a rancher (Herman Brix), a land-grabber (Wheeler Oakman) places the blame on a cowboy (Jack Randall).

Running time: 53 min. Release date: March 11, 1938.

143. Rose of the Rio Grande (adventure) Directed by William Nigh. Produced by George E. Kann. Screenplay by Ralph Bettinson. Story by Johnston McCulley.

Jack Randall and Louise Stanley in "Land of Fighting Men" (1938).

Cast: Movita, John Carroll, Antonio Moreno, Don Alvarado, Lina Basquette, Duncan Renaldo, George Cleveland, Gino Corrado, Martin Garralaga, Rosa Turich.

Unbeknownst to the woman (Movita) who loves him, an aristocrat (John Carroll) masquerades as an outlaw soldier in order to fight against a bandit chieftain.

Running time: 60 minutes. Release date: March 16, 1938.

144. Code of the Rangers (western) Directed by Sam Newfield. Produced by Maurice Conn. Original story and screenplay by Stanley Roberts.

Cast: Tim McCoy, Rex Lease, Judith Ford, Wheeler Oakman, Frank LaRue, Roger Williams, Kit Guard, Frank McCarroll, Jack Ingram, Loren Riebe, Budd Buster, Edward Peil, Sr., Hal Price, Zeke Clemens, Herman Hack.

A U.S. Ranger (Tim McCoy) tries to straighten out his brother (Rex Lease), also a lawman, when the latter turns outlaw.
Running time: 56 minutes. Release date: April 8, 1938.

145. Female Fugitive (drama) Directed by William Nigh. Produced by E.B. Derr. Original story and screenplay by John T. Neville and Bennett R. Cohen. A Crescent Pictures Production.

Cast: Evelyn Venable, Craig Reynolds, Reed Hadley, John Kelly, Martha Tibbetts, Charlotte Treadway, Reginald Sheffield, Rafael Bennett, John Merton, Emmett Vogan, Lee Phelps.

Leaving her husband (Craig Reynolds) after discovering he's a truck hijacker and murderer, Peggy Mallory (Evelyn Venable) becomes involved with a bachelor artist (Reed Hadley).
Running time: 58 minutes. Release date: April 15, 1938.

146. Two Gun Justice (western) Directed by Alan James. Produced by Maurice Conn. Story and screenplay by Fred Myton. A Concord Production.

Cast: Tim McCoy, Betty Compson, John Merton, Joan Barclay, Lane Chandler, Al Bridge, Tony Paton, Allan Cavan, Harry Strang, Earl Dwire, Enid Parrish, Olin Francis, Curley Dresden, Jack Ingram.

Ex-ranger Tim Carson (Tim McCoy) is called upon to bring a gang of murderous cattle rustlers to justice.
Running time: 58 minutes. Release date: April 30, 1938.

147. Numbered Woman (drama) Directed by Karl Brown. Produced by E.B. Derr. Original screenplay by John T. Neville.

Cast: Sally Blane, Lloyd Hughes, Mayo Methot, Clay Clement, J. Farrell MacDonald, John Arledge, Ward Bond, Morgan Wallace, Mary MacLaren, Gordon Hart, Robert Fiske, Ralph Dunn, Oscar O'Shea, Mary Lou Lender, Howard Hickman, Kathryn Sheldon.

An empty-handed Tim McCoy (left) watches as Betty Compson and Joan Barclay (right) restrain John Merton in "Two Gun Justice" (1938).

After her brother (John Arledge) is arrested for a bond theft, a nurse (Sally Blane) sets out to prove his innocence by trapping the real thieves.

Running time: 63 minutes. Release date: May 22, 1938.

Working title: **Private Nurse.**

148. Gunsmoke Trail (western) Directed by Sam Newfield. Produced by Maurice Conn. Screenplay by Fred Myton. Story by Robert Emmett (Tansey).

Cast: Jack Randall, Louise Stanley, Al St. John, John Merton, Henry Rocquemore, Ted Adams, Al Bridge, Hal Price, Harry Strang, Kit Guard, Jack Ingram, Charles "Slim" Whitaker, Art Dillard, Carleton Young, Sherry Tansey, George Morrell, Oscar Gahan, Blackjack Ward, Glenn Strange.

A cowboy (Jack Randall) clashes with a greedy land-grabber who has abused an orphan girl. Running time: 57 minutes. Release date: May 27, 1938.

149. Phantom Ranger (western) Directed by Sam Newfield. Produced by Maurice Conn. Screenplay by Joseph O'Donnell. Story by Stanley Roberts and Joseph O'Donnell.

Cast: Tim McCoy, Suzanne Kaaren, John St. Polis, Karl Hackett, Charles King, Tom London, John Merton, Dick Cramer, Herbert Holcombe, Harry Strang, Wally West, Horace B. Carpenter, Sherry Tansey, George Morrell, Herman Hack.

An undercover government investigator (Tim McCoy) poses as an outlaw in order to break up the operations of a counterfeiting ring. Running time: 54 minutes. Release date: May 27, 1938.

150. The Marines Are Here (action-drama) Directed by Phil Rosen. Produced by Scott R. Dunlap. Screenplay by Jack Knapp and J. Benton Cheney. Original story by Edwin C. Parsons and Charles Logue.

Cast: Gordon Oliver, June Travis, Ray Walker, Guinn "Big Boy" Williams, Ronnie Cosbey, Billy Dooley, Pat Gleason, Edward Earle, Wade Boteler.

A young marine (Gordon Oliver) changes his bad attitude and helps his comrades against a bandit attack. Running time: 60 minutes. Release date: June 8, 1938.

151. Romance of the Limberlost (drama) Directed by William Nigh. Screenplay by Marion Orth. From the story "Her Father's Daughter" by Gene Stratton-Porter.

Cast: Jean Parker, Eric Linden, Marjorie Main, Betty Blythe, Edward Pawley, Hollis Jewell, George Cleveland, Sarah Padden, Guy Usher, Jack Kennedy, Jean O'Neill.

An orphan girl (Jean Parker) falls in love with a young law school graduate (Eric Linden), but her cruel aunt (Marjorie Main) wants her to marry a rich widower. Running time: 81 min. Release date: June 22, 1938.

Jean Parker and Eric Linden in "Romance of the Limberlost" (1938).

152. Man's Country (western) Directed by Robert Hill. Produced by Robert Tansey. Screenplay by Robert Emmett (Tansey).

Cast: Jack Randall, Marjorie Reynolds, Walter Long, Ralph Peters, Forrest Taylor, David Sharpe, Harry Harvey, Charles King, Bud Osborne, Dave O'Brien, Sherry Tansey, Ernie Adams.

A U.S. Ranger (Jack Randall) poses as an outlaw in order to gather evidence against a gang of desperados.

Running time: 53 minutes. Release date: July 6, 1938.

153. Barefoot Boy (drama) Directed by Karl Brown. Produced by E.B. Derr. Story and screenplay by John T. Neville.

Cast: Jackie Moran, Marcia Mae Jones, Ralph Morgan,

Claire Windsor, Matty Fain, Frank Puglia, Charles D. Brown, Helen MacKellar, Marilyn Knowlden, Henry Rocquemore, Roger Gray, Earle Hodgins, Johnnie Morris.

A country boy (Jackie Moran) finds stolen bonds in an abandoned house; before long, gangsters are after him, trying to recover the loot.

Running time: 63 minutes. Release date: August 3, 1938.

154. Under the Big Top (drama) Directed by Karl Brown. Produced by William T. Lackey. Screenplay by Marion Orth. Story by Llewellyn Hughes.

Cast: Anne Nagel, Grant Richmond, Jack LaRue, Marjorie Main, George Cleveland, Herbert Rawlinson, Rolfe Sedan, Betty Compson, Fred "Snowflake" Toones, Harry Harvey, Charlene Wyatt, Speed Hansen.

The success of a circus trapeze trio is threatened when the two men (Grant Richmond, Jack LaRue) both fall in love with the girl (Anne Nagel).

Running time: 63 min. Release date: Aug. 31, 1938.

Working title: **The Circus Comes to Town.**

155. Starlight Over Texas (western) Directed by Al Herman. Produced by Edward Finney. Screenplay by John Rathmell. Original story by Harry MacPherson.

Cast: Tex Ritter, Carmen LaRoux, Snub "Pee Wee" Pollard, Salvatore Damino, Horace Murphy, Karl Hackett, Charles King, Martin Garralaga, George Chesebro, Carlos Villarias, Edward Cassidy, Jerry Gomez, Sherry Tansey, Bob Terry, Horace B. Carpenter, Dave O'Brien, Denver Dixon (Victor Adamson), Chick Hannon, Tex Palmer, Rosa Turich, Fred Velasco, Stelita, Carmen Alvarez, Eduardo Chaves, The Northwesterners (Merle and Ray Scobee, Shorty Brier, Buck Rasch, Chuck Davis), "White Flash."

Tex tries to restore law and order along the Mexican border when a bandit (Karl Hackett) assumes the identity of a slain marshal.

Running time: 58 min. Release date: Sept. 7, 1938.

156. Mexicali Kid (western) Directed by Wallace Fox.

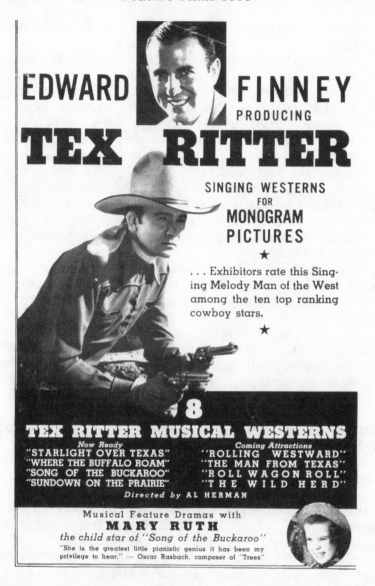

A trade advertisement for the Tex Ritter series, produced by Edward Finney. "The Wild Herd," listed among the coming attractions, was the working title for "Down the Wyoming Trail (1939).

Produced by Robert Tansey. Screenplay by Robert Emmett (Tansey).

Cast: Jack Randall, Wesley Barry, Eleanor Stewart, Edward Cassidy, Bud Osborne, George Chesebro, Ernie Adams, William von Brincken, Frank LaRue, Sherry Tansey.

A cowboy (Jack Randall) teams with a reformed outlaw known as "The Mexicali Kid" (Wesley Barry) and together they help save a young woman's ranch.

Running time: 51 minutes. Release date: September 14, 1938.

157. Wanted by the Police (drama) Directed by Howard Bretherton. Produced by Lindsley Parsons. Screenplay by Wellyn Totman. Original story by Donn Mullaly and Renaud Hoffman.

Cast: Frankie Darro, Evalyn Knapp, Robert Kent, Lillian Elliott, Matty Fain, Don Rowan, Sam Bernard, Maurice Hugo, Thelma White, Willy Costello, Walter Merrill, Ralph Peters.

To help support his mother (Lillian Elliott), Danny Murphy (Frankie Darro) gets a job in a garage; before long, he finds himself implicated in a car-stealing racket.

Running time: 59 minutes. Release date: September 21, 1938.

158. Mr. Wong, Detective (mystery) Directed by William Nigh. Produced by William T. Lackey. Screenplay by Houston Branch. Based on the character "James Lee Wong" created by Hugh Wiley.

Cast: Boris Karloff, Grant Withers, Maxine Jennings, Evelyn Brent, Lucien Prival, John St. Polis, William Gould, Hooper Atchley, John Hamilton, Frank Bruno, Lee Tong Fu, George Lloyd, Wilbur Mack, Grace Wood.

Chinese criminologist Mr. Wong (Boris Karloff) investigates the successive deaths of three partners (William Gould, Hooper Atchley, John Hamilton) in the poison gas export trade—each death occurring while the individual was alone in his quarters and each without visible cause.

Running time: 69 minutes. Release date: October 5, 1938.

Remade as **Docks of New Orleans** (Monogram, 1948).

74

159. Where the Buffalo Roam (western) Directed by Al Herman. Produced by Edward Finney. Story and screenplay by Robert Emmett (Tansey).

Cast: Tex Ritter, Dorothy Short, Horace Murphy, Snub Pollard, John Merton, Richard Alexander, Karl Hackett, Dave O'Brien, Louise Massey, Bob Terry, Charles King, John "Blackie" Whiteford, Denver Dixon (Victor Adamson), Ernie Adams, Hank Worden, Curt Massey, Edward Cassidy, Louise Massey's Westerners, "White Flash."

Tex goes after a gang responsible for the wanton slaughter of buffalo herds.

Running time: 61 minutes. Release date: October 21, 1938.

160. Gang Bullets (drama) Directed by Lambert Hillyer. Produced by E.B. Derr. Original screenplay by John T. Neville.

Cast: Anne Nagel, Robert Kent, Charles Trowbridge, Morgan Wallace, J. Farrell MacDonald, John T. Murray, Arthur Loft, John Merton, Donald Kerr, Carleton Young, Isabelle LaMal, Benny Bartlett.

A young couple (Anne Nagel, Robert Kent) are involved in a crusade against crime; the girl's father (Charles Trowbridge), a district attorney, tries to jail a racketeer (Morgan Wallace) when anonymous notes cast aspersions on the D.A.'s honesty.

Running time: 63 minutes. Release date: November 16, 1938.

161. Gangster's Boy (drama) Directed by William Nigh. Produced by William T. Lackey. Screenplay by Robert Andrews. Story by Robert Andrews and Karl Brown.

Cast: Jackie Cooper, Lucy Gilman, Robert Warwick, Louise Lorimer, Tommy Wonder, Selmer Jackson, Bobby Stone, Betty Blythe, Bradley Metcalfe, Huntley Gordon, William Gould, Jack Kennedy, Herbert Evans.

A young man (Jackie Cooper), the prize student and athlete of his high school, is ostracized when his father (Robert Warwick), a former racketeer, comes to town.

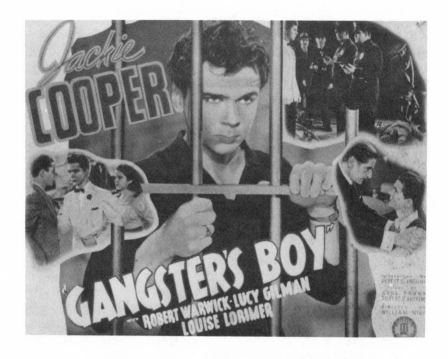

Lobby card for "Gangster's Boy" (1938).

Running time: 80 minutes. Release date: November 16, 1938.

162. Gun Packer (western) Directed by Wallace Fox. Produced by Robert Tansey. Original story and screenplay by Robert Emmett (Tansey).

Cast: Jack Randall, Louise Stanley, Charles King, Barlowe Borland, Glenn Strange, Raymond Turner, Lloyd Ingraham, Lowell Drew, Ernie Adams, Forrest Taylor, Curley Dresden, Sherry Tansey, "Rusty."

Jack Dinton (Jack Randall) pursues a bandit gang who is robbing stagecoaches of their gold bullion shipments. Running time: 51 min. Release date: Nov. 16, 1938.

163. The Sin of Lena Rivers (drama) Directed by Phil Rosen. Produced by Sam Bischoff. Screenplay by Stuart Anthony and Warren B. Duff. Story by Mary J. Holmes.

Cast: Charlotte Henry, Beryl Mercer, James Kirkwood, Morgan Galloway, Betty Blythe, John St. Polis, Joyce Compton, Clarence Muse, John Larkin, Russell Simpson, The Kentucky Jubilee Singers.

Lena Rivers (Charlotte Henry), the child of an unmarried couple, goes to live with a rich uncle whose wife (Betty Blythe) and daughter (Joyce Compton) openly show their dislike and distrust of her.

Running time: 57 minutes. Release date: December 1, 1938.

A reissue of **Lena Rivers** (1932), which was originally produced and released by Tiffany.

164. **I Am a Criminal** (drama) Directed by William Nigh. Produced by E.B. Derr. Screenplay by John Krafft. Story by Harrison Jacobs. A Crescent Pictures Production.

Cast: John Carroll, Kay Linaker, Martin Spellman, Craig Reynolds, Lester Mathews, Mary Kornman, Mary Beatty, Robert Fiske, Byron Foulger, Edward Earle, Jack Kennedy, Allan Cavan.

Seeking to win public favor, a big-time racketeer (John Carroll), about to be tried for murder, adopts an orphan newsboy (Martin Spellman).

Running time: 73 minutes. Release date: December 7, 1938.

Remade as **Smart Guy** (Monogram, 1943).

165. **Wild Horse Canyon** (western) Directed by Robert Hill. Produced by Robert Tansey. Original screenplay by Robert Emmett (Tansey).

Cast: Jack Randall, Dorothy Short, Frank Yaconelli, Dennis Moore, Warner Richmond, Edward Cassidy, Walter Long, Charles King, Earl Douglas, Sherry Tansey, "Rusty."

A cowboy (Jack Randall) pursues the horse rustlers who killed his brother.

Running time: 56 minutes. Release date: December 21, 1938.

166. **Tough Kid** (drama) Directed by Howard Bretherton. Produced by Lindsley Parsons. Screenplay by Wellyn Totman. Story by Brenda Weisberg.

Cast: Frankie Darro, Dick Purcell, Judith Allen, Lillian Elliott, Don Rowan, William Ruhl, Lew Kelly, Ralph Peters, Max Marx, Jean Joyce, Cliff Howell, Joe Lynch, Wilbur Mack.

A young man (Frankie Darro) tries to keep his brother (Dick Purcell), a prizefighter, from falling in with a gang trying to get him to throw some fights.

Running time: 59 minutes. Release date: December 28, 1938.

Released in Great Britain as **The Fifth Round.**

1939

167. Song of the Buckaroo (western) Directed by Al Herman. Produced by Edward Finney. Story and screenplay by John Rathmell.

Cast: Tex Ritter, Jinx Falkenberg, Mary Ruth, Frank LaRue, Tom London, Snub Pollard, Horace Murphy, Dave O'Brien, Dorothy Fay, George Chesebro, Ernie Adams, Bob Terry, Charles King, "White Flash."

Texas Dan (Tex Ritter), an outlaw, assumes the identity of a dead man and, after being elected mayor of a small western town, decides to go straight.

Running time: 58 minutes. Release date: January 12, 1939.

Working title: **Little Tenderfoot.**

168. Convict's Code (drama) Directed by Lambert Hillyer. Produced by E.B. Derr. Original screenplay by John Krafft. A Crescent Pictures Production.

Cast: Robert Kent, Anne Nagel, Sidney Blackmer, Norman Willis, Victor Kilian, Maude Eburne, Ben Alexander, Pat Flaherty, Carleton Young, Howard Hickman, Joan Barclay, Harry Strang.

Framed into a jail sentence but out on restricted parole, a man (Robert Kent) is determined to clear his name.

Running time: 62 minutes. Release date: January 18, 1939.

169. Drifting Westward (western) Directed by Robert Hill. Produced by Scott R. Dunlap. Screenplay by Robert Emmett (Tansey).

Cast: Jack Randall, Frank Yaconelli, Edna Duran, Stanley Blystone, Carmen Bailey, Julian Rivero, Dave O'Brien, Octavio Giraud, Dean Spencer, James Sheridan (Sherry Tansey), Rusty the Wonder Horse.

Jack Randall goes to the aid of a Spanish family who are being terrorized by an outlaw gang seeking a map that reveals the location of a valuable mine.

Running time: 58 minutes (this is the time most frequently listed, although **Variety** clocked the film at 47 minutes). Release date: January 25, 1939.

170. Navy Secrets (adventure) Directed by Howard Bretherton. Produced by William T. Lackey. Screenplay by Harvey Gates. From the original Cosmopolitan Magazine story by Steve Fisher.

Cast: Grant Withers, Fay Wray, Craig Reynolds, Dewey Robinson, Andre Cheron, Robert Frazer, George Sorell, William von Brincken, Joseph Crehan, Duke York, Arthur Housman, Joseph Girard.

Two government agents (Grant Withers, Fay Wray) investigate a traitorous seaman, who leads them to a spy ring.

Running time: 62 minutes. Release date: February 8, 1939.

171. Sundown on the Prairie (western) Directed by Al Herman. Produced by Edward Finney. Screenplay by William Nolte and Edmond Kelso.

Cast: Tex Ritter, Dorothy Fay, Horace Murphy, Karl Hackett, Charles King, Hank Worden, Frank Ellis, Wally West, Ernie Adams, Frank LaRue, Edward Peil, Sr., The Musical Tornadoes featuring Juanita Street.

A ranger (Tex Ritter) tries to put a halt to the activities of smugglers operating near the U.S. border.

Running time: 58 minutes. Release date: February 8, 1939.

172. Star Reporter (drama) Directed by Howard

Grant Withers and Fay Wray in "Navy Secrets" (1939).

Bretherton. Produced by E.B. Derr. Original screenplay by John T. Neville.

Cast: Warren Hull, Marsha Hunt, Morgan Wallace, Virginia Howell, Clay Clement, Wallis Clarke, Paul Fix, Joseph Crehan, Eddie Kane.

A newspaper publisher (Warren Hull) doggedly keeps on trying to get a confession from a murderer (Morgan Wallace), unaware that the man is his father.

Running time: 62 minutes. Release date: February 22, 1939.

173. Rollin' Westward (western) Directed by Al Herman. Produced by Edward Finney. Original screenplay by Fred Myton.

Cast: Tex Ritter, Dorothy Fay, Horace Murphy, Charles "Slim" Whitaker, Herbert Corthell, Harry Harvey, Charles King, Jr., Hank Worden, Dave O'Brien, Tom London, Estrelita Novarro, "White Flash."

Tex helps a cattleman (Herbert Corthell) and his daughter (Dorothy Fay) to thwart a swindle by landgrabbers (Harry Harvey, Charles King, Jr.).

Running time: 55 min. Release date: March 1, 1939.

174. The Mystery of Mr. Wong (mystery) Directed by William Nigh. Produced by William T. Lackey. Screenplay by W. Scott Darling. Based on the "James Lee Wong" series in Collier's Magazine written by Hugh Wiley.

Cast: Boris Karloff, Grant Withers, Dorothy Tree, Craig Reynolds, Lotus Long, Morgan Wallace, Holmes Herbert, Ivan Lebedeff, Hooper Atchley, Bruce Wong, Lee Tong Foo, Chester Gan.

Chinese criminologist Mr. Wong (Boris Karloff) investigates the murder of a curio collector (Morgan Wallace) who had obtained a famous gem known as the "Eye of the Moon."

Running time: 68 minutes. Release date: March 8, 1939.

175. Mystery Plane (adventure) Directed by George Waggner. Produced by Paul Malvern. Screenplay by Paul Schofield and Joseph West (George Waggner). Original story from the cartoon strip "Tailspin Tommy" by Hal Forrest.

Cast: John Trent, Marjorie Reynolds, Milburn Stone, Jason Robards (Sr.), Pete George Lynn, Lucien Littlefield, Polly Ann Young, Tommy Bupp, Betsy Gay, Sayre Dearing, John Peters.

Aerialist Tailspin Tommy (John Trent), aided by his friends Betty Lou (Marjorie Reynolds) and Skeeter (Milburn Stone), develops a radio-controlled bomb-dropping device; foreign agents kidnap the trio to gain access to the invention.

AMERICA'S FAVORITE COMIC STRIP IS ON THE SCREEN!

TAILSPIN TOMMY

"MYSTERY PLANE"

JOHN TRENT
MARJORIE REYNOLDS
MILBURN STONE
Produced by PAUL MALVERN
Directed by GEORGE WAGGNER
Screenplay by PAUL SCHOFIELD & JOSEPH WEST
Original Story by HAL FORREST
A Monogram

John Trent and Marjorie Reynolds are pictured on this poster for "Mystery Plane" (1939), the first of four Monogram features based on the Tailspin Tommy comic strip.

Running time: 60 minutes. Release date: March 8, 1939.
Also known as **Sky Pilot.**

176. Trigger Smith (western) Directed by Alan James. Produced by Robert Tansey. Original screenplay by Robert Emmett (Tansey).

Cast: Jack Randall, Joyce Bryant, Frank Yaconelli, Forrest Taylor, Dennis Moore, Dave O'Brien, Sherry Tansey, Edward Cassidy, Jim Corey, Reed Howes, Warner Richmond, Milton Kibbee.

A drifter (Jack Randall) goes after the gang of stage-coach robbers responsible for murdering his brother.

Running time: 59 minutes. Release date: March 22, 1939.

177. Undercover Agent (drama) Directed by Howard Bretherton. Produced by E.B. Derr. Screenplay by Milton Raison. Original story by Martin Mooney.

Cast: Russell Gleason, Shirley Deane, J.M. Kerrigan, Maude Eburne, Oscar O'Shea, Selmer Jackson, Ralf Harolde, Ray Bennett, Ralph Sanford.

A railway postal clerk (Russell Gleason) exposes a sweepstakes counterfeiting ring.

Running time: 56 minutes. Release date: April 5, 1939.

178. Streets of New York (drama) Directed by William Nigh. Produced by William T. Lackey. Original screenplay by Robert D. Andrews.

Cast: Jackie Cooper, Dick Purcell, Marjorie Reynolds, Martin Spellman, Sidney Miller, Buddy Pepper, Bobby Stone, David Durand, William Bucker, Robert Tucker, Kent Rogers, George Cleveland.

Ambitious to be a lawyer, a young man (Jackie Cooper) runs a newsstand by day and goes to law school at night; while studying, he organizes his street hustlers legitimately.

Running time: 73 minutes. Release date: April 15, 1939.

179. Man from Texas (western) Directed by Al Herman. Produced by Edward Finney. Screenplay by Robert Emmett (Tansey).

Cast: Tex Ritter, Ruth Rogers, Hal Price, Charles B. Wood, Charles King, Kenne Duncan, Vic Demourelle, Jr., Roy Barcroft, Frank Wayne, Tom London, Nelson McDowell, Sherry Tansey, Chick Hannon, "White Flash."

A railroad agent (Tex Ritter) reforms an outlaw known as "The Shootin' Kid" and together they thwart a landgrabber (Roy Barcroft) who is using unscrupulous tactics to buy up valuable land.

Running time: 56 minutes. Release date: April 19, 1939.

180. Wanted by Scotland Yard (drama) Directed by Norman Lee.

Cast: James Stephenson, Betty Lynne, Leslie Perrins, Nadine March, Sally Stuart, D.A. Clarke-Smith, George Merritt, Bryan Herbert, Florence Groves, Phil Ray.

After being released from prison, a safecracker (James Stephenson) falls in love with a woman (Betty Lynne) who tries to reform him.

Running time: 65 minutes. Release date: April 19, 1939.

A British-Pathe production, produced and released in Great Britain as **Dangerous Fingers** (1937); released in the U.S. under the title **Wanted by Scotland Yard** by Monogram.

181. Boys' Reformatory (drama) Directed by Howard Bretherton. Produced by Lindsley Parsons. Screenplay by Ray Trampe and Wellyn Totman. Story by Ray Trampe and Norman S. Hill.

Cast: Frankie Darro, Grant Withers, David Durand, Ben Welden, Warren McCollum, Albert Hill, Jr., Bob McClung, George Offerman, Jr., Frank Coghlan, Jr., Lillian Elliott, Tempe Pigott, John St. Polis, Jack McHugh, Kathryn Sheldon, Robert Smith.

In order to protect the son (Frank Coghlan, Jr.) of his foster mother (Lillian Elliott), a young man (Frankie Darro) confesses to a crime he didn't commit and is sent to reform school.

Running time: 61 minutes. Release date: May 1, 1939.

182. Wolf Call (adventure) Directed by George Waggner. Produced by Paul Malvern. Screenplay by Joseph West (George Waggner). From the novel by Jack London.

Cast: John Carroll, Movita, Polly Ann Young, George Cleveland, Wheeler Oakman, Peter George Lynn, Guy Usher, Holmes Herbert, John Sheehan, Charles Irwin, Roger Williams, Pat O'Malley, Grey Shadow the dog.

A New York playboy (John Carroll) journeys to the Canadian mountains where he learns that unscrupulous partners are trying to defraud his father (Guy Usher) out of a valuable radium mine.

Running time: 62 min. Release date: May 22, 1939.

84

183. Across the Plains (western) Directed by Spencer Gordon Bennet. Produced by Robert Tansey. Original screenplay by Robert Emmett (Tansey).

Cast: Jack Randall, Joyce Bryant, Frank Yaconelli, Hal Price, Dennis Moore, Glenn Strange, Robert Cord, Bud Osborne, Dean Spencer, James Sheridan (Sherry Tansey), Wylie Grant.

Two small boys are orphaned when a band of white raiders destroy their wagon caravan and murder their parents. The raiders adopt one of the boys, friendly Indians raise the other; thus Cherokee (Jack Randall) and the Kansas Kid (Dennis Moore) wind up on opposite sides during a battle between outlaws and Indians.

Running time: 59 minutes. Release date: June 1, 1939.

Working title: **Riders of the Rio Grande.**

184. Should a Girl Marry? (drama) Directed by Lambert Hillyer. Original screenplay by Gayl Newbury and David Silverstein.

Cast: Anne Nagel, Warren Hull, Mayo Methot, Lester Mathews, Sarah Padden, Robert Elliott, Weldon Heyburn.

An innocent woman (Anne Nagel) and her doctor husband (Warren Hull) are blackmailed when it is learned that she was born in prison.

Running time: 61 min. Release date: June 10, 1939.

Working title: **Girl from Nowhere.**

185. Down the Wyoming Trail (western) Directed by Al Herman. Produced by Edward Finney. Original story and screenplay by Peter Dixon.

Cast: Tex Ritter, Mary Brodel, Horace Murphy, Bobby Lawson, Charles King, Bob Terry, Jack Ingram, Earl Douglas, Frank LaRue, Ernie Adams, Charles Sergeant, Ed Coxen, Jean Southern, The Northwesterners (Merle Scobee, A.J. Brier, Wilson Rasch, Ray Scobee, Charles Davis), "White Flash."

An honest cowboy (Tex Ritter) is framed by cattle rustlers who are stampeding elk and reindeer herds to cover their tracks; to prove his innocence, the cowboy is forced to bring the rustlers in.

Running time: 56 minutes. Release date: June 14, 1939.
Working title: **The Wild Herd.**

186. Stunt Pilot (adventure) Directed by George Waggner. Produced by Paul Malvern. Screenplay by W. Scott Darling and Joseph West (George Waggner). Based on the cartoon strip "Tailspin Tommy" by Hal Forrest.

Cast: John Trent, Marjorie Reynolds, Milburn Stone, Jason Robards (Sr.), Pat O'Malley, George Meeker, Wesley Barry, George Cleveland, Johnny Day, Charles Morton, Mary Fields, Buddy Cox.

Tailspin Tommy (John Trent) joins a movie company as a stunt pilot; when a murder occurs, Tommy tries to solve the mystery.

Running time: 62 minutes. Release date: July 1, 1939.

187. Mr. Wong in Chinatown (mystery) Directed by William Nigh. Produced by Scott R. Dunlap. Screenplay by W. Scott Darling. Based on the character "James Lee Wong" created by Hugh Wiley.

Cast: Boris Karloff, Grant Withers, Marjorie Reynolds, Peter George Lynn, William Royle, Huntley Gordon, James Flavin, Lotus Long, Richard Loo, Bessie Loo, Lee Tong Loo, Little Angelo (Rossitto), Guy Usher.

Criminologist Mr. Wong (Boris Karloff) investigates the murder of a Chinese princess (Lotus Long) who was killed by a poisoned dart.

Running time: 70 minutes. Release date: August 1, 1939.

Remade as **The Chinese Ring** (Monogram, 1947).

188. Girl from the Rio (mystery) Directed by Lambert Hillyer. Produced by E.B. Derr. Original screenplay by Milton Raison and John T. Neville.

Cast: Movita, Warren Hull, Alan Baldwin, Kay Linaker, Clay Clement, Adele Pearce, Soledad Jiminez, Richard Tucker, Dennis Moore, Byron Foulger.

A South American singer (Movita) is called to New York to help clear her brother of arson and murder charges.

Running time: 62 minutes. Release date: August 7, 1939.

189. Riders of the Frontier (western) Directed by Spencer Gordon Bennet. Produced by Edward Finney. Screenplay by Jesse Duffy and Joseph Levering.

Cast: Tex Ritter, Jack Rutherford, Hal Taliaferro (Wally Wales), Jean Joyce, Marin Sais, Mantan Moreland, Olin Francis, Roy Barcroft, Merrill McCormick, Maxine Leslie, Nolan Willis, Nelson McDowell, Charles King, Forrest Taylor, Robert Frazer, "White Flash."

In order to gather evidence, Tex masquerades as a desperado and joins a cut-throat band of outlaws led by a crooked ranch foreman (Roy Barcroft).

Running time: 58 minutes. Release date: August 16, 1939.

190. Roll, Wagons, Roll (western) Directed by Al Herman. Produced by Edward Finney. Story and screenplay by Victor Adamson, Edmond Kelso and Roger Merton.

Cast: Tex Ritter, Nelson McDowell, Muriel Evans, Nolan Willis, Steve Clark, Tom London, Reed Howes, Frank Ellis, Keene Duncan, Frank LaRue, Chick Hannon.

Tex leads wagon trains of settlers trying to reach Oregon.

Running time: 55 minutes. Release date: August 16, 1939.

191. Irish Luck (mystery-comedy) Directed by Howard Bretherton. Produced by Grant Withers. Screenplay by Mary C. McCarthy. Story by Charles M. Brown.

Cast: Frankie Darro, Dick Purcell, Lillian Elliott, Sheila Darcy, Mantan Moreland, James Flavin, Dennis Moore, Howard Mitchell.

A bellhop (Frankie Darro) who fancies himself an amateur detective takes off on the trail of gangsters who are selling hot bonds.

Running time: 58 minutes. Release date: August 22, 1939.

Released in Great Britain as **Amateur Detective.**

192. Oklahoma Terror (western) Directed by Spencer Gordon Bennet. Produced Lindsley Parsons. Screenplay by Joseph West (George Waggner). Story by Lindsley Parsons.

Cast: Jack Randall, Virginia Carroll, Al "Fuzzy" St. John, Davidson Clark, Nolan Willis, Glenn Strange, Warren McCollum, Don Rowan, Brandon Beach, Tristram Coffin, Ralph Peters, Charles "Slim" Whitaker, Rusty the Wonder Horse.

After the Civil War, a Yankee army captain (Jack Randall) returns west; learning that his father, the manager of a stagecoach line, had been killed by an outlaw band, the captain sets out to bring the culprits to justice.

Running time: 50 minutes. Release date: August 25, 1939.

193. Sky Patrol (adventure) Directed by Howard Bretherton. Produced by Paul Malvern. Screenplay by Joseph West (George Waggner) and Norton S. Parker. Based on the cartoon strip "Tailspin Tommy" by Hal Forrest.

Cast: John Trent, Marjorie Reynolds, Milburn Stone, Jason Robards (Sr.), Jackie Coogan, Boyd Irwin, Bryant Washburn, LeRoy Mason, John Peters, Johnny Day, Dickie Jones.

Tailspin Tommy (John Trent) tangles with a gang smuggling guns and ammunition out of the country by means of a hydroplane.

Running time: 61 minutes. Release date: September 12, 1939.

194. The Fight for Peace (documentary) Narrated by David Ross.

A documentary on the horrors of war, focusing on Hitler, Mussolini and Stalin.

Running time: 65 minutes. Release date: September 30, 1939.

A Warwick Picture, originally released in 1938.

195. Mutiny in the Big House (drama) Directed by William Nigh. Produced by Grant Withers. Screenplay by Robert D. Andrews. Original story by Martin Mooney.

Cast: Charles Bickford, Barton MacLane, Pat Moriarity, Dennis Moore, William Royle, George Cleveland, Charles Foy, Russell Hopton, Jeffrey Sayre, Eddie Foster, Jack Daley, Dave O'Brien, Wheeler Oakman, Charles King, Nigel de Brulier, Merrill McCormick.

Father Joe (Charles Bickford), a crusading prison chaplain, and Red Manson (Barton MacLane), a hardened convict, both make a play to win the friendship of a new prisoner (Dennis Moore), who has been sentenced for forging a check to pay for his sick mother's medical bills.

Running time: 83 minutes. Release date: October 25, 1939.

196. Danger Flight (adventure) Directed by Howard Bretherton. Produced by Paul Malvern. Screenplay by Byron Morgan and Edwin C. Parsons. Based on the cartoon strip "Tailspin Tommy" by Hal Forrest.

Cast: John Trent, Marjorie Reynolds, Milburn Stone, Jason Robards (Sr.), Tommie Baker, Dennis Moore, Julius Tanner, Edwin Parker, Joe Bernard, Harry Harvey, Jr., Walter Wills.

Crooks set a trap for aerialist Tailspin Tommy (John Trent), who is flying through a storm to deliver a payroll.

Running time: 65 minutes. Release date: November 1, 1939.

197. Fighting Mad (adventure) Directed by Sam Newfield. Produced by Philip N. Krasne. Screenplay by George Rosener and John Rathmell. Based on the story "Renfrew Rides Again" by Laurie York Erskine. A Criterion Production.

Cast: James Newill, Sally Blane, Dave O'Brien, Benny Rubin, Milburn Stone, Walter Long, Warner Richmond, Ted Adams, Chief Thunder Cloud, Ole Olson, Horace Murphy.

Renfrew (James Newill) and a fellow Mountie (Dave O'Brien) pursue American gangsters on the lam.

Running time: 60 minutes. Release date: November 5, 1939.

198. Heroes in Blue (drama) Directed by William Watson. Produced by T.R. Williams. Screenplay by C.B. Williams. Based on the story "Detective First Class" by Charles Curran and C.B. Williams.

Cast: Dick Purcell, Charles Quigley, Bernadene Hayes, Edward Keane, Julie Warren, Lillian Elliott, Frank Sheridan.

Two brothers are on the police force; one (Dick Purcell) has a reputation for integrity, while the other (Frank Sheridan) follows the easy money path.

Running time: 61 minutes. Release date: November 7, 1939.

199. The Phantom Strikes (mystery) Directed by Walter Forde. Produced by Michael Balcon. Screenplay by Sidney Gilliat. Based on the novel "The Ringer" by Edgar Wallace.

Cast: Sonnie Hale, Wilfred Lawson, Alexander Knox, Louise Henry, Patrick Barr, John Longden, Patricia Roc, Peter Croft, Charles Eaton, George Merritt, Arthur Hambling.

Inspector Wembury (Patrick Barr) is summoned to protect Maurice Meister (Wilfred Lawson), a criminal lawyer with a shady reputation, who has been threatened with death within 48 hours by "The Ringer."

Running time: 58 minutes. Release date: November 15, 1939.

Produced and released in Great Britain as **The Gaunt Stranger** (1938); released in the U.S. under the title **The Phantom Strikes** by Monogram.

200. Overland Mail (western) Directed by Robert Hill. Produced by Robert Tansey. Story and screenplay by Robert Emmett (Tansey).

Cast: Jack Randall, Vince Barnett, Jean Joyce, Tristram Coffin, Glenn Strange, George Cleveland, Dennis Moore, Merrill McCormick, Joe Garcia, Maxine Leslie, James Sheridan (Sherry Tansey), Hal Price, Harry Semels, Rusty the Wonder Horse.

Jack Randall solves an Indian murder and clears out a band of counterfeiters.

Running time: 51 min. Release date: Nov. 16, 1939.

201. Crashing Thru (adventure) Directed by Elmer Clifton. Produced by Philip N. Krasne. Screenplay by Sherman L. Lowe. Based on a story by Laurie York Erskine. A Criterion Production.

Cast: James Newill, Jean Carmen, Warren Hull, Iron Eyes Cody, Milburn Stone, Walter Byron, Stanley Blystone, Robert Frazer, Joseph Girard, Dave O'Brien, Earl Douglas, Ted Adams, Roy Barcroft.

Renfrew (James Newill), of the Royal Canadian Mounted Police, tracks down the robbers of a gold shipment.

Running time: 65 minutes. Release date: December 11, 1939.

Originally produced for release through Grand National; released by Monogram.

202. Westbound Stage (western) Directed by Spencer Gordon Bennet. Produced by Edward Finney. Screenplay by Robert Emmett (Tansey). Story by John Foster.

Cast: Tex Ritter, Nelson McDowell, Muriel Evans, Nolan Willis, Steve Clark, Tom London, Reed Howes, Frank Ellis, Frank LaRue, Kenne Duncan, Hank Bell, Chester Gan, Phil Dunham, Chick Hannon.

Tex Wallace (Tex Ritter) guards a shipment of money on the westbound stage and helps round up a gang who wiped out an army patrol.

Running time: 56 minutes. Release date: December 15, 1939.

203. The Gentleman from Arizona (western) Directed by Earl Haley. Produced by Charles E. Goetz. Screenplay by Earl Haley and Jack O'Donnell. In Cinecolor.

Cast: John King, J. Farrell MacDonald, Joan Barclay, Craig Reynolds, Ruth Reece, Johnny Morris, Nora Lane, Doc Pardee.

The story of a singing caballero (John King), an outlaw stallion untamed by man, and the fiery senorita (Joan Barclay) who loved them both.

Running time: 71 minutes. Release date: December 25, 1939.

Left to right: Dave O'Brien, Louise Stanley and James Newill in "Yukon Flight" (1940), one in a series of Renfrew of the Royal Canadian Mounted Police adventures.

1940

204. Yukon Flight (adventure) Directed by Ralph Staub. Produced by Philip N. Krasne. Screenplay by Edward Halperin. Based on the story "Renfrew Rides North" by Laurie York Erskine. A Criterion Production.

Cast: James Newill, Louise Stanley, Dave O'Brien, Warren Hull, William Pawley, Karl Hackett, Jack Clifford, Roy Barcroft, Bob Terry, Earl Douglas.

Renfrew (James Newill), of the Northwest Canadian Mounted Police, learns that a so-called "trading company" is handling stolen gold and sets out to bring the owner (William Pawley) to justice.

Running time: 57 minutes. Release date: January 2, 1940.

205. The Fatal Hour (mystery) Directed by William Nigh. Produced by William T. Lackey. Screenplay by W. Scott Darling. Adaptation by Joseph West (George Waggner). Based on the character "James Lee Wong" created by Hugh Wiley.

Cast: Boris Karloff, Grant Withers, Marjorie Reynolds, Charles Trowbridge, John Hamilton, Craig Reynolds, Jack Kennedy, Lita Chevret, Frank Puglia, I. Stanford Jolley, Jason Robards (Sr.), Pauline Drake.

Mr. Wong (Boris Karloff) investigates the death of a police detective who was working on a smuggling case.

Running time: 68 minutes. Release date: January 15, 1940.

Working title: **Mr. Wong at Headquarters.**

Released in Great Britain as **Mr. Wong at Headquarters.**

206. The Secret Four (mystery) Directed by Walter Forde. Produced by Michael Balcon. Screenplay by Angus MacPhail, Sergei Nolbandov and Roland Pertwee. From the story "The Four Just Men" by Edgar Wallace.

Cast: Hugh Sinclair, Griffith Jones, Francis L. Sullivan, Frank Lawton, Anna Lee, Alan Napier, Basil Sydney, Lydia Sherwood, Edward Chapman, Athole Stewart, George Merritt, Arthur Hambling, Ellaline Terriss, Garry Marsh, Roland Pertwee, Elliot Makeham, Henrietta Watson.

The Four Just Men (Hugh Sinclair, Griffith Jones, Francis L. Sullivan, Frank Lawton), a group of modern–day Robin Hoods, become involved with spying, counterspying and a newspaper reporter (Anna Lee).

Running time: 85 minutes. Release date: January 15, 1940.

A CAPAD Production, produced and released in Great Britain as **The Four Just Men** (1939); released in the U.S. under the title **The Secret Four** by Monogram.

207. Hidden Enemy (mystery-drama) Directed by Howard Bretherton. Produced by T.R. Williams. Screenplay by C.B. Williams and Marion Orth. Story by C.B. Williams.

Cast: Warren Hull, Kay Linaker, William von Brincken,

George Cleveland, William Castello, Fern Emmett, Ed Keane.

A newspaper reporter (Warren Hull) encounters German spies who are after an experimental metal that is three times lighter than aluminum and stronger than steel.

Running time: 63 minutes. Release date: January 20, 1940.

208. Danger Ahead (adventure) Directed by Ralph Staub. Produced by Philip N. Krasne. Screenplay by Edward Halperin. Based on the story "Renfrew's Long Trail" by Laurie York Erskine. A Criterion Production.

Cast: James Newill, Dorothea Kent, Dave O'Brien, Guy Usher, Maude Allen, Harry Depp, John Dilson, Al Shaw, Dick Rich, Bob Terry, Lester Dorr, Earl Douglas.

Renfrew (James Newill), of the Royal Canadian Mounted Police, investigates the theft of a gold shipment and the murder of the driver of an armored truck.

Running time: 60 minutes. Release date: January 22, 1940.

209. Pioneer Days (western) Produced and directed by Harry S. Webb. Original screenplay by Bennett Cohen.

Cast: Jack Randall, June Wilkins, Frank Yaconelli, Nelson McDowell, Ted Adams, Bud Osborne, Robert Walker, Glenn Strange, Jimmy Aubrey, Lafe McKee, George Chesebro, Denver Dixon (Victor Adamson), Dick Cramer.

A private investigator (Jack Randall) for an express company is wrongfully accused of murder.

Running time: 51 minutes. Release date: January 25, 1940.

210. Chasing Trouble (mystery-comedy) Directed by Howard Bretherton. Produced by Grant Withers. Original screenplay by Mary McCarthy.

Cast: Frankie Darro, Marjorie Reynolds, Mantan Moreland, Milburn Stone, Cheryl Walker, Donald Kerr, George Cleveland, Alex Callam, Lillian Elliot, Tristram Coffin, I. Stanford Jolley, William Castello.

A florist's delivery boy (Frankie Darro), who fancies himself an amateur sleuth, discovers that the shop's owner transmits messages for a foreign government in the flowers he delivers.

Running time: 64 minutes. Release date: January 30, 1940.

211. East Side Kids (drama) Directed by Robert F. Hill. Produced by Sam Katzman. Screenplay by William Lively. A Four-Bell Production.

Cast: Harris Berger, Hally (Hal E.) Chester, Frankie Burke, Donald Haines, Eddie Brian, Sam Edwards, Leon Ames, Dennis Moore, Joyce Bryant, Jack Edwards, David O'Brien, Vince Barnett, Richard Adams, Maxine Lewis, James Farley, Robert Fiske, Alden (Stephen) Chase, Fred Hoose, Eric Burtis, Frank Yaconelli, David Durand.

When Knuckles Dolan (David O'Brien) is framed on a murder rap, his brother Danny (Harris Berger) and the other East Side Kids (Hally Chester, Frankie Burke, Donald Haines, Eddie Brian, Sam Edwards) set out to bring the real culprits to justice.

Running time: 62 minutes. Release date: February 10, 1940.

212. The Cheyenne Kid (western) Directed by Raymond K. Johnson. Produced by Harry S. Webb. Original screenplay by Tom Gibson.

Cast: Jack Randall, Louise Stanley, Kenne Duncan, Frank Yaconelli, Reed Howes, Charles King, George Chesebro, Forrest Taylor, Tex Palmer.

The Cheyenne Kid (Jack Randall) handles complications arising from the sale of some steers and a gambling debt.

Running time: 50 minutes. Release date: February 20, 1940.

213. Murder on the Yukon (adventure) Directed by Louis Gasnier. Produced by Philip N. Krasne. Screenplay by Milton Raison. Based on the story "Renfrew Rides North" by Laurie York Erskine. A Criterion Production.

Cast: James Newill, Polly Ann Young, Dave O'Brien,

Al St. John, William Royle, Chief Thunder Cloud, Budd Buster, Karl Hackett, Snub Pollard, Kenne Duncan, Earl Douglas, Jack Clifford.

Renfrew (James Newill) and a fellow Mountie (Dave O'Brien) investigate the murders of two prospectors.

Running time: 58 minutes. Release date: February 25, 1940.

214. Torpedo Raider (action-drama) Directed by Walter Forde. Screenplay by J.O.C. Orton. Story by C.S. Forester. Dialogue by Michael Hogan and Gerald Fairlie.

Cast: Betty Balfour, John Mills, Barry Mackay, Jimmy Hanley, Howard Marion-Crawford, H.G. Stoker, Percy Walsh.

The story of the briny battles waged between the Britannic flotilla and the Nordic squadrons in South American waters.

Running time: 55 minutes. Release date: February 28, 1940.

A British production, released in Great Britain as **Born for Glory** (1935); released in the U.S. under the title **Torpedo Raider** by Monogram.

215. Rhythm of the Rio Grande (western) Directed by Al Herman. Produced by Edward Finney. Screenplay by Robert Emmett (Tansey).

Cast: Tex Ritter, Suzan Dale, Warner Richmond, Martin Garralaga, Lloyd "Arkansas Slim" Andrews, Frank Mitchell, Mike J. Rodriquez, Juan Duval, Tristram Coffin, Chick Hannon, Earl Douglas, Forrest Taylor, Glenn Strange, James McNally, Wally West, "White Flash."

Tex arrives in Cinco Valley and finds it being raided, presumably by a Mexican bandit (Martin Garralaga). After capturing him, Tex enlists his aid to trap the real marauder.

Running time: 53 minutes. Release date: March 2, 1940.

216. The Human Monster (horror) Directed by Walter Summers. Screenplay by Patrick Irwin, Walter Summers and John Argyle. Based on a novel by Edgar Wallace.

Cast: Bela Lugosi, Hugh Williams, Greta Gynt, Edmond Ryan, Wilfred Walter, Alexander Field, Arthur E. Owen, Julie Suedo, Gerald Pring, Bryan Herbert, May Haliatt, Charles Penrose.

The evil Dr. Orloff (Bela Lugosi) commits a series of brutal murders, then collects from the insurance policies of the victims.

Running time: 76 minutes. Release date: March 9, 1940.

An Argyle British Production, released in Great Britain as **Dark Eyes of London** (1939); released in the U.S. by Monogram.

217. Midnight Limited (mystery) Directed by Howard Bretherton. Produced by T.R. Williams. Screenplay by Harrison Carter and C.B. Williams.

Cast: John King, Marjorie Reynolds, George Cleveland, Edward Keane, Pat Flaherty, Monte Collins, Herb Ashley, I. Stanford Jolley, Buck Woods.

A private detective (John King) investigates a series of robberies aboard a Montreal train.

Running time: 61 minutes. Release date: March 20, 1940.

218. Son of the Navy (comedy-drama) Directed by William Nigh. Produced by Grant Withers. Screenplay by Marion Orth and Joseph West (George Waggner). Original story by True Boardman and Grover Jones.

Cast: James Dunn, Jean Parker, Martin Spellman, William Royle, Selmer Jackson, Dave O'Brien, Sarah Padden, Craig Reynolds, Charles King, Gene Morgan.

An 11-year-old orphan (Martin Spellman) "adopts" a naval officer (James Dunn) as his father and another sailor's daughter (Jean Parker) as his mother.

Running time: 72 minutes. Release date: March 30, 1940.

Also known as **The Young Recruit.**

219. Covered Wagon Trails (western) Directed by Raymond K. Johnson. Produced by Harry S. Webb. Story and screenplay by Tom Gibson.

Cast: Jack Randall, Sally Cairns, David Sharpe, Lafe McKee, Budd Buster, Glenn Strange, Kenne Duncan, Hank Bell, Frank Ellis, George Chesebro, Carl Mathews, Edward Hearn, Art Mix, Jack Montgomery, Frank McCarroll.

Trying to deliver a herd of horses to a wagon train, Jack and his pal Manny (Budd Buster) run afoul with fur traders who don't want civilization to come to the West.

Running time: 52 minutes. Release date: April 10, 1940.

220. Tomboy (drama) Directed by Robert McGowan. Produced by William T. Lackey. Screenplay by Dorothy (Mrs. Wallace) Reid and Marion Orth.

Cast: Jackie Moran, Marcia Mae Jones, Grant Withers, George Cleveland, Charlotte Wynters, Marvin Stephens, Clara Blandick, Gene Morgan.

A tomboy (Marcia Mae Jones) tries to defend a young farm lad (Jackie Moran) against the cruelty of his hardbitten uncle (George Cleveland).

Running time: 70 minutes. Release date: April 20, 1940.

221. Pals of the Silver Sage (western) Directed by Al Herman. Produced by Edward Finney. Screenplay by Robert Emmett (Tansey). Story by George Martin.

Cast: Tex Ritter, Sugar Dawn, Lloyd "Arkansas Slim" Andrews, Clarissa Curtis, Glenn Strange, Carleton Young, Joe McGuinn, Warner Richmond, Betty Miles, Chester Gann, John Merton, Evelyn Daw, Gene Alsace (Rocky Camron), Harry Harvey, Fred Parker, "White Flash."

Tex Wright (Tex Ritter) and Cactus (Lloyd "Arkansas Slim" Andrews), employed on a ranch owned by a six-year-old girl (Sugar Dawn), save the property from rustlers who are stealing the livestock.

Running time: 52 minutes. Release date: April 22, 1940.

Working title: **The Colorado Trail.**

222. The Mysterious Mr. Reeder (mystery) Produced and directed by Jack Raymond. Screenplay by Bryan Wallace, Marjorie Gaffney and Michael Hogan. From the story by Edgar Wallace.

Cast: Will Fyffe, Kay Walsh, George Curzon, Chili Bouchier, John Warwick, Leslie Waring, Romilly Lunge, Bettey Astell, Derek Gorst, Ronald Shiner, Wally Patch, George Hayes, Dorothy Dewhurst.

J.G. Reeder (Will Fyffe), an elderly eccentric employed by the Director of Public Prosecutions, sets out to expose a counterfeiting ring.

Running time: 77 minutes. Release date: April 30, 1940.

Produced and released in Great Britain as **The Mind of Mr. Reeder** (1939); originally released in the U.S. by Grand National in 1939 under its original title; released in the U.S. under the title **The Mysterious Mr. Reeder** by Monogram.

223. Cowboy from Sundown (western) Directed by Spencer Gordon Bennet. Produced by Edward Finney. Screenplay by Roland Lynch and Robert Emmett (Tansey). Original story by Roland Lynch.

Cast: Tex Ritter, Roscoe Ates, Pauline Hadden, Carleton Young, George Pembroke, Dave O'Brien, Patsy Moran, James Farrar, Chick Hannon, Lloyd "Arkansas Slim" Andrews, Bud Osborne, Glenn Strange, Wally West, Sherry Tansey, Tristram Coffin, "White Flash."

A sheriff (Tex Ritter) finds trouble when he has to quarantine ranches because of an epidemic of hoof and mouth disease.

Running time: 58 minutes. Release date: May 9, 1940.

224. Land of the Six Guns (western) Directed by Raymond K. Johnson. Produced by Harry S. Webb. Original screenplay by Tom Gibson.

Cast: Jack Randall, Louise Stanley, Glenn Strange, Bud Osborne, Kenne Duncan, George Chesebro, Steve Clark, Frank LaRue, Carl Mathews, Jimmy Aubrey, Jack Perrin.

Jack Randall investigates the smuggling of cattle from Mexico into the U.S.

Running time: 54 minutes. Release date: May 9, 1940.

225. The Kid from Santa Fe (western) Directed by Raymond K. Johnson. Produced by Harry S. Webb. Screenplay by Carl Krusada. Story by Joseph P. Murphy.

Cast: Jack Randall, Clarence Logan, Forrest Taylor, Claire Rochelle, Tom London, George Chesebro, Dave O'Brien, Jimmy Aubrey, Kenne Duncan, Carl Mathews, Steve Clark, Buzz Barton, Tex Palmer.

After Sheriff Holt (Forrest Taylor) appoints him deputy, the Santa Fe Kid (Jack Randall) goes after smugglers operating near the Mexican border.

Running time: 57 minutes. Release date: May 23, 1940.

226. Riders from Nowhere (western) Directed by Raymond K. Johnson. Produced by Harry S. Webb. Screenplay by Carl Krusada. Story by Richard Piersall.

Cast: Jack Randall, Margaret Roach, Ernie Adams, Tom London, Charles King, Nelson McDowell, George Chesebro, Dorothy Vernon, Ted Adams, Carl Mathews, Jack Evans, Herman Hack, Archie Ricks, Ray Henderson.

Jack Rankin (Jack Randall) steps in to tame the town of Brimstone after the sheriff is murdered.

Running time: 55 minutes. Release date: May 30, 1940.

227. On the Spot (mystery-comedy) Directed by Howard Bretherton. Produced by Grant Withers. Screenplay by Joseph West (George Waggner) and Dorothy (Mrs. Wallace) Reid. Original story by Joseph West (George Waggner).

Cast: Frankie Darro, Mantan Moreland, Mary Kornman, John St. Polis, Robert Warwick, Maxine Leslie, Lillian Elliot.

A soda jerk (Frankie Darro) and his pal (Mantan Moreland) are in hot water when gangsters believe that they know the whereabouts of $300,000 in missing stolen loot.

Running time: 62 minutes. Release date: June 11, 1940.
Working title: **Amateur Detective.**

228. The Last Alarm (drama) Directed by William West. Produced by T.R. Williams. Original screenplay by Al Martin.

Cast: J. Farrell MacDonald, Polly Ann Young, Warren Hull, Mary Gordon, George Pembroke, Joel Friedkin, Bruce MacFarlane, Eddie Hart.

Fireman Jim Hadley (J. Farrell MacDonald) is retired from the force because of an age regulation. After his best friend dies in a blaze started by a pyromaniac, Hadley, with the help of his daughter (Polly Ann Young) and her finance (Warren Hull), an investigator for a fire insurance company, tracks down the arsonist.

Running time: 61 minutes. Release date: June 25, 1940.

229. Wild Horse Range (western) Directed by Raymond K. Johnson. Produced by Harry S. Webb. Screenplay by Carl Krusada.

Cast: Jack Randall, Phyllis Ruth, Frank Yaconelli, Charles King, Tom London, Marin Sais, Ralph Hoopes, Forrest Taylor, George Chesebro, Carl Mathews, Steve Clark, Ted Adams, Tex Palmer.

Two horse traders (Jack Randall, Frank Yaconelli) encounter a gang of horse thieves and try to restore the animals to their rightful owner.

Running time: 58 minutes. Release date: June 25, 1940.

230. Sky Bandits (adventure) Directed by Ralph Staub. Produced by Phil Goldstone. Screenplay by Edward Halperin. Based on the story "Renfrew Rides the Sky" by Laurie York Erskine. A Criterion Production.

Cast: James Newill, Louise Stanley, Dave O'Brien, William Pawley, Ted Adams, Bob Terry, Dwight Frye, Joseph Stefani, Dewey Robinson, Jack Clifford, Kenne Duncan.

Renfrew (James Newill), of the Royal Canadian

Mounted Police, investigates the mysterious disappearances of planes carrying gold. Running time: 62 minutes. Release date: July 3, 1940.

231. The Golden Trail (western) Directed by Al Herman. Produced by Edward Finney. Screenplay by Roland Lynch, Roger Merton and Robert Emmett (Tansey).

Cast: Tex Ritter, Lloyd "Arkansas Slim" Andrews, Ina Guest, Patsy Moran, Stanley Price, Warner Richmond, Eddie Dean, Gene Alsace (Rocky Camron), Sugar Dawn, Bill Wells, Forrest Taylor, Jack Pierce, Denver Dixon (Victor Adamson), Chuck Morrison, Art Mix, Tex Palmer, Chick Hannon, Frank LaRue, Sherry Tansey, "White Flash."

Prospecting for gold, Tex encounters a murderous gang of claim jumpers who are in league with a crooked county clerk.

Running time: 52 minutes. Release date: July 8, 1940.

232. Boys of the City (comedy) Directed by Joseph H. Lewis. Produced by Sam Katzman. Screenplay by William Lively. A Four-Bell Production.

Cast: Leo Gorcey, Bobby Jordan, "Sunshine Sammy" Morrison, David Gorcey, Donald Haines, Hally (Hal E.) Chester, Frankie Burke, David O'Brien, Inna Gest (Ina Guest), Dennis Moore, Vince Barnett, Eugene Francis, Forrest Taylor, Minerva Urecal, Alden (Stephen) Chase, George Humbert, Jerry Mandy.

En route to a mountain camp, the East Side Kids (Leo Gorcey, Bobby Jordan, "Sunshine Sammy" Morrison, David Gorcey, Donald Haines, Hally Chester, Frankie Burke) stop at an eerie mansion where they become involved in a murder mystery.

Running time: 63 minutes. Release date: July 15, 1940.

Released in the Northeast under the title **The Ghost Creeps.**

233. Haunted House (mystery) Directed by Robert McGowan. Produced by William T. Lackey. Screenplay

Marcia Mae Jones and Jackie Moran are pictured on this poster for "Haunted House" (1940). These child stars were paired for a number of juvenile adventures.

by Dorothy (Mrs. Wallace) Reid. Story by Jack Leonard and Monty Collins.

Cast: Jackie Moran, Marcia Mae Jones, George Cleveland, Henry Hall, John St. Polis, Jessie Arnold, Henry Rocquemore, Marcelle Ray, Buddy Swan.

Jimmy (Jackie Moran), an office boy for the local newspaper, and Millie (Marcia Mae Jones), the niece of the paper's publisher (George Cleveland), turn sleuthing reporters in order to help a friend who's been wrongfully accused of murder.

Running time: 70 minutes. Release date: July 22, 1940.

234. Rainbow Over the Range (western) Directed by Al Herman. Produced by Edward Finney. Screenplay by Roland Lynch, Roger Merton and Robert Emmett (Tansey).

Cast: Tex Ritter, Dorothy Fay, Warner Richmond, Dennis Moore, Lloyd "Arkansas Slim" Andrews, Jim Pierce, Chuck Morrison, John Merton, Tommy Southworth, Steve Lorber, Romaine Loudermilk and His Ranch House Cowboys, "White Flash."

A U.S. Marshal (Tex Ritter) helps a young woman (Dorothy Fay) and her brother (Dennis Moore) in their fight against rustlers who are stealing horses from their ranch.

Running time: 58 minutes. Release date: July 29, 1940.

235. Doomed to Die (mystery) Directed by William Nigh. Produced by Paul Malvern. Screenplay by Michael Jacoby. Original story by Ralph Bettinson. Based on the character "James Lee Wong" created by Hugh Wiley.

Cast: Boris Karloff, Marjorie Reynolds, Grant Withers, Melvin Lang, Guy Usher, Catherine Craig, William Stelling, Kenneth Harlan, Wilbur Mack, Henry Brandon, Richard Loo.

Mr. Wong (Boris Karloff) attempts to solve the murder of a shipping tycoon (Melvin Lang) and the theft of contraband bonds.

Running time: 68 minutes. Release date: August 12, 1940.

Released in Great Britain as **Mystery of the Wentworth Castle.**

236. Laughing at Danger (mystery-comedy) Directed by Howard Bretherton. Produced by Lindsley Parsons. Screenplay by Joseph West (George Waggner) and John Krafft. Story by Joseph West (George Waggner).

Cast: Frankie Darro, Joy Hodges, Mantan Moreland, George Houston, Kay Sutton, Veda Ann Borg, Guy Usher, Lillian Elliott, Rolfe Sedan, Betty Compson, Maxine Leslie, Ralph Peters, Gene O'Donnell.

A pageboy (Frankie Darro) delves into the mystery surrounding the death of a beauty parlor operator.

Running time: 62 min. Release date: Aug. 12, 1940.

Boris Karloff as Chinese detective James Lee Wong in "Doomed to Die" (1940), one in a series of "Mr. Wong" mysteries.

237. Arizona Frontier (western) Directed by Al Herman. Produced by Edward Finney. Screenplay by Robert Emmett (Tansey).

Cast: Tex Ritter, Evelyn Finley, Lloyd "Arkansas Slim" Andrews, Jim Thorpe, Tristram Coffin, Frank LaRue, Gene Alsace (Rocky Camron), Dick Cramer, Jim Pierce, Hal Price, Chick Hannon, Art Wilcox and His Arizona Rangers, "White Flash."

A government agent (Tex Ritter), appointed to choose a spot where the east and west branches of a railroad will meet, encounters treachery by an army lieutenant. Running time: 60 minutes. Release date: August 19, 1940.

238. The Range Busters (western) Directed by S. Roy Luby. Produced by George W. Weeks. Screenplay by John Rathmell.

Cast: Ray "Crash" Corrigan, John "Dusty" King, Max "Alibi" Terhune, LeRoy Mason, Luana Walters, Earle Hodgins, Frank LaRue, Kermit Maynard, Bruce King, Duke (Carl) Mathews, Horace Murphy, Karl Hackett.

The Range Busters (Ray "Crash" Corrigan, John "Dusty" King, Max "Alibi" Terhune) try to find out the identity of a supposed "ghost" responsible for a series of murders on a ranch owned by a young woman (Luana Walters).

Running time: 56 min. Release date: Aug. 22, 1940.

239. Queen of the Yukon (adventure) Directed by Phil Rosen. Produced by Paul Malvern. Screenplay by Joseph West (George Waggner). From a story by Jack London.

Cast: Charles Bickford, Irene Rich, Melvin Lang, George Cleveland, Guy Usher, June Carlson, Dave O'Brien, Tristram Coffin, Jack Daley, John Merton, Johnny Morris, J.M. Holmes, Cap Anderson, Gene O'Donnell.

Sadie (Irene Rich), the owner of a riverboat, strives to keep her daughter (June Carlson) from following in her footsteps, but the young girl is determined to do so nevertheless.

Running time: 73 minutes. Release date: August 26, 1940.

240. Who Is Guilty? (mystery) Directed by Fred Zelnik. Produced by I. Goldsmith. Screenplay by Laurence Huntington. From the play by Alec Coppel.

Cast: Syd Walker, Ben Lyon, Terence de Marney, Barbara Blair, Athole Stewart, Antoinette Cellier, Leslie Perrins, Dave Burns, Kathleen Harrison, Gus McNaughton, Ronald Shiner, Aubrey Mallalieu, Robert Adair.

Frankie Darro (left) and Mantan Moreland are pictured on this poster for "Up in the Air" (1940), one of several Darro-Moreland teamings. Darro was frequently teamed with Moreland in the series of actioners in which he starred.

Inspector Davidson (Syd Walker) of Scotland Yard is called in when four people confess to have murdered Count Mattoni (Leslie Perrins), each of them with a plausible motive.

Running time: 89 minutes. Release date: September 2, 1940.

A Grafton Production, produced and released in Great Britain as **I Killed the Count** (1939); originally released in the U.S. by Grand National in 1939; released in the U.S. under the title **Who Is Guilty?** by Monogram.

241. Up in the Air (mystery-comedy) Directed by Howard Bretherton. Produced by Lindsley Parsons. Screenplay by Edmond Kelso.

Cast: Frankie Darro, Marjorie Reynolds, Mantan Moreland, Lorna Gray (Adrian Booth), Gordon Jones, Tristram Coffin, Clyde Dilson, Dick Elliott, John Holland, Carleton Young.

When a murder is committed at a radio station, two friends (Frankie Darro, Mantan Moreland) set out to solve the crime.

Running time: 61 minutes. Release date: September 9, 1940.

242. That Gang of Mine (comedy-drama) Directed by Joseph H. Lewis. Produced by Sam Katzman. Screenplay by William Lively. Story by Alan Whitman. A Four-Bell Production.

Cast: Leo Gorcey, Bobby Jordan, "Sunshine Sammy" Morrison, David Gorcey, Donald Haines, Clarence Muse, David O'Brien, Joyce Bryant, Eugene Francis, Milton Kibbee, Richard R. Terry, Wilbur Mack, Hazel Keener.

Mugs Maloney (Leo Gorcey) trains to become a jockey, even though his decision to do so is ridiculed by the other East Side Kids (Bobby Jordan, "Sunshine Sammy" Morrison, David Gorcey, Donald Haines).

Running time: 62 minutes. Release date: September 23, 1940.

243. The Ape (horror) Directed by William Nigh. Produced by William T. Lackey. Screenplay by Curt Siodmak and Richard Carroll. Suggested by the play "The Ape" by Adam Hull Shirk. Adaptation by Curt Siodmak.

Cast: Boris Karloff, Maris Wrixon, Gertrude Hoffman, Henry Hall, Gene O'Donnell, Dorothy Vaughn, Jack Kennedy, Jessie Arnold, Selmer Jackson, George Cleveland.

A country doctor (Boris Karloff), disguised as an ape, slays two women and attempts to kill a third in order to obtain their spinal fluids to cure a young girl (Maris Wrixon) of paralysis.

Running time: 61 minutes. Release date: September 30, 1940.

244. Drums of the Desert (adventure) Directed by George Waggner. Produced by Paul Malvern. Screenplay by Dorothy

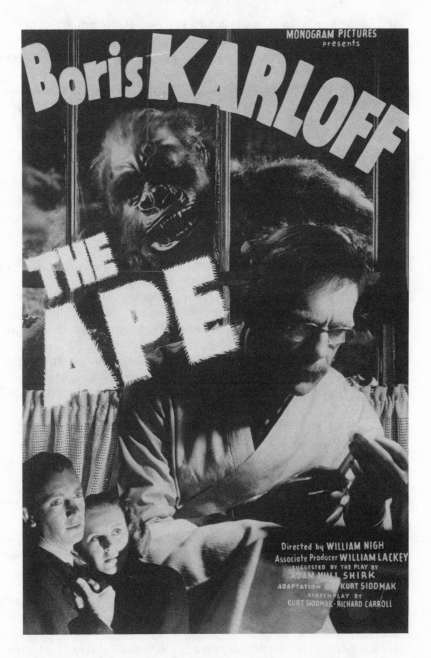

A poster for "The Ape" (1940) starring Boris Karloff.

(Mrs. Wallace) Reid and Joseph West (George Waggner). Original story by John T. Neville.

Cast: Ralph Byrd, Lorna Gray (Adrian Booth), Mantan Moreland, George Peter Lynn, Willie Castello.

A French Foreign Legion officer (Ralph Byrd), en route to his post as special advisor for parachute troops, meets and falls in love with a woman (Lorna Gray) who's already engaged to be married.

Running time: 64 minutes. Release date: October 7, 1940.

245. Trailing Double Trouble (western) Directed by S. Roy Luby. Produced by George W. Weeks. Screenplay by Oliver Drake. Story by George Plympton. A Phoenix Production.

Cast: Ray "Crash" Corrigan, John "Dusty" King, Max "Alibi" Terhune, Lita Conway, Nancy Louise King, Roy Barcroft, Jack Rutherford, Tom London, William Kellogg, Carl Mathews, Forrest Taylor, Kenne Duncan, Dick Cramer, Tex Felker, Jimmy Wakely and His Rough Riders.

Finding a baby (Nancy Louise King) in a runaway wagon, the Range Busters (Ray "Crash" Corrigan, John "Dusty" King, Max "Alibi" Terhune) investigate the murder of the child's father (Kenne Duncan).

Running time: 56 minutes. Release date: October 10, 1940.

246. Old Swimmin' Hole (drama) Directed by Robert McGowan. Produced by Scott R. Dunlap. Screenplay by Dorothy (Mrs. Wallace) Reid. Original story by Gerald Breitigam.

Cast: Jackie Moran, Marcia Mae Jones, Leatrice Joy, Charles Brown, Theodore von Eltz, George Cleveland, Dix Davis, Dorothy Vaughn.

Romance blossoms between a widow (Leatrice Joy) and a widower (Charles Brown) thanks to the efforts of their respective children (Jackie Moran, Marcia Mae Jones).

Running time: 80 minutes. Release date: October 21, 1940.

Released in Great Britain as **When Youth Conspires.**

247. Missing People (mystery) Directed by Jack Raymond. Produced by Charles Q. Steel. Screenplay by Lydia Hayward. Based on a short story by Edgar Wallace.

Cast: Will Fyffe, Kay Walsh, Lyn Harding, Ronald Shiner, Ronald Adam, Patricia Roc, Anthony Holles, Reginald Purdell, Laurence Hanray.

Gentleman-detective J.G. Reeder (Will Fyffe) appoints himself official investigator to locate the whereabouts of 27 well-to-do citizens whose absence under similar circumstances arouses his suspicion.

Running time: 69 minutes. Release date: November 6, 1940.

Produced and released in Great Britain in 1939; released in the U.S. by Monogram.

248. Take Me Back to Oklahoma (western) Directed by Al Herman. Produced by Edward Finney. Screenplay by Robert Emmett (Tansey).

Cast: Tex Ritter, Lloyd "Arkansas Slim" Andrews, Terry Walker, Karl Hackett, George Eldredge, Bob McKenzie, Olin Francis, Carleton Young, Sherry Tansey, Gene Alsace (Rocky Camron), Don Curtis, Bob Wills and His Texas Playboys, Tex Cooper, Rose Plummer, Chick Hannon, "White Flash."

Tex and his sidekick (Lloyd "Arkansas Slim" Andrews) go after a gang which has been systematically destroying stagecoaches in order to get a coach line franchise.

Running time: 57 min. Release date: Nov. 11, 1940.

Working title: **Oklahoma Bound.**

249. Phantom of Chinatown (mystery) Directed by Phil Rosen. Produced by Paul Malvern. Screenplay by Joseph West (George Waggner). Original story by Ralph Bettinson. Based on the character "James Lee Wong" created by Hugh Wiley.

Cast: Keye Luke, Lotus Long, Grant Withers, Paul McVey, Charles Miller, Virginia Carpenter, John Dilson, John Holland, Dick Terry, Huntley Gordon, Roy Kellard, William Castello, Victor Wong.

Mr. Wong (Keye Luke) investigates the murder of an explorer who had discovered a scroll showing the location of a large oil deposit.

Running time: 62 minutes. Release date: November 18, 1940.

250. Chamber of Horrors (mystery) Directed by Norman Lee. Produced by John Argyle. Screenplay by Norman Lee and Gilbert Gunn. Based on the novel "The Door with Seven Locks" by Edgar Wallace.

Cast: Leslie Banks, Lilli Palmer, Romilly Lunge, Gina Malo, Richard Bird, R. Montgomery, Dave Horne, J.H. Roberts, Cathleen Nesbitt, Harry Hutchinson, Phil Ray, Aubrey Mallalieu.

Upon the death of their benefactor, a group of trusted friends and servants steal the keys to his tomb, in which his jewels have been placed. Seven keys are necessary to open the tomb; one of the keys finds its way to a girl (Lilli Palmer) and her detective friend (Romilly Lunge).

Running time: 79 minutes. Release date: December 20, 1940.

Produced and released in Great Britain as **The Door with Seven Locks**; released in the U.S. under the title **Chamber of Horrors** by Monogram.

251. Her First Romance (musical-drama) Directed by Edward Dmytryk. Produced by I.E. Chadwick. Screenplay by Adele Comandini. Based on the novel "His First Daughter" by Gene Stratton-Porter.

Cast: Edith Fellows, Wilbur Evans, Jacqueline Wells (Julie Bishop), Alan Ladd, Roger Daniel, Judith Linden, Marion Kerby, Marlo Dwyer, Otila Nesmith, Ray Hirsch, Alexandria Moreland, Julie Sheldon, John Adamson.

A young girl (Edith Fellows) gets invited to a college dance, only to learn that it's part of an initiation stunt; she is brokenhearted, but a visiting singer (Wilbur Evans), considered to be the "catch" of the season, takes her.

Running time: 77 minutes. Release date: December 25, 1940.

Reissued as **The Right Man.**

112

252. West of Pinto Basin (western) Directed by S. Roy Luby. Produced by George W. Weeks. Screenplay by Earle Snell. Original story by Elmer Clifton. A Phoenix Production.

Cast: Ray "Crash" Corrigan, John "Dusty" King, Max "Alibi" Terhune, Gwen Gaze, Tristram Coffin, Jack Perrin, Carl Mathews, George Chesebro, Dirk Thane, Bud Osborne, Dick Cramer, Phil Dunham, Jerry Smith, Budd Buster.

The Range Busters (Ray "Crash" Corrigan, John "Dusty" King, Max "Alibi" Terhune) foil a plot by a saloon owner who's trying to prevent the completion of an irrigation project.

Running time: 60 minutes. Release date: December 25, 1940.

Working title: **Triple Threat.**

253. Rollin' Home to Texas (western) Directed by Al Herman. Produced by Edward Finney. Screenplay by Robert Emmett (Tansey).

Cast: Tex Ritter, Cal Shrum and His Rhythm Rangers, Lloyd "Arkansas Slim" Andrews, Virginia Carpenter, Eddie Dean, Jack Rutherford, Minta Durfee, Walt Shrum, I. Stanford Jolley, Charles Phillips, Harry Harvey, Olin Francis, Gene Alsace (Rocky Camron), Harold Landon, Bob Battier, Donald Kerr, Rusty Cline, Gene Haas, Tony Flores, Mack Williams, Robert Hoag, Hal Blaire, "White Flash."

A U.S. Marshal (Tex Ritter) has an uncle (a prison warden) who institutes an honor system among the convicts. The Marshal swears in the convicts as his deputies and gets them to aid in the capture of a criminal gang responsible for helping prisoners to escape and then murdering them for the reward money.

Running time: 63 minutes. Release date: December 30, 1940.

1941

254. Trail of the Silver Spurs (western) Directed by

113

"CRASH" CORRIGAN   "DUSTY" KING   "ALIBI" TERHUNE
"RANGE BUSTERS"
BOX OFFICE CHAMPIONS OF 1941

A trade announcement for The Range Busters series.

S. Roy Luby. Produced by George W. Weeks. Screenplay by Earle Snell. Story by Elmer Clifton.

Cast: Ray "Crash" Corrigan, John "Dusty" King, Max "Alibi" Terhune, Dorothy Short, Milburn Morante, George Chesebro, Eddie Dean, I. Stanford Jolley, Kermit Maynard, Steve Clark, Frank Ellis, Carl Mathews.

The Range Busters (Ray "Crash" Corrigan, John "Dusty" King, Max "Alibi" Terhune) pursue a gold thief and wind up in a ghost town; there they encounter a mysterious figure who uses the clicking of spurs as a warning of death.

Running time: 58 minutes. Release date: January 4, 1941.

255. Dead Man's Shoes (drama) Directed by Thomas Bentley. Produced by Walter C. Mycroft. Screenplay by Hans Hafka and Nina Jarvis.

Cast: Leslie Banks, Wilfred Lawson, Judy Kelly, George Atkin, Nancy Price, Walter Hudd, Peter Bull, Henry Oscar, Ludwig Stossel.

An amnesia victim (Leslie Banks), unaware of his criminal past, tries to save his reputation when confronted by a blackmailer (Wilfred Lawson).

Running time: 70 minutes. Release date: January 15, 1941.

An Associated British Picture Corp. production, released in Great Britain in 1939; released in the U.S. by Monogram.

256. You're Out of Luck (mystery-comedy) Directed by Howard Bretherton. Produced by Lindsley Parsons. Original screenplay by Edmond Kelso.

Cast: Frankie Darro, Mantan Moreland, Kay Sutton, Billy Snyder, Tristram Coffin, Richard Bond, Willie Castello, Ralph Peters, Gene O'Donnell, Vickie Lester, Janet Shaw.

An elevator operator (Frankie Darro) and a janitor (Mantan Moreland) become involved in two murders stemming from the activities of a gambling ring.

Running time: 62 minutes. Release date: January 20, 1941.

257. Pride of the Bowery (comedy-drama) Directed by Joseph H. Lewis. Produced by Sam Katzman. Screenplay by George Plympton. Story by Steven Clensos. A Banner Production.

Cast: Leo Gorcey, Bobby Jordan, Donald Haines, Carleton Young, David Gorcey, "Sunshine Sammy" Morrison, Eugene Francis, Mary Ainslee, Kenneth Howell, Bobby Stone, Kenneth Harlan, Nick Stuart, Lloyd Ingraham, Steve Clensos.

The East Side Kids wind up at a Civilian Conservation

Corps camp when Mugs (Leo Gorcey) is convinced that it's a "Free Training Camp" for the furtherance of his boxing career.

Running time: 61 minutes. Release date: January 31, 1941.

Released in Great Britain as **Here We Go Again.**

258. **The Kid's Last Ride** (western) Directed by S. Roy Luby. Produced by George W. Weeks. Story and screenplay by Earle Snell.

Cast: Ray "Crash" Corrigan, John "Dusty" King, Max "Alibi" Terhune, Luana Walters, Edwin Brian, Al Bridge, Glenn Strange, Frank Ellis, John Elliott, George Havens, Tex Palmer, Carl Mathews, George Morrell.

The Range Busters (Ray "Crash" Corrigan, John "Dusty" King, Max "Alibi" Terhune) try to stop a blackmailing crook from taking over a girl's ranch.

Running time: 55 minutes. Release date: February 10, 1941.

259. **Ridin' the Cherokee Trail** (western) Directed by Spencer Gordon Bennet. Produced by Edward F. Finney. Screenplay by Edmond Kelso.

Cast: Tex Ritter, Lloyd "Arkansas Slim" Andrews, Betty Miles, Forrest Taylor, Jack Roper, Fred Burns, Bruce Nolan, Edward Cassidy, Gene Alsace (Rocky Camron), Bob Card, Nolan Willis, The Tennessee Ramblers, Hal Price, Chuck Baldra, "White Flash."

A Texas Ranger (Tex Ritter) pursues an outlaw (Forrest Taylor) operating in the Cherokee strip.

Running time: 62 min. Release date: Feb. 25, 1941.

Also known as **Arizona Ranch Hands.**

260. **Flying Wild** (comedy-drama) Directed by William West. Produced by Sam Katzman. Story and screenplay by Al Martin. A Banner Production.

Cast: Leo Gorcey, Bobby Jordan, Donald Haines, David Gorcey, Bobby Stone, "Sunshine Sammy" Morrison, Eugene Francis, Joan Barclay, Herbert Rawlinson, George Pembroke, Forrest Taylor, Alden (Stephen) Chase, David O'Brien, Dennis Moore, Mary Bovard, Bob Hill.

The East Side Kids are working at an airplane factory when Mugs (Leo Gorcey) accidentally stumbles into a sabotage plot.
Running time: 64 minutes. Release date: March 10, 1941. Working title: **Air Devils.**

261. Sign of the Wolf (adventure–drama) Directed by Howard Bretherton. Produced by Paul Malvern. Screenplay by Edmond Kelso and Elizabeth Hopkins. From the story "That Spot" by Jack London.

Cast: Michael Whalen, Grace Bradley, Darryl Hickman, Mantan Moreland, Louise Beavers, Wade Crosby, Tony Paton, Joseph Bernard, Ed Brady, Brandon Hurst, Eddie Kane.

Canadian hijackers of fox furs train an Alsatian shepherd to steal pelts from a local fox camp.

Running time: 69 minutes. Release date: March 25, 1941.

262. Break the News (comedy) Produced and directed by Rene Clair. Screenplay by Geoffrey Kerr. Adapted by Carlo Rima. From the novel "La Mort En Fuite" by Lois le Guriadec. A Jack Buchanan Production. A Trio Picture.

Cast: Maurice Chevalier, Jack Buchanan, June Knight, Marta Labarr, Gertrude Musgrove, Charles Lefeaux, Gary Marsh, Wallace Douglas, Felix Aylmer, C. Denier Warren, D.J. Williams, Robb Wilton, Gibb McLaughlin, Elliot Mason, Athole Stewart, J. Abercromie, Guy Middleton, George Hayes, W. Fazan, Mark Daly, George Benson, Joss Ambler, H.R. Hignett, Wally Patch, Hall Gordon.

A publicity stunt concocted by two song–and–dance men (Maurice Chevalier, Jack Buchanan) goes hopelessly awry.

Running time: 72 minutes. Release date: April 10, 1941.

Made in England; released in Great Britain in 1938 by General Film Distributors; released in the U.S. by Monogram.

263. Tumbledown Ranch in Arizona (western) Directed by S. Roy Luby. Produced by George W. Weeks. Screenplay by Milton Raison.

Cast: Ray "Crash" Corrigan, John "Dusty" King, Max "Alibi" Terhune, Sheila Darcy, Marion Kerby, Quen Ramsey, James Craven, John Elliott, Jack Holmes, Steve Clark, Sam Bernard, Carl Mathews, Tex Palmer, Tex Cooper, Frank Ellis, Nick Thompson, Frank McCarroll, Chick Hannon, The University of Arizona Glee Club.

The sons of the Range Busters are participating in a collegiate rodeo show in 1941; a blow on the head sends one of them back into the past--by a sort of application of what he calls fourth dimension--and it is in this past that the Range Busters (Ray "Crash" Corrigan, John "Dusty" King, Max "Alibi" Terhune) thwart a plot to steal a ranch.

Running time: 60 min. Release date: April 20, 1941.

264. The Invisible Ghost (mystery-horror) Directed by Joseph H. Lewis. Produced by Sam Katzman. Screenplay by Al and Helen Martin.

Cast: Bela Lugosi, Polly Ann Young, John McGuire, Clarence Muse, Terry Walker, Betty Compson, Ernie Adams, George Pembroke, Fred Kelsey, Jack Mulhall.

The gentle Mr. Kessler (Bela Lugosi) sees his supposedly dead wife (Betty Compson), who is actually a victim of amnesia, and goes on a homicidal rampage.

Running time: 66 minutes. Release date: April 25, 1941.

Working titles: **Murder by the Stars** and **The Phantom Killer.**

265. Roar of the Press (drama) Directed by Phil Rosen. Produced by Scott R. Dunlap. Screenplay by Albert Duffy. Original story by Al Bloch.

Cast: Wallace Ford, Jean Parker, Jed Prouty, Suzanne Kaaren, Harlan Tucker, Robert Frazer, John Holland, Paul Fix, Eddie Foster, Matty Fain, Betty Compson, Dorothy Lee, Donald Kerr, Evalyn Knapp, Willie Costello, Maxine Leslie, Wilbur Mack, Bob Pittard, Charles King, Frank O'Connor, Dennis Moore.

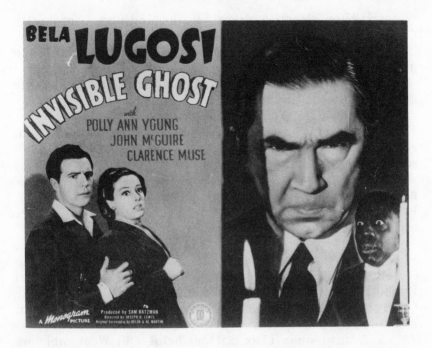

Bela Lugosi is prominently featured in this poster for "The Invisible Ghost" (1941). Also pictured: John McGuire (left), Polly Ann Young and Clarence Muse. This was the first of nine Monogram films Lugosi made that were produced by Sam Katzman, a veteran "quickie" producer who was also responsible for Monogram's East Side Kids and Teen Agers series.

While on their honeymoon, a reporter (Wallace Ford) and his bride (Jean Parker) encounter a group of fifth columnists.

Running time: 72 minutes. Release date: April 30, 1941.

Working title: **Widows of the Press.**

266. House of Mystery (mystery-drama) Directed by Walter Summers. Screenplay by Doreen Montgomery. Based on the novel "At the Villa Rose" by A.E.W. Mason.

Cast: Kenneth Kent, Judy Kelly, Peter Murray Hill,

Walter Rilla, Martita Hunt, Ruth Maitland, Antoinette Cellier, Clifford Evans, Ronald Adam, Arthur Hambling.

A police inspector (Kenneth Kent) investigates the abduction of a wealthy woman's companion (Judy Kelly).

Running time: 62 minutes (74 minutes in Great Britain). Release date: May 5, 1941.

Working title: **The Human Ghost.**

An Associated British Picture Corp. production, released in Great Britain as **At the Villa Rose** (1939); released in the U.S. by Monogram.

267. The Pioneers (western) Directed by Al Herman. Produced by Edward Finney. Screenplay by Charles Alderson. Based on a story by James Fenimore Cooper.

Cast: Tex Ritter, Lloyd "Arkansas Slim" Andrews, Red Foley and his Saddle Pals, Wanda McKay, Doyle O'Dell, George Chesebro, Del Lawrence, Post Park, Karl Hackett, Lynton Brent, Chick Hannon, Gene Alsace (Rocky Camron), Jack Smith, Chief Many Treaties, Chief Soldani, Art Dillard, "White Flash."

A frontiersman (Tex Ritter) helps Old West pioneers settle in the new land.

Running time: 58 minutes. Release date: May 10, 1941.

268. King of the Zombies (horror) Directed by Jean Yarbrough. Produced by Lindsley Parsons. Screenplay by Edmond Kelso.

Cast: Dick Purcell, Joan Woodbury, Mantan Moreland, Henry Victor, John Archer, Patricia Stacey, Guy Usher, Marguerite Whitten, Leigh Whipper, Madame Sul-Te-Wan, Jimmy Davis, Laurence Criner.

On an island near Puerto Rico, a mad scientist (Henry Victor) creates an army of zombies; foreign powers plan to use them to control the world.

Running time: 67 minutes. Release date: May 14, 1941.

269. Redhead (comedy) Directed by Edward L. Cahn. Produced by I.E. Chadwick. Screenplay by Conrad Seiler and Dorothy Reid. From the novel by Vera Brown.

120

Cast: June Lang, Johnny Downs, Eric Blore, Weldon Heyburn, Anna Chandler, Frank Jaquet, Kalina Zarova, Baron Emerson, Harry Burns.

Two young people (June Lang, Johnny Downs) marry in a plot to obtain $20,000 from the boy's father (Frank Jaquet) who they think will buy off the bride. Instead the father makes a deal with the girl to reform his playboy son.

Running time: 64 minutes. Release date: May 21, 1941.

A remake of **Redhead** (Monogram, 1934).

270. Silver Stallion (western) Produced and directed by Edward Finney. Screenplay by Robert Emmett (Tansey).

Cast: David Sharpe, LeRoy Mason, Chief Thunder Cloud, Janet Waldo, Fred Hoose, Thornton Edwards, Walter Long, Thunder the Wonder Horse, Captain Boots the Police Dog.

Forced by circumstances, three pals (David Sharpe, LeRoy Mason, Chief Thunder Cloud) become horse thieves and are hunted by every law agency in the West.

Running time: 57 minutes. Release date: May 28, 1941.

271. Wrangler's Roost (western) Directed by S. Roy Luby. Produced by George W. Weeks. Screenplay by John Vlahos and Robert Finkle. Story by Earle Snell.

Cast: Ray "Crash" Corrigan, John "Dusty" King, Max "Alibi" Terhune, Forrest Taylor, Gwen Gaze, George Chesebro, Frank Ellis, Jack Holmes, Walter Shumway, Frank McCarroll, Carl Mathews, Hank Bell, Tex Palmer, Jim Corey, Al Haskell, Ray Jones, Horace B. Carpenter, Tex Cooper, Herman Hack, Chick Hannon.

The Range Busters (Ray "Crash" Corrigan, John "Dusty" King, Max "Alibi" Terhune) are assigned to track down a stagecoach robber who is impersonating Black Bart, a reformed outlaw.

Running time: 57 minutes. Release date: June 4, 1941.

272. The Gang's All Here (mystery-comedy) Directed

by Jean Yarbrough. Produced by Lindsley Parsons. Screenplay by Edmond Kelso.

Cast: Frankie Darro, Marcia Mae Jones, Jackie Moran, Mantan Moreland, Keye Luke, Robert Homans, Irving Mitchell, Edward Cassidy, Pat Gleason, Jack Kenney, Laurence Criner, Paul Bryar, Jack Ingram.

A pair of truck drivers (Frankie Darro, Mantan Moreland) become involved in a war between two rival trucking companies.

Running time: 61 minutes. Release date: June 11, 1941.

Released in Great Britain as **In the Night.**

273. Murder by Invitation (mystery-comedy) Directed by Phil Rosen. Produced by A.W. Hackel. Screenplay by George Bricker.

Cast: Wallace Ford, Marian Marsh, Sarah Padden, George Guhl, Wallis Clark, Gavin Gordon, Minerva Urecal, J. Arthur Young, Herbert Vigran, Philip Trent, Dave O'Brien, Hazel Keener, Isabelle LaMal, Lee Shumway, John James, Kay Deslys.

A newspaper columnist (Wallace Ford) befriends a wealthy old spinster (Sarah Padden) whose greedy relatives are trying to have her committed to a mental institution.

Running time: 67 minutes. Release date: June 30, 1941.

Working title: **Murder by Appointment.**

274. Arizona Bound (western) Directed by Spencer Gordon Bennet. Produced by Scott R. Dunlap. Screenplay by Jess Bowers (Adele Buffington). Story by Oliver Drake.

Cast: Buck Jones, Tim McCoy, Raymond Hatton, Luana Walters, Tristram Coffin, Charles "Slim" Whitaker, Gene Alsace (Rocky Camron), Ben Corbett, Horace Murphy, Kathryn Sheldon, Dennis Moore, Jack Daley, Hal Price, I. Stanford Jolley, Augie Gomez, Artie Ortego, "Silver."

The "Rough Riders"—an ex-U.S. Marshal (Buck Jones) and his pals (Tim McCoy, Raymond Hatton)—clean up a gang of gold thieves in Mesa City.

Running time: 57 minutes. Release date: July 19, 1941.

Working title: **Rough Riders.**

275. Father Steps Out (comedy) Directed by Jean Yarbrough. Produced by Lindsley Parsons. Screenplay by Joseph West (George Waggner).

Cast: Frank Albertson, Lorna Gray (Adrian Booth), Jed Prouty, Kathryn Sheldon, Frank Faylen, Charles Hall, John Maxwell, John Dilson, Mary Field, Paul Maxey, Tristram Coffin, J. Arthur Young, Gene O'Donnell, Frank Melton.

A reporter (Frank Albertson) poses as a doctor's assistant in order to obtain a story from a railroad president (Jed Prouty). The railroad magnate later meets two hoboes (Frank Faylen, Charles Hall) who teach the high-strung businessman how to really enjoy life.

Running time: 63 minutes. Release date: July 19, 1941.

Working title: **City Limits.**

A remake of **City Limits** (Monogram, 1934).

276. Wanderers of the West (western) Directed by Robert Hill. Produced by Robert Tansey. Screenplay by Robert Emmett (Tansey).

Cast: Tom Keene, Betty Miles, Sugar Dawn, Lloyd "Arkansas Slim" Andrews, Tom Seidel, Stanley Price, Gene Alsace (Rocky Camron), Tom London, Fred Hoose, James Sheridan (Sherry Tansey).

Tom Mallory (Tom Keene) hits the western trail, searching for the cattle rustlers who killed his father.

Running time: 58 minutes. Release date: July 25, 1941.

277. Fugitive Valley (western) Directed by S. Roy Luby. Produced by George W. Weeks. Screenplay by John Vlahos and Robert Finkle. Story by Oliver Drake.

Cast: Ray "Crash" Corrigan, John "Dusty" King, Max "Alibi" Terhune, Julie Duncan, Glenn Strange, Bob Kortman, Ed Brady, Tom London, Reed Howes, Carl Mathews, Edward Peil, Sr., Doyle O'Dell, Frank McCarroll.

The Range Busters (Ray "Crash" Corrigan, John "Dusty" King, Max "Alibi" Terhune) go to Fugitive Valley to capture "The Whip," a notorious bandit. Running time: 61 minutes. Release date: July 30, 1941.

278. The Deadly Game (drama) Directed by Phil Rosen. Produced by Dixon R. Harwin. Screenplay by Wellyn Totman.

Cast: Charles Farrell, June Lang, John Miljan, J. Arthur Young, Dave Clark, Bernadene Hayes, Dave O'Brien, Fred Gierman, Hans von Morhart, Tom Herbert, Kenne Duncan, John Harmon, Jack Gardner, Walter Bonn, William Vaughn, Ottola Nesmith, Knud Kreuger, Harold Daniels.

An F.B.I. agent (Charles Farrell) pursues a gang of German spies who've kidnapped a scientist (J. Arthur Young) working on the invention of a night air-raid detector.

Running time: 63 min. Release date: Aug. 8, 1941.

279. Dynamite Canyon (western) Produced and directed by Robert Tansey. Story and screenplay by Robert Emmett (Tansey) and Frances Kavanaugh.

Cast: Tom Keene, Evelyn Finley, Sugar Dawn, Lloyd "Arkansas Slim" Andrews, Stanley Price, Kenne Duncan, Tom London, Gene Alsace (Rocky Camron), Fred Hoose, "Rusty."

A U.S. Ranger (Tom Keene), disguised as a desperado, joins a gang of outlaws responsible for the murder of a rancher.

Running time: 58 minutes. Release date: August 8, 1941.

280. Saddle Mountain Roundup (western) Directed by S. Roy Luby. Produced by George W. Weeks. Screenplay by John Vlahos. Story by Earle Snell.

Cast: Ray "Crash" Corrigan, John "Dusty" King, Max "Alibi" Terhune, Jack Mulhall, Lita Conway, Willie Fung, John Elliott, George Chesebro, Jack Holmes, Harold Goodman, Carl Mathews, Al Ferguson, Charles "Slim" Whitaker, Tex Palmer, Steve Clark.

The Range Busters (Ray "Crash" Corrigan, John "Dusty" King, Max "Alibi" Terhune) go to the aid of an old rancher who's targeted for murder.
Running time: 55 minutes. Release date: August 29, 1941.

281. Gentleman from Dixie (drama) Directed by Al Herman. Produced by Edward Finney. Story and screenplay by Fred Myton.

Cast: Jack LaRue, Marian Marsh, Clarence Muse, Mary Ruth, Robert Kellard, John Holland, Lillian Randolph, Harold Gerard, Herbert Rawlinson, I. Stanford Jolley, Joe Hernandez, Phyllis Barry, Mist-A-Shot, The Clarence Muse Singers.

When a convict (Jack LaRue), framed for murder, is released from prison, he returns to the Southern farm where his brother (Robert Kellard) raises horses.
Running time: 63 min. Release date: Sept. 2, 1941.
Working title: **Li'l Louisiana Belle.**
This film was produced by Producers Releasing Corporation (PRC), but released by Monogram.

282. Bowery Blitzkrieg (comedy-drama) Directed by Wallace Fox. Produced by Sam Katzman. Screenplay by Sam Robins. Story by Brendan Wood and Donn Mullahy. A Banner Production.

Cast: Leo Gorcey, Bobby Jordan, Huntz Hall, Keye Luke, Warren Hull, Charlotte Henry, Bobby Stone, Donald Haines, "Sunshine Sammy" Morrison, David Gorcey, Martha Wentworth, Eddie Foster, Dennis Moore, Tony Carson, Dick Ryan, Pat Costello, Minerva Urecal, Jack Mulhall.

Crooked gamblers try to persuade East Side Kid Muggs McGinnis (Leo Gorcey) to throw an upcoming boxing match.
Running time: 62 minutes. Release date: September 8, 1941.
Released in Great Britain as **Stand and Deliver.**

283. Let's Go Collegiate (musical-comedy) Directed by Jean Yarbrough. Produced by Lindsley Parsons. Story and screenplay by Edmond Kelso.

Cast: Frankie Darro, Jackie Moran, Marcia Mae Jones, Mantan Moreland, Gale Storm, Keye Luke, Frank Sully, Billy Griffith, Barton Yarborough, Frank Faylen, Marguerite Whitten, Paul Maxey, Tristram Coffin, Gene O'Donnell.

Two fraternity brothers (Frankie Darro, Jackie Moran) pass off a truck driver (Frank Sully) as a collegiate athlete. Running time: 62 minutes. Release date: September 12, 1941.

Released in Great Britain as **Farewell to Fame.**

284. The Gunman from Bodie (western) Directed by Spencer Gordon Bennet. Produced by Scott R. Dunlap. Original screenplay by Jess Bowers (Adele Buffington).

Cast: Buck Jones, Tim McCoy, Raymond Hatton, Christine McIntyre, Dave O'Brien, Charles King, Robert Frazer, Lynton Brent, Max Waxman, Gene Alsace (Rocky Camron), John Merton, Frank LaRue, Jerry Sheldon, Jack King, Earl Douglas, Warren Jackson, Billy Carro, Frederick Gee, "Silver."

A U.S. Marshal (Buck Jones), one of the "Rough Riders," poses as "the gunman from Bodie" in order to infiltrate a gang of cattle rustlers.

Running time: 62 minutes. Release date: September 26, 1941.

Working title: **Bad Man from Bodie.**

285. Tonto Basin Outlaws (western) Directed by S. Roy Luby. Produced by George W. Weeks. Screenplay by John Vlahos. Story by Earle Snell.

Cast: Ray "Crash" Corrigan, John "Dusty" King, Max "Alibi" Terhune, Jan Wiley, Tristram Coffin, Edmund Cobb, Ted Mapes, Art "Dustbowl" Fowler, Carl Mathews, Reed Howes, Rex Lease, Edward Peil, Sr., Budd Buster, Tex Palmer, Hank Bell, Denver Dixon (Victor Adamson), Jim Corey.

Set during the Spanish-American War, the Range Busters (Ray "Crash" Corrigan, John "Dusty" King, Max "Alibi" Terhune) enlist in Teddy Roosevelt's Rough Riders and are promptly assigned to clean up the cattle-rustling in Wyoming, which is affecting the army's meat supply.

126

Running time: 60 minutes. Release date: October 10, 1941.

286. The Driftin' Kid (western) Produced and directed by Robert Tansey. Story and screenplay by Robert Emmett (Tansey) and Frances Kavanaugh.

Cast: Tom Keene, Betty Miles, Lloyd "Arkansas Slim" Andrews, Frank Yaconelli, Glenn Strange, Stanley Price, Fred Hoose, Gene Alsace (Rocky Camron), Steve Clark, Frank Yaconelli, James Sheridan (Sherry Tansey), Wally West, Frank McCarroll.

A government agent (Tom Keene), in his search for a gang of rustlers who have stolen a herd of two hundred wild horses, poses as a rancher.

Running time: 57 minutes. Release date: October 17, 1941.

287. Top Sergeant Mulligan (comedy) Directed by Jean Yarbrough. Produced by Lindsley Parsons. Screenplay by Edmond Kelso.

Cast: Nat Pendleton, Carol Hughes, Sterling Holloway, Marjorie Reynolds, Frank Faylen, Charles Hall, Tom Neal, Betty Blythe, Dick Elliott, Maynard Holmes, Wonderful Smith.

A top sergeant (Nat Pendleton) is continually exasperated by the antics of two bumbling rookies (Frank Faylen, Charles Hall).

Running time: 70 minutes. Release date: October 17, 1941.

288. Spooks Run Wild (comedy) Directed by Phil Rosen. Produced by Sam Katzman. Screenplay by Carl Foreman and Charles R. Marion. Additional dialogue by Jack Henley. A Banner Production.

Cast: Bela Lugosi, Leo Gorcey, Huntz Hall, Bobby Jordan, David Gorcey, "Sunshine Sammy" Morrison, Donald Haines, Dave O'Brien, Dorothy Short, Dennis Moore, Rosemary Portia, Guy Wilkerson, Angelo Rossitto, Joe Kirk, Jack Carr, P.J. Kelley, Pat Costello.

The East Side Kids (Leo Gorcey, Huntz Hall, Bobby Jordan, David Gorcey, "Sunshine Sammy" Morrison, Donald

127

Haines) wind up at a holiday camp for underprivileged boys; stumbling onto an old mansion, they encounter a mysterious stranger (Bela Lugosi) and his dwarf companion (Angelo Rossitto).
Running time: 64 minutes. Release date: October 24, 1941.
Working title: **Ghosts in the Night.**

289. Stolen Paradise (drama) Directed by Louis Gasnier. Produced by George A. Hirliman. Screenplay by Arthur Hoerl. Story by Lawrence Meade.
Cast: Leon Janney, Eleanor Hunt, Esther Muir, Wilma Francis, Doris Blaine, Herbert Fisher, Roy Tracy, Fred Meilsey, Maime Smith, Larry Hodges, Billy Birnes, Charles Shaw, Gilda Lynch.
A young man (Leon Janney) studies for the priesthood, but is sidetracked when he falls in love with his stepsister (Eleanor Hunt).
Running time: 62 minutes. Release date: October 30, 1941.
Working title: **Adolescence.**

290. Riding the Sunset Trail (western) Produced and directed by Robert Tansey. Screenplay by Robert Emmett (Tansey) and Frances Kavanaugh.
Cast: Tom Keene, Betty Miles, Lloyd "Arkansas Slim" Andrews, Frank Yaconelli, Sugar Dawn, Kenne Duncan, Tom Seidel, James Sheridan (Sherry Tansey), Earl Douglas, Tom London, Gene Alsace (Rocky Camron), Fred Hoose, "Rusty."
The leader of an outlaw gang (Kenne Duncan) tries to use a fake will to seize control of his half-brother's ranch; Tom Sterling (Tom Keene) sets out to prevent him from doing so.
Running time: 56 minutes. Release date: October 31, 1941.

291. Zis Boom Bah (musical-comedy) Directed by William Nigh. Produced by Sam Katzman. Screenplay by Harvey Gates and Jack Henley. Original story by Connie Lee and Harvey Gates.

Cast: Grace Hayes, Peter Lind Hayes, Mary Healy, Huntz Hall, Jan Wiley, Skeets Gallagher, Benny Rubin, Betty Compson, Lois Landon, Eddie Kane, Leonard Sues, Roland Dupree.

A musical-comedy performer (Grace Hayes) attempts a reconciliation with her estranged son (Peter Lind Hayes) by organizing a show at the college he attends.

Running time: 62 minutes. Release date: November 7, 1941.

292. Double Trouble (comedy) Directed by William West. Produced by Dixon R. Harwin. Screenplay by Jack Natteford.

Cast: Harry Langdon, Charles Rogers, Catherine Lewis, Louise Currie, Dave O'Brien, Frank Jaquet, Mira McKinney, Wheeler Oakman, Benny Rubin, Edward Kane, David Cavendish, Dick Alexander, Ruth Hiatt, Alfred Hall, Guy Kingsford, Fred Santley, Richard Cramer, Art Hamberger.

Two British refugees (Harry Langdon, Charles Rogers) get jobs at a canned bean manufacturing plant and manage to lose a valuable gem in one of the cans.

Running time: 63 minutes. Release date: November 21, 1941.

293. Underground Rustlers (western) Directed by S. Roy Luby. Produced by George W. Weeks. Screenplay by Bud Tuttle, Elizabeth Beecher and John Vlahos. Story by John Rathmell.

Cast: Ray "Crash" Corrigan, John "Dusty" King, Max "Alibi" Terhune, Gwen Gaze, Robert Blair, Forrest Taylor, Tom London, Steve Clark, Bud Osborne, Dick Cramer, John Elliott, Tex Palmer, Edward Peil, Sr., Carl Mathews, Tex Cooper, Frank McCarroll.

Stagecoaches carrying gold are being held up, so the Range Busters (Ray "Crash" Corrigan, John "Dusty" King, Max "Alibi" Terhune) are called in to remedy the situation at an important bullion dispensing center.

Running time: 56 minutes. Release date: November 21, 1941.

Working title: **Bullets and Bullion.**

A trade advertisement for "I Killed That Man" (1941).

294. I Killed That Man (mystery) Directed by Phil Rosen. Produced by Maurice and Franklin King. Screenplay by Henry Bancroft. Story by Leonard Fields and David Silverstein.

Cast: Ricardo Cortez, Joan Woodbury, Pat Gleason, Iris Adrian, George Pembroke, Herbert Rawlinson, Ralf Harolde, Jack Mulhall, Vince Barnett, Gavin Gordon, John Hamilton, Harry Holman.

A man condemned to die in the electric chair is killed by a poisoned dart in front of witnesses to the scheduled execution; an assistant district attorney (Ricardo Cortez) and a newspaper reporter (Joan Woodbury) set out to track down the murderer.

Running time: 71 minutes. Release date: November 28, 1941.

A remake of **Devil's Mate** (Monogram, 1933).

295. Borrowed Hero (drama) Directed by Lewis D. Collins. Produced by A.W. Hackel. Screenplay by Earle Snell. Story by Ben Roberts and Sidney Sheldon.

Cast: Alan Baxter, Florence Rice, John Hamilton, Stanley Andrews, Constance Worth, Wilma Francis, Mary Gordon, Richard Terry, Jerry Marlowe, Paul Everton, John Maxwell, Guy Usher, George Dobbs, Dorothy Gulliver, Eba Larson, Eddie Kane, Dudley Dickerson, James Deliso, Gene O'Donnell, Ted Stanhope, Robert Street, Charles King, Syd Saylor.

A struggling young lawyer (Alan Baxter) is appointed special prosecutor in the district attorney's office when he captures the murderer of a newspaperman who had uncovered evidence against the Civic League, a corrupt organization.

Running time: 65 minutes. Release date: December 5, 1941.

296. Lone Star Law Men (western) Produced and directed by Robert Tansey. Screenplay by Robert Emmett (Tansey) and Frances Kavanaugh.

Cast: Tom Keene, Betty Miles, Frank Yaconelli, Sugar Dawn, Glenn Strange, Charles King, Gene Alsace (Rocky Camron), James Sheridan (Sherry Tansey), Stanley Price, Fred Hoose, Franklyn Farnum, Jack Ingram, Reed Howes.

A cowpoke (Tom Keene) is appointed sheriff of a western town when he pretends to be on the side of the lawless element in control.

Running time: 61 minutes. Release date: December 5, 1941.

Working title: **Lone Star Law.**

297. Riot Squad (drama) Produced and directed by Edward Finney. Story and screenplay by C.C. Coons.

Cast: Richard Cromwell, Rita Quigley, John Miljan, Mary Ruth, Herbert Rawlinson, Mary Gordon, Donald Kerr, Jack C. Smith, Richard Clarke, Noel Cravat, Arthur Space.

An intern (Richard Cromwell) takes a job as doctor for a gang of criminals in order to trap them for the police.

Running time: 55 minutes. Release date: December 12, 1941.

298. Road to Happiness (drama) Directed by Phil Rosen. Produced by Scott R. Dunlap. Screenplay by Robert D. Andrews. From the American Magazine story "First Performance" by Matt Taylor.

Cast: John Boles, Mona Barrie, Billy Lee, Roscoe Karns, Lillian Elliott, Paul Porcasi, Sam Flint, Brandon Hurst, Byron Foulger, Selmer Jackson, Harlan Tucker, Antonio Filauri.

Returning to New York after spending four years in Europe, an aspiring opera singer (John Boles) learns that his wife (Mona Barrie) had divorced him eight months earlier and placed their ten-year-old son (Billy Lee) in a military school.

Running time: 83 minutes. Release date: December 19, 1941.

299. Forbidden Trails (western) Directed by Robert N. Bradbury. Produced by Scott R. Dunlap. Screenplay by Jess Bowers (Adele Buffington). Story by Oliver Drake.

Cast: Buck Jones, Tim McCoy, Raymond Hatton, Tristram Coffin, Christine McIntyre, Charles King, Glenn Strange, Lynton Brent, Jerry Sheldon, Hal Price, Dave O'Brien, Dick Alexander, "Silver."

The Rough Riders (Buck Jones, Tim McCoy, Raymond Hatton) help a mine owner who's being forced by outlaws to sign a hauling contract.

Running time: 54 minutes. Release date: December 26, 1941.

1942

300. Freckles Comes Home (comedy) Directed by Jean Yarbrough. Produced by Lindsley Parsons. Screenplay by Edmond Kelso. Suggested by the story by Gene Stratton-Porter.

Cast: Johnny Downs, Gale Storm, Mantan Moreland, Bradley Page, Betty Blythe, Marvin Stephens, Walter Sande.

Freckles (Johnny Downs), on his way home from college, inadvertently becomes acquainted with a big-time gangster.

Running time: 63 minutes. Release date: January 2, 1942.

301. Thunder River Feud (western) Directed by S. Roy Luby. Produced by George W. Weeks. Screenplay by John Vlahos and Earle Snell. Story by Earle Snell.

Cast: Ray "Crash" Corrigan, John "Dusty" King, Max "Alibi" Terhune, Jan Wiley, Jack M. Holmes, Rick Anderson, Carleton Young, Carl Mathews, George Chesebro, Budd Buster, Steve Clark, Ted Mapes, Tex Palmer, Hal Price, Dick Cramer.

The Range Busters (Ray "Crash" Corrigan, John "Dusty" King, Max "Alibi" Terhune) feud over a girl (Jan Wiley) just returned from an eastern school, but get together when a scheming band of men try to profit from a dispute between the girl's relatives and a neighboring family.

Running time: 51 minutes. Release date: January 9, 1942.

302. Private Snuffy Smith (comedy) Directed by Edward Cline. Produced by Edward Gross and Jack Dietz. Original screenplay by Jack Grey, Jack Henley, Lloyd French and Doncho Hall. From the comic strip "Barney Google and Snuffy Smith" by Billy DeBeck. A Capitol Production.

Cast: Bud Duncan, Edgar Kennedy, Sarah Padden, Doris Linden, Andraia Palmer, J. Farrell MacDonald, Pat McVeigh, Frank Austin, Jimmy Dodd.

After saving the life of an army sergeant, hillbilly

133

Top: Frank Albertson and Joan Woodbury in "Man from Headquarters" (1942). Bottom, pictured in a "Private Snuffy Smith" poster: Bud Duncan (as Snuffy Smith), Sarah Padden (as Loweezy) and Edgar Kennedy.

134

Snuffy Smith (Bud Duncan) is allowed to join the army as a "yard bird," a sort of servant around the camp.

Running time: 67 minutes. Release date: January 16, 1942.

Working title: **Snuffy Smith, the Yard Bird.** Released in Great Britain as **Snuffy Smith.**

303. Man from Headquarters (mystery) Directed by Jean Yarbrough. Produced by Lindsley Parsons. Screenplay by John Krafft and Rollo Lloyd.

Cast: Frank Albertson, Joan Woodbury, Dick Elliott, Byron Foulger, John Maxwell, Robert Kellard, Mel Ruick, Gwen Kenyon, Jack Mulhall, Christine McIntyre, Max Hoffman, Jr., Paul Bryar, Arthur O'Connell, Maynard Holmes, Charles Hall.

A revolver belonging to a reporter (Frank Albertson) falls into the hands of crooks; when the gun is used in a holdup, the reporter is suspected of the crime.

Running time: 63 minutes. Release date: January 23, 1942.

A remake of **The Mystery Man** (Monogram, 1935).

304. Maxwell Archer, Detective (mystery) Directed by John Paddy Carstairs. Produced by William Sistrom. Screenplay by Katherine Strueby and Hugh Clevely. From the novel by Hugh Clevely.

Cast: John Loder, Leueen MacGrath, Athole Stewart, Marta Labarr, George Merritt, Ronald Adam, Peter E. Hobbs, Ralph Roberts.

Amateur detective Maxwell Archer (John Loder) comes to the aid of a young RAF flyer wrongfully accused of murder.

Running time: 73 minutes. Release date: January 26, 1942.

Produced and released in Great Britain as **Meet Maxwell Archer** (1939); released in the U.S. by Monogram.

305. Below the Border (western) Directed by Howard Bretherton. Produced by Scott R. Dunlap. Original screenplay by Jess Bowers (Adele Buffington).

Cast: Buck Jones, Tim McCoy, Raymond Hatton,

Linda Brent, Eva Puig, Charles King, Dennis Moore, Roy Barcroft, Ted Mapes, Bud Osborne, Merrill McCormack, Jack Rockwell, "Silver."

The Rough Riders (Buck Jones, Tim McCoy, Raymond Hatton) check on rustling activities in Border City and round up a gang of outlaws who have stolen the famous Garcia jewels from Senorita Rosita (Linda Brent).

Running time: 57 minutes. Release date: January 30, 1942.

306. Law of the Jungle (adventure) Directed by Jean Yarbrough. Produced by Lindsley Parsons. Original screenplay by George Bricker.

Cast: Arline Judge, John King, Mantan Moreland, Martin Wilkins, Arthur O'Connell, C. Montague Shaw, Guy Kingsford, Victor Kendal, Feodor Chaliapin, Lawrence Criner.

On safari in Africa, a singer (Arline Judge) and an explorer (John King) encounter foreign agents who are stirring up trouble among the natives.

Running time: 61 min. Release date: Feb. 6, 1942.

307. Western Mail (western) Produced and directed by Robert Tansey. Screenplay by Robert Emmett (Tansey) and Frances Kavanaugh.

Cast: Tom Keene, Frank Yaconelli, Jean Trent, Glenn Strange, LeRoy Mason, Fred Kohler, Jr., James Sheridan (Sherry Tansey), Gene Alsace (Rocky Camron), Karl Hackett, Tex Palmer, "Prince."

After a stagecoach is robbed, Tom Keene goes after the culprits.

Running time: 55 minutes. Release date: February 13, 1942.

308. Shadows of the Underworld (mystery) Directed by David MacDonald. Produced by Anthony Havelock-Allan. Story by Allan MacKinnon and Roger MacDougall.

Cast: Barry K. Barnes, Valerie Hobson, Alastair Sim, Jacques Max Michel, Mona Goya, Edward Lexy, Garry Marsh, Anthony Shaw, Cyril Chamberlain, Charles Oliver, Paul Sheridan.

While in Paris, a British crime reporter (Barry K. Barnes) and his wife (Valerie Hobson) encounter a gang of counterfeiters.

Running time: 86 minutes. Release date: February 15, 1942.

Produced at the Pinebrook-Paramount studio in England; released by Paramount as **This Man in Paris** (1939), a sequel to **This Man Is News** (1939); released under the title **Shadows of the Underworld** by Monogram.

309. Mr. Wise Guy (comedy) Directed by William Nigh. Produced by Sam Katzman and Jack Dietz. Screenplay by Sam Robins, Harvey Gates and Jack Henley. Story by Martin Mooney. A Banner Production.

Cast: Leo Gorcey, Bobby Jordan, Huntz Hall, Billy Gilbert, Guinn "Big Boy" Williams, Gabriel Dell, Douglas Fowley, Joan Barclay, Ann Doran, Jack Mulhall, David Gorcey, "Sunshine Sammy" Morrison, Bill Lawrence, Bobby Stone, Dick Ryan, Warren Hymer, Benny Rubin, Sidney Miller, Joe Kirk.

The East Side Kids (Leo Gorcey, Bobby Jordan, Huntz Hall, David Gorcey, "Sunshine Sammy" Morrison, Bill Lawrence) are sent to the Wilton Reform School after they are unjustly convicted of stealing a truck.

Running time: 70 minutes. Release date: February 20, 1942.

310. Rock River Renegades (western) Directed by S. Roy Luby. Produced by George W. Weeks. Screenplay by John Vlahos and Earle Snell. Story by Faith Thomas.

Cast: Ray "Crash" Corrigan, John "Dusty" King, Max "Alibi" Terhune, Christine McIntyre, John Elliott, Weldon Heyburn, Kermit Maynard, Frank Ellis, Carl Mathews, Dick Cramer, Tex Palmer, Hank Bell, Budd Buster, Steve Clark.

The Range Busters (Ray "Crash" Corrigan, John "Dusty" King, Max "Alibi" Terhune) pursue a band of renegades operating near the Rock River territory.

Running time: 56 minutes. Release date: February 27, 1942.

Monogram Checklist

311. Continental Express (mystery-drama) Directed by Herbert Mason. Produced by Anthony Havelock-Allan. Screenplay by Rodney Ackland and Wolfgang Wilhelm. From the novel "Le Poisson Chinois" by Jean Bommart.

Cast: Rex Harrison, Valerie Hobson, John Loder, Muriel Aked, George Devine, John Salew, Kay Seeley, Carl Jaffe, Megs Jenkins.

A secret service man (Rex Harrison) foils a plot by terrorists to use the daughter (Valerie Hobson) of a political figure as a dupe in their plans to assassinate a prime minister.

Running time: 73 minutes. Release date: March 1, 1942.

Produced at the Pinebrook-Paramount studio in England. Released in Great Britain as **The Silent Battle** (1939); released in the U.S. under the title **Continental Express** by Monogram.

312. Arizona Roundup (western) Produced and directed by Robert Tansey. Screenplay by Robert Emmett (Tansey) and Frances Kavanaugh.

Cast: Tom Keene, Hope Blackwood, Frank Yaconelli, Sugar Dawn, Jack Ingram, Steve Clark, Tom Seidel, Nick Moro, Hal Price, I. Stanford Jolley, Edward Cassidy, Tex Palmer, Gene Alsace (Rocky Camron), Fred Hoose, Horace B. Carpenter, Sherry Tansey.

Tom Keene clashes with a railroad owner who is charging exorbitant prices for the use of the right-of-way road out of town.

Running time: 56 minutes. Release date: March 6, 1942.

313. Black Dragons (mystery) Directed by William Nigh. Produced by Sam Katzman and Jack Dietz. Story and screenplay by Harvey Gates. A Banner Production.

Cast: Bela Lugosi, Joan Barclay, Clayton Moore, George Pembroke, Robert Frazer, I. Stanford Jolley, Max Hoffman, Jr., Irving Mitchell, Edward Peil, Sr., Robert Fiske, Joseph Eggenton, Kenneth Harlan, Bernard Gorcey, Frank Melton.

A plastic surgeon (Bela Lugosi) operates on six

138

Japanese enemy agents, transforming them into American industrialists.

Running time: 64 minutes. Release date: March 6, 1942.

Working title: **Yellow Menace.**

314. Man with Two Lives (drama) Directed by Phil Rosen. Produced by A.W. Hackel. Original screenplay by Joseph Hoffman.

Cast: Edward Norris, Marlo Dwyer, Eleanor Lawson, Frederick Burton, Addison Richards, Edward Keene, Hugh Sothern, Tom Seidel, Elliott Sullivan, Anthony Warde, Ernie Adams, Kenne Duncan, George Dobbs, Lois Landon, Frances Richards, Jack Buckley, Jack Ingraham, George Kirby.

A wealthy young man (Edward Norris) is killed in an auto accident and is restored to life by a scientist (Edward Keene) at the same minute that a gangster is being executed; a transmigration of souls takes place, and the youth "inherits" the personality of the cold-blooded gangster.

Running time: 65 minutes. Release date: March 13, 1942.

315. Klondike Fury (drama) Directed by William K. Howard. Produced by Maurice King. Screenplay by Henry Blankfort. Adapted from the story "Klondike" by Tristram Tupper.

Cast: Edmund Lowe, Lucile Fairbanks, Bill Henry, Ralph Morgan, Robert Middlemass, Jean Brooks, Mary Forbes, Vince Barnett, Clyde Cook, Marjorie Wood, Kenneth Harlan.

A brain specialist (Edmund Lowe), ousted from the medical profession when he performed a delicate operation that was unsuccessful, enters an airplane ferrying service. On a return flight, he crashes in the Alaskan wilderness, where new problems and romance await.

Running time: 68 minutes. Release date: March 20, 1942.

Working title: **Klondike Victory.**

A remake of **Klondike** (Monogram, 1932).

A trade ad for "Klondike Fury" (1942).

316. Ghost Town Law (western) Directed by Howard Bretherton. Produced by Scott R. Dunlap. Screenplay by Jess Bowers (Adele Buffington).

Cast: Buck Jones, Tim McCoy, Raymond Hatton, Virginia Carpenter, Murdock McQuarrie, Charles King, Howard Masters, Ben Corbett, Tom London, "Silver."

In a Nevada ghost town, the Rough Riders (Buck Jones, Tim McCoy, Raymond Hatton) clash with a band of outlaws who, having discovered a rich vein of gold in an old mine, are attempting to kill the last remaining heir (Virginia Carpenter) to the property.

Running time: 62 minutes. Release date: March 27, 1942.

317. Tower of Terror (drama) Directed by Lawrence Huntington. Produced by John Argyle. Screenplay by John Reinhardt.

Cast: Michael Rennie, Movita, Wilfred Lawson, Morland Graham, John Longden, George Woodbridge, Richard George, Edward Sinclair, Charles Rolfe, Eric Clavering, J. Victor Weske.

An English secret agent (Michael Rennie) in Germany takes the post as assistant to a lighthouse-keeper (Wilfred Lawson) on the coast, hoping to make his escape with valuable documents when a British boat arrives.

Running time: 62 min. Release date: April 1, 1942.

Produced and released in Great Britain in 1941; released in the U.S. by Monogram.

318. Where Trails End (western) Produced and directed by Robert Tansey. Screenplay by Robert Emmett (Tansey) and Frances Kavanaugh.

Cast: Tom Keene, Joan Curtis, Frank Yaconelli, Charles King, Donald Stewart, Steve Clark, William Vaughn, Horace B. Carpenter, Nick Moro, Gene Alsace (Rocky Camron), Fred Hoose, James Sheridan (Sherry Tansey), Steve Clensos, Tex Palmer, Tom Seidel, Chick Hannon, "Prince."

A U.S. Marshal (Tom Keene) is assigned to protect ranchers against outlaws working for enemy agents who are trying to seize land for the tungsten it contains.

Running time: 58 minutes. Release date: April 1, 1942.

319. Three Wise Brides (comedy) Produced and directed by Walter C. Mycroft. Adapted from a stage play by M. J. Farrell and John Perry.

Cast: Nova Pilbeam, Sarah Churchill, Basil Sydney, Michael Wilding, Enid Stamp-Taylor, Henry Edwards, Hugh McDermott.

Although his mother wishes him to marry an heiress (Sarah Churchill), a young man (Michael Wilding) falls in love with the girl's sister (Nova Pilbeam).

Running time: 83 minutes. Release date: April 15, 1942.

Produced and released in Great Britain as **Spring Meeting**; released in the U.S. by Monogram.

320. So's Your Aunt Emma! (comedy) Directed by Jean Yarbrough. Produced by Lindsley Parsons. Screenplay by George Bricker and Edmond Kelso. Based on the original story "Aunt Emma Paints the Town" by Harry Hervey.

Cast: Zasu Pitts, Roger Pryor, Warren Hymer, Gwen Kenyon, Douglas Fowley, Elizabeth Russell, Tristram Coffin, Bud McTaggart, Lester Dorr, Wheeler Oakman, Gene O'Donnell, Irvin Mitchell.

A spinster (Zasu Pitts), in town to see a prizefight, gets mixed up with gangsters.

Running time: 62 minutes. Release date: April 17, 1942.

Working title: **Aunt Emma Paints the Town**. Also known as **Meet the Mob**.

321. Boot Hill Bandits (western) Directed by S. Roy Luby. Produced by George W. Weeks. Screenplay by Arthur Durlam.

Cast: Ray "Crash" Corrigan, John "Dusty" King, Max "Alibi" Terhune, Jean Brooks (Jeanne Kelly), John Merton, Glenn Strange, I. Stanford Jolley, Steve Clark, Dick Cramer, George Chesebro, Budd Buster, Milburn Morante, Jimmy Aubrey, Charles King, Carl Mathews, Tex Palmer, Merrill McCormack.

The Range Busters (Ray "Crash" Corrigan, John "Dusty" King, Max "Alibi" Terhune) pursue a gang of bandits who are looting the Wells Fargo stage. Running time: 58 minutes. Release date: April 24, 1942.

322. The Corpse Vanishes (horror) Directed by Wallace Fox. Produced by Sam Katzman and Jack Dietz. Screenplay by Harvey Gates. Original story by Sam Robins and Gerald Schnitzer. A Banner Production.

Cast: Bela Lugosi, Luana Walters, Tristram Coffin, Elizabeth Russell, Minerva Urecal, Kenneth Harlan, Vince Barnett, Joan Barclay, Frank Moran, Angelo Rossitto, Gwen Kenyon, George Eldredge, Gladys Faye, Pat Costello.

A mad scientist (Bela Lugosi) kidnaps young brides at their wedding ceremonies and drains them of blood in order to restore his wife's youth and beauty. Running time: 63 minutes. Release date: May 8, 1942.

Released in Great Britain as **The Case of the Missing Brides.**

323. She's in the Army (comedy) Directed by Jean Yarbrough. Produced by Ted Richmond. Story and screenplay by Sidney Sheldon.

Cast: Veda Ann Borg, Marie Wilson, Lyle Talbot, Robert Lowery, Lucile Gleason, Charlotte Henry, Warren Hymer, Maxine Leslie.

A debutante (Veda Ann Borg) joins the Women's Ambulance Corps for publicity and to win a $5,000 bet with a newspaper columnist who is confident that she won't last six weeks. Running time: 63 minutes. Release date: May 15, 1942.

324. Down Texas Way (western) Directed by Howard Bretherton. Produced by Scott R. Dunlap. Screenplay by Jess Bowers (Adele Buffington).

Cast: Buck Jones, Tim McCoy, Raymond Hatton, Luana Walters, Dave O'Brien, Glenn Strange, Lois Austin,

Harry Woods, Tom London, Kansas Moehring, Jack Daley, "Silver."

Rough Riders Buck and Tim investigate when they learn that their friend (Raymond Hatton) is missing and under suspicion of murder.

Running time: 57 minutes. Release date: May 22, 1942.

325. Let's Get Tough! (comedy) Directed by Wallace Fox. Produced by Sam Katzman and Jack Dietz. Screenplay by Harvey Gates, based on his story "I Am an American." A Banner Production.

Cast: Leo Gorcey, Bobby Jordan, Huntz Hall, Tom Brown, Florence Rice, Robert Armstrong, Gabriel Dell, "Sunshine Sammy" Morrison, Bobby Stone, David Gorcey, Philip Ahn, Sam Bernard, Jerry Bergen, Pat Costello.

The East Side Kids (Leo Gorcey, Bobby Jordan, Huntz Hall, "Sunshine Sammy" Morrison, Bobby Stone, David Gorcey) stumble on a clue which leads them to a spy ring preparing to cripple U.S. war production efforts.

Running time: 62 minutes. Release date: May 22, 1942.

Working title: **Little MacArthurs.**

326. One Thrilling Night (mystery-comedy) Directed by William Beaudine. Produced by A.W. Hackel. Original screenplay by Joseph Hoffman.

Cast: John Beal, Wanda McKay, Warren Hymer, J. Farrell MacDonald, Barbara Pepper, Tom Neal, Ernie Adams, Lynton Brent.

A honeymoon couple (John Beal, Wanda McKay), in New York for one night of wedded bliss before he's to join the army, become involved with gangsters after they find a cadaver under their bed.

Running time: 69 minutes. Release date: June 5, 1942.

Working titles: **No Time for Love** and **Do Not Disturb.**

327. Texas Trouble Shooters (western) Directed by S. Roy Luby. Produced by George W. Weeks. Screenplay by Arthur Hoerl. Story by Elizabeth Beecher.

Cast: Ray "Crash" Corrigan, John "Dusty" King, Max "Alibi" Terhune, Julie Duncan, Glenn Strange, Roy Harris (Riley Hill), Kermit Maynard, Eddie Phillips, Frank Ellis, Ted Mapes, Steve Clark, Gertrude Hoffman, Jack Holmes, Dick Cramer, Carl Mathews.

The Range Busters (Ray "Crash" Corrigan, John "Dusty" King, Max "Alibi" Terhune) take on assumed identities in order to follow the activities of a crooked lawyer who's posing as the owner of oil-rich property.

Running time: 55 minutes. Release date: June 12, 1942.

328. Rubber Racketeers (drama) Directed by Harold Young. Produced by Maurice King. Screenplay by Henry Blankfort.

Cast: Ricardo Cortez, Rochelle Hudson, Bill Henry, Barbara Reed, John Abbott, Dick Rich, Dewey Robinson, Sam Edwards, Kam Tong, Milburn Stone, Pat Gleason, Alex Callam.

A former bootlegger (Ricardo Cortez) starts a new racket: stealing automobile tires and selling them, as well as selling recapped tires made with crude rubber his gang has stolen.

Running time: 67 minutes. Release date: June 26, 1942.

329. Lure of the Islands (adventure) Directed by Jean Yarbrough. Produced by Lindsley Parsons. Original screenplay by Edmond Kelso, George Bricker and Scott Littleton.

Cast: Margie Hart, Robert Lowery, Guinn "Big Boy" Williams, Gale Storm, Ivan Lebedeff, John Bleifer, Warren Hymer.

On the island of Tanukai, two FBI agents (Robert Lowery, Guinn "Big Boy" Williams), disguised as ship-wrecked sailors, meet a half-caste native girl (Margie Hart) who agrees to help them in their search for pro-Japanese activity.

Running time: 61 minutes. Release date: July 3, 1942.

330. Smart Alecks (comedy-drama) Directed by Wallace

Fox. Produced by Sam Katzman and Jack Dietz. Screenplay by Harvey H. Gates and Jack Dietz. A Banner Production.

Cast: Leo Gorcey, Bobby Jordan, Huntz Hall, Maxie Rosenbloom, Gale Storm, Roger Pryor, Walter Woolf King, Gabriel Dell, Stanley Clements, "Sunshine Sammy" Morrison, David Gorcey, Bobby Stone, Herbert Rawlinson, Joe Kirk, Sam Bernard, Dick Ryan, Marie Windsor, Betty Sinclair.

Trying to raise enough money to buy baseball uniforms, the East Side Kids (Leo Gorcey, Bobby Jordan, Huntz Hall, Stanley Clements, "Sunshine Sammy" Morrison, David Gorcey, Bobby Stone) become involved with a notorious criminal (Maxie Rosenbloom).

Running time: 63 min. Release date: Aug. 7, 1942.

331. Hillbilly Blitzkrieg (comedy) Directed by Roy Mack. Produced by Edward Gross. Screenplay by Ray S. Harris. From the comic strip "Barney Google and Snuffy Smith" by Billy DeBeck. A Capitol Production.

Cast: Bud Duncan, Edgar Kennedy, Cliff Nazarro, Lucien Littlefield, Doris Linden, Alan Baldwin, Jimmy Dodd, Frank Austin, Nicolle Andre, Manart Kippen, Jerry Jerome, Jack Carr, Teddy Mangean.

Snuffy Smith (Bud Duncan) becomes involved with a rocket ship invention designed to aid the war effort.

Running time: 63 minutes. Release date: August 14, 1942.

332. Riders of the West (western) Directed by Howard Bretherton. Produced by Scott R. Dunlap. Screenplay by Jess Bowers (Adele Buffington).

Cast: Buck Jones, Tim McCoy, Raymond Hatton, Sarah Padden, Dennis Moore, Christine McIntyre, Harry Woods, Walter McGrail, Harry Frazer, Bud Osborne, Charles King, Lee Phelps, Kermit Maynard, Milburn Morante, Edward Peil, Sr., Lynton Brent, J. Merrill Holmes, George Morrell, Tom London, "Silver."

The Rough Riders (Buck Jones, Tim McCoy, Raymond Hatton) are called in when cattle rustlers try to bankrupt local ranchers in an effort to obtain their land cheaply.

Running time: 58 minutes. Release date: August 21, 1942.

333. Arizona Stagecoach (western) Directed by S. Roy Luby. Produced by George W. Weeks. Screenplay by Arthur Hoerl. Story by Oliver Drake.

Cast: Ray "Crash" Corrigan, John "Dusty" King, Max "Alibi" Terhune, Nell O'Day, Kermit Maynard, Charles King, Carl Mathews, Charles "Slim" Whitaker, Slim Harvey, Steve Clark, Frank Ellis, Roy Harris (Riley Hill), Jack Ingram, Stanley Price, Forrest Taylor, Dick Cramer, Eddie Dean.

The Range Busters (Ray "Crash" Corrigan, John "Dusty" King, Max "Alibi" Terhune) help to prove the innocence of a man falsely accused of murder.

Running time: 58 minutes. Release date: September 4, 1942.

334. Isle of Missing Men (drama) Produced and directed by Richard Oswald. Screenplay by Robert Chapin. From the play "Isle of Terror" by Gina Kauss and Ladislaus Fodor. Adaptation by Richard Oswald and Robert Chapin.

Cast: John Howard, Gilbert Roland, Helen Gilbert, Alan Mowbray, Bradley Page, George Chandler, Geraldine Gray, Egon Brecher, Kitty O'Neill, Dewey Robinson.

A woman (Helen Gilbert) goes to a penal island to help her convict husband (Gilbert Roland) to escape.

Running time: 67 minutes. Release date: September 18, 1942.

Working titles: **Isle of Terror** and **Isle of Fury**.

335. King of the Stallions (western) Produced and directed by Edward Finney. Screenplay by Sherman Lowe and Arthur St. Clair.

Cast: Chief Thunder Cloud, Chief Yowlachie, Dave O'Brien, Barbara Felker, Sally Cairns, Rick Vallin, Ted Adams, Gordon DeMain, Forrest Taylor, Joe Cody, Bill Wilkerson, Chief Many Treaties, George Sky Eagle, Charles Brunner, Iron Eyes Cody, Willow Bird, Nakoma the horse.

A beautiful stallion, the leader of wild horses, is sought after by cowboys and Indians.

Running time: 63 minutes. Release date: September 18, 1942.

336. Police Bullets (comedy-drama) Directed by Jean Yarbrough. Produced by Lindsley Parsons. Screenplay by Edmond Kelso and Ande Lamb.

Cast: John Archer, Joan Marsh, Milburn Stone, Warren Hymer, Pat Gleason, Tristram Coffin, Ann Eavers, Charles Jordan, Gene O'Donnell, Ben Taggart, Irving Mitchell, Fern Emmett.

The head of a protection racket, hearing of his possible prosecution on tax evasion charges, hires a man with a photographic mind to memorize his books and then destroys the ledgers.

Running time: 61 minutes. Release date: September 25, 1942.

337. The Phantom Killer (mystery) Directed by William Beaudine. Produced by A.W. Hackel. Screenplay by Karl Brown.

Cast: Dick Purcell, Joan Woodbury, John Hamilton, Warren Hymer, Mantan Moreland, J. Farrell MacDonald, Gayne Whitman, Kenneth Harlan, George Lewis, Karl Hackett, Isabel LaMal, Robert Carson, Frank Ellis, Harry Depp.

A mute goes on the witness stand to provide alibis for his homicidal twin brother (John Hamilton plays both roles).

Running time: 61 minutes. Release date: October 2, 1942.

A remake of **The Sphinx** (Monogram, 1933).

338. West of the Law (western) Directed by Howard Bretherton. Produced by Scott R. Dunlap. Screenplay by Jess Bowers (Adele Buffington).

Cast: Buck Jones, Tim McCoy, Raymond Hatton, Evelyn Cook, Milburn Morante, Harry Woods, Roy Barcroft, Bud McTaggart, George DeNormand, Jack Daley, Bud Osborne, Lynton Brent, "Silver."

Rough Riders Buck Roberts (Buck Jones), Tim McCall (Tim McCoy) and Sandy (Raymond Hatton) pose as an

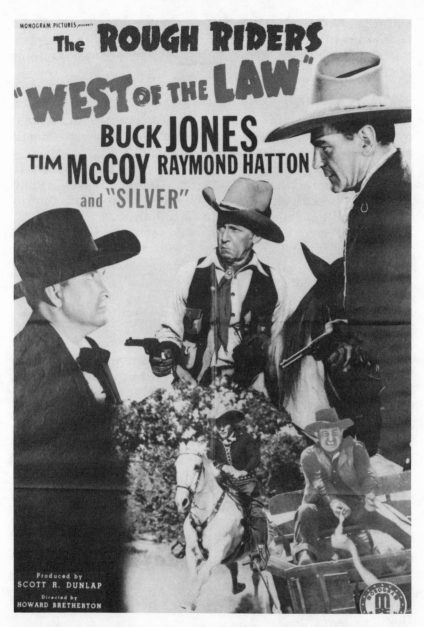

One-sheet poster for "West of the Law" (1942), one of Monogram's "Rough Riders" westerns. Pictured: Tim McCoy, Raymond Hatton and Buck Jones.

outlaw, a minister and an undertaker, respectively, in order to capture bandits who are hijacking gold shipments. Running time: 60 minutes. Release date: October 2, 1942.

339. Foreign Agent (drama) Directed by William Beaudine. Produced by Martin Mooney and Max King. Screenplay by Martin Mooney and John Krafft. Story by Martin Mooney.

Cast: John Shelton, Gale Storm, Ivan Lebedeff, Hanz Schumm, William Halligan, George Travell, Patsy Moran, Lyly Lattel, Herbert Rawlinson, Kenneth Harlan, Jack Mulhall, David Clarke, Edward Peil, Sr.

Enemy agents in Hollywood seek the plans for a searchlight filter that a film studio technician has been working on.

Running time: 64 min. Release date: Oct. 9, 1942.

340. Texas to Bataan (western) Directed by Robert Tansey. Produced by George W. Weeks. Screenplay by Arthur Hoerl.

Cast: John "Dusty" King, David Sharpe, Max "Alibi" Terhune, Marjorie Manners, Budd Buster, Kenne Duncan, Escolastico Baucin, Frank Ellis, Carl Mathews, Guy Kingsford, Steve Clark, Al Ferguson, Tom Steele, Tex Palmer.

The Range Busters (John "Dusty" King, David Sharpe, Max "Alibi" Terhune) encounter Japanese spies while escorting a shipment of horses to the Philippines.

Running time: 56 minutes. Release date: October 16, 1942.

341. Criminal Investigator (mystery) Directed by Jean Yarbrough. Produced by Lindsley Parsons. Screenplay by George Jeske and Edmond Kelso.

Cast: Robert Lowery, Edith Fellows, John Miljan, Jan Wiley, Charles Jordan, Gloria Faye, Paul Bryar, George O'Hanlon, Vivian Wilcox, Charles Hall, Maurice Hugo.

A cub reporter (Robert Lowery) investigates the murder of a showgirl (Vivian Wilcox) who was the widow of a millionaire.

Running time: 61 minutes. Release date: October 23, 1942.

Working title: **Crime Reporter.**

342. Bowery at Midnight (drama) Directed by Wallace Fox. Produced by Sam Katzman and Jack Dietz. Original story and screenplay by Gerald Schnitzer. A Banner Production.

Cast: Bela Lugosi, John Archer, Wanda McKay, Tom Neal, Dave O'Brien, Vince Barnett, John Berkes, Ray Miller, J. Farrell MacDonald, Lew Kelly, Lucille Vance, Anna Hope, George Eldredge, Wheeler Oakman, Ray Miller, Bernard Gorcey, Pat Costello, Eddie Kane, Snub Pollard.

A psychology professor (Bela Lugosi) uses a Bowery mission as a front for his criminal activities.

Running time: 61 minutes. Release date: October 30, 1942.

343. War Dogs (adventure-drama) Directed by S. Roy Luby. Produced by George W. Weeks. Screenplay by John Vlahos. Story by Ande Lamb.

Cast: Billy Lee, Addison Richards, Kay Linaker, Bradley Page, Herbert Rawlinson, Lee Phelps, Bryant Washburn, John Berkes, George Neise, Don Curtis, Hal Price, Steve Clark.

A young boy (Billy Lee) donates his pet police dog to the army for training.

Running time: 63 minutes. Release date: November 13, 1942.

Also known as **Pride of the Army** and **Unsung Heroes.**

344. 'Neath Brooklyn Bridge (comedy) Directed by Wallace Fox. Produced by Sam Katzman and Jack Dietz. Screenplay by Harvey H. Gates. A Banner Production.

Cast: Leo Gorcey, Bobby Jordan, Huntz Hall, Ann Gillis, Noah Beery, Jr., Marc Lawrence, David O'Brien, Gabriel Dell, "Sunshine Sammy" Morrison, Stanley Clements, Bobby Stone, Jack Raymond, Bud Osborne, Patsy Moran, Dewey Robinson, Betty Wells, Snub Pollard, Jack Mulhall, Betty Sinclair, J. Arthur Young.

The East Side Kids (Leo Gorcey, Bobby Jordan, Huntz Hall, "Sunshine Sammy" Morrison, Stanley Clements, Bobby Stone) help a girl (Ann Gillis) track down the murderer of her guardian (Bud Osborne).

Running time: 61 minutes. Release date: November 20, 1942.

345. The Living Ghost (mystery-horror) Directed by William Beaudine. Produced by A.W. Hackel. Screenplay by Joseph Hoffman. Story by Howard Dimsdale.

Cast: James Dunn, Joan Woodbury, Paul McVey, Vera Gordon, Norman Willis, J. Farrell MacDonald, Minerva Urecal, George Eldredge, Jan Wiley, Edna Johnson, Danny Beck, Gus Glassmire, Lawrence Grant, Howard Banks, J. Arthur Young, Frances Richards, Harry Depp.

An investigator (James Dunn) seeks a madman who paralyzes the brains of his victims.

Running time: 61 minutes. Release date: November 27, 1942.

346. Trail Riders (western) Directed by Robert Tansey. Produced by George W. Weeks. Screenplay by Frances Kavanaugh

Cast: John "Dusty" King, David Sharpe, Max "Alibi" Terhune, Evelyn Finley, Forrest Taylor, Lynton Brent, Charles King, Kermit Maynard, John Curtis, Steve Clark, Kenne Duncan, Frank LaRue, Bud Osborne, Tex Palmer, Dick Cramer, Frank Ellis.

The Range Busters (John "Dusty" King, David Sharpe, Max "Alibi" Terhune) try to bring law and order to the town of Gila Springs, where the leader of the outlaws is also the head of the vigilantes.

Running time: 55 minutes. Release date: December 4, 1942.

347. Rhythm Parade (musical) Directed by Howard Bretherton and Dave Gould. Produced by Sydney Williams. Story and screenplay by Carl Foreman and Charles R. Marion.

Cast: Gale Storm, Robert Lowery, Nils T. Granlund, Margaret Dumont, Chick Chandler, Cliff Nazarro, Jan

Wiley, Candy Candido, Julie Milton, Sugar Geise, Jean Foreman, the Florentine Gardens Revue, the Mills Brothers, Ted Fio Rito and His Orchestra.

A jealous nightclub performer (Jan Wiley) tries to spoil the professional chances of an aspiring singer (Gale Storm).

Running time: 68 minutes. Release date: December 11, 1942.

348. Dawn on the Great Divide (western) Directed by Howard Bretherton. Produced by Scott R. Dunlap. Screenplay by Jess Bowers (Adele Buffington). Based on a story by James Oliver Curwood.

Cast: Buck Jones, Raymond Hatton, Rex Bell, Mona Barrie, Robert Lowery, Harry Woods, Christine McIntyre, Betty Blythe, Robert Frazer, Tristram Coffin, Jan Wiley, Roy Barcroft, Dennis Moore, Steve Clark, Reed Howes, Bud Osborne, I. Stanford Jolley, Artie Ortego, George Morrell, Milburn Morante, Ray Jones, "Silver."

The Rough Riders (Buck Jones, Raymond Hatton, Rex Bell) pursue a gang of bandits who are attacking wagon trains and placing the blame on the Indians.

Running time: 63 minutes. Release date: December 18, 1942.

1943

349. Two-Fisted Justice (western) Directed by Robert Tansey. Produced by George W. Weeks. Screenplay by William L. Nolte.

Cast: John "Dusty" King, David Sharpe, Max "Alibi" Terhune, Gwen Gaze, Joel Davis, John Elliott, Charles King, George Chesebro, Frank Ellis, Cecil Weston, Hal Price, Carl Mathews, Lynton Brent, Kermit Maynard, Dick Cramer, Tex Palmer, John Curtis.

The Wells Fargo Company sends the Range Busters (John "Dusty" King, David Sharpe, Max "Alibi" Terhune) to the town of Dry Gulch to restore law and order.

Running time: 61 minutes. Release date: January 8, 1943.

350. Silent Witness (drama) Directed by Jean Yarbrough. Produced by Max M. King. Story and screenplay by Martin Mooney.

Cast: Frank Albertson, Maris Wrixon, Lucien Littlefield, Evelyn Brent, Vince Barnett, Bradley Page, Milburn Stone, John Ince, Anthony Warde, Kenneth Harlan, Jack Mulhall, Ace the Wonder Dog.

With the aid of Ace the Wonder Dog, two investigators (Frank Albertson, Maris Wrixon) break up a crime ring.

Running time: 62 minutes. Release date: January 15, 1943.

Released in Great Britain as **Attorney for the Defense.**

351. Cosmo Jones in the Crime Smasher (mystery) Directed by James Tinling. Produced by Lindsley Parsons. Screenplay by Michael L. Simmons and Walter Gering. Original story by Walter Gering. Based on the CBS radio program "Cosmo Jones" created by Frank Graham.

Cast: Frank Graham, Edgar Kennedy, Gale Storm, Richard Cromwell, Mantan Moreland, Gwen Kenyon, Herbert Rawlinson, Tristram Coffin, Charles Jordan, Vince Barnett, Emmett Vogan, Maxine Leslie, Mauritz Hugo, Sam Bernard.

Cosmo Jones (Frank Graham), a somewhat addled psychologist-criminologist, investigates the kidnapping of the daughter of the town's most influential citizen.

Running time: 62 minutes. Release date: January 29, 1943.

Also known as **Cosmo Jones–Crime Smasher.** Released in Great Britain as **Crime Smasher.**

352. You Can't Beat the Law (drama) Directed by Phil Rosen. Produced by Lindsley Parsons. Screenplay by Albert Reich.

Cast: Edward Norris, Joan Woodbury, Jack LaRue, Milburn Stone, Robert Homans, Charles Jordan, Kenneth Harlan, Bryant Washburn, Selmer Jackson, Paul McVey, Inna Guest (Ina Guest), George Kamel.

A playboy (Edward Norris), framed for a robbery by the real crooks, is sent to prison.

Running time: 61 min. Release date: Jan. 29, 1943.

353. Kid Dynamite (comedy) Directed by Wallace Fox. Produced by Sam Katzman and Jack Dietz. Screenplay by Gerald Schnitzer. Additional dialogue by Morey Amsterdam. Based on the Saturday Evening Post story "The Old Gang" by Paul Ernst. A Banner Production.

Cast: Leo Gorcey, Huntz Hall, Bobby Jordan, Gabriel Dell, Pamela Blake, Bennie Bartlett, "Sunshine Sammy" Morrison, Bobby Stone, David Durand, Vince Barnett, Daphne Pollard, Charles Judels, Dudley Dickerson, Henry Hall, Minerva Urecal, Wheeler Oakman, Margaret Padula, Jack Mulhall, Ray Miller, Kay Marvis Gorcey, Snub Pollard, Mike Riley's Orchestra with Marion Miller.

Muggs McGinnis (Leo Gorcey), the champion boxer of the East Side Kids gang, is kidnapped by thugs just before a big fight.

Running time: 67 min. Release date: Feb. 12, 1943. Working title: **Little Mobsters.**

354. Haunted Ranch (western) Directed by Robert Tansey. Produced by George W. Weeks. Screenplay by Elizabeth Beecher. Story by Arthur Hoerl.

Cast: John "Dusty" King, David Sharpe, Max "Alibi" Terhune, Rex Lease, Julie Duncan, Bud Osborne, Budd Buster, Steve Clark, Glenn Strange, Tex Palmer, Charles King, Fred "Snowflake" Toones, Carl Mathews, Jimmy Aubrey, Hank Bell, Augie Gomez, Jim Corey.

The Range Busters (John "Dusty" King, David Sharpe, Max "Alibi" Terhune) investigate the death of an outlaw and try to recover the stolen property which was known to have been kept in his home.

Running time: 57 minutes. Release date: February 19, 1943.

355. Silver Skates (musical) Directed by Leslie Goodwins. Produced by Lindsley Parsons. Story and screenplay by Jerry Cady.

Cast: Kenny Baker, Patricia Morison, Belita, Frick and Frack, Irene Dare, Danny Shaw, Eugene Turner, Joyce Compton, Frank Faylen, Paul McVey, Ruth Lee, John Maxwell, Henry Wadsworth, George Stewart, Jo Ann Dean, Ted Fio Rito and His Orchestra.

Top: Minerva Urecal comforts a troubled Bela Lugosi in "The Ape Man" (1943). Bottom: Jack Dietz (left), Bela Lugosi and Emil Van Horn (in gorilla suit) in a publicity shot for "The Ape Man." Dietz, with Sam Katzman, produced several pictures for Monogram under the "Banner Productions" label.

A singer (Kenny Baker) romances an ice skating star (Belita) in an effort to keep her from leaving a skating revue badly in need of funds.

Running time: 75 min. Release date: Feb. 26, 1943.

356. The Ape Man (horror) Directed by William Beaudine. Produced by Sam Katzman and Jack Dietz. Screenplay by Barney Sarecky. Based on the story "They Creep in the Dark" by Karl Brown. A Banner Production.

Cast: Bela Lugosi, Louise Currie, Wallace Ford, Henry Hall, Minerva Urecal, Ralph Littlefield, J. Farrell MacDonald, George Kirby, Wheeler Oakman, Charles Hall, Emil Van Horn, Ray Miller, Jack Mulhall, Charles Jordan.

A scientist (Bela Lugosi) concocts a formula that transforms him into a man-beast; he commits a series of murders in order to obtain spinal fluid which he hopes will restore himself to normalcy.

Running time: 64 minutes. Release date: March 19, 1943.

Working title: **The Gorilla Strikes.** Released in Great Britain as **Lock Your Doors.**

Return of the Ape Man (Monogram, 1944) is <u>not</u> a sequel to this film.

357. Land of Hunted Men (western) Directed by S. Roy Luby. Produced by George W. Weeks. Screenplay by Elizabeth Beecher. Story by William Nolte.

Cast: Ray "Crash" Corrigan, Dennis Moore, Max "Alibi" Terhune, Phyllis Adair, Charles King, John Merton, Ted Mapes, Frank McCarroll, Forrest Taylor, Steve Clark, Fred "Snowflake" Toones, Carl Sepulveda.

The Range Busters (Ray "Crash" Corrigan, Dennis Moore, Max "Alibi" Terhune) pursue an outlaw gang responsible for payroll robberies.

Running time: 58 minutes. Release date: March 26, 1943.

358. The Ghost Rider (western) Directed by Wallace Fox. Produced by Scott R. Dunlap. Screenplay by Jess Bowers (Adele Buffington).

A trade advertisement for "Wild Horse Stampede" (1943), the first in a series of "Trail Blazers" westerns featuring veteran cowboy stars Ken Maynard and Hoot Gibson. Later in the year, Bob Steele was recruited for the series, making the Trail Blazers a trio. When Maynard left Monogram in 1944, Chief Thundercloud took his place.

158

Cast: Johnny Mack Brown, Raymond Hatton, Beverly Boyd, Tom Seidel, Bud Osborne, Milburn Morante, Harry Woods, Edmund Cobb, Charles King, Artie Ortego, George DeNormand, Jack Daley, George Morrell.

Nevada (Johnny Mack Brown), known as the "Ghost Rider," sets out to bring to justice all members of the gang which murdered his family.

Running time: 58 minutes. Release date: April 2, 1943.

359. Wild Horse Stampede (western) Directed by Alan James. Produced by Robert Tansey. Screenplay by Elizabeth Beecher. Story by Frances Kavanaugh.

Cast: Ken Maynard, Hoot Gibson, Betty Miles, Bob Baker, Ian Keith, Si Jenks, Donald Stewart, John Bridges, Glenn Strange, Reed Howes, Kenneth Harlan, Tom London, Tex Palmer, Forrest Taylor, I. Stanford Jolley, Kenne Duncan, Bob McKenzie, Chick Hannon.

Disguised as cowboys, the Trail Blazers (Ken Maynard, Hoot Gibson) go after a gang seeking to prevent the completion of a new railroad line.

Running time: 59 minutes. Release date: April 16, 1943.

360. Clancy Street Boys (comedy) Directed by William Beaudine. Produced by Sam Katzman and Jack Dietz. Screenplay by Harvey H. Gates. A Banner Production.

Cast: Leo Gorcey, Huntz Hall, Bobby Jordan, Noah Beery, Sr., Amelita Ward, Bennie Bartlett, Rick Vallin, Billy Benedict, J. Farrell MacDonald, Jan Rubini, Martha Wentworth, "Sunshine Sammy" Morrison, Dick Chandlee, Eddie Mills, George DeNormand, Johnny Duncan, Bernard Gorcey, Jack Normand, Gino Corrado, Symona Boniface.

Muggs McGinnis (Leo Gorcey) has the other East Side Kids (Huntz Hall, Bobby Jordan, Bennie Bartlett, "Sunshine Sammy" Morrison, Dick Chandlee, Eddie Mills) pose as his relatives in order to deceive a rich uncle (Noah Beery, Sr.) who's been sending money to a non-existent McGinnis clan for years.

Running time: 66 minutes. Release date: April 23, 1943.

Working title: **Grand Street Boys.**

361. I Escaped from the Gestapo (mystery-drama) Directed by Harold Young. Produced by Maurice King. Screenplay by Martin Mooney. Story by Gertrude Walker and Edgar G. Ulmer.

Cast: Dean Jagger, John Carradine, Mary Brian, William Henry, Sidney Blackmer, Ian Keith, Isabel Jewell, Wanda McKay, Betty Compson, Cobina Wright, Sr., Allan Byron (Jack Randall), Warren Hymer, Michael Kirk, Vince Barnett, Anthony Warde, William Vine, Charles Waggenheim, Billy Marshall, Norman Willis, Spanky McFarland, Ed Keane, Greta Granstedt.

A counterfeiter (Dean Jagger) falls in with a gang of Nazi saboteurs who want him to engrave forged plates of various securities of both the United States and neutral countries.

Running time: 75 minutes. Release date: May 14, 1943.

Working title: **No Escape.** Released in Great Britain as **No Escape.**

362. Sarong Girl (musical-comedy) Directed by Arthur Dreifuss. Produced by Philip N. Krasne. Story and screenplay by Charles R. Marion and Arthur Hoerl. Additional dialogue by Tim Ryan.

Cast: Ann Corio, Tim and Irene Ryan, Mantan Moreland, Bill Henry, Johnny "Scat" Davis, Damian O'Flynn, Gwen Kenyon, Henry Kolker, Mary Gordon, Charles Williams, Betty Blythe, Charles Jordan, Lorraine Krueger, Paul Bryar.

A burlesque queen (Ann Corio) is placed on probation after her show is raided by the vice squad; securing work as a nightclub singer, she plots revenge on the reformer (Henry Kolker) responsible for the raid.

Running time: 55 minutes. Release date: May 28, 1943.

363. Cowboy Commandos (western) Directed by S. Roy Luby. Produced by George W. Weeks. Screenplay by Elizabeth Beecher. Story by Clark Paylow.

Cast: Ray "Crash" Corrigan, Dennis Moore, Max "Alibi" Terhune, Evelyn Finley, Johnny Bond, Budd Buster, John Merton, Edna Bennett, Steve Clark, Bud Osborne, Frank Ellis, Hank Bell, Denver Dixon (Victor Adamson), Artie Ortego, Ray Jones, Augie Gomez, George Chesebro, Carl Sepulveda.

The Range Busters (Ray "Crash" Corrigan, Dennis Moore, Max "Alibi" Terhune) tangle with a group of Nazis who believe they have located magnesium deposits in a western community.

Running time: 55 minutes. Release date: June 4, 1943.

364. Spy Train (drama) Directed by Harold Young. Produced by Max King. Screenplay by Leslie Schwabacher, Wallace Sullivan and Bart Lytton. Story by Scott Littlefield.

Cast: Richard Travis, Catherine Craig, Chick Chandler, Evelyn Brent, Thelma White, Paul Movey, Gerald Brock, Steve Roberts, Fred "Snowflake" Toones, Bill Hunter, Warren Hymer, John Hamilton.

A newspaper publisher's daughter (Catherine Craig) falls into possession of a traveling bag, unaware that it contains a time bomb planted by Nazi agents.

Running time: 60 minutes. Release date: July 9, 1943.

Working title: **Time Bomb.**

365. The Stranger from Pecos (western) Directed by Lambert Hillyer. Produced by Scott R. Dunlap. Story and screenplay by Jess Bowers (Adele Buffington).

Cast: Johnny Mack Brown, Raymond Hatton, Kirby Grant, Christine McIntyre, Steve Clark, Sam Flint, Roy Barcroft, Robert Frazer, Edmund Cobb, Charles King, Bud Osborne, Artie Ortego, Tom London, Kermit Maynard, Milburn Morante, Lynton Brent, Carol Henry, George Morrell.

Two U.S. Marshals (Johnny Mack Brown, Raymond Hatton) go after a gang of robber barons preying upon small landowners.

Running time: 56 min. Release date: July 16, 1943.

366. Wings Over the Pacific (action-drama) Directed by Phil Rosen. Produced by Lindsley Parsons. Original screenplay by George Wallace Sayre.

Cast: Inez Cooper, Edward Norris, Montagu Love, Robert Armstrong, Henry Guttman, Ernie Adams, Satini Pauiloa, John Roth, James Lono, Hawksha Paia, George Kamel, Alex Havier.

An American lieutenant (Edward Norris) foils a Nazi plot to seize control of an oil-rich Pacific island.

Running time: 60 minutes. Release date: July 23, 1943.

367. Ghosts on the Loose (comedy) Directed by William Beaudine. Produced by Sam Katzman and Jack Dietz. Original screenplay by Kenneth Higgins. A Banner Production.

Cast: Leo Gorcey, Huntz Hall, Bobby Jordan, Bela Lugosi, Ava Gardner, Rick Vallin, "Sunshine Sammy" Morrison, Billy Benedict, Stanley Clements, Bobby Stone, Minerva Urecal, Wheeler Oakman, Peter Seal, Bill Bates, Frank Moran, Jack Mulhall, Kay Marvis Gorcey, Robert F. Hill, Blanche Payson.

Planning to decorate a newlywed couple's home, The East Side Kids (Leo Gorcey, Huntz Hall, Bobby Jordan, "Sunshine Sammy" Morrison, Billy Benedict, Stanley Clements, Bobby Stone, Bill Bates) go to the wrong house, which turns out to be the headquarters for a Nazi spy ring.

Running time: 63 minutes. Release date: July 30, 1943.

Released in Great Britain as **Ghosts in the Night.**

368. The Law Rides Again (western) Directed by Alan James. Produced by Robert Tansey. Screenplay by Frances Kavanaugh.

Cast: Ken Maynard, Hoot Gibson, Betty Miles, Jack LaRue, Chief Thunder Cloud, Hank Bell, Bryant Washburn, Emmett Lynn, Kenneth Harlan, John Bridges, Fred Hoose, Charles Murray, Jr., Chief Many Treaties, John Merton.

The Trail Blazers (Ken Maynard, Hoot Gibson) try

Ava Gardner struggles to maintain her composure while being manhandled by Huntz Hall and Leo Gorcey in this publicity shot for the East Side Kids comedy "Ghosts on the Loose" (1943).

to quell threats of an Indian uprising in the Arizona territory.

Running time: 58 minutes. Release date: August 6, 1943.

369. Black Market Rustlers (western) Directed by S. Roy Luby. Produced by George W. Weeks. Screenplay by Patricia Harper.

Cast: Ray "Crash" Corrigan, Dennis Moore, Max "Alibi" Terhune, Evelyn Finley, Steve Clark, Glenn Strange,

Carl Sepulveda, George Chesebro, Hank Worden, Frank Ellis, John Merton, Frosty Royce, Hal Price, Stanley Price, Wally West, Carl Mathews, Tex Cooper, Claire McDowell, Foxy Callahan.

The Range Busters (Ray "Crash" Corrigan, Dennis Moore, Max "Alibi" Terhune) are summoned to a town where cattle is being rustled in order to supply the black market with meat.

Running time: 58 minutes. Release date: August 27, 1943.

370. Melody Parade (musical) Directed by Arthur Dreifuss. Produced by Lindsley Parsons. Screenplay by Tim Ryan and Charles R. Marion.

Cast: Mary Beth Hughes, Eddie Quillan, Tim and Irene Ryan, Mantan Moreland, Andre Charlot, Kenneth Harlan, Cyril Ring, Jerry Cooper, Armida, Anson Weeks and His Orchestra, Ted Fio Rito and His Orchestra, Loumell Morgan Trio, Ramon Ros, Ruloff, Follette and Lunard.

A bus boy (Eddie Quillan) is determined to see that a nightclub hat check girl (Mary Beth Hughes) gets a break as a singer.

Running time: 73 minutes. Release date: August 27, 1943.

371. Six-Gun Gospel (western) Directed by Lambert Hillyer. Produced by Scott R. Dunlap. Screenplay by Ed Earl Repp and Jess Bowers (Adele Buffington).

Cast: Johnny Mack Brown, Raymond Hatton, Inna Guest (Ina Guest), Eddie Dew, Roy Barcroft, Kenneth MacDonald, Edmund Cobb, Milburn Morante, L.W. (Lynton) Brent, Bud Osborne, Kernan Cripps, Jack Daley, Mary MacLaren.

U.S. Marshals Nevada (Johnny Mack Brown) and Sandy (Raymond Hatton) are sent to round up a gang of gold hijackers; the townspeople mistake Sandy for a preacher who aids in the hunt.

Running time: 59 minutes. Release date: September 3, 1943.

372. Here Comes Kelly (comedy) Directed by William

Beaudine. Produced by William T. Lackey. Screenplay by Charles R. Marion. Original story by Jeb (Dore) Schary.

Cast: Eddie Quillan, Joan Woodbury, Maxie Rosenbloom, Armida, Sidney Miller, Mary Gordon, Ian Keith, Luis Alberni, Charles Jordan, Emmett Vogan, Sugar Geise.

A brash, hot-headed young man (Eddie Quillan), who can't seem to hold a job for very long, becomes a process server.

Running time: 64 minutes. Release date: September 10, 1943.

A remake of **He Couldn't Take It** (Monogram, 1934).

Remade as **Live Wires** (Monogram, 1946).

373. Revenge of the Zombies (horror) Directed by Steve Sekely. Produced by Lindsley Parsons. Original screenplay by Edmond Kelso and Van Norcross.

Cast: John Carradine, Veda Ann Borg, Bob Steele, Robert Lowery, Gale Storm, Mantan Moreland, Wanda McKay, Mauritz Hugo, Barry Macollum, James Baskett, Mme. Sul-Te-Wan, Sybil Lewis, Robert Cherry.

Dr. Von Altermann (John Carradine), a scientist collaborating with the Nazis, turns human beings into zombies in hopes of creating an invincible army.

Running time: 61 minutes. Release date: September 17, 1943.

Released in Great Britain as **The Corpse Vanished.**

374. Spotlight Scandals (musical-comedy) Directed by William Beaudine. Produced by Sam Katzman and Jack Dietz. Screenplay by William X. Crowley and Beryl Sachs.

Cast: Billy Gilbert, Frank Fay, Bonnie Baker, Butch and Buddy (Billy Lenhart and Kenneth Brown), Harry Langdon, Iris Adrian, James Bush, Claudia Dell, The Radio Rogues (Jimmy Hollywood, Eddie Bartell, Syd Chalton), Herb Miller and His Orchestra, Henry King and His Orchestra, Lottie Harrison, Jim Hope, Jack Boyle Eddie Parks, Betty Blythe.

A barber (Billy Gilbert) and a stranded actor (Frank Fay) team up to do a vaudeville act that leads them to musical comedy stardom on Broadway.

Running time: 73 minutes. Release date: September 24, 1943.
Also known as **Spotlight Revue** and **Spotlight on Scandal.**

375. Blazing Guns (western) Produced and directed by Robert Tansey. Original story and screenplay by Frances Kavanaugh.

Cast: Ken Maynard, Hoot Gibson, Cay Forrester, LeRoy Mason, Roy Brent, Lloyd Ingraham, Charles King, Weldon Heyburn, Dan White, Frank Ellis, Kenne Duncan, Emmett Lynn.

The Trail Blazers (Ken Maynard, Hoot Gibson) are summoned to clean up Willow Springs, a town being ravaged by a greedy landgrabber (LeRoy Mason) who seeks to drive out all the honest ranchers.

Running time: 55 minutes. Release date: October 8, 1943.

376. Outlaws of Stampede Pass (western) Directed by Wallace Fox. Produced by Scott R. Dunlap. Screenplay by Jess Bowers (Adele Buffington). Story by Johnston McCulley.

Cast: Johnny Mack Brown, Raymond Hatton, Ellen Hall, Harry Woods, Milburn Morante, Edmund Cobb, Sam Flint, Jon Dawson, Charles King, Mauritz Hugo, Art Mix, Cactus Mack, Artie Ortego, Eddie Burns, Bill Wolfe, Hal Price, Dan White, Kansas Moehring, Tex Cooper.

Two U.S. Marshals (Johnny Mack Brown, Raymond Hatton) operate undercover as they go to a frontier town to stop a bad cattle rustling situation threatening to break the local ranchers.

Running time: 58 minutes. Release date: October 15, 1943.

377. The Unknown Guest (mystery) Directed by Kurt Neumann. Produced by Maurice King. Screenplay by Philip Yordan.

Cast: Victor Jory, Pamela Blake, Veda Ann Borg, Paul Fix, Frank Faylen, Phil Van Zandt, Harry Hayden,

Feature Films 1943

Emory Parnell, Nora Cecil, Lee White, Ray Walker, Edwin Mills.

A man (Victor Jory) is suspected of murdering relatives (Lee White, Nora Cecil) at a hunting lodge.

Running time: 64 minutes. Release date: October 22, 1943.

Working title: **I Was a Criminal.**

378. Bullets and Saddles (western) Directed by Anthony Marshall. Produced by George W. Weeks. Screenplay by Elizabeth Beecher. Story by Arthur Hoerl.

Cast: Ray "Crash" Corrigan, Dennis Moore, Max "Alibi" Terhune, Julie Duncan, Budd Buster, Rose Plummer, Forrest Taylor, Glenn Strange, Steve Clark, John Merton, Edward Cassidy, Joe Garcia, Silver Harr, Carl Mathews.

The Range Busters (Ray "Crash" Corrigan, Dennis Moore, Max "Alibi" Terhune) clean out a greedy land-grabber (Glenn Strange) who is buying up all the surrounding ranches in order to gain right-of-way to a contemplated railroad line.

Running time: 54 minutes. Release date: October 29, 1943.

379. Mr. Muggs Steps Out (comedy) Directed by William Beaudine. Produced by Sam Katzman and Jack Dietz. Story and screenplay by William X. Crowley and Beryl Sachs. A Banner Production.

Cast: Leo Gorcey, Huntz Hall, Gabriel Dell, Billy Benedict, Joan Marsh, Noah Beery, Sr., Betty Blythe, Nick Stuart, Patsy Moran, Eddie Gribbon, David Durand, Stanley Brown, Halliwell Hobbes, Bobby Stone, Bud Gorman, Jimmy Strand, Emmett Vogan, Lottie Harrison, Kay Marvis Gorcey.

The East Side Kids (Huntz Hall, Billy Benedict, Bobby Stone, Bud Gorman, David Durand, Jimmy Strand) wind up on Park Avenue when a society matron (Betty Blythe) hires Muggs McGinnis (Leo Gorcey) as her chauffeur.

Running time: 63 minutes. Release date: October 29, 1943.

Working title: **The Honor System.**

380. The Mystery of the 13th Guest (mystery) Directed by William Beaudine. Produced by Lindsley Parsons. Screenplay by Tim Ryan, Charles R. Marion and Arthur Hoerl. From the Armitage Trail novel "The 13th Guest."

Cast: Dick Purcell, Helen Parrish, Tim Ryan, Frank Faylen, John Duncan, John Dawson, Paul McVey, Jacqueline Dalya, Cyril Ring, Addison Richards, Lloyd Ingraham, Fred "Snowflake" Toones.

Thirteen years after her father died suddenly at a dinner party he had hosted for 13 guests, someone is trying to kill Marie Morgan (Helen Parrish).

Running time: 60 minutes. Release date: November 5, 1943.

A remake of **The Thirteenth Guest** (Monogram, 1932).

381. Nearly Eighteen (comedy) Directed by Arthur Dreifuss. Produced by Lindsley Parsons. Screenplay by George Wallace Sayre. Original story by Margaret Englander.

Cast: Gale Storm, Rick Vallin, Bill Henry, Luis Alberni, Ralph Hodges, Jerry Rush, George O'Hanlon, Bebe Fox.

A young woman (Gale Storm), nearly 18, poses as a child so she can attend a singing and dancing school offering free tuition to youngsters 15 and under.

Running time: 61 minutes. Release date: November 12, 1943.

382. Campus Rhythm (musical) Directed by Arthur Dreifuss. Produced by Lindsley Parsons. Screenplay by Charles R. Marion. Story by Ewart Adamson and Jack White. Additional dialogue by Albert Beich and Frank Tarloff.

Cast: Gale Storm, Robert Lowery, Johnny Downs, GeGe Pierson, Candy Candido, Douglas Leavitt, Herbert Hayes, Marie Blake, Johnny Duncan, Claudia Drake.

A radio songstress (Gale Storm) runs away from her sponsor and guardian to enroll in college under an assumed name.

Running time: 63 minutes. Release date: November 19, 1943.

A poster for "Campus Rhythm" (1943). Pictured (lower right): Johnny Downs, Gale Storm and Robert Lowery.

Also known as **Fraternity Sweetheart**.

383. The Texas Kid (western) Directed by Lambert Hillyer. Produced by Scott R. Dunlap. Screenplay by Jess Bowers (Adele Buffington). Story by Lynton W. Brent.

Cast: Johnny Mack Brown, Raymond Hatton, Shirley Patterson, Marshall Reed, Kermit Maynard, Edmund Cobb, Robert Fiske, Stanley Price, Lynton Brent, Bud Osborne, John Judd, Charles King, Cyril Ring, George J. Lewis.

Two U.S. Marshals (Johnny Mack Brown, Raymond Hatton) are assigned to wipe out the infamous Scully Gang, a band of highwaymen who are staging a series of stagecoach holdups, preventing ranch owners from meeting payrolls and carrying on their operations.

Running time: 59 minutes. Release date: November 26, 1943.

384. Death Valley Rangers (western) Produced and directed by Robert Tansey. Screenplay by Elizabeth Beecher. Original story by Robert Emmett (Tansey) and Frances Kavanaugh.

Cast: Ken Maynard, Hoot Gibson, Bob Steele, Linda Brent, Kenneth Harlan, Bob Allen, Charles King, George Chesebro, John Bridges, Al Ferguson, Steve Clark, Wally West, Glenn Strange, Forrest Taylor, Lee Roberts, Weldon Heyburn, Karl Hackett.

A succession of stagecoach robberies prompts the citizens of a Death Valley outpost to send for the Trail Blazers (Ken Maynard, Hoot Gibson, Bob Steele), a trio of law-enforcing plainsmen.

Running time: 59 min. Release date: Dec. 3, 1943.

385. Smart Guy (drama) Directed by Lambert Hillyer. Produced by John T. Coyle. Screenplay by Charles R. Marion and John W. Krafft. Original story by Harrison Jacobs.

Cast: Rick Vallin, Bobby Larson, Veda Ann Borg, Wanda McKay, Jack LaRue, Mary Gordon, Paul McVey, Addison Richards, Roy Darmour, John Dawson.

A gambler (Rick Vallin), about to stand trial for a crime he is innocent of, adopts a newsboy (Bobby Larson) in an effort to improve his public image.

Running time: 63 minutes. Release date: December 17, 1943.

A remake of **I Am a Criminal** (Monogram, 1938).

1944

386. The Sultan's Daughter (musical-comedy) Directed by Arthur Dreifuss. Produced by Philip N. Krasne and James S. Burkett. Screenplay by Tim Ryan and Milton Raison.

Cast: Ann Corio, Charles Butterworth, Tim and Irene Ryan, Edward Norris, Fortunio Bonanova, Jack LaRue, Gene Stutenroth (Roth), Chris-Pin Martin, Joseph J. Greene, Freddie "Schnickelfritz" Fisher and his orchestra.

A sultan's daughter (Ann Corio), the owner of vast oil lands of great importance to the Nazis, refuses to lease her property to anyone but Americans. The Germans try to trick her by getting a couple of Americans (Edward Norris, Tim Ryan) to obtain the lease.

Running time: 64 minutes. Release date: January 2, 1944.

387. Women in Bondage (drama) Directed by Steve Sekely. Produced by Herman Millakowsky. Screenplay by Houston Branch. Original story by Frank Bentick Wisbar.

Cast: Gail Patrick, Nancy Kelly, Bill Henry, Tala Birell, Gertrude Michael, Alan Baxter, Maris Wrixon, Rita Quigley, Anne Nagel, Mary Forbes, Felix Basch, H.B. Warner, Frederic Brunn, Roland Varno, Ralph Linn, Francine Bordeaux, Anne Franks, Gesila Werbiseck.

A story of the degradation and brutalizing of women in Germany where members of the SS Elite Troops are appointed to become fathers of children by women who are selected for motherhood by the Reich.

Running time: 72 minutes. Release date: January 10, 1944.

Working title: **Hitler's Women.**

388. Westward Bound (western) Produced and directed by Robert Tansey. Story and screenplay by Frances Kavanaugh.

Cast: Ken Maynard, Hoot Gibson, Bob Steele, Betty Miles, John Bridges, Harry Woods, Karl Hackett, Weldon Heyburn, Hal Price, Roy Brent, Frank Ellis, Curley Dresden, Dan White, Al Ferguson.

The Trail Blazers (Ken Maynard, Hoot Gibson, Bob Steele) are called to Big Horn territory to nab a gang of desperadoes who are destroying ranches.

Running time: 54 minutes. Release date: January 17, 1944.

389. Where Are Your Children? (drama) Directed by William Nigh. Produced by Jeffrey Bernerd. Screenplay by Hilary Lynn and George Wallace Sayre. Story by Hilary Lynn.

Nancy Kelly (left) and Gail Patrick in "Women in Bondage" (1944).

Cast: Jackie Cooper, Gale Storm, Patricia Morison, John Litel, Gertrude Michael, Addison Richards, Herbert Rawlinson, Betty Blythe, Anthony Warde, Sarah Edwards, Evelyn Eaton, Jimmy Zaner, Charles Williams, John Laurenz, Neyle Marx.

A high school girl (Gale Storm) is accused of murdering a gas station operator.

Running time: 72 minutes. Release date: January 17, 1944.

172

390. Raiders of the Border (western) Directed by John P. McCarthy. Produced by Scott R. Dunlap. Screenplay by Jess Bowers (Adele Buffington). Story by Johnston McCulley.

Cast: Johnny Mack Brown, Raymond Hatton, Ellen Hall, Craig Woods, Stanley Price, Ray Bennett, Edmund Cobb, Lynton Brent, Dick Alexander, Kermit Maynard, Ernie Adams.

U.S. Marshal Nevada (Johnny Mack Brown) and his officer pal Sandy (Raymond Hatton) hunt down cattle rustlers who are exchanging the stolen beef for equally illicit Mexican jewels.

Running time: 58 min. Release date: Jan. 31, 1944.

391. What a Man! (comedy) Directed by William Beaudine. Produced by Barney A. Sarecky. Original screenplay by William X. Crowley and Beryl Sachs.

Cast: Johnny Downs, Wanda McKay, Robert Kent, Etta McDaniels, Harry Holman, Lillian Bronson, Wheeler Oakman, John Ince, I. Stanford Jolley, Jack Gardner.

A meek accountant (Johnny Downs) in a big accounting firm becomes involved in a murder when he finds that an attractive blonde (Wanda McKay) has moved into his apartment.

Running time: 73 minutes. Release date: January 31, 1944.

Working title: **Her Bachelor Husband.**

392. Charlie Chan in the Secret Service (mystery) Directed by Phil Rosen. Produced by Philip N. Krasne. Screenplay by George Callahan. Based on the character "Charlie Chan" created by Earl Derr Biggers.

Cast: Sidney Toler, Gwen Kenyon, Mantan Moreland, Arthur Loft, Benson Fong, Marianne Quon, Lela Tyler, John Elliott, Eddie Chandler, George Lewis, Barry Bernard, Gene Stutenroth (Roth), George Lessey, Muni Seroff.

Called in by the Secret Service, detective Charlie Chan (Sidney Toler) investigates the murder of a scientist who was working on new explosive devices.

Running time: 65 minutes. Release date: February 14, 1944.

393. Arizona Whirlwind (western) Produced and directed by Robert Tansey. Screenplay by Frances Kavanaugh.

Cast: Ken Maynard, Hoot Gibson, Bob Steele, Ian Keith, Myrna Dell, Donald Stewart, Charles King, Karl Hackett, George Chesebro, Dan White, Charles Murray, Jr., Frank Ellis, Chief Soldani, Willow Bird.

The Trail Blazers (Ken Maynard, Hoot Gibson, Bob Steele) take jobs as telegraph linemen to get the goods on a local banker who is head of a band of counterfeiters.

Running time: 59 minutes. Release date: February 21, 1944.

394. Voodoo Man (mystery-horror) Directed by William Beaudine. Produced by Sam Katzman and Jack Dietz. Screenplay by Robert Charles. A Banner Production.

Cast: Bela Lugosi, John Carradine, George Zucco, Michael Ames, Wanda McKay, Ellen Hall, Louise Currie, Henry Hall, Dan White, Pat McKee, Terry Walker, Claire James, Ethelreda Leopold, Ralph Littlefield, Dorothy Bailer.

A doctor (Bela Lugosi) resorts to voodoo practices in an effort to bring his deceased wife (Ellen Hall) back to life.

Running time: 62 minutes. Release date: February 21, 1944.

Working title: **The Tiger Man.**

395. Million Dollar Kid (comedy) Directed by Wallace Fox. Produced by Sam Katzman and Jack Dietz. Story and screenplay by Frank H. Young. A Banner Production.

Cast: Leo Gorcey, Huntz Hall, Gabriel Dell, Billy Benedict, Louise Currie, Noah Beery, Sr., Iris Adrian, Herbert Hayes (Heyes), Robert Greig, Johnny Duncan, Stanley Brown, Patsy Moran, Mary Gordon, Al Stone, Dave Durand, Bud Gorman, Jimmy Strand, Pat Costello, Bobby Stone.

The East Side Kids (Leo Gorcey, Huntz Hall, Billy Benedict, Al Stone, Dave Durand, Bud Gorman, Jimmy Strand, Bobby Stone) learn that a millionaire's son (Johnny Duncan) is associating with mobsters and try to put him back on the path of respectability.

Feature Films 1944

Running time: 65 minutes. Release date: February 28, 1944.

396. Sweethearts of the U.S.A. (musical-comedy) Directed by Lewis D. Collins. Produced by Lester Cutler. Screenplay by Arthur St. Clare, Sherman Lowe and Mary Sheldon. Original story by Mary Sheldon.

Cast: Una Merkel, Parkyakarkus (Harry Einstein), Donald Novis, Lillian Cornell, Joel Friend, Ralph Sanford, Cobina Wright, Sr., Judith Gibson, Joe Devlin, Vince Barnett, Forrest Taylor, Marion Martin, Joseph Kirk, Georgann Smith, Edmund Cobb, Dorothy Bradshaw, Charles Williams, Jan Garber and his orchestra, Henry King and his orchestra, Phil Ohman and his orchestra.

A defense worker (Una Merkel) is knocked unconscious and dreams of a detective's (Parkyakarkus) hunt for some bank robbers.

Running time: 63 minutes. Release date: March 7, 1944.

British title: **Sweethearts on Parade.**

397. Partners of the Trail (western) Directed by Lambert Hillyer. Produced by Scott R. Dunlap. Story and screenplay by Frank H. Young.

Cast: Johnny Mack Brown, Raymond Hatton, Christine McIntyre, Craig Woods, Robert Frazer, Harry (Hal) L. Price, Jack Ingram, Lynton Brent, Ben Corbett, Steve Clark, Marshall Reed, Lloyd Ingraham, Ted Mapes.

U.S. Marshal Nevada (Johnny Mack Brown) and Sandy (Raymond Hatton) help a young woman (Christine McIntyre) track down her father's killer.

Running time: 57 minutes. Release date: March 28, 1944.

398. Lady, Let's Dance (musical) Directed by Frank Woodruff. Produced by Scott R. Dunlap. Screenplay by Peter Milne and Paul Gerard Smith. Story by Bradbury Foote and Scott R. Dunlap.

Cast: Belita, James Ellison, Frick and Frack, Walter Catlett, Lucien Littlefield, Maurice St. Clair, Eugene Mikeler, Harry Harvey, Jack Rice, Emmett Vogan, Barbara

175

Belita in "Lady, Let's Dance" (1944). When it came to cinema ice skaters, 20th Century-Fox had Sonia Henie, Republic had Vera Hruba Ralston, and Monogram had Belita, who was referred to (by Monogram, if no one else) as "Hollywood's drama, skating, swimming and dancing star."

Woodell, Jimmy Alexander, Eddie LeBaron and his orchestra, Henry Busse and his orchestra, Mitch Ayres and his orchestra, Lou Bring.

The entertainment director (James Ellison) of a

California resort turns a refugee (Belita) into a big star attraction.
Running time: 88 minutes. Release date: April 11, 1944.

399. Hot Rhythm (musical-comedy) Directed by William Beaudine. Produced by Lindsley Parsons. Story and screenplay by Tim Ryan and Charles R. Marion.

Cast: Dona Drake, Robert Lowery, Tim and Irene Ryan, Sidney Miller, Jerry Cooper, Robert Kent, Harry Langdon, Lloyd Ingraham, Cyril Ring, Joan Curtis, Paul Porcasi, Fred Skinner, Fred Cook.

Two radio jingle-writers (Robert Lowery, Sidney Miller) help an aspiring vocalist (Dona Drake) by recording an orchestra's music off the air for her to sing. Trouble begins when a number of recordings are mistakenly offered for sale.
Running time: 79 min. Release date: April 22, 1944.

400. Law Men (western) Directed by Lambert Hillyer. Produced by Charles J. Bigelow. Screenplay by Glenn Tryon.

Cast: Johnny Mack Brown, Raymond Hatton, Jan Wiley, Kirby Grant, Robert Frazer, Edmund Cobb, Art Fowler, Hal Price, Marshall Reed, Isabel Withers, Ted Mapes, Steve Clark, Bud Osborne, Ben Corbett, Jack Rockwell, George Morrell, Ray Jones.

Two U.S. Marshals (Johnny Mack Brown, Raymond Hatton) secretly arrive into town to investigate various bank and stagecoach holdups.
Running time: 58 minutes. Release date: April 25, 1944.

401. Outlaw Trail (western) Produced and directed by Robert Tansey. Screenplay by Frances Kavanaugh. Story by Alvin J. Neitz (Alan James).

Cast: Hoot Gibson, Bob Steele, Chief Thunder Cloud, Jennifer Holt, Cy Kendall, Rocky Camron, George Eldredge, Charles King, Hal Price, John Bridges, Bud Osborne, Jim Thorpe, Frank Ellis, Al Ferguson, Warner Richmond, Tex Palmer.

The Trail Blazers (Hoot Gibson, Bob Steele, Chief Thunder Cloud) go to the aid of ranchers who are being oppressed by a town boss (Cy Kendall) and his henchmen. Running time: 53 minutes. Release date: April 29, 1944.

402. Detective Kitty O'Day (mystery-comedy) Directed by William Beaudine. Produced by Lindsley Parsons. Screenplay by Tim Ryan and Victor Hammond. Original story by Victor Hammond.

Cast: Jean Parker, Peter Cookson, Tim Ryan, Veda Ann Borg, Edward Gargan, Douglas Fowley, Edward Earle, Herbert Heyes, Pat Gleason, Olaf Hytten.

Kitty O'Day (Jean Parker) and her boyfriend (Peter Cookson) try to clear themselves when they're suspected of murdering her employer.

Running time: 63 min. Release date: May 13, 1944.

403. The Chinese Cat (mystery) Directed by Phil Rosen. Produced by Philip N. Krasne and James S. Burkett. Screenplay by George Callahan. Based on the character "Charlie Chan" created by Earl Derr Biggers.

Cast: Sidney Toler, Benson Fong, Mantan Moreland, Weldon Heyburn, Joan Woodbury, Ian Keith, Sam Flint, Cy Kendall, Anthony Warde, Dewey Robinson, Betty Blythe, John Davidson.

Charlie Chan (Sidney Toler) pursues murderous jewel thieves who are using an abandoned fun house as a hideout.

Running time: 65 minutes. Release date: May 20, 1944.

404. Follow the Leader (comedy) Directed by William Beaudine. Produced by Sam Katzman and Jack Dietz. Screenplay by William X. Crowley and Beryl Sachs. Original story by Ande Lamb. A Banner Production.

Cast: Leo Gorcey, Huntz Hall, Gabriel Dell, Billy Benedict, Joan Marsh, Jack LaRue, Mary Gordon, J. Farrell MacDonald, Dave Durand, Bobby Stone, Jimmy Strand, Bud Gorman, Bernard Gorcey, Bryant Washburn, Gene Austin and the Sherrill Sisters, "Sunshine Sammy" Morrison.

East Side Kids Muggs McGinnis (Leo Gorcey) and Glimpy Freedhoff (Huntz Hall), on furlough from the army, conduct a private investigation into a series of medical warehouse robberies.
Running time: 65 minutes. Release date: June 3, 1944.
Working title: **East of the Bowery.**

405. Sonora Stagecoach (western) Produced and directed by Robert Tansey. Screenplay by Frances Kavanaugh. Original story by Robert Emmett (Tansey).
Cast: Hoot Gibson, Bob Steele, Chief Thunder Cloud, Rocky Camron, Betty Miles, Glenn Strange, George Eldredge, Karl Hackett, Henry Hall, Charles King, Bud Osborne, Charles Murray, Jr., John Bridges, Al Ferguson, Forrest Taylor, Frank Ellis, Hal Price, Rodd Redwing, John (Bob) Cason, Horace B. Carpenter.
The Trail Blazers (Hoot Gibson, Bob Steele, Chief Thunder Cloud) are bringing in a prisoner to stand trial for bank robbery when several attempts are made to kill him; convinced of the man's innocence, they arrange a trap for the real thieves.
Running time: 61 minutes. Release date: June 10, 1944.

406. Range Law (western) Directed by Lambert Hillyer. Produced by Charles J. Bigelow. Story and screenplay by Frank H. Young.
Cast: Johnny Mack Brown, Raymond Hatton, Sarah Padden, Ellen Hall, Lloyd Ingraham, Marshall Reed, Steve Clark, Jack Ingram, Hugh Prosser, Stanley Price, Art Fowler, Harry (Hal) L. Price, Ben Corbett, Bud Osborne, Tex Palmer, George Morrell, Lynton Brent, Forrest Taylor, Horace B. Carpenter.
"Boots" Annie (Sarah Padden), a gun-toting frontier woman, sends for U.S. Marshals Nevada (Johnny Mack Brown) and Sandy (Raymond Hatton) when a friend is wrongfully convicted of cattle rustling.
Running time: 57 minutes. Release date: June 24, 1944.

407. Johnny Doesn't Live Here Anymore (comedy) Directed by Joe May. Produced by Maurice and Franklin King. Screenplay by Philip Yordan and John Kafka. From the Liberty Magazine story by Alice Means Reeve.

Cast: Simone Simon, James Ellison, William Terry, Minna Gombel, Chick Chandler, Alan Dinehart, Gladys Blake, Robert Mitchum, Dorothy Granger, Grady Sutton, Chester Clute, Fern Emmett, Jerry Maren, Janet Shaw.

A young girl (Simone Simon) rents an apartment from an enlisting marine (William Terry) who has given keys to half a dozen friends—all of whom drop in.

Running time: 79 minutes. Release date: July 8, 1944.

408. Are These Our Parents? (drama) Directed by William Nigh. Produced by Jeffrey Bernerd. Screenplay by Michael Jacoby. Original story by Hilary Lynn.

Cast: Helen Vinson, Lyle Talbot, Ivan Lebedeff, Noel Neill, Richard Byron, Addison Richards, Anthony Warde, Emma Dunne, Ian Wolfe, Robin Raymond, Jean Carlin, Claire McDowell, Emmett Vogan, Edgar Norton, Jimmy Strand.

A young girl (Noel Neill), neglected by her mother (Helen Vinson), sneaks away to a roadhouse; she becomes involved with a boy (Richard Byron) whose father (Lyle Talbot) is neglecting his defense job for a woman.

Running time: 73 minutes. Release date: July 15, 1944.

409. Return of the Ape Man (horror) Directed by Phil Rosen. Produced by Sam Katzman and Jack Dietz. Screenplay by Robert Charles. A Banner Production.

Cast: Bela Lugosi, John Carradine, Frank Moran, Judith Gibson, Michael Ames (Tod Andrews), Mary Currier, Ed Chandler, Mike Donovan, George Eldredge, Horace B. Carpenter, Ernie Adams, Frank Leigh. (Although he is given third billing, George Zucco does not appear in the film—see photo and caption, page 181.)

A scientist (Bela Lugosi) revives a prehistoric ape man (Frank Moran), then attempts to civilize him via brain surgery.

180

Left to right: Bela Lugosi, George Zucco and John Carradine in a preproduction publicity shot used to promote "Return of the Ape Man" (1944). Zucco, seen here in "ape man" makeup, became ill prior to actual filming and did not appear in the completed picture, although he did receive third billing (Frank Moran played the role of the ape man throughout).

Running time: 60 minutes. Release date: July 17, 1944.

410. Block Busters (comedy) Directed by Wallace Fox. Produced by Sam Katzman and Jack Dietz. Screenplay by Houston Branch. A Banner Production.

Cast: Leo Gorcey, Huntz Hall, Gabriel Dell, Billy Benedict, Jimmy Strand, Bill Chaney, Minerva Urecal, Roberta Smith, Noah Beery, Sr., Harry Langdon, Frederick Pressel, Jack Gilman, Kay Marvis, Bernard Gorcey, Tom Herbert, Robert F. Hill, Charles Murray, Jr., Jimmy Noone and his orchestra, The Ashburns.

The East Side Kids take a rich kid (Frederick Pressel) under their wing so he can learn the values of fellowship by associating with other boys.
Running time: 60 minutes. Release date: July 22, 1944.

411. Three of a Kind (comedy) Directed by Ross Lederman. Produced by Sam Katzman and Jack Dietz. Screenplay by Earle Snell and Arthur Caesar. A Banner Production.

Cast: Billy Gilbert, Shemp Howard, Maxie Rosenbloom, Helen Gilbert, June Lang, Robert "Buzzy" Henry, Paul Phillips, Wheeler Oakman.

Two vaudeville acrobats (Billy Gilbert, Shemp Howard) adopt an actor pal's son (Robert "Buzzy" Henry).
Running time: 67 minutes. Release date: July 22, 1944.

Also known as **Cooking Up Trouble.**

412. Marked Trails (western) Directed by John P. McCarthy. Produced by William Strohbach. Screenplay by John P. McCarthy and Victor Hammond.

Cast: Bob Steele, Hoot Gibson, Veda Ann Borg, Ralph Lewis, Mauritz Hugo, Steve Clark, Charles Stevens, Lynton Brent, Bud Osborne, George Morrell, Allen B. Sewell, Ben Corbett.

Two cowboys (Bob Steele, Hoot Gibson), posing as outlaw and reformer respectively, round up a gang of oil swindlers.
Running time: 58 minutes. Release date: July 29, 1944.

413. West of the Rio Grande (western) Directed by Lambert Hillyer. Produced by Charles J. Bigelow. Story and screenplay by Betty Burbridge.

Cast: Johnny Mack Brown, Raymond Hatton, Dennis Moore, Christine McIntyre, Lloyd Ingraham, Kenneth MacDonald, Frank LaRue, Art Fowler, Hugh Prosser, Edmund Cobb, Steve Clark, Jack Rockwell, Hal Price, John Merton, Bob Kortman, Bud Osborne, Pierce Lyden, Lynton Brent.

A unique publicity photo for "Three of a Kind" (1944), starring Shemp Howard, Billy Gilbert and Maxie Rosenbloom.

U.S. Marshal Nevada (Johnny Mack Brown) disguises himself as a gunman hired by a crooked politician to take control of a town.

Running time: 57 minutes. Release date: August 5, 1944.

414. Black Magic (mystery) Directed by Phil Rosen. Produced by Philip N. Krasne and James S. Burkett. Screenplay by George Callahan. Based on the character "Charlie Chan" created by Earl Derr Biggers.

Cast: Sidney Toler, Mantan Moreland, Frances Chan, Joe Crehan, Jacqueline DeWit, Ralph Peters, Helen Beverley, Frank Jaquet, Dick Gordon, Charles Jordan, Claudia Dell, Geraldine Wall, Harry Depp, Edward Earle.

Charlie Chan (Sidney Toler) investigates the murder of a phony spiritualist.

Running time: 67 minutes. Release date: August 19, 1944.

Also known as **Charlie Chan in Black Magic** and **Meeting at Midnight.**

415. Call of the Jungle (mystery-adventure) Directed by Phil Rosen. Produced by Philip N. Krasne and James S. Burkett. Screenplay by George Callahan.

Cast: Ann Corio, James Bush, John Davidson, Claudia Dell, Edward Chandler, Muni Seroff, I. Stanford Jolley, J. Alex Havier, Phil Van Zandt, Harry Burns.

On a South Sea isle, a native girl (Ann Corio) aids a police officer (James Bush) in recovering a pair of sacred pearls stolen from a native temple.

Running time: 60 minutes. Release date: August 19, 1944.

416. Leave It to the Irish (mystery-comedy) Directed by William Beaudine. Produced by Lindsley Parsons. Original story and screenplay by Tim Ryan and Eddie Davis.

Cast: James Dunn, Wanda McKay, Ralph Lewis, Dick Purcell, Arthur Loft, Vince Barnett, Barbara Woodell, Jack LaRue, Joe DeVillard, Eddie Allen, Dick Scott, Ted Stanhope, Olaf Hytten.

A private investigator (James Dunn), hired to solve the murder of a fur dealer, finds a gang of fur thieves operating under the cover of a nightclub.

Running time: 71 minutes. Release date: August 26, 1944.

417. The Utah Kid (western) Directed by Vernon Keays. Produced by William Strohbach. Screenplay by Victor Hammond.

Cast: Hoot Gibson, Bob Steele, Beatrice Gray, Evelyn Eaton, Ralph Lewis, Mike Letz, Mauritz Hugo, Jamesson Shade, Dan White, George Morrell, Bud Osborne.

Two U.S. Marshals (Hoot Gibson, Bob Steele) pursue a gang using snake venom to poison other entrants in rodeo events.

Running time: 53 min. Release date: Aug. 26, 1944.

418. Oh, What a Night! (drama) Directed by William Beaudine. Produced by Scott R. Dunlap. Screenplay by Paul Gerard Smith. Story by Marion Orth.

Cast: Edmund Lowe, Marjorie Rambeau, Jean Parker, Pierre Watkin, Alan Dinehart, Claire DuBrey, Ivan Lebedeff, Karin Lang, Charles Miller, Olaf Hytten, George Lewis, Crane Whitley, Charles Jordan, Dick Rush.

A young woman (Jean Parker) is unaware that her uncle (Edmund Lowe) is an international jewel thief.

Running time: 72 minutes. Release date: September 2, 1944.

419. Land of the Outlaws (western) Directed by Lambert Hillyer. Produced by Charles J. Bigelow. Screenplay by Joseph O'Donnell.

Cast: Johnny Mack Brown, Raymond Hatton, Stephen Keyes, Nan Holliday, Hugh Prosser, Charles King, John Merton, Steve Clark, Art Fowler, Tom Quinn, Ray Elder, Chick Hannon, Bob Cason, Kansas Moehring, Ben Corbett, George Morrell.

A U.S. Marshal (Johnny Mack Brown) steps in when a crooked saloonkeeper begins hijacking ore shipments.

Running time: 56 minutes. Release date: September 16, 1944.

420. Shadows of Suspicion (mystery-comedy) Directed by William Beaudine. Produced by A.W. Hackel. Screenplay by Albert DeMond and Earle Snell.

Cast: Marjorie Weaver, Peter Cookson, Tim Ryan, Pierre Watkin, Clara Blandick, J. Farrell MacDonald, John Hamilton, Tom Herbert, Anthony Warde, George Lewis, Frank Scanell, Ralph Lewis, Lester Dorr, Frank Stephens, Wilbur Mack, Charlotte Treadway.

A private detective (Peter Cookson) and his partner (Tim Ryan) investigate the theft of a valuable necklace.

Running time: 68 minutes. Release date: September 23, 1944.

421. Trigger Law (western) Directed by Vernon Keays. Produced by Charles J. Bigelow. Screenplay by Victor Hammond.

Cast: Hoot Gibson, Bob Steele, Beatrice Gray, Ralph Lewis, Edward Cassidy, Jack Ingram, George Eldredge, Pierce Lyden, Lane Chandler, Bud Osborne, George Morrell.

A U.S. Marshal (Bob Steele), arriving in a small western town to investigate the mysterious death of his father, finds that a band of lawless men are trying to acquire all the land thereabouts and gain control of the town.

Running time: 56 minutes. Release date: September 30, 1944.

422. A Wave, a Wac and a Marine (comedy) Directed by Philip N. Karlstein (Phil Karlson). Produced by Edward Sherman. Screenplay by Hal Fimberg. A Biltmore Production (financed by comedian Lou Costello).

Cast: Henny Youngman, Elyse Knox, Ann Gillis, Sally Eilers, Ramsay Ames, Richard Lane, Marjorie Woodworth, Alan Dinehart, Billy Mack, Charles "Red" Marshall, Freddie Rich and His Orchestra (with Connie Haines), Cy Kendall, Aileen Pringle.

A Hollywood talent agent (Henny Youngman) mistakes a pair of understudies (Elyse Knox, Ann Gillis) for the stars of a Broadway production and signs them for leads in a picture.

Running time: 70 minutes. Release date: November 3, 1944.

423. Law of the Valley (western) Directed by Howard Bretherton. Produced by Charles J. Bigelow. Screenplay by Joseph O'Donnell.

Cast: Johnny Mack Brown, Raymond Hatton, Lynne Carver, Edmund Cobb, Charles King, Kirk Barton, Tom Quinn, Marshall Reed, Hal Price, George DeNormand, Steve Clark, George Morrell, Charles McMurphy.

In answer to a letter from an old friend, two cowboys (Johnny Mack Brown, Raymond Hatton) journey to Green Valley; there they find their friend murdered and the town controlled by crooks.

Running time: 52 minutes. Release date: November 4, 1944.

424. Enemy of Women (drama) Directed by Alfred Zeisler. Produced by W.R. Frank. Original story and screenplay by Alfred Zeisler and Herbert O. Phillips. Additional dialogue by Elizabeth Peroix.

Cast: Claudia Drake, Paul Andor, Donald Woods, H.B. Warner, Sigrid Gurie, Ralph Morgan, Gloria Stuart, Robert Barrat, Beryl Wallace, Charles Halton, Douglas Fowley, Byron Foulger, Erskine Sanford, Reid Kilpatrick, Jerry Michelsen, Erskine Johnson, Walter Brooke, Lester Dorr, Stephen Roberts, Dell Henderson, Kalina Zarova, George Meader, Howard Johnson, Gene Stutenroth (Roth).

The rise of Dr. Paul Joseph Goebbels (Paul Andor), Hitler's minister of propaganda, focusing on his infatuation with a young actress (Claudia Drake).

Running time: 72 minutes. Release date: November 10, 1944.

An independent production (W.R. Frank) distributed by Monogram. Original title: **The Private Life of Dr. Paul Joseph Goebbels.** Also known as **Mad Lover** and **Dr. Paul Joseph Goebbels.**

425. Ghost Guns (western) Directed by Lambert Hillyer. Produced by Charles J. Bigelow. Screenplay by Frank H. Young. Story by Bennett Cohen.

Cast: Johnny Mack Brown, Raymond Hatton, Evelyn Finley, Sarah Padden, Riley Hill, Ernie Adams, Jack Ingram, Tom Quinn, Frank LaRue, John Merton, Bob Cason, Marshall Reed, Steve Clark, George Morrell.

Two U.S. Marshals (Johnny Mack Brown, Raymond Hatton) go after landgrabbers who are killing off ranchers in an attempt to take possession of a fertile valley.

Running time: 60 minutes. Release date: November 17, 1944.

426. Alaska (adventure) Directed by George Archainbaud. Produced by Lindsley Parsons. Screenplay by George Wallace Sayre, Harrison Orkow and Malcolm Stuart Boylan. From the story " Flush of Gold" by Jack London.

Cast: Kent Taylor, Margaret Lindsay, John Carradine, Dean Jagger, Nils Asther, Iris Adrian, George Cleveland, Lee "Lasses" White, Dewey Robinson, John Rogers, Jack

Kim Hunter and Robert Mitchum in "When Strangers Marry" (1944).

Norton, John Maxwell, Warren Jackson, Dick Scott, Glenn Strange, Tex Cooper.

An innocent man (Kent Taylor), framed on a murder charge, is remanded in the custody of a crooked U.S. Marshal (Dean Jagger) who is the brains behind a claim-jumping gang.

Running time: 76 minutes. Release date: November 18, 1944.

427. When Strangers Marry (mystery-drama) Directed by William Castle. Produced by Maurice and Franklin King. Screenplay by Philip Yordan and Dennis J. Cooper. Original story by George V. Moscov.

Cast: Dean Jagger, Kim Hunter, Robert Mitchum, Neil Hamilton, Lou Lubin, Milton Kibbee, Dewey Robinson, Claire Whitney, Edward Keane, Virginia Sale, Dick Elliott, Lee "Lasses" White.

Two strangers (Dean Jagger, Kim Hunter) get married after only three meetings and then are separated; when the girl begins searching for her spouse, she learns that he may be a wanted killer.

Running time: 67 minutes. Release date: November 24, 1944.

Reissue title: **Betrayed.**

428. Bowery Champs (comedy) Directed by William Beaudine. Produced by Sam Katzman and Jack Dietz. Original story and screenplay by Earle Snell. Additional dialogue by Morey Amsterdam. A Banner Production.

Cast: Leo Gorcey, Huntz Hall, Billy Benedict, Gabriel Dell, Thelma White, Evelyn Brent, Bobby Jordan, Ian Keith, Frank Jaquet, Fred Kelsey, Ann Sterling, Bill Ruhl, Wheeler Oakman, Buddy Gorman, Jimmy Strand, Francis Ford, Eddie Cherkose, Bernard Gorcey, Betty Sinclair, Charles Jordan, Joe Bautista.

When a former Broadway star (Evelyn Brent) is suspected of murdering her ex-husband (Wheeler Oakman), the East Side Kids (Leo Gorcey, Huntz Hall, Billy Benedict, Buddy Gorman, Jimmy Strand) set out to find the real killer.

Running time: 62 minutes. Release date: November 25, 1944.

Working title: **Mr. Muggs Meets a Deadline.**

429. Song of the Range (western) Directed by Wallace Fox. Produced by Philip N. Krasne. Screenplay by Betty Burbridge.

Cast: Jimmy Wakely, Dennis Moore, Lee "Lasses" White, Cay Forester, Bud Osborne, George Eldredge, Hugh Prosser, Carl Mathews, Pierre Watkin, Steve Clark, Edmund Cobb, Ken Terrell, Carl Sepulveda, Johnny Bond and His Red River Boys, The Sunshine Girls, Jimmie Dean, Wesley Tuttle.

Jimmy Wakely and his pals (Dennis Moore, Lee "Lasses" White) help a government agent (Cay Forester) track down crooks engaged in transporting gold bullion across the state line.

Running time: 55 min. Release date: Dec. 1, 1944.

430. **Crazy Knights** (comedy) Directed by William Beaudine. Produced by Sam Katzman and Jack Dietz. Original screenplay by Tim Ryan. A Banner Production.

Cast: Billy Gilbert, Shemp Howard, Maxie Rosenbloom, Tim Ryan, Jayne Hazard, Tay Dunn, Minerva Urecal, John Hamilton, Bernard Sell, Betty Sinclair, Art Miles.

Two carnival performers (Billy Gilbert, Shemp Howard) and a chauffeur (Maxie Rosenbloom) wind up in a mysterious mansion and foil a plot to murder a young heiress (Jayne Hazard).

Running time: 63 minutes. Release date: December 8, 1944.

Working title: **Murder in the Family.** Also known as **Ghost Crazy.**

1945

431. **The Navajo Trail** (western) Directed by Howard Bretherton. Produced by Charles J. Bigelow. Screenplay by Jess Bowers (Adele Buffington). Story by Frank H. Young.

Cast: Johnny Mack Brown, Raymond Hatton, Jennifer Holt, Riley Hill, Edmund Cobb, Charles King, Ray Bennett, Bud Osborne, Tom Quinn, Edward Cassidy, John Carpenter.

Two U.S. Marshals (Johnny Mack Brown, Raymond Hatton) step in when a band of cattle rustlers begin preying upon the settlers.

Running time: 60 min. Release date: Jan. 5, 1945.

432. **Army Wives** (comedy) Directed by Phil Rosen. Produced by Lindsley Parsons. Original screenplay by B. Harrison Orkow. Based on an idea by Sergeant Joel Levy, Jr.

Cast: Elyse Knox, Marjorie Rambeau, Rick Vallin, Dorothea Kent, Hardie Albright, Murray Alper, Ralph Lewis, Ralph Sanford, Jimmy Collins, Butch and Buddy (Billy Lenhart and Kenneth Brown), Danny Guthrie, Patsy Creighton, Susan Lester, Eilene Janssen, Phil Warren, Gladys Blake, Dorothy Christy, John Hamilton, Robert Homans.

A young woman (Elyse Knox) is engaged to marry a soldier (Rick Vallin), but they cannot obtain a marriage license because she will not be 21 years of age for four days.

Running time: 67 minutes. Release date: January 12, 1945.

433. Adventures of Kitty O'Day (mystery-comedy) Directed by William Beaudine. Produced by Lindsley Parsons. Screenplay by Tim Ryan, George Callahan and Victor Hammond.

Cast: Jean Parker, Peter Cookson, Tim Ryan, Jan Wiley, William Forrest, Lorna Gray (Adrian Booth), Ralph Sanford, William Ruhl, Hugh Prosser, Dick Elliott, Byron Foulger, Shelton Brooks.

Kitty O'Day (Jean Parker), a switchboard operator at a swank hotel, tries to solve three murders and a number of robberies committed there.

Running time: 62 minutes. Release date: January 19, 1945.

434. Forever Yours (drama) Directed by William Nigh. Produced by Jeffrey Bernerd. Screenplay by William Nigh and George Wallace Sayre. Original story by William Nigh, Neil Rau and George Wallace Sayre.

Cast: Gale Storm, Johnny Mack Brown, Sir Aubrey Smith, Frank Craven, Johnny Downs, Conrad Nagel, Mary Boland, Catherine McLeod, Selmer Jackson, Matt Willis, Maurice St. Clair, Leo Diamond and his Harmonaires.

A young society girl (Gale Storm) is striken with infantile paralysis and threatens to "will herself to die" as a consequence; a medical officer (Johnny Mack Brown), who has been experimenting with paralyzed nerves, is convinced that he can cure the girl.

Running time: 83 minutes. Release date: January 26, 1945.

Working title: **They Shall Have Faith.** Released in Great Britain as **The Right to Live.**

435. The Jade Mask (mystery) Directed by Phil Rosen.

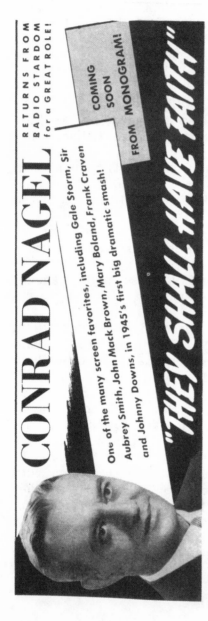

CONRAD NAGEL

One of the many screen favorites, including Gale Storm, Sir Aubrey Smith, John Mack Brown, Mary Boland, Frank Craven and Johnny Downs, in 1945's first big dramatic smash!

"THEY SHALL HAVE FAITH"

"THEY SHALL HAVE FAITH"

COMING SOON FROM MONOGRAM!

FRANK CRAVEN

HEART-WARMING, HUMAN and DELIGHTFUL!

One of the many screen favorites, including Gale Storm, John Mack Brown, Mary Boland Aubrey Smith, Conrad Nagel, 1945's first great and Johnny Downs, in 1945's first great dramatic hit!

Produced by James S. Burkett. Screenplay by George Callahan. Based on the character "Charlie Chan" created by Earl Derr Biggers.

Cast: Sidney Toler, Mantan Moreland, Edwin Luke, Janet Warren, Edith Evanson, Hardie Albright, Ralph Lewis, Frank Reicher, Cyril Delevanti, Alan Bridge, Dorothy Granger, Joe Whitehead, Lester Dorr, Henry Hall.

Charlie Chan (Sidney Toler) is called in to investigate the murder of a scientist who had discovered a method of treating wood so that it becomes as durable as steel.

Running time: 66 minutes. Release date: January 26, 1945.

436. The Cisco Kid Returns (western) Directed by John P. McCarthy. Produced by Philip N. Krasne. Screenplay by Betty Burbridge. Based on the characters created by O. Henry (William Sydney Porter).

Cast: Duncan Renaldo, Martin Garralaga, Cecilia Callejo, Roger Pryor, Anthony Warde, Fritz Leiber, Vicky Lane, Jan Wiley, Sharon Smith, Cy Kendall, Eva Puig, Bud Osborne, Bob Duncan, Elmer Napier, Carl Mathews, Jerry Fields, Neyle Marx, Cedric Stevens, Walter Clinton.

The Cisco Kid (Duncan Renaldo) finds himself the guardian of a four-year old girl whose father has been shot to death.

Running time: 64 minutes. Release date: February 16, 1945.

Working title: **The Cisco Kid Comes Through.**

437. Gun Smoke (western) Directed by Howard Bretherton. Produced by Charles J. Bigelow. Screenplay by Frank H. Young.

Cast: Johnny Mack Brown, Raymond Hatton, Jennifer Holt, Riley Hill, Frank Ellis, Ray Bennett, Marshall Reed, Steve Clark, Bob Cason, Elmer Napier, Roy Butler, Wen

Opposite: A trade advertisement for the Monogram production of "They Shall Have Faith," featuring veteran actors Conrad Nagel and Frank Craven in supporting roles. The film was released as "Forever Yours" (1945).

Wright, Demas Sotello, Kansas Moehring, Louis Hart, Chick Hannon.

U.S. Marshals Nevada (Johnny Mack Brown) and Sandy (Raymond Hatton) try to recover valuable gold Indian relics that were stolen from an archeologist.

Running time: 57 minutes. Release date: February 16, 1945.

438. There Goes Kelly (mystery-comedy) Directed by Phil Karlstein (Phil Karlson). Produced by William Strohbach. Screenplay by Edmond Kelso.

Cast: Jackie Moran, Wanda McKay, Sidney Miller, Ralph Sanford, Dewey Robinson, Jan Wiley, Anthony Warde, Harry Depp, George Eldredge, Edward Emerson, John Gilbreath, Pat Gleason, Don Kerr, Charlie Jordan, Terry Frost, Ralph Linn, Gladys Blake.

Two page boys (Jackie Moran, Sidney Miller) working at a radio station try to get an audition for an aspiring singer (Wanda McKay). When the station's star vocalist is murdered, they try to solve the crime.

Running time: 61 minutes. Release date: February 16, 1945.

439. Docks of New York (comedy) Directed by Wallace Fox. Produced by Sam Katzman and Jack Dietz. Original screenplay by Harvey Gates. A Banner Production.

Cast: Leo Gorcey, Huntz Hall, Billy Benedict, Gloria Pope, Carlyle Blackwell, Jr., Betty Blythe, Cyrus Kendall, George Meeker, Joy Reese, Pierre Watkin, Patsy Moran, Buddy Gorman, Mendie Koenig, Leo Borden, Bernard Gorcey, Betty Sinclair, Maurice St. Clair.

The East Side Kids (Leo Gorcey, Huntz Hall, Billy Benedict, Buddy Gorman, Mendie Koenig) befriend a pretty refugee (Gloria Pope) who is a princess.

Running time: 62 minutes. Release date: February 24, 1945.

Working title: **Bowery Boys.**

440. Dillinger (drama) Directed by Max Nosseck. Produced by Maurice and Franklin King. Original screenplay by Philip Yordan.

Lawrence Tierney (center, seated) played the title role in "Dillinger" (1945); also pictured: Elisha Cook, Jr., Eduardo Cianelli, Edmund Lowe and Marc Lawrence. Several civic groups were outraged by the film's brutal, sensational subject matter (according to "Variety", "Dillinger" was banned in Chicago for two years); because of this uproar, Monogram officials promised that future productions would avoid such "off-color material." Nevertheless, "Dillinger" was a box office success, and Philip Yordan received an Academy Award nomination for his original screenplay.

Cast: Lawrence Tierney, Edmund Lowe, Anne Jeffreys, Eduardo Cianelli, Marc Lawrence, Elisha Cook, Jr., Ralph Lewis, Else Jannsen, Ludwig Stossel, Constance Worth, Hugh Prosser, Dewey Robinson, Bob Perry, Kid Chisel, Billy Nelson, Lee "Lasses" White, Lou Lubin, Victor Kilian, Jack "Tiny" Lipson, Dick Elliott, William Davidson, Sam McDaniel.

The life of notorious criminal John Dillinger (Lawrence Tierney), "Public Enemy Number One" during the 1930s. Running time: 72 minutes. Release date: March 2, 1945.
Working title: **John Dillinger, Killer.**
Uses footage from **Sherlock Holmes** (Fox, 1932) and **You Only Live Once** (United Artists, 1937).

441. Fashion Model (mystery-comedy) Directed by William Beaudine. Produced by William Strohbach. Screenplay by Tim Ryan and Victor Hammond. Story by Victor Hammond.

Cast: Robert Lowery, Marjorie Weaver, Tim Ryan, Lorna Gray (Adrian Booth), Dorothy Christy, Dewey Robinson, Sally Yarnell, Jack Norton, Harry Depp, Nell Craig, Edward Keane, John Valentine, Cedric Stevens.

When a fashion model is killed, a stock boy (Robert Lowery) suspected of the murder and another model (Marjorie Weaver) set out to solve the crime.
Running time: 61 min. Release date: Mar. 2, 1945.
Working title: **The Model Murder.**

442. G.I. Honeymoon (comedy) Directed by Phil Karlstein (Karlson). Produced by Lindsley Parsons. Screenplay by Richard Weil, Jr. Additional dialogue by Tim Ryan. Adapted from the play by A.J. Rubien, Robert Chapin and Marion Page Johnson.

Cast: Gale Storm, Peter Cookson, Arline Judge, Frank Jenks, Jerome Cowan, Virginia Brissac, Ralph Lewis, Earl Hodgins, Ruth Lee, Andrew Tombes, Jonathan Hale, Lois Austin, John Valentine, Claire Whitney, Frank Stevens, Jack Overman.

The efforts of a G.I. couple (Gale Storm, Peter Cookson) to consummate their marriage are constantly being frustrated by various Army emergencies.
Running time: 70 minutes. Release date: April 6, 1945.

443. Stranger from Santa Fe (western) Directed by Lambert Hillyer. Produced by Charles J. Bigelow. Screenplay by Frank H. Young.

Cast: Johnny Mack Brown, Raymond Hatton, Beatrice Gray, Jo Ann Curtis, Jack Ingram, Bud Osborne, Jimmie Martin, Steve Clark, Hal Price, John Merton, Tom Quinn, Ray Elder, Eddie Parker, Louis Hart, Jack Rockwell.

A U.S. Marshal (Johnny Mack Brown) is captured by a gang of bandits and forced by them to cooperate in a stagecoach holdup.

Running time: 57 minutes. Release date: April 15, 1945.

444. The Scarlet Clue (mystery) Directed by Phil Rosen. Produced by James S. Burkett. Screenplay by George Callahan. Based on the character "Charlie Chan" created by Earl Derr Biggers.

Cast: Sidney Toler, Benson Fong, Mantan Moreland, Helen Devereaux, Robert Homans, Virginia Brissac, I. Stanford Jolley, Reid Kilpatrick, Jack Norton, Charles Sherlock, Janet Shaw, Milton Kibbee, Ben Carter, Victoria Faust, Charles Jordan, Leonard Mudie, Kernan Cripps.

While Charlie Chan (Sidney Toler) is investigating a plot to steal radar plans from the government, one of the suspects is murdered.

Running time: 64 minutes. Release date: May 11, 1945.

445. In Old New Mexico (western) Directed by Phil Rosen. Produced by Philip N. Krasne. Screenplay by Betty Burbridge. Based on the characters created by O. Henry (William Sydney Porter).

Cast: Duncan Renaldo, Martin Garralaga, Gwen Kenyon, Norman Willis, Lee "Lasses" White, Pedro DeCordoba, Frank Jaquet, Bud Osborne, Artie Ortego, Aurora Roche, Edward Earle, Donna Day, Kenneth Terrell, John Laurenz, Richard Gordon, Harry Depp, James Farley, Car-Bert Dancers.

The Cisco Kid (Duncan Renaldo) comes to the aid of a pretty young nurse (Gwen Kenyon) who has been falsely accused of murder.

Running time: 62 minutes. Release date: May 15, 1945.

Also known as **The Cisco Kid in Old New Mexico.**

Gwen Kenyon cheerfully accepts a note from Duncan Renaldo, playing the Cisco Kid, in "In Old New Mexico" (1945).

446. China's Little Devils (adventure-drama) Directed by Monta Bell. Produced by Grant Withers. Screenplay by Sam Ornitz.

Cast: Paul Kelly, Harry Carey, Ducky Louie, Hayward Soo Hoo, Gloria Ann Chew.

Mission children-commandos aid U.S. pilots when they are forced down over Japanese-held territory in China.

Running time: 74 minutes. Release date: May 27, 1945.

Working title: **Little Devils.**

447. Springtime in Texas (western) Produced and directed by Oliver Drake. Screenplay by Frances Kavanaugh.

Cast: Jimmy Wakely, Dennis Moore, Lee "Lasses"

White, Marie Harmon, Rex Lease, Horace Murphy, I. Stanford Jolley, Hal Taliaferro (Wally Wales), Budd Buster, Ted French, Pat Patterson, Rusty McDonald, Spud Goodale, Frankie Marvin, Terry Frost, Roy Butler, Lloyd Ingraham, Pearl Early, Johnny Bond, The Callahan Brothers and their Blue Ridge Mountain Boys.

In the small town of Pecos, Jimmy Wakely and his pals (Dennis Moore, Lee "Lasses" White) become involved in an election campaign after one of the candidates is murdered in a barroom brawl.

Running time: 55 minutes. Release date: June 2, 1945.

448. Trouble Chasers (comedy) Directed by Lew Landers. Produced by Sam Katzman and Jack Dietz. Original story and screenplay by George Plympton and Ande Lamb. A Banner Production.

Cast: Billy Gilbert, Shemp Howard, Maxie Rosenbloom, Patsy Moran, Wheeler Oakman, I. Stanford Jolley.

A pair of gangsters (Wheeler Oakman, I. Stanford Jolley) think that three goofs (Billy Gilbert, Shemp Howard, Maxie Rosenbloom) know the whereabouts of a stolen necklace.

Running time: 63 minutes. Release date: June 2, 1945.

Working title: **Here Comes Trouble.**

449. Flame of the West (western) Directed by Lambert Hillyer. Produced by Scott R. Dunlap. Screenplay by Adele Buffington. Story by Bennett Foster.

Cast: Johnny Mack Brown, Raymond Hatton, Joan Woodbury, Douglas Dumbrille, Lynne Carver, Harry Woods, Riley Hill, Jack Ingram, John Merton, Tom Quinn, Jack Rockwell, Ted Mapes, Bob Duncan, Pierce Lyden, Frank McCarroll, Raphael Bennett, Steve Clark, Bud Osborne, Hal Price, Bob Cason, Eddie Parker, Horace B. Carpenter, Pee Wee King and his Golden West Cowboys.

A peace-loving doctor (Johnny Mack Brown) settles in a small western town; when his friend the marshal (Douglas Dumbrille) is killed, the doctor undertakes the responsibility of ridding the town of its vicious elements.

Running time: 70 minutes. Release date: June 25, 1945.

450. Mr. Muggs Rides Again (comedy) Directed by Wallace Fox. Produced by Sam Katzman and Jack Dietz. Original story and screenplay by Harvey H. Gates. A Banner Production.

Cast: Leo Gorcey, Huntz Hall, Billy Benedict, Nancy Brinkman, Bernard B. Brown, George Meeker, Minerva Urecal, Pierre Watkin, Johnny Duncan, Mendie Koenig, Bud Gorman, John H. Allen, Milton Kibbee, Frank Jaquet, Bernard Gorcey, I. Stanford Jolley, Michael Owen, Betty Sinclair.

The East Side Kids (Leo Gorcey, Huntz Hall, Billy Benedict, Johnny Duncan, Mendie Koenig, Bud Gorman) nurse an ailing thoroughbred back to health and enter her in a big race.

Running time: 63 minutes. Release date: July 15, 1945.

451. Saddle Serenade (western) Produced and directed by Oliver Drake. Screenplay by Frances Kavanaugh.

Cast: Jimmy Wakely, Lee "Lasses" White, Johnny James, Nancy Brinkman, Alan Foster, Jack Ingram, Jack Spears, Carl Mathews, Jack Hendricks, Frank McCarroll, Al Sloey, Jimmie Dean, Pat Gleason, Roy Butler, Kay Deslys, Elmer Napier, Johnny Paul, Claire James, Bob Duncan, Dee Cooper, Foy Willing and his Riders of the Purple Sage.

Jimmy Wakely and his pals (Lee "Lasses" White, Johnny James) try to find out why a make-believe stagecoach holdup--arranged for the entertainment of some dude ranchers--resulted in the death of one of the participants.

Running time: 57 minutes. Release date: August 11, 1945.

452. Divorce (drama) Directed by William Nigh. Produced by Jeffrey Bernerd and Kay Francis. Screenplay by Sidney Sutherland and Harvey H. Gates. Original story by Harvey H. Gates.

Cast: Kay Francis, Bruce Cabot, Helen Mack, Jerome Cowan, Craig Reynolds, Ruth Lee, Jean Fenwick, Mary Gordon, Larry Olsen, Johnny Calkins, Jonathan Hale, Addison Richards, Reed Kilpatrick, Virginia Ware.

A woman (Kay Francis) who has been married and divorced five times returns to her old home town, where she wrecks the marriage of her childhood sweetheart (Bruce Cabot).

Running time: 71 minutes. Release date: August 18, 1945.

453. South of the Rio Grande (western) Directed by Lambert Hillyer. Produced by Philip N. Krasne. Screenplay by Victor Hammond and Ralph Bettinson. Story by Johnston McCulley. Based on the characters created by O. Henry (William Sydney Porter).

Cast: Duncan Renaldo, Martin Garralaga, Armida, George J. Lewis, Lillian Molieri, Francis McDonald, Charles Stevens, Pedro Regas, Soledad Jiminez, Tito Renaldo, The Guadalajara Trio.

The Cisco Kid (Duncan Renaldo) goes after a dishonest Mexican official (George J. Lewis) who is burning down the homes of the landlords and taking their land, after falsely accusing the owners of cattle rustling.

Running time: 62 minutes. Release date: September 8, 1945.

454. Riders of the Dawn (western) Produced and directed by Oliver Drake. Screenplay by Louise Rousseau.

Cast: Jimmy Wakely, Lee "Lasses" White, Johnny James, Phyllis Adair, Sarah Padden, Horace Murphy, Jack Baxley, Bob Shelton, Dad Pickard, Arthur (Fiddlin') Smith, Eddie Taylor, Brooks Temple, Bill Hammond, Michael Joseph Ward, Wesley Tuttle and his Texas Stars.

Jimmy Wakely befriends a child (Michael Joseph Ward) whose parents have been poisoned; Jimmy discovers that the crime was committed by the child's guardian (Jack Baxley), a doctor who is aware that the child is heir to some oil-rich property.

Running time: 58 minutes. Release date: September 22, 1945.

455. Come Out Fighting (comedy) Directed by William Beaudine. Produced by Sam Katzman and Jack Dietz. Original story and screenplay by Earle Snell. A Banner Production.

Cast: Leo Gorcey, Huntz Hall, Billy Benedict, Gabriel Dell, June Carlson, Amelita Ward, Addison Richards, George Meeker, Johnny Duncan, Fred Kelsey, Mendie Koenig, Bud Gorman, Douglas Wood, Milton Kibbee, Pat Gleason, Robert Homans, Patsy Moran, Alan Foster, Davidson Clark, Meyer Grace, Betty Sinclair.

The East Side Kids (Leo Gorcey, Huntz Hall, Billy Benedict, Gabriel Dell, Mendie Koenig, Bud Gorman) try to make a man of the police commissioner's dandy son (Johnny Duncan).

Running time: 62 min. Release date: Sept. 29, 1945.

456. The Shanghai Cobra (mystery) Directed by Phil Karlson. Produced by James S. Burkett. Screenplay by George Callahan and George Wallace Sayre. Story by George Callahan. Based on the character "Charlie Chan" created by Earl Derr Biggers.

Cast: Sidney Toler, Benson Fong, Mantan Moreland, Joan Barclay, Walter Fenner, James Cardwell, James Flavin, Addison Richards, Arthur Loft, Gene Stutenroth (Roth), Joe Devlin, Roy Gordon, Janet Warren, George Chandler, William Ruhl.

Charlie Chan (Sidney Toler) thwarts a plot to steal a quantity of radium stored in a bank vault.

Running time: 64 minutes. Release date: September 29, 1945.

457. Sensation Hunters (drama) Directed by Christy Cabanne. Produced by Joseph Kaufman. Screenplay by Dennis Cooper.

Cast: Robert Lowery, Doris Merrick, Eddie Quillan, Constance Worth, Isabel Jewell, Wanda McKay, Nestor Paiva, Byron Foulger, Vince Barnett, Minerva Urecal.

A sweet and wholesome young woman (Doris Merrick), seeking escape from sordid family surroundings, falls in love with a scoundrel (Robert Lowery) who leads her to ruin.

Running time: 62 minutes. Release date: October 13, 1945.
Working titles: **Party Girl** and **Main Street Girl.** Also known as **Club Paradise.**

458. The Lost Trail (western) Directed by Lambert Hillyer. Produced by Charles J. Bigelow. Original screenplay by Jess Bowers (Adele Buffington).

Cast: Johnny Mack Brown, Raymond Hatton, Jennifer Holt, Kenneth MacDonald, Riley Hill, Lynton Brent, John Ince, John Bridges, Eddie Parker, Frank McCarroll, Dick Dickinson, Milburn Morante, Frank LaRue, Steve Clark, George Morrell, Carl Mathews, Victor Cox, Cal Shrum and his Rhythm Rangers.

U.S. Marshals Nevada (Johnny Mack Brown) and Sandy (Raymond Hatton) go to the aid of a young woman (Jennifer Holt) who is attempting to operate a stagecoach line after her father is killed by bandits.

Running time: 53 minutes. Release date: October 20, 1945.

459. Frontier Feud (western) Directed by Lambert Hillyer. Produced by Charles J. Bigelow. Screenplay by Jess Bowers (Adele Buffington). Story by Charles N. Heckelmann.

Cast: Johnny Mack Brown, Raymond Hatton, Christine McIntyre, Dennis Moore, Jack Ingram, Eddie Parker, Frank LaRue, Steve Clark, Jack Rockwell, Mary MacLaren, Edmund Cobb, Lloyd Ingraham, Ted Mapes, Stanley Price, Terry Frost, Dan White, Ray Jones, Charles King, Lynton Brent.

After her father is murdered by a cattle rustler, a young woman (Christine McIntyre) appeals to a U.S. Marshal (Johnny Mack Brown) for help.

Running time: 54 minutes. Release date: November 24, 1945.

460. Lonesome Trail (western) Produced and directed by Oliver Drake. Screenplay by Louise Rousseau. Original story by Oliver Drake.

Cast: Jimmy Wakely, Lee "Lasses" White, Lorraine Miller, Iris Clive, Johnny James, Horace Murphy, Eddie

Majors, Zon Murray, Roy Butler, Jasper Palmer, Frank McCarroll, Jack Rivers, Tom Smith, The Sunshine Girls, Arthur (Fiddlin') Smith, The Saddle Pals.

Jimmy Wakely clashes with an unscrupulous gang who are selling land to settlers, claiming it contains valuable mineral deposits.

Running time: 57 minutes. Release date: December 8, 1945.

461. Sunbonnet Sue (musical) Directed by Ralph Murphy. Produced by Scott R. Dunlap. Screenplay by Ralph Murphy and Richard A. Carroll. Story by Paul Gerard and Bradford Ropes.

Cast: Gale Storm, Phil Regan, George Cleveland, Alan Mowbray, Minna Gombell, Raymond Hatton, Charles Judels, Billy Green, Charles D. Brown, Edna M. Holland, Gerald O. Smith, Jerry Franks.

In the Gay 90s, a pedigree-minded society woman (Minna Gombell) tries to stop her niece (Gale Storm) from singing and dancing in a Bowery saloon.

Running time: 89 minutes. Release date: December 8, 1945.

Working title: **Belle of the Bowery.**

462. Black Market Babies (drama) Directed by William Beaudine. Produced by Jeffrey Bernerd. Screenplay by George Wallace Sayre. Original story by George Morris.

Cast: Ralph Morgan, Kane Richmond, Teala Loring, Marjorie Hoshelle, George Meeker, Jayne Hazard, Dewey Robinson, Alan Foster, Selmer Jackson, Nana Bryant, Maris Wrixon, John Gallaudet, Addison Richards, Parker Gee, Terry Frost.

An alcoholic doctor (Ralph Morgan) and a two-bit racketeer (Kane Richmond) join forces and set up a maternity home whose facilities are extended free to expectant mothers, with the proviso that the women will sign away all rights to their children.

Running time: 71 minutes. Release date: December 15, 1945.

463. Allotment Wives (drama) Directed by William

Kay Francis (right) consoles Teala Loring in "Allotment Wives" (1945), the second of three pictures Francis made for Monogram.

Nigh. Produced by Jeffrey Bernerd and Kay Francis. Screenplay by Harvey H. Gates and Sidney Sutherland. Original story by Sidney Sutherland.

Cast: Kay Francis, Paul Kelly, Otto Kruger, Gertrude Michael, Teala Loring, Bernard Nedell, Matty Fain, Anthony Warde, Jonathan Hale, Selmer Jackson, Evelyn (Evelynne) Eaton, Pierre Watkin, Marcelle Corday.

An army officer (Paul Kelly) is sent to the Pacific Coast to investigate the bigamy racket of women who marry soldiers and sailors for their allotment checks; he discovers that the leader of the syndicate is a prominent society woman (Kay Francis).

Running time: 80 minutes. Release date: December 29, 1945.

Also known as **Allotment Wives, Inc.,** and **Woman in the Case.**

1946

464. Border Bandits (western) Directed by Lambert Hillyer. Produced by Charles J. Bigelow. Screenplay by Frank H. Young.

Cast: Johnny Mack Brown, Raymond Hatton, Riley Hill, Rosa del Rosario, John Merton, Tom Quinn, Frank LaRue, Steve Clark, Charles Stevens, Lucio Villegas, Bud Osborne, Pat R. McGee, I. Stanford Jolley, Ray Jones, Terry Frost, Julia Vilirea.

The owner of a large hacienda is robbed of some valuable jewels; his granddaughter (Rosa del Rosario) prevails upon two U.S. Marshals (Johnny Mack Brown, Raymond Hatton) to join in the search for the thieves.

Running time: 58 minutes. Release date: January 12, 1946.

465. Live Wires (comedy) Directed by Phil Karlson. Produced by Lindsley Parsons and Jan Grippo. Screenplay by Tim Ryan and Joseph Mischel. Based on an original story by Jeb (Dore) Schary.

Cast: Leo Gorcey, Huntz Hall, Bobby Jordan, Billy Benedict, William Frambes, Pamela Blake, Claudia Drake, Mike Mazurki, Patti Brill, John Eldredge, Pat Gleason, William Ruhl, Rodney Bell, Bernard Gorcey, Frank Marlowe, Gladys Blake, Bill Christy, Nancy Brinkman, Robert Emmett Keane, Earle Hodgins, George Eldredge, Eddie Borden, Charlie Sullivan, Henry Russell, John Indrisano, Steve Taylor, Beverly Hawthorne, Jack Chefe, Malcolm McClean.

Slip Mahoney (Leo Gorcey), the hot-tempered leader of the Bowery Boys, lands a job as a process server and becomes involved with gangsters.
Running time: 64 minutes. Release date: January 12, 1946.
A remake of **He Couldn't Take It** (Monogram, 1933) and **Here Comes Kelly** (Monogram, 1943).

466. The Strange Mr. Gregory (mystery) Directed by Phil Rosen. Produced by Louis Berkoff. Screenplay by Charles S. Belden. Story by Myles Connolly.
Cast: Edmund Lowe, Jean Rogers, Don Douglas, Frank Reicher, Marjorie Hoshelle, Robert Emmett Keane, Jonathan Hale, Frank Mayo, Fred Kelsey, Jack Norton, Anita Turner, Tom Leffingwell.
A theatrical magician (Edmund Lowe) who dabbles in psychic matters falls in love with a married woman (Jean Rogers); he arranges a phony murder, making it appear that he is the victim and the woman's husband (Don Douglas) the killer.
Running time: 63 minutes. Release date: January 12, 1946.

467. The Face of Marble (horror) Directed by William Beaudine. Produced by Jeffrey Bernerd. Screenplay by Michael Jacoby. Original story by William Thiele and Edmund Hartman.
Cast: John Carradine, Claudia Drake, Robert Shayne, Maris Wrixon, Willie Best, Thomas E. Jackson, Rosa Rey, Neal Burns, Donald Kerr, Allan Ray.
A brain surgeon (John Carradine) and his assistant (Robert Shayne) conduct life-rejuvenating experiments on recently deceased persons. In trying to restore life, the doctor succeeds in a sort of death-in-life, a state in which the victim, deranged and disembodied, is capable only of violence and evil.
Running time: 72 min. Release date: Jan. 19, 1946.

468. Drifting Along (western) Directed by Derwin M. Abrahams. Produced by Scott R. Dunlap. Screenplay by Adele Buffington.

Robert Shayne and John Carradine examine one of their experimental victims in "The Face of Marble" (1946).

Cast: Johnny Mack Brown, Raymond Hatton, Lynne Carver, Douglas Fowley, Smith Ballew, Milburn Morante, Thornton Edwards, Steve Clark, Marshall Reed, Jack Rockwell, Lynton Brent, Terry Frost, Leonard St. Leo, Ted Mapes, Curt Barrett and the Trailsmen.

U.S. Marshals Nevada (Johnny Mack Brown) and Sandy (Raymond Hatton) help a young woman (Lynne Carver) fight an unscrupulous gang resorting to murder and cattle rustling in an attempt to get a valuable ranch away from her.

Running time: 60 minutes. Release date: January 26, 1946.

469. The Red Dragon (mystery) Directed by Phil Rosen. Produced by James S. Burkett. Original screenplay by George Callahan. Based on the character "Charlie Chan" created by Earl Derr Biggers.

Cast: Sidney Toler, Benson Fong, Willie Best, Fortunio Bonanova, Robert Emmett Keane, Carol Hughes, Marjorie Hoshelle, Barton Yarborough, George Meeker, Don Costello, Charles Trowbridge, Mildred Boyd, Jean Wong, Donald Dexter Taylor.

Charlie Chan (Sidney Toler) journeys to Mexico City, where people interested in an atomic bomb secret are being murdered by mysterious means while attempting to obtain possession of it.

Running time: 64 minutes. Release date: February 2, 1946.

Working title: **Charlie Chan in Mexico.**

470. Moon Over Montana (western) Produced and directed by Oliver Drake. Screenplay by Earle Snell and Betty Burbridge. Original story by Norman Sheldon.

Cast: Jimmy Wakely, Lee "Lasses" White, Jennifer Holt, Terry Frost, Jack Ingram, Jesse Ashlock, Jack Rivers, Woody Woodell and his Riding Rangers, Kenne Duncan, Arthur (Fiddlin') Smith, Art Mix, Ray Jones, Eddie Majors, Brad Slavin, Stanley Blystone, Louise Arthur, John Elliott, Bob Duncan, Denver Dixon (Victor Adamson).

A young woman (Jennifer Holt) owns a small branch railroad used for transporting cattle to the market; a cowboy (Jimmy Wakely) comes to her aid when crooks try to gain control of the railroad.

Running time: 56 minutes. Release date: February 16, 1946.

471. The Shadow Returns (mystery) Directed by Phil Rosen. Produced by Joe Kaufman. Screenplay by George Callahan. Based on the "Shadow" stories by Maxwell Grant (Walter B. Gibson).

Cast: Kane Richmond, Barbara Reed, Tom Dugan, Joseph Crehan, Pierre Watkin, Robert Emmett Keane, Frank Reicher, Lester Dorr, Rebel Randall, Emmett Vogan, Sherry Hall, Cyril Delevanti.

Super-sleuth Lamont Cranston (Kane Richmond), alias "The Shadow," investigates the theft of jewels spirited from an open grave.

Running time: 61 min. Release date: Feb. 16, 1946.

472. Fear (mystery-drama) Directed by Alfred Zeisler. Produced by Lindsley Parsons. Original screenplay by Alfred Zeisler and Dennis Cooper (the scenario was heavily influenced by Dostoyevski's novel "Crime and Punishment").

Cast: Warren William, Anne Gwynne, Peter Cookson, James Cardwell, Nestor Paiva, Francis Pierlot, William Moss, Almira Sessions, Darren McGavin, Henry Clay, Ernie Adams, Johnny Strong, Charles Calvert, Fairfax Burger.

A medical student (Peter Cookson) is driven by poverty to the murder-for-money of a loan shark (Francis Pierlot), only to be haunted by the deed. A detective (Warren William) plays upon the young man's guilt feelings, hoping to get him to confess.

Running time: 68 minutes. Release date: March 2, 1946.

473. The Haunted Mine (western) Directed by Derwin M. Abrahams. Produced by Charles J. Bigelow. Screenplay by Frank H. Young.

Cast: Johnny Mack Brown, Raymond Hatton, Linda Johnson, Ray Bennett, Riley Hill, Claire Whitney, John Merton, Marshall Reed, Terry Frost, Lynton Brent, Leonard St. Leo, Frank LaRue, Ray Jones.

Two U.S. Marshals (Johnny Mack Brown, Raymond Hatton) step in when a gang of landgrabbers try to rob a widow of her gold mine.

Running time: 51 minutes. Release date: March 2, 1946.

474. Swing Parade of 1946 (musical-comedy) Directed by Phil Karlson. Produced by Lindsley Parsons and Harry A. Romm. Screenplay by Tim Ryan. Story by Edmond Kelso. Additional dialogue by Nicholas Ray.

Cast: Gale Storm, Phil Regan, The Three Stooges (Moe Howard, Larry Fine, Jerry "Curly" Howard), Connee Boswell, Ed Brophy, Mary Treen, John Eldredge, Russell Hicks, Leon Belasco, Windy Cook, Jack Boyle, Will Osborne and His Orchestra, Louis Jordan and his Tympany Five, Emmett Vogan, Dewey Robinson.

An aspiring singer (Gale Storm), a bandleader (Phil

The Three Stooges (from bottom: Jerry "Curly" Howard, Moe Howard, Larry Fine) in "Swing Parade of 1946."

Regan) and three zany waiters (The Three Stooges) help save a nightclub from going out of business.

Running time: 74 minutes. Release date: March 16, 1946.

475. The Gay Cavalier (western) Directed by William

Nigh. Produced by Scott R. Dunlap. Original screenplay by Charles S. Belden. Based on the characters created by O. Henry (William Sydney Porter).

Cast: Gilbert Roland, Martin Garralaga, Nacho Galindo, Ramsay Ames, Helen Gerald, Drew Allen, Tristram Coffin, Iris Flores, Gabriel Peralta, Pierre Andre, Iris Bocigon, John Merton, Frank LaRue, Ray Bennett, Artie Ortego.

The Cisco Kid (Gilbert Roland) has two prime goals: to rescue a maiden who is about to marry a supposedly wealthy suitor in order to save the family hacienda and to capture the outlaws who held up a stagecoach bearing gold for a mission.

Running time: 65 minutes. Release date: March 30, 1946.

476. West of the Alamo (western) Produced and directed by Oliver Drake. Screenplay by Louise Rousseau.

Cast: Jimmy Wakely, Lee "Lasses" White, Iris Clive, Jack Ingram, Red Holton, Budd Buster, Eddie Majors, Early Cantrell, Betty Lou Head, Ray Whitley, Billy Dix, Betty Majors, Jack Rivers, Ted French, Steven Keys, Ray Jones, Rudy Bowman, Arthur (Fiddlin') Smith Trio, The Saddle Pals.

Two undercover agents (Jimmy Wakely, Lee "Lasses" White) stop a crime wave launched by the town's bank president (Jack Ingram).

Running time: 58 minutes. Release date: April 20, 1946.

477. Under Arizona Skies (western) Directed by Lambert Hillyer. Produced by Scott R. Dunlap. Screenplay by J. Benton Cheney.

Cast: Johnny Mack Brown, Raymond Hatton, Reno Blair (Browne), Riley Hill, Tristram Coffin, Reed Howes, Ted Adams, Ray Bennett, Frank LaRue, Steve Clark, Jack Rockwell, Bud Geary, Ted Mapes, Kermit Maynard, Ray Jones, Smith Ballew and the Sons of the Sage.

U.S. Marshals "Dusty" Smith (Johnny Mack Brown) and Santa Fe Jones (Raymond Hatton) help prove the innocence of a rancher accused of cattle rustling.

Running time: 59 minutes. Release date: April 27, 1946.

478. Junior Prom (musical-comedy) Directed by Arthur Dreifuss. Produced by Sam Katzman. Story and screenplay by Erna Lazarus and Hal Collins.

Cast: Freddie Stewart, June Preisser, Judy Clark, Noel Neill, Jackie Moran, Frankie Darro, Warren Mills, Murray Davis, Mira Mae McKinney, Belle Mitchell, Milton Kibbee, Sam Flint, Charles Evans, Hank Henry, Abe Lyman and His Orchestra, Eddie Heywood and His Orchestra, Harry "The Hipster" Gibson, The Airliners.

A high school lad (Freddie Stewart), one of the "Teen Agers" gang, campaigns for student body president of Whitney High, but the father of another candidate threatens to withhold his annual donation unless his son wins the election.

Running time: 69 minutes. Release date: May 11, 1946.

479. Behind the Mask (mystery) Directed by Phil Karlson. Produced by Joe Kaufman. Screenplay by George Callahan. Story by Arthur Hoerl. Based on the "Shadow" stories by Maxwell Grant (Walter B. Gibson).

Cast: Kane Richmond, Barbara Reed, George Chandler, Dorothea Kent, Joseph Crehan, Pierre Watkin, Robert Shayne, June Clyde, James Cardwell, Marjorie Hoshelle, Joyce Compton, Edward Gargan, Lou Crosby, Bill Christy, Nancy Brinkman, Dewey Robinson, Jean Carlin, Alura Stevens, Christine McIntyre, Marie Harmon, Ruth Cherrington, James Nataro.

Amateur sleuth Lamont Cranston (Kane Richmond), alias "The Shadow," is called upon to solve the murder of a blackmailing columnist (Robert Shayne).

Running time: 67 min. Release date: May 25, 1946.

Also known as **The Shadow Behind the Mask.**

480. Dark Alibi (mystery) Directed by Phil Karlson. Produced by James S. Burkett. Story and screenplay by George Callahan. Based on the character "Charlie Chan" created by Earl Derr Biggers.

213

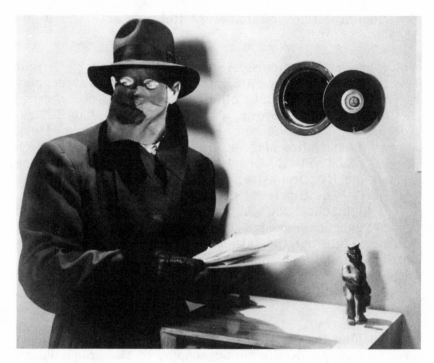

Kane Richmond as "The Shadow" in "Behind the Mask" (1946).

Cast: Sidney Toler, Benson Fong, Mantan Moreland, Teala Loring, George Holmes, Edward Earle, Ben Carter, Joyce Compton, Janet Shaw, Edna Holland, John Eldredge, William Ruhl, Milton Parsons, Ray Walker, Russell Hicks, Anthony Warde, Tim Ryan, Frank Marlowe, George Eldredge.

Three men are convicted of a bank robbery on the strength of fingerprints found at the scene of the crime. Charlie Chan (Sidney Toler), believing these men innocent, investigates and discovers that others have forged the fingerprints and planted them there, using prison files for that purpose.

Running time: 61 minutes. Release date: May 25, 1946.

Working titles: **Charlie Chan in Alcatraz** and **Fatal Fingertips.**

A poster for "Joe Palooka, Champ" (1946), the first in a series of Monogram features based on the Ham Fisher comic strip "Joe Palooka."

481. Joe Palooka, Champ (comedy-drama) Directed by Reginald LeBorg. Produced by Hal E. Chester. Screenplay by Cyril Endfield and Albert DePina. Original story by Hal E. Chester. Based on the "Joe Palooka" comic strip by Ham Fisher.

Cast: Leon Errol, Elyse Knox, Joe Kirkwood, Jr., Eduardo Cianelli, Joe Sawyer, Elisha Cook, Jr., Sam McDaniel, Robert Kent, Sarah Padden, Michael Mark, Lou Nova, Russ Vincent, Alexander Laszlo, Carole Dunne, Carol Hughes, Betty Blythe, Phil Van Zandt, Jimmy Mc-Larnin, Joe Louis, Henry Armstrong, Manuel Ortiz.

After gangsters take away his championship fighter, boxing manager Knobby Walsh (Leon Errol) discovers a young man named Joe Palooka (Joe Kirkwood, Jr.) working at a gas station and develops him into a contender.

Running time: 70 minutes. Release date: May 28, 1946.

482. The Gentleman from Texas (western) Directed by Lambert Hillyer. Produced by Scott R. Dunlap. Screenplay by J. Benton Cheney.

Cast: Johnny Mack Brown, Raymond Hatton, Claudia Drake, Reno Blair (Browne), Christine McIntyre, Curt Barrett and the Trailsmen, Tristram Coffin, Marshall Reed, Terry Frost, Jack Rockwell, Steve Clark, Pierce Lyden, Wally West, Artie Ortego, Bill Wolfe, Ted Adams, Lynton Brent, Frank LaRue.

A Wells Fargo agent (Johnny Mack Brown) is sent to the small western town of Rimrock to stop stagecoach holdups being perpetrated by a saloon owner and his henchmen.

Running time: 55 minutes. Release date: June 8, 1946.

Working title: **The Fighting Texan.**

483. South of Monterey (western) Directed by William Nigh. Produced by Scott R. Dunlap. Screenplay by Charles S. Belden. Based on the characters created by O. Henry (William Sydney Porter).

Cast: Gilbert Roland, Martin Garralaga, Frank Yaconelli, Marjorie Riordan, Iris Flores, George J. Lewis, Harry Woods, Terry Frost, Wheaton Chambers, Rosa Turich.

The Cisco Kid (Gilbert Roland) sets out to stop a land-swindling scheme devised by the police captain and the tax collector in a small western town.

Running time: 63 minutes. Release date: June 15, 1946.

484. Suspense (mystery) Directed by Frank Tuttle. Produced by Maurice and Frank King. Original screenplay by Philip Yordan.

Cast: Belita, Barry Sullivan, Bonita Granville, Albert Dekker, Eugene Pallette, George E. Stone, Edith Angold, Leon Belasco, Miguelito Valdes, Bobby Ramos and His Band.

When an ambitious heel (Barry Sullivan) begins romancing a successful ice-skating star (Belita), her husband (Albert Dekker) plots his murder.
Running time: 101 minutes. Release date: June 15, 1946.

485. Don't Gamble with Strangers (drama) Directed by William Beaudine. Produced by Jeffrey Bernerd. Screenplay by Caryl Coleman and Harvey H. Gates.

Cast: Kane Richmond, Bernadene Hayes, Peter Cookson, Gloria Warren, Charles Trowbridge, Frank Dae, Anthony Caruso, Phil Van Zandt, Harold Goodwin, Leonard Mudie, Bill Kennedy, Addison Richards, Ferris Taylor, Mary Field, Edith Evanson, Steve Darrell, Robert Barron, Sayre Dearing.

Two card sharks (Kane Richmond, Bernadene Hayes), posing as brother and sister, fleece a small-town banker and take over a gambling joint.
Running time: 68 minutes. Release date: June 22, 1946.

486. In Fast Company (comedy) Directed by Del Lord. Produced by Lindsley Parsons and Jan Grippo. Screenplay by Edmond Seward, Tim Ryan, Victor Hammond and Ray Schrock. Story by Martin Mooney.

Cast: Leo Gorcey, Huntz Hall, Bobby Jordan, Billy Benedict, Judy Clark, Jane Randolph, David Gorcey, Douglas Fowley, Charles D. Brown, Paul Harvey, Marjorie Woodworth, Frank Marlowe, Dick Wessel, William Ruhl, Luis Alberni, Mary Gordon, Bernard Gorcey, Judy Schenz, George Eldredge, Stanley Price, Marcel de la Brosse, Lee Phelps, Walter Soderling, Jack Cheatham, Fred Aldrich, Mike Pat Donovan, John Indrisano.

The Bowery Boys (Leo Gorcey, Huntz Hall, Bobby Jordan, Billy Benedict, David Gorcey) become involved in a war between two rival taxi cab companies.
Running time: 63 minutes. Release date: June 22, 1946.
Working title: **High Gear.**

487. Freddie Steps Out (musical-comedy) Directed

217

by Arthur Dreifuss. Produced by Sam Katzman. Original screenplay by Hal Collins.

Cast: Freddie Stewart, June Preisser, Jackie Moran, Frankie Darro, Noel Neill, Ann Rooney, Warren Mills, Murray Davis, Milton Kibbee.

When a radio singer disappears, the "Teen Agers" gang try to pass Freddie (Freddie Stewart) off as the missing vocalist.

Running time: 75 minutes. Release date: June 29, 1946.

Working title: **Sweet Sixteen.**

488. Trail to Mexico (western) Produced and directed by Oliver Drake. Screenplay by Oliver Drake.

Cast: Jimmy Wakely, Lee "Lasses" White, Delores Castelli, Julian Rivero, Terry Frost, Forrest Matthews, Jonathan McCall, Alex Montoya, Dora Del Rio, Juan Duval, Jack Rivers, Don Weston, Arthur (Fiddlin') Smith, Brad Slavin, Cactus Mack, Wheaton Chambers, Dee Cooper, Billy Dix, The Saddle Pals, The Guadalajara Trio.

A stagecoach driver (Jimmy Wakely) joins a gang of outlaws in order to find out who's been hijacking gold shipments.

Running time: 56 minutes. Release date: June 29, 1946.

489. Strange Voyage (drama) Directed by Irving Allen. Produced by Louis B. Appleton, Jr. Screenplay by Andrew Holt. A Signal Pictures presentation (the joint venture of a group of ex-servicemen).

Cast: Eddie Albert, Forrest Taylor, Ray Teal, Matt Willis, Martin Garralaga, Elena Verdugo, Bobby Cooper, Clyde Fillmore, Daniel Kerry, Henry Orosco.

A group of men go on a treasure-hunting cruise, only to run into difficulties from the elements and each other.

Running time: 80 minutes. Release date: July 6, 1946.

490. Bowery Bombshell (comedy) Directed by Phil Karlson. Produced by Jan Grippo. Screenplay by Edmond

Seward. Story by Edmond Seward and Victor Hammond. Additional dialogue by Tim Ryan.

Cast: Leo Gorcey, Huntz Hall, Bobby Jordan, Billy Benedict, David Gorcey, Teala Loring, Sheldon Leonard, Dawn Kennedy, James Burke, Vince Barnett, Emmett Vogan, William Newell, Milton Parsons, Bernard Gorcey, William "Wee Willie" Davis, Lester Dorr, William Ruhl, Eddie Dunn, Bud Gorman.

When Sach (Huntz Hall) is mistaken for a bank robber, the Bowery Boys set out to trap the real culprits.

Running time: 65 minutes. Release date: July 20, 1946.

491. Shadows Over Chinatown (mystery) Directed by Terry Morse. Produced by James S. Burkett. Original screenplay by Raymond Schrock. Based on the character "Charlie Chan" created by Earl Derr Biggers.

Cast: Sidney Toler, Mantan Moreland, Victor Sen Yung, Tanis Chandler, John Gallaudet, Paul Bryar, Bruce Kellogg, Alan Bridge, Mary Gordon, Dorothy Granger, Jack Norton, Charles Jordan.

In San Francisco's Chinatown, detective Charlie Chan (Sidney Toler) uncovers a murder ring which has been collecting life insurance on its victims.

Running time: 64 minutes. Release date: July 27, 1946.

Working title: **The Mandarin Secret.**

492. Below the Deadline (drama) Directed by William Beaudine. Produced by Lindsley Parsons. Screenplay by Harvey H. Gates and Forrest Judd. Original story by Ivan Tors.

Cast: Warren Douglas, Ramsay Ames, Jan Wiley, Paul Maxey, Phil Van Zandt, John Harmon, Bruce Edwards, George Meeker, Clancy Cooper, Cay Forester, Alan Bridge, George Eldredge, William Ruhl.

After the death of his brother (George Meeker), who was a bigshot gambler, an embittered war veteran (Warren Douglas) follows in his sibling's footsteps, determined to parlay a fortune to make up for his years in the service.

Running time: 65 minutes. Release date: August 3, 1946.

493. The Missing Lady (mystery) Directed by Phil Karlson. Produced by Joe Kaufman. Original screenplay by George Callahan. Based on the "Shadow" stories by Maxwell Grant (Walter B. Gibson).

Cast: Kane Richmond, Barbara Reed, George Chandler, James Flavin, Pierre Watkin, Dorothea Kent, Jack Overman, George Lewis, James Cardwell, Bert Roach, Cary Owen, Ray Teal, Jo Carroll Dennison, Ralph Dunn, Dewey Robinson.

Amateur sleuth Lamont Cranston (Kane Richmond), "The Shadow," solves a series of mysterious killings which are linked together by a valuable jade statuette of Kwan Yin, the Chinese Goddess of Mercy.

Running time: 60 minutes. Release date: August 17, 1946.

Also known as **The Shadow and the Missing Lady.**

494. Spook Busters (comedy) Directed by William Beaudine. Produced by Jan Grippo. Screenplay by Edmond Seward and Tim Ryan.

Cast: Leo Gorcey, Huntz Hall, Bobby Jordan, Douglass Dumbrille, Gabriel Dell, Billy Benedict, David Gorcey, Tanis Chandler, Bernard Gorcey, Maurice Cass, Vera Lewis, Charles Middleton, Chester Clute, Richard Alexander, Charles Millfield, Arthur Miles, Tom Coleman.

The Bowery Boys (Leo Gorcey, Huntz Hall, Bobby Jordan, Billy Benedict, David Gorcey), recent exterminating school graduates, go out on their first assignment, which turns out to be an old deserted mansion where a mad scientist (Douglass Dumbrille) is conducting brain-transplant experiments.

Running time: 68 minutes. Release date: August 24, 1946.

495. High School Hero (musical comedy) Directed by Arthur Dreifuss. Produced by Sam Katzman. Screenplay by Hal Collins and Arthur Dreifuss.

Cast: Freddie Stewart, June Preisser, Noel Neill,

Ann Rooney, Jackie Moran, Frankie Darro, Warren Mills, Milton Kibbee, Belle Mitchell, Douglas Fowley, Edythe Elliott, Leonard Penn, Pierre Watkin, Dick Elliott, Joe DeRita, Freddie Slack and His Orchestra, Jan Savitt and His Orchestra featuring Isabelita.

The "Teen Agers" gang (Freddie Stewart, June Preisser, Ann Rooney, Noel Neill, Jackie Moran, Frankie Darro, Warren Mills) at Whitney High have three major concerns: to win a big football game, to boost the circulation of the school paper, and to make their student show a success.

Running time: 69 minutes. Release date: September 7, 1946.

496. Decoy (mystery-drama) Directed by Jack Bernhard. Produced by Jack Bernhard and Bernard Brandt. Screenplay by Ned Young. Original story by Stanley Rubin.

Cast: Jean Gillie, Edward Norris, Robert Armstrong, Herbert Rudley, Sheldon Leonard, Marjorie Woodworth, Phil Van Zandt, Carole Dunne, John Shay, Bert Roach, Rosemary Bertrand.

A ruthless gun moll (Jean Gillie) resorts to murder to uncover the whereabouts of some buried holdup loot.

Running time: 76 minutes. Release date: September 14, 1946.

497. Trigger Fingers (western) Directed by Lambert Hillyer. Produced by Charles J. Bigelow. Screenplay by Frank H. Young.

Cast: Johnny Mack Brown, Raymond Hatton, Jennifer Holt, Riley Hill, Steve Clark, Eddie Parker, Pierce Lyden, Ted Adams, Cactus Mack, Edward Cassidy, Ray Jones, George Morrell, Frank McCarroll.

A U.S. Marshal (Johnny Mack Brown) protects a blacksmith's son (Riley Hill) from an outlaw gang trying to frame the youth on a murder charge.

Running time: 56 min. Release date: Sept. 21, 1946.

498. Gentleman Joe Palooka (comedy-drama) Directed by Cyril Endfield. Produced by Hal E. Chester. Screenplay by Cyril Endfield. Based on the "Joe Palooka" comic strip by Ham Fisher.

Cast: Leon Errol, Joe Kirkwood, Jr., Elyse Knox, Guy Kibbee, Lionel Stander, H.B. Warner, Stanley Prager, Richard Lane, Warren Hymer, Cliff Nazarro, Fritz Feld.

Two state senators, anxious to obtain oil-rich land, use boxer Joe Palooka (Joe Kirkwood, Jr.) in a publicity campaign to get the land transferred to the state, supposedly for a park.

Running time: 72 minutes. Release date: October 5, 1946.

499. Dangerous Money (mystery) Directed by Terry Morse. Produced by James S. Burkett. Screenplay by Miriam Kissinger. Based on the character "Charlie Chan" created by Earl Derr Biggers.

Cast: Sidney Toler, Victor Sen Yung, Willie Best, Joseph Crehan, Dick Elliott, Elaine Lange, Amira Moustafa, Gloria Warren, Joe Allen, Jr., Rick Vallin, Bruce Edwards, Emmett Vogan, John Harmon, Alan Douglas, Leslie Denison, Dudley Dickerson, Tristram Coffin, Rito Punay, Selmer Jackson.

An agent of the U.S. Treasury Department, who is investigating a transfer of stolen currency and art works from the Philippines, enlists the aid of detective Charlie Chan (Sidney Toler) while aboard a ship bound for Samoa. During the voyage, the agent is murdered and several passengers are suspected of the crime.

Running time: 66 minutes. Release date: October 12, 1946.

500. Shadows on the Range (western) Directed by Lambert Hillyer. Produced by Scott R. Dunlap. Screenplay by Jess Bowers (Adele Buffington).

Cast: Johnny Mack Brown, Raymond Hatton, Jan Bryant, Marshall Reed, John Merton, Jack Perrin, Steve Clark, Terry Frost, Cactus Mack, Pierce Lyden, Ted Adams, Lane Bradford.

Steve Mason (Johnny Mack Brown), a representative of the Cattleman's Association, comes to the aid of a young woman (Jan Bryant) when a band of cattle rustlers murder her father and try to force her off her property.

Running time: 58 min. Release date: Oct. 16, 1946.

501. Wife Wanted (drama) Directed by Phil Karlson. Produced by Jeffrey Bernerd and Kay Francis. Screenplay by Caryl Coleman and Sidney Sutherland.

Cast: Kay Francis, Paul Cavanaugh, Robert Shayne, Veda Ann Borg, Teala Loring, Edgar Hayes, John Gallaudet, Jonathan Hale, Tim Ryan, Barton Yarborough.

A movie star (Kay Francis) buys a partnership in a real estate office which, unbeknownst to her, is a front for a fraudulent matrimonial agency.

Running time: 73 minutes. Release date: November 2, 1946.

Also known as **Shadow of Blackmail.**

502. Beauty and the Bandit (western) Directed by William Nigh. Produced by Scott R. Dunlap. Screenplay by Charles S. Belden. Additional dialogue by Gilbert Roland. Based on the character created by O. Henry (William Sydney Porter).

Cast: Gilbert Roland, Martin Garralaga, Frank Yaconelli, Ramsay Ames, Vida Aldana, George J. Lewis, William Gould, Dimas Sotello, Felipe Turich, Glenn Strange, Alex Montoya, Artie Ortego.

The Cisco Kid (Gilbert Roland) meets a female bandit (Ramsay Ames) and brings out the hidden nobility in her.

Running time: 77 minutes. Release date: November 9, 1946.

Working title: **Cisco and the Angel.**

503. Mr. Hex (comedy) Directed by William Beaudine. Produced by Jan Grippo. Screenplay by Cyril Endfield. Story by Jan Grippo.

Cast: Leo Gorcey, Huntz Hall, Bobby Jordan, Gabriel Dell, Billy Benedict, David Gorcey, Gale Robbins, Ben Welden, Ian Keith, Sammy Cohen, Bernard Gorcey, William Ruhl, Danny Beck, Rita Lynn, Joe Gray, Eddie Gribbon, Gene Stutenroth (Roth), John Indrisano, Dewey Robinson, Jimmy Aubrey, Meyer Grace, Knox Manning.

Horace Debussy "Sach" Jones (Huntz Hall) is hypnotized into believing he has the strength of ten men, so the Bowery Boys turn him into a championship boxer.

Running time: 63 minutes. Release date: November 9, 1946.

504. Silver Range (western) Directed by Lambert Hillyer. Produced by Charles J. Bigelow. Original screenplay by J. Benton Cheney.

Cast: Johnny Mack Brown, Raymond Hatton, Jan Bryant, I. Stanford Jolley, Terry Frost, Eddie Parker, Ted Adams, Frank LaRue, Cactus Mack, Lane Bradford, Dee Cooper, Billy Dix, Bill Willmering, George Morrell.

A former U.S. Marshal (Johnny Mack Brown) and his partner (Raymond Hatton) expose a band of smugglers who have been bringing silver across the Mexican border illegally.

Running time: 53 minutes. Release date: November 16, 1946.

505. Bringing Up Father (comedy) Directed by Eddie Cline. Produced by Barney Gerard. Screenplay by Jerry Warner. Original story by Barney Gerard. Based on the King Features comic strip "Bringing Up Father" by George McManus.

Cast: Joe Yule, Renie Riano, George McManus, Tim Ryan, June Harrison, Wallace Chadwell, Tom Kennedy, Laura Treadwell, William Frambes, Pat Goldin, Jack Norton, Ferris Taylor, Tom Dugan, Joe Devlin, Fred Kelsey, Charles Wilson, Herbert Evans, Dick Ryan, Mike Pat Donovan, Bob Carleton, George Hickman.

Jiggs (Joe Yule) and Maggie (Renie Riano) unwittingly become involved in a crooked real estate tycoon's plot to tear down Dinty Moore's (Tim Ryan) restaurant.

Running time: 68 minutes. Release date: November 23, 1946.

506. Song of the Sierras (western) Produced and directed by Oliver Drake. Screenplay by Elmer Clifton. Original story by Oliver Drake.

Cast: Jimmy Wakely, Lee "Lasses" White, Jean Carlin, Jack Baxley, Iris Clive, Jonathan Black, Bob Duncan, Jasper Palmer, Zon Murray, Ray Jones, Budd Buster, Billy Dix, Robert Gilbert, Horace Mathews, Brad Slavin,

Jack Rivers, Wesley Tuttle and his Texas Stars, Carl Sepulveda, Jessie Ashlock, Artie Ortego, Ben Corbett, Ben Jones.

A cowboy (Jimmy Wakely) wants to sell the government a group of mustangs he has trained as race horses; however, the owner of a nearby ranch wishes the government to buy her thoroughbreds instead. The government decides to buy the winning horses of an upcoming cross-country race, so both parties prepare for the competition.

Running time: 58 minutes. Release date: November 28, 1946.

507. The Trap (mystery) Directed by Howard Bretherton. Produced by James S. Burkett. Screenplay by Miriam Kissinger. Based on the character "Charlie Chan" created by Earl Derr Biggers.

Cast: Sidney Toler, Victor Sen Yung, Mantan Moreland, Tanis Chandler, Larry Blake, Kirk Alyn, Rita Quigley, Anne Nagel, Helen Gerald, Howard Negley, Lois Austin, Barbara Jean Wong, Minerva Urecal, Margaret Brayton, Bettie Best, Jan Bryant, Walden Boyle.

When two members of a show troupe are murdered, detective Charlie Chan (Sidney Toler) is called in on the case.

Running time: 62 minutes. Release date: November 30, 1946.

Released in Great Britain as **Murder at Malibu Beach.**

508. Sweetheart of Sigma Chi (musical) Directed by Jack Bernhard. Produced by Jeffrey Bernerd. Screenplay by Michel Jacoby. Original story by George Waggner.

Cast: Elyse Knox, Phil Regan, Phil Brito, Ross Hunter, Tom Harmon, Paul Guilfoyle, Anne Gillis, Edward Brophy, Fred Colby, Alan Hale, Jr., David Holt, Marjorie Hoerner, William Beaudine, Jr., Emmett Vogan, Jr., Ruth Allen, Robert Arthur, Fred Datig, Jr., Slim Gaillard Trio, Frankie Carle and His Orchestra.

A college girl (Eylse Knox) wins the love of a campus athlete (Ross Hunter), the key man on the crew team. Professional gamblers (Paul Guilfoyle, Edward Brophy),

**Left to right: Sidney Toler (as Charlie Chan), Victor
Sen Yung and Mantan Moreland in "The Trap" (1946).
This was Toler's last film (he died in 1947); he had played
the role of Charlie Chan since 1938 (the Chan character
became the property of Monogram in 1944). Roland Winters
took over the role until the series ended in 1949.**

who have made heavy bets on the rival crew, try to blackmail the girl into using her influence to make her boyfriend throw the big rowing race.

Running time: 75 minutes. Release date: December
21, 1946.

1947

509. Ginger (drama) Directed by Oliver Drake. Produced by Lindsley Parsons. Screenplay by Oliver Drake.

Cast: Frank Albertson, Barbara Reed, Johnny Calkins, Janet Burston, Gene Collins, Lee "Lasses" White, Dick Elliott, Oliver Blake, Edythe Elliott, Wally Walker, Napoleon.

A retired boxer (Frank Albertson) is made poundmaster in a small town; his ten-year old nephew (Johnny Calkins) adopts Ginger, one of the stray dogs. When Ginger is jailed after biting the mayor (Dick Elliott), the boy engineers the dog's escape and runs away with him.

Running time: 67 minutes. Release date: January 4, 1947.

510. Riding the California Trail (western) Directed by William Nigh. Produced by Scott R. Dunlap. Story and screenplay by Clarence Upson Young. Based on the characters created by O. Henry (William Sydney Porter).

Cast: Gilbert Roland, Martin Garralaga, Frank Yaconelli, Teala Loring, Inez Cooper, Ted Hecht, Marcelle Granville, Eve Whitney, Frank Marlowe, Alex Montoya, Rosa Turich, Julia Kent, Gerald Echevirria.

The Cisco Kid (Gilbert Roland) aids a young woman (Inez Cooper) who is being tricked out of an inheritance by a scheming uncle.

Running time: 59 minutes. Release date: January 11, 1947.

511. Raiders of the South (western) Directed by Lambert Hillyer. Produced by Scott R. Dunlap. Screenplay by J. Benton Cheney.

Cast: Johnny Mack Brown, Raymond Hatton, Evelyn Brent, Reno Blair (Browne), Marshall Reed, John Hamilton, John Merton, Eddie Parker, Frank LaRue, Ted Adams, Pierce Lyden, Cactus Mack, George Morrell, Ray Jones, Artie Ortego, Curt Barrett and the Trailsmen, Billy Dix, Dee Cooper.

A former Confederate officer-turned-federal agent (Johnny Mack Brown) is assigned to obtain evidence against

227

a gang of raiders, headed by a Yankee-hating widow (Evelyn Brent), who have been making life difficult for the local carpetbaggers.

Running time: 55 minutes. Release date: January 18, 1947.

512. Vacation Days (comedy) Directed by Arthur Dreifuss. Produced by Sam Katzman. Screenplay by Hal Collins.

Cast: Freddie Stewart, June Preisser, Frankie Darro, Warren Mills, Noel Neill, Milt Kibbee, Belle Mitchell, John Hart, Hugh Prosser, Terry Frost, Edythe Elliott, Claire James, Jerry Wald and his orchestra, Spade Cooley and his orchestra, Jay Silverheels, Harold Brauer, Joe Palma.

While spending their vacation on a ranch inherited by one of their teachers, the Teen Agers gang (Freddie Stewart, June Preisser, Frankie Darro, Warren Mills, Noel Neill) become involved with a bank robbery.

Running time: 66 minutes. Release date: January 25, 1947.

513. Rainbow Over the Rockies (western) Produced and directed by Oliver Drake. Screenplay by Elmer Clifton. Original story by Oliver Drake.

Cast: Jimmy Wakely, Lee "Lasses" White, Dennis Moore, Pat Starling, Carl Sepulveda, Budd Buster, John Baxley, Zon Murray, Billy Dix, Jasper Palmer, Robert L. Gilbert, Wesley Tuttle and his Texas Stars.

A trail boss (Jimmy Wakely) exposes a conspiracy of rustlers who are instigating a range war between cattlemen and a land owner.

Running time: 54 min. Release date: Feb. 8, 1947.

514. Valley of Fear (western) Directed by Lambert Hillyer. Produced by Charles J. Bigelow. Original screenplay by J. Benton Cheney.

Cast: Johnny Mack Brown, Raymond Hatton, Christine McIntyre, Tristram Coffin, Edward Cassidy, Eddie Parker, Edward Peil, Sr., Ted Adams, Pierce Lyden, Steve Darrell, Cactus Mack, Budd Buster, Gary Garrett, Robert O'Bryne, Matty Roubert.

Feature Films 1947

Johnny Williams (Johnny Mack Brown) and Rusty Peters (Raymond Hatton) look into a conspiracy by a gang of landgrabbers to swindle money from ranchers and then foreclose mortgages on their property.
Running time: 54 minutes. Release date: February 15, 1947.

515. Fall Guy (mystery) Directed by Reginald LeBorg. Produced by Walter Mirisch. Screenplay by Jerry Warner. Based on the story "Cocaine" by Cornell Woolrich.
Cast: Clifford Penn, Robert Armstrong, Teala Loring, Elisha Cook, Jr., Douglas Fowley, Charles Arnt, Virginia Dale, Iris Adrian, Jack Overman, John Harmon, Christian Rub, Bob Carleton.
A man (Clifford Penn) becomes the "fall guy" for a murder he didn't commit and, with the aid of his fiancee (Teala Loring), fights to clear himself.
Running time: 64 minutes. Release date: March 15, 1947.

516. The Guilty (mystery) Directed by John Reinhardt. Produced by Jack Wrather. Screenplay by Robert Presnell, Sr. From a story "He Looked Like Murder" by Cornell Woolrich.
Cast: Bonita Granville, Don Castle, Wally Cassell, Regis Toomey, John Litel, Thomas Jackson, Netta Packer, Oliver Blake, Caroline Andrews.
Twin sisters (both played by Bonita Granville)—one good, one bad—fall in love with a psychoneurotic war veteran (Don Castle). When one of the girls is found murdered, her sister and the veteran are among the suspects.
Running time: 71 minutes. Release date: March 22, 1947.

517. Trailing Danger (western) Directed by Lambert Hillyer. Produced by Barney Sarecky. Screenplay by J. Benton Cheney.
Cast: Johnny Mack Brown, Raymond Hatton, Peggy Wynn, Marshall Reed, Patrick Desmond, Steve Darrell, Eddie Parker, Bonnie Jean Parker, Ernie Adams, Bud

Osborne, Cactus Mack, Kansas Moehring, Gary Garrett, Dee Cooper, Jack Hendricks, Artie Ortego.

A U.S. Marshal (Johnny Mack Brown) goes after an escaped convict (Steve Darrell) who is plotting to murder the superintendent of a nearby stagecoach line.

Running time: 58 minutes. Release date: March 29, 1947.

518. Violence (mystery) Directed by Jack Bernhard. Produced by Jack Bernhard and Bernard Brandt. Story and screenplay by Stanley Rubin and Lois Lantz.

Cast: Nancy Coleman, Michael O'Shea, Sheldon Leonard, Peter Whitney, Emory Parnell, Pierre Watkin, Frank Reicher, Cay Forester, John Hamilton, Richard Irving, Carol Donne, Jimmy Clark, William Gould.

An undercover operator (Nancy Coleman) for a photo magazine and an FBI agent (Michael O'Shea) are out to bust an organization known as United Defenders, a front for a secret fascist outfit whose objective is to spread civic discord under the cloak of patriotism.

Running time: 72 minutes. Release date: April 12, 1947.

519. Six Gun Serenade (western) Directed by Ford Beebe. Produced by Barney Sarecky. Original screenplay by Bennett Cohen.

Cast: Jimmy Wakely, Lee "Lasses" White, Kay Morley, Cactus Mack, Chick Hannon, Jimmie Martin, Bud Osborne, Steve Clark, Pierce Lyden, Jack Rivers, Jack Hendricks, Stanley Ellison, Arthur (Fiddlin') Smith, Rivers Lewis.

Jimmy Wakely tangles with cattle rustlers who, in an effort to gain control of property belonging to a young woman (Kay Morley), have been killing off ranch hands.

Running time: 54 minutes. Release date: April 15, 1947.

520. Hard Boiled Mahoney (comedy) Directed by William Beaudine. Produced by Jan Grippo. Story and screenplay by Cyril Endfield. Additional dialogue by Edmond Seward and Tim Ryan.

Cast: Leo Gorcey, Huntz Hall, Bobby Jordan, Billy Benedict, Gabriel Dell, David Gorcey, Teala Loring, Dan Seymour, Bernard Gorcey, Patti Brill, Betty Compson, Danny Beck, Pierre Watkin, Noble Johnson, Carmen D'Antonio, Byron Foulger, Teddy Pavelec, Pat O'Malley, Jack Cheatham, William Ruhl, Tom Faust, Lew Davis, voice of Tim Ryan.

Mistaken for private detectives, Bowery Boys Slip (Leo Gorcey) and Sach (Huntz Hall) become involved with an extortion ring.

Running time: 63 minutes. Release date: April 26, 1947.

521. Land of the Lawless (western) Directed by Lambert Hillyer. Produced by Barney Sarecky. Screenplay by J. Benton Cheney.

Cast: Johnny Mack Brown, Raymond Hatton, Christine McIntyre, Tristram Coffin, June Harrison, Marshall Reed, I. Stanford Jolley, Steve Clark, Edmund Cobb, Roy Butler, Cactus Mack, Gary Garrett, Carl Sepulveda, Victor Cox.

A cowboy (Johnny Mack Brown) agrees to help clean up a frontier town where his friend was killed and thwarts a plot to ship a hoard of money stolen from miners and settlers.

Running time: 54 minutes. Release date: April 26, 1947.

522. Sarge Goes to College (musical-comedy) Produced and directed by Will Jason. Screenplay by Hal Collins. Original story by Henry Edwards.

Cast: Freddie Stewart, June Preisser, Frankie Darro, Warren Mills, Noel Neill, Arthur Walsh, Alan Hale, Jr., Russ Morgan, Monte Collins, Frank Cady, Margaret Brayton, Selmer Jackson, Earl Bennett, Margaret Burt, Harry Tyler, Pat Goldin, William Forrest, Irwin Kauffman, Russ Morgan and his orchestra, Jack McVea and his orchestra, Abe Lyman, Wingy Manone, Les Paul, Candy Candido, Jess Stacy, Jerry Wald, Joe Venuti.

Before facing a critical operation, a Marine sergeant (Alan Hale, Jr.) is sent to college for relaxation. On his arrival he makes the acquaintance of the Teen Agers

Left to right: Warren Mills, Alan Hale, Jr., June Preisser, Freddie Stewart, Noel Neill and Frankie Darro in "Sarge Goes to College" (1947), an entry in the "Teen Agers" series.

gang (Freddie Stewart, June Preisser, Frankie Darro, Warren Mills, Noel Neill, Arthur Walsh) who are preparing for a big college show.

Running time: 63 minutes. Release date: May 17, 1947.

523. The Law Comes to Gunsight (western) Directed by Lambert Hillyer. Produced by Barney Sarecky. Screenplay by J. Benton Cheney.

Cast: Johnny Mack Brown, Raymond Hatton, Reno Blair (Browne), Lanny Rees, Zon Murray, Frank LaRue, Ernie Adams, Kermit Maynard, Ted Adams, Gary Garrett, Lee Roberts, Willard Willingham, Artie Ortego.

Johnny arrives in Gunsight, where the mayor mistakes him for a thug hired to run a gambler and his henchmen out of town.

232

Running time: 56 minutes. Release date: May 24, 1947.

Working title: **Backfire.**

524. Song of the Wasteland (western) Directed by Thomas Carr. Produced by Barney Sarecky. Screenplay by J. Benton Cheney.

Cast: Jimmy Wakely, Lee "Lasses" White, Holly Bane, Dottye Brown, John James, Henry Hall, Marshall Reed, Gary Garrett, Pierce Lyden, Chester Conklin, Ted Adams, John Carpenter, George Chesebro, Jack Rivers, Milburn Morante, The Saddle Pals (Johnny Bond, Dick Reinhart, Rivers Lewis), Jessie Ashlock, Cotton Thompson, Ray Jones.

A Ranger (Jimmy Wakely) clashes with vigilantes who are trying to murder one rancher and frame another for thievery.

Running time: 56 minutes. Release date: May 31, 1947.

525. High Conquest (drama) Produced and directed by Irving Allen. Screenplay by Max Troll. Original story by Aben Kandel. Based on the novel by James Ramsey Ullman.

Cast: Anna Lee, Gilbert Roland, Warren Douglas, Beulah Bondi, Sir C. Aubrey Smith, Alan Napier, John Qualen, Helene Thimig, Eric Feldary, Mickey Kuhn, Louis Mercier, Richard Flato, Gezade Rosner, Al Mathews, John Good, John Vosper, Wilton Graff, Maurice Cass, Fritz Leiber, Eddie Parks, Minerva Urecal, John Bleifer, Douglas Walton, Regina Wallace.

A young man (Warren Douglas) returns to the Matterhorn site where his father was killed years before; there he overcomes his reluctance to climb the mountain with the help of a Swiss girl (Anna Lee).

Running time: 79 minutes. Release date: June 21, 1947.

526. Code of the Saddle (western) Directed by Thomas Carr. Produced by Barney Sarecky. Original screenplay by Eliot Gibbons.

Monogram Checklist

Cast: Johnny Mack Brown, Raymond Hatton, Riley Hill, Kay Morley, William Norton Bailey, Zon Murray, Ted Adams, Bud Osborne, Kenne Duncan, Jr., Gary Garrett, Curley Gibson, Jack Hendricks, Boyd Stockman, Bob McElroy, Ray Jones, Chick Hannon.

Two U.S. Marshals (Johnny Mack Brown, Raymond Hatton), en route to a ranch to investigate a range war, stop to probe the killings of two ranch owners whose cattle have been stolen.

Running time: 53 minutes. Release date: June 28, 1947.

527. Flashing Guns (western) Directed by Lambert Hillyer. Produced by Barney Sarecky. Screenplay by Frank H. Young.

Cast: Johnny Mack Brown, Raymond Hatton, Jan Bryant, Douglas Evans, James E. Logan, Ted Adams, Edmund Cobb, Norman Jolley, Ken Adams, Gary Garrett, Ray Jones, Jack O'Shea, Steve Clark, Frank LaRue, Jack Rockwell, Riley Hill, Bob Woodward.

Johnny fights to keep a heavily mortgaged ranch from falling into the hands of a crooked banker (Douglas Evans).

Running time: 59 minutes. Release date: July 16, 1947.

528. Kilroy Was Here (comedy) Directed by Phil Karlson. Produced by Dick Irving Hyland and Sidney Luft. Screenplay by Dick Irving Hyland. Original story by Dick Irving Hyland and Lee Wainer. Additional dialogue by Louis Quinn.

Cast: Jackie Cooper, Jackie Coogan, Wanda McKay, Frank Jenks, Norman Phillips, Rand Brooks, Barton Yarborough, Frank Scannell, Patti Brill, Robert Coogan, Joe Forte, Allen Mathews, Sidney Melton, Pat Goldin.

This film revolves around the popular wartime phrase "Kilroy Was Here." John J. Kilroy (Jackie Cooper) enrolls in college under the G.I. Bill; a snobbish fraternity accepts him because he is the Kilroy, but then wants to drop him when he insists on associating with his taxi-driving buddies.

234

Running time: 68 minutes. Release date: July 19, 1947.

529. Thunderbolt (documentary) Directed by Lt. Col. William Wyler. Produced under the command of Lt. General Ira C. Eaker. In Technicolor.

Introduced by James Stewart; narrated by Lloyd Bridges.

An Army Air Forces documentary showing how Allied air power finally broke the stalemate that held the United States Fifth and British Eighth Armies for five months at the Gustav Line in Italy during World War II.

Running time: 44 minutes. Release date: July 26, 1947 (made in 1945, distributed by Monogram in 1947).

530. News Hounds (comedy) Directed by William Beaudine. Produced by Jan Grippo. Screenplay by Edmond Seward and Tim Ryan. Original story by Tim Ryan, Edmond Seward and George Cappy.

Cast: Leo Gorcey, Huntz Hall, Bobby Jordan, Billy Benedict, David Gorcey, Gabriel Dell, Christine McIntyre, Anthony Caruso, Bernard Gorcey, Tim Ryan, Bill Kennedy, Robert Emmett Keane, Ralph Dunn, John Hamilton, Nita Bieber, Terry Goodman, Bud Gorman, Russ Whiteman, Emmett Vogan, Jr., John H. Elliott, Meyer Grace, Leo Kaye.

Bowery Boys Slip (Leo Gorcey) and Sach (Huntz Hall) secure jobs with a local newspaper and attempt to expose a philanthropist (John Hamilton) who has ties with organized crime.

Running time: 68 min. Release date: Aug. 13, 1947.

Working title **Newshounds**.

531. Robin Hood of Monterey (western) Directed by Christy Cabanne. Produced by Jeffrey Bernerd. Screenplay by Bennett Cohen. Based on the characters created by O. Henry (William Sydney Porter).

Cast: Gilbert Roland, Chris-Pin Martin, Evelyn Brent, Jack LaRue, Travis Kent, Donna DeMario, Ernie Adams, Pedro deCordoba, Nestor Paiva, Thornton Edwards, Julian Rivero, Alex Montoya, Fred Cordova, Felipe Turich.

The Cisco Kid (Gilbert Roland) steps in when a woman (Evelyn Brent) kills her husband and frames her stepson (Ernie Adams) for the crime.

Running time: 55 minutes. Release date: September 6, 1947.

532. Ridin' Down the Trail (western) Directed by Howard Bretherton. Produced by Bennett Cohen. Screenplay by Bennett Cohen.

Cast: Jimmy Wakely, Dub "Cannonball" Taylor, Beverly Jons, Charles King, Milburn Morante, Douglas Fowley, John James, Kermit Maynard, Don Weston, Stanley Ellison, Doug Aylesworth, Brad Slavin, Harry Carr, Ted French, Post Park, Dick Reinhart, Jesse Ashlock, Wayne Burson.

After being shot, a dying ranger (Doug Aylesworth) entrusts Jimmy Wakely with a money belt to be given to the ranger's sister (Beverly Jons). Upon arriving in town, Jimmy discovers that someone there is posing as the dead man; the imposter accuses Wakely of murder since he has the money belt in his possession.

Running time: 53 minutes. Release date: October 4, 1947.

533. High Tide (mystery) Directed by John Reinhardt. Produced by Jack Wrather. Screenplay by Robert Presnell, Sr. Story by Raoul Whitfield. Additional dialogue by Peter Milne.

Cast: Lee Tracy, Don Castle, Julie Bishop, Anabel Shaw, Regis Toomey, Douglas Walton, Francis Ford, Anthony Warde, Wilson Wood, Argentina Brunetti, George H. Ryland.

An ex-reporter turned bodyguard (Don Castle) is called in when a crusading newspaper editor (Lee Tracy) starts receiving death threats.

Running time: 72 min. Release date: Oct. 11, 1947.

534. Joe Palooka in the Knockout (comedy-drama) Directed by Reginald LeBorg. Produced by Hal E. Chester. Screenplay by Nedrick Young. Based on the Ham Fisher comic strip.

Beverly Jons and Jimmy Wakely in "Ridin' Down the Trail" (1947).

Cast: Joe Kirkwood, Leon Errol, Morris Carnovsky, Elyse Knox, Billy House, Trudy Marshall, Marc Lawrence, Whitford Kane, Benny Baker, Donald MacBride, Danny Morton, Vince Barnett, Sarah Padden, Clarence Muse, Chester Clute, Eddie Gribbon, James Flavin, Suni Chorre.

After knocking out a contender who later dies, boxer Joe Palooka (Joe Kirkwood) threatens to give up the fight game. But when the fiancee (Trudy Marshall) of

237

the dead man suspects his death was caused by a drug administered by crooked gamblers, Palooka and his manager Knobby Walsh (Leon Errol) decide to investigate. Running time: 72 minutes. Release date: October 18, 1947. Also known as **The Knockout.**

535. Prairie Express (western) Directed by Lambert Hillyer. Produced by Barney Sarecky. Screenplay by Anthony Coldeway and J. Benton Cheney.

Cast: Johnny Mack Brown, Raymond Hatton, Virginia Belmont, Marshall Reed, William Ruhl, Robert Winkler, Frank LaRue, Ted Adams, Steve Darrell, Ken Adams, Gary Garrett, Hank Worden, Bob McElroy, Carl Mathews, Boyd Stockman, Jack Gibson, Steve Clark, Artie Ortego, I. Stanford Jolley, Jack Hendricks.

Johnny Hudson (Johnny Mack Brown) helps save an express company when outlaws attempt to break it up in order to bankrupt a ranch owned by one of the express partners. Running time: 55 minutes. Release date: October 25, 1947.

536. Louisiana (drama) Directed by Phil Karlson. Produced by Lindsley Parsons. Screenplay by Jack DeWitt. Original story by Steve Healey. Additional dialogue by Vick Knight and W. Scott Darling.

Cast: Jimmie Davis, Margaret Lindsay, John Gallaudet, Freddie Stewart, Dottye Brown, Mollie Miller, Ralph Freeto, Russell Hicks, Lee "Lasses" White, John Harmon, Tristram Coffin, Eddy Waller, Mary Field, Joseph Crehan, Charles Lane, Raymond Largay, Ford Pearson, The Sunshine Serenaders (Charlie Mitchell, Jimmy Thompson, Lloyd Ellis, Logan Conger, Gib Thompson, Slim Herbert).

The story of Jimmie Davis (playing himself), recounting his rise from a poor sharecropper's son to the governor of Louisiana. Running time: 85 minutes. Release date: November 1, 1947.

Feature Films 1947

537. King of the Bandits (western) Directed by Christy Cabanne. Produced by Jeffrey Bernerd. Screenplay by Bennett R. Cohen. Original story by Christy Cabanne. Additional dialogue by Gilbert Roland. Based on the characters created by O. Henry (William Sydney Porter).

Cast: Gilbert Roland, Chris-Pin Martin, Angela Greene, Anthony Warde, Laura Treadwell, William Bakewell, Rory Mallison, Pat Goldin, Cathy Carter, Boyd Irwin, Antonio Filauri, Jasper Palmer, Bill Cabanne, Jack O'Shea.

The Cisco Kid (Gilbert Roland) pursues a stagecoach robber (Anthony Warde) who's been impersonating him.

Running time: 66 min. Release date: Nov. 8, 1947.

538. Bowery Buckaroos (comedy) Directed by William Beaudine. Produced by Jan Grippo. Screenplay by Edmond Seward, Tim Ryan and Jerry Warner.

Cast: Leo Gorcey, Huntz Hall, Bobby Jordan, Gabriel Dell, Billy Benedict, David Gorcey, Julie Gibson, Bernard Gorcey, Jack Norman (Norman Willis), Minerva Urecal, Russell Simpson, Chief Yowlachie, Iron Eyes Cody, Rosa Turich, Sherman Sanders, Billy Wilkerson, Jack O'Shea, Bud Osborne, Cathy Carter.

The Bowery Boys (Leo Gorcey, Huntz Hall, Bobby Jordan, Gabriel Dell, Billy Benedict, David Gorcey) journey out to the Wild West in order to clear the name of Sweet Shop proprietor Louis Dumbrowski (Bernard Gorcey), alias "Louie the Lout."

Running time: 66 minutes. Release date: November 22, 1947.

539. The Chinese Ring (mystery) Directed by William Beaudine. Produced by James S. Burkett. Screenplay by W. Scott Darling. Based on the character "Charlie Chan" created by Earl Derr Biggers.

Cast: Roland Winters, Mantan Moreland, Victor Sen Yung, Warren Douglas, Louise Currie, Philip Ahn, Byron Foulger, Thayer Roberts, Jean Wong, Chabing, Paul Bryar, George L. Spaulding, Charmienne Harker, Thornton Edwards, Lee Tung Foo, Richard Wang, Spencer Chan, Kenneth Chuck.

Joe Yule is on the receiving end of a swift kick delivered by Renie Riano on this poster for "Jiggs and Maggie in Society" (1947), one of a series of Monogram features based on the George McManus comic strip "Bringing Up Father."

Charlie Chan (Roland Winters) investigates the murder of a Chinese princess (Jean Wong) who was in the United States to purchase airplanes.

Running time: 68 minutes. Release date: December 6, 1947.

Working title: **The Red Hornet.**

A remake of **Mr. Wong in Chinatown** (Monogram, 1939).

540. Jiggs and Maggie in Society (comedy) Directed by Eddie Cline. Produced by Barney Gerard. Screenplay by Eddie Cline and Barney Gerard. Based on the King Features comic strip "Bringing Up Father" by George McManus.

Cast: Joe Yule, Renie Riano, Dale Carnegie, Arthur Murray, Sheilah Graham, Tim Ryan, Wanda McKay, Lee Bonnell, Pat Goldin, Herbert Evans, June Harrison, Scott Taylor, Jimmy Aubrey, Thayer Roberts, Richard Irving, William Cabanne, Dick Ryan, Constance Purdy, Edith Leslie, Helena Dare, Lesley Farley, Betty Blythe, Marcelle Imhof.

Jiggs (Joe Yule) and Maggie (Renie Riano) crash society and round up a gang of jewel thieves in the process.

Running time: 66 minutes. Release date: December 12, 1947.

541. Gun Talk (western) Directed by Lambert Hillyer. Produced by Barney A. Sarecky. Screenplay by J. Benton Cheney.

Cast: Johnny Mack Brown, Raymond Hatton, Christine McIntyre, Douglas Evans, Geneva Gray, Wheaton Chambers, Frank LaRue, Ted Adams, Carl Mathews, Zon Murray, Cactus Mack, Carol Henry, Bill Hale, Boyd Stockman, Roy Butler, Bob McElroy.

Johnny foils a plot by an outlaw leader (Wheaton Chambers), who is posing as a barber, to seize control of a gold mine.

Running time: 57 minutes. Release date: December 20, 1947.

1948

542. Smart Politics (musical comedy) Produced and directed by Will Jason. Screenplay by Hal Collins. Original story by Monte F. Collins and Hal Collins.

Cast: Freddie Stewart, June Preisser, Frankie Darro, Warren Mills, Noel Neill, Donald MacBride, Martha Davis, Butch Stone, Don Ripps, Candy Candido, Harry Tyler, Monte F. Collins, George Offerman, Jr., George Fields, Dick Paxton, Tommy Mack, Bill Snyder, Gene Krupa and his Orchestra, Cappy Barra Harmonica Boys.

The "Teen Agers" gang (Freddie Stewart, June Preisser, Frankie Darro, Warren Mills, Noel Neill) launch a campaign to turn an old warehouse into a youth center,

but run into opposition from the mayor (Donald MacBride), who wants the property for his own use.
Running time: 65 minutes. Release date: January 3, 1948.
Working title: **The Old Gray Mayor.**

543. Rocky (western-drama) Directed by Phil Karlson. Produced by Lindsley Parsons. Screenplay by Jack DeWitt. Story by George Wallace Sayre.
Cast: Roddy McDowall, Gale Sherwood, Nita Hunter, Edgar Barrier, Jonathan Hale, Irving Bacon, William Ruhl, Claire Whitney, John Alvin.
Rocky is a shaggy, oversized poodle which, because of his resemblance to another dog, is suspected of being a sheep killer. Rocky's young master (Roddy McDowall) protects his beloved pet when ranchers try to eliminate the canine.
Running time: 76 minutes. Release date: January 17, 1948.

544. Song of the Drifter (western) Directed by Lambert Hillyer. Produced by Louis Gray. Screenplay by Frank H. Young.
Cast: Jimmy Wakely, Dub "Cannonball" Taylor, Mildred Coles, Patsy Moran, Bud Osborne, William Ruhl, Marshall Reed, Frank LaRue, Carl Mathews, Steve Clark, Wheaton Chambers, Bob Woodward, Dick Reinhart, Cliffie Stone, Arthur (Fiddlin') Smith, Wayne Burson, Bill Callahan, Jimmie Martin, Gary Garrett.
Jimmy Wakely runs up against a couple of gangsters who are trying to bluff ranchers out of their land by telling them that the water reservoir is polluted.
Running time: 53 minutes. Release date: January 17, 1948.

545. Overland Trails (western) Directed by Lambert Hillyer. Produced by Barney A. Sarecky. Screenplay by Jess Bowers (Adele Buffington).
Cast: Johnny Mack Brown, Raymond Hatton, Virginia Belmont, Bill Kennedy, Virginia Carroll, Holly Bane, Ted Adams, Steve Darrell, Sonny Rees, Carl Mathews,

Milburn Morante, Bob Woodward, Boyd Stockman, George Peters, Tom London, Pierce Lyden, Roy Butler, Post Park, Marshall Reed, Artie Ortego.

Johnny encounters a pair of crooks (Bill Kennedy, Steve Darrell) who murder gold prospectors in order to gain full ownership of their claims.

Running time: 58 minutes. Release date: January 31, 1948.

546. Joe Palooka in Fighting Mad (comedy-drama) Directed by Reginald LeBorg. Produced by Hal E. Chester. Screenplay by John Bright. Original story by Ralph S. Lewis and Bernard D. Shamberg. Additional dialogue by Monte F. Collins. Based on the "Joe Palooka" comic strip by Ham Fisher.

Cast: Leon Errol, Joe Kirkwood, Elyse Knox, John Hubbard, Patricia Dane, Charles Cane, Wally Vernon, Frank Hyers, Jack Shea, Jack Roper, Horace McMahon, Jack Overman, Eddie Gribbon, Sarah Padden, Michael Mark, Evelynne Smith, Geneva Gray, Johnny Indrisano, Frank Reicher, Jay Norris, Paul Scardon, Virginia Belmont, Larry Steers, Robert Conway, Herb Vigran, Dewey Robinson, Emil Sitka, Murray Leonard, Robert C. McCracken, Cy Kendall, Bill McLean, Jack Mower, Paul Bryar, Sammy Wolfe, Reid Kilpatrick, Ted Pavelec.

While boxer Joe Palooka (Joe Kirkwood) is recuperating after an eye operation, his manager Knobby Walsh (Leon Errol) buys a piece of another promising prizefighter, who turns out to be in league with corrupt gamblers.

Running time: 75 minutes. Release date: February 7, 1948.

Also known as **Fighting Mad.**

547. Perilous Waters (drama) Directed by Jack Bernhard. Produced by Jack Wrather. Screenplay by Richard Wormser and Francis Rosenwald. From the Good Housekeeping story "Search" by Leon Ware.

Cast: Don Castle, Audrey Long, Peggy Knudsen, Samuel S. Hinds, Gloria Holden, John Miljan, Walter Sande, Stanley Andrews, Cy Kendall, Gene Garrick, George Ramsey, Mike Kilian, Julian Rivero.

A hired killer (Don Castle) slips aboard a yacht headed for Mexico, with the intention of murdering the vessel's owner (Samuel S. Hinds), a newspaper publisher who's been on an anti-gambling crusade.
Running time: 66 minutes. Release date: February 14, 1948.
Working title: **In Self Defense.**

548. Angels' Alley (comedy) Directed by William Beaudine. Produced by Jan Grippo. Story and screenplay by Edmond Seward, Tim Ryan and Gerald Schnitzer.

Cast: Leo Gorcey, Huntz Hall, Gabriel Dell, Frankie Darro, Billy Benedict, David Gorcey, Nestor Paiva, Rosemary LaPlanche, Geneva Gray, Bennie Bartlett, John Eldredge, Nelson Leigh, Tommie Menzies, Mary Gordon, Dick Paxton, Robert Emmett Keane, Buddy Gorman, Dewey Robinson, John H. Elliott, William Ruhl, Wade Crosby, Meyer Grace.

The Bowery Boys (Leo Gorcey, Huntz Hall, Billy Benedict, David Gorcey) take on a gang of car thieves when Slip's cousin Jimmy (Frankie Darro) becomes involved with the crooks.

Running time: 67 minutes. Release date: March 21, 1948.

549. Docks of New Orleans (mystery) Directed by Derwin Abrahams. Produced by James S. Burkett. Screenplay by W. Scott Darling. Based on the character "Charlie Chan" created by Earl Derr Biggers.

Cast: Roland Winters, Mantan Moreland, Victor Sen Yung, Virginia Dale, John Gallaudet, Carol Forman, Douglas Fowley, Harry Hayden, Howard Negley, Stanley Andrews, Emmett Vogan, Boyd Irwin, Rory Mallison, George J. Lewis, Dian Fauntelle, Ferris Taylor, Haywood Jones, Eric Wilton, Forrest Matthews, Wally Walker, Larry Steers, Paul Conrad, Frank Stephens, Fred Miller.

Charlie Chan (Roland Winters) investigates the murder of the head of a chemical firm.

Running time: 64 minutes. Release date: March 21, 1948.

A remake of **Mr. Wong, Detective** (Monogram, 1938).

550. Oklahoma Blues (western) Directed by Lambert Hillyer. Produced by Louis Gray. Screenplay by Bennett Cohen.

Cast: Jimmy Wakely, Dub "Cannonball" Taylor, Virginia Belmont, Charles King, George J. Lewis, Zon Murray, I. Stanford Jolley, Steve Clark, Frank LaRue, Milburn Morante, Don Weston, Arthur (Fiddlin') Smith, Bob Woodward, J.C. Lytton.

A group of outlaws capture Jimmy Wakely after he is mistaken for a fictitious bandit called "The Melody Kid."

Running time: 56 minutes. Release date: March 28, 1948.

551. Campus Sleuth (musical-comedy) Produced and directed by Will Jason. Screenplay by Hal Collins. Story by Max Wilson and Hal Collins.

Cast: Freddie Stewart, June Preisser, Warren Mills, Noel Neill, Donald MacBride, Monte Collins, Stan Rose, Bobby Sherwood, Billy Snyder, William Norton Bailey, Charles Campbell, Paul Bryar, George Eldredge, Dottye D. Brown, Harry Taylor, Margaret Bert, Lane Chandler, Joey Preston, Mildred Jorman, Jimmy Grisson, George Fields, Bobby Sherwood and His Orchestra, Gerri Gallian.

The "Teen Agers" gang (Freddie Stewart, June Preisser, Warren Mills, Noel Neill) try to solve the campus murder of a visiting photographer.

Running time: 57 minutes. Release date: April 4, 1948.

552. Crossed Trails (western) Directed by Lambert Hillyer. Produced by Louis Gray. Screenplay by Colt Remington ("probably Adele Buffington," say Les Adams and Buck Rainey in **Shoot 'Em Ups** [New Rochelle, New York: Arlington House, 1978]).

Cast: Johnny Mack Brown, Raymond Hatton, Lynne Carver, Douglas Evans, Kathy Frye, Steve Clark, Ted Adams, Zon Murray, Mary MacLaren, Frank LaRue, Milburn Morante, Robert (Bob) D. Woodward, Pierce Lyden, Henry Hall, Hugh Murray, Bud Osborne, Artie Ortego, Boyd Stockman.

Johnny comes to the aid of a rancher (Raymond Hatton) who has been framed on a murder charge by two badmen (Douglas Evans, Steve Clark) after his property.
Running time: 53 minutes. Release date: April 11, 1948.

553. French Leave (comedy) Directed by Frank McDonald. Produced by Sid Luft. Screenplay by Jameson Brewer and Jack Rubin.

Cast: Jackie Cooper, Jackie Coogan, Ralph Sanford, Curt Bois, Renee Godfrey, William Dembrosi, Claire DuBrey, John Bleifer, Larry Blake.

Two carefree merchant seamen (Jackie Cooper, Jackie Coogan) become involved with a French black market ring which systematically loots food cargoes on the Marseilles waterfront.
Running time: 63 minutes. Release date: April 11, 1948.

554. Partners of the Sunset (western) Directed by Lambert Hillyer. Produced by Louis Gray. Screenplay by J. Benton Cheney.

Cast: Jimmy Wakely, Dub "Cannonball" Taylor, Christine Larson, Ray Whitley, Leonard Penn, Steve Darrell, Marshall Reed, Bob Woodward, Boyd Stockman, Don Weston, Jack Rivers, Jay Kirby, Arthur (Fiddlin') Smith, J.C. Lytton, Carl Mathews, Carl Sepulveda, Agapito Martinez.

A ranch foreman (Jimmy Wakely) tries to prove the innocence of a man framed for a murder committed by his stepmother's sweetheart.
Running time: 53 minutes. Release date: May 6, 1948.

555. Frontier Agent (western) Directed by Lambert Hillyer. Produced by Barney Sarecky. Screenplay by J. Benton Cheney.

Cast: Johnny Mack Brown, Raymond Hatton, Reno Blair (Browne), Dennis Moore, Kenneth MacDonald, Riley Hill, Frank LaRue, Ted Adams, Virginia Carroll, William

Ruhl, Kansas Moehring, Bill Hale, Lane Bradford, Bob Woodward, Boyd Stockman.

Johnny, a trouble shooter for the Overland Telegraph, foils a corrupt land promoter's plot to sabotage the company's construction work.

Running time: 56 minutes. Release date: May 16, 1948.

556. I Wouldn't Be in Your Shoes (mystery) Directed by William Nigh. Produced by Walter Mirisch. Screenplay by Steve Fisher. From the story "I Wouldn't Be in Your Shoes" by Cornell Woolrich.

Cast: Don Castle, Elyse Knox, Regis Toomey, Charles D. Brown, Rory Mallison, Bill Kennedy, Ray Dolciame, William Ruhl, Esther Michelson, Steve Darrell, Wally Walker, John Sheehan, Herman Cantor, John H. Elliott, Tito Vuolo, Jimmy Aubrey, John Shay, Donald Kerr, Joe Bernard, Stanley Blystone, Dorothy Vaughn, Robert Lowell, Matty Fain, John Doucette, Bill Walker, Dan White, Ray Teal, Paul Bryar, Lou Marcelle, Walden Boyle, Hugh Charles, Laura Treadwell.

A dancer (Don Castle) is convicted of robbery and murder after a print of one of his shoes is found at the scene of the crime. His wife (Elyse Knox), convinced of her husband's innocence, sets out to track down the real culprit.

Running time: 70 minutes. Release date: May 23, 1948.

557. Range Renegades (western) Directed by Lambert Hillyer. Produced by Louis Gray. Screenplay by Ronald Davidson and William Lively.

Cast: Jimmy Wakely, Dub "Cannonball" Taylor, Jennifer Holt, Dennis Moore, John James, Riley Hill, Steve Clark, Frank LaRue, Cactus Mack, Milburn Morante, Don Weston, Arthur (Fiddlin') Smith, Bob Woodward, Carl Mathews, Roy Garrett, Agapito Martinez.

Jimmy's a new marshal; his deputy (Dennis Moore) becomes interested in Belle (Jennifer Holt), who secretly heads an outlaw band.

Running time: 54 min. Release date: June 6, 1948.

Working title: **Arizona Sunset.**

558. Stage Struck (mystery) Directed by William Nigh. Produced by Jeffrey Bernerd. Screenplay by Wallace Sayre and Agnes Christine Johnston. Original story by George Wallace Sayre.

Cast: Kane Richmond, Audrey Long, Conrad Nagel, Ralph Byrd, Evelyn Brent, John Gallaudet, Anthony Warde, Pamela Blake, Charles Trowbridge, Nana Bryant, Selmer Jackson, Wanda McKay, Jacqueline Thomas, Wilbur Mack.

After her stagestruck sister is murdered, a young woman (Audrey Long) tries to solve the crime; her search leads to a shady nightclub where girls end up as customer conveniences.

Running time: 71 minutes. Release date: June 13, 1948.

559. Triggerman (western) Directed by Howard Bretherton. Produced by Barney Sarecky. Screenplay by Ronald Davidson.

Cast: Johnny Mack Brown, Raymond Hatton, Virginia Carroll, Bill Kennedy, Marshall Reed, Forrest Mathews, Bob Woodward, Dee Cooper.

A Wells Fargo agent (Johnny Mack Brown), posing as a ranch hand, uncovers half of a map which shows the location where a chest of gold has been buried.

Running time: 56 minutes. Release date: June 20, 1948.

560. Jinx Money (comedy) Directed by William Beaudine. Produced by Jan Grippo. Original screenplay by Edmond Seward, Tim Ryan and Gerald Schnitzer. From a story suggested by Jerome T. Gollard.

Cast: Leo Gorcey, Huntz Hall, Gabriel Dell, Sheldon Leonard, Donald MacBride, Betty Caldwell, Billy Benedict, Bennie Bartlett, David Gorcey, John Eldredge, Ben Welden,

Opposite: Top: Audrey Long and Kane Richmond in "Stage Struck" (1948). Bottom: Ben Welden (right) menaces the Bowery Boys (Leo Gorcey, Huntz Hall, David Gorcey, Bennie Bartlett, Billy Benedict) in "Jinx Money" (1948).

Lucien Littlefield, Bernard Gorcey, Benny Baker, Ralph Dunn, Wanda McKay, Tom Kennedy, William Ruhl, Stanley Andrews, George Eldredge, William H. Vedder, Mike Pat Donovan.

The Bowery Boys (Leo Gorcey, Huntz Hall, Gabriel Dell, Billy Benedict, Bennie Bartlett, David Gorcey) fall into possession of $50,000 which is being sought after by a mysterious stranger who commits murder using a sword-tipped umbrella.

Running time: 68 minutes. Release date: June 27, 1948.

561. Cowboy Cavalier (western) Directed by Derwin Abrahams. Produced by Louis Gray. Screenplay by Ronald Davidson and J. Benton Cheney.

Cast: Jimmy Wakely, Dub "Cannonball" Taylor, Jan Bryant, Bud Osborne, Douglas Evans, Steve Darrell, Carol Henry, Steve Clark, Bob Woodward, William Ruhl, Milburn Morante, Claire Whitney, Louis Armstrong (not the famed musician), Don Weston.

Jimmy Wakely clashes with a tricky outlaw (Douglas Evans) who resorts to hijacking and blackmail in an effort to gain possession of a freight line.

Running time: 57 minutes. Release date: July 11, 1948.

562. The Shanghai Chest (mystery) Directed by William Beaudine. Produced by James S. Burkett. Screenplay by W. Scott Darling and Sam Newman. Story by Sam Newman. Based on the character "Charlie Chan" created by Earl Derr Biggers. Additional dialogue by Tim Ryan.

Cast: Roland Winters, Mantan Moreland, Victor Sen Yung, Tim Ryan, Deannie Best, Tristram Coffin, John Alvin, Russell Hicks, Pierre Watkin, Phil Van Zandt, Milton Parsons, Olaf Hytten, Erville Alderson, George Eldredge, Louis Mason, Edward Coke, Charlie Sullivan, Paul Scardon, William Ruhl, Lois Austin, Chabing, John Shay, Willie Best.

Charlie Chan (Roland Winters) investigates the strange case of a dead criminal whose fingerprints are in plain view after each of three murders.

Running time: 56 minutes. Release date: July 11, 1948.

563. Back Trail (western) Directed by Christy Cabanne. Produced by Barney Sarecky. Screenplay by J. Benton Cheney.

Cast: Johnny Mack Brown, Raymond Hatton, Mildred Coles, Ted Adams, Pierce Lyden, Jimmy Horne, Jr., Snub Pollard, Marshall Reed, Bob Woodward, Carol Henry, George Holmes, William Norton Bailey, George Morrell.

A State Protective League representative (Johnny Mack Brown) goes after a saloonkeeper (Pierce Lyden) who's blackmailing a local banker (Ted Adams) into revealing the routes of stagecoaches carrying payrolls.

Running time: 57 minutes. Release date: July 18, 1948.

564. 16 Fathoms Deep (action-drama) Directed by Irving Allen. Produced by James S. Burkett and Irving Allen. Screenplay by Max Trell. Adaptation by Forrest Judd. From the American Magazine story "16 Fathoms Deep" by Eustace L. Adams. An Arthur Lake Production. In Ansco color (the first feature film to be released in this color process).

Cast: Lon Chaney, Jr., Lloyd Bridges, Arthur Lake, Eric Feldary, Tanis Chandler, John Qualen, Ian MacDonald, Dickie Moore, Harry Cheshire, John Bleifer, Grant Means, John Gonatos, Allen Mathews.

An ex-Navy diver (Lloyd Bridges) becomes involved in the highly competitive sponge-diving industry when he joins with a new boat owner (Eric Feldary) and his crew; a crooked sponge dealer (Lon Chaney, Jr.) tries his best to sabotage the vessel.

Running time: 82 minutes. Release date: July 25, 1948.

A remake of **16 Fathoms Deep** (Monogram, 1934).

565. Michael O'Halloran (drama) Directed by John Rawlins. Produced by Julian Lesser and Frank Melford. Screenplay by Emma Lazarus. From the novel by Gene Stratton-Porter. A Windsor Pictures Production.

Cast: Scotty Beckett, Allene Roberts, Tommy Cook, Isabel Jewell, Charles Arnt, Jonathan Hale, Gladys Blake, Roy Gordon, Florence Auer, William Haade, Dorothy Granger, Douglas Evans, Beverly Jons, Greg Barton, Lee Phelps, Harry Strang, Bob Scott, Ethyl Halls, Ralph Brooks, Rob Haines.

Michael O'Halloran (Scotty Beckett), an orphan making it on his own as a newsboy, takes in a crippled girl (Allene Roberts) after her drunkard mother (Isabel Jewell) is injured.

Running time: 79 minutes. Release date: August 8, 1948.

566. The Fighting Ranger (western) Directed by Lambert Hillyer. Produced by Barney Sarecky. Screenplay by Ronald Davidson.

Cast: Johnny Mack Brown, Raymond Hatton, Christine Larson, Marshall Reed, Steve Clark, I. Stanford Jolley, Bob Woodward, Eddie Parker, Charlie Hughes, Milburn Morante, Peter Perkins.

A U.S. Ranger (Johnny Mack Brown) poses as a cowhand in order to bring a crooked rancher (Marshall Reed) to justice.

Running time: 57 minutes. Release date: August 15, 1948.

567. Silver Trails (western) Directed by Christy Cabanne. Produced by Louis Gray. Original screenplay by J. Benton Cheney.

Cast: Jimmy Wakely, Dub "Cannonball" Taylor, Whip Wilson, Christine Larson, George J. Lewis, George Meeker, Pierce Lyden, William Norton Bailey, Fred Edwards, Glenn Strange, Bob Woodward, Bud Osborne, Consuelo Asnis.

A group of landgrabbers try to ruin Jimmy Wakely's attempts to have settlers and native Californians iron out their differences.

Running time: 53 minutes. Release date: August 22, 1948.

568. The Golden Eye (mystery) Directed by William

Beaudine. Produced by James S. Burkett. Screenplay by W. Scott Darling. Based on the character "Charlie Chan" created by Earl Derr Biggers.

Cast: Roland Winters, Mantan Moreland, Victor Sen Yung, Wanda McKay, Bruce Kellogg, Tim Ryan, Evelyn Brent, Ralph Dunn, Lois Austin, Forrest Taylor, Tom Tyler, George L. Spaulding, Barbara Jean Wong, Lee Tung Foo, Richard Loo, Bill Walker, Herman Cantor, Edmund Cobb, John Merton, Lee "Lasses" White.

Charlie Chan (Roland Winters) journeys to Arizona to investigate the attempted murder of the owner of the Golden Eye mine.

Running time: 69 minutes. Release date: August 29, 1948.

Also known as **The Mystery of the Golden Eye.**

569. Music Man (musical-comedy) Produced and directed by Will Jason. Original screenplay by Sam Mintz.

Cast: Freddie Stewart, June Preisser, Phil Brito, Jimmy Dorsey and His Orchestra, Noel Neill, Alan Hale, Jr., Grazia Narisco, Chick Chandler, Norman Leavitt, Helen Woodford, Gertrude Astor.

Two brothers (Freddie Stewart, Phil Brito), a successful songwriting team, quarrel and split up; their secretary (June Preisser) gets them into an unknowing collaboration on a musical show by letting each think that the other collaborator is another person.

Running time: 66 minutes. Release date: September 5, 1948.

570. Winner Take All (comedy-drama) Directed by Reginald LeBorg. Produced by Hal E. Chester. Screenplay by Stanley Rubin. Additional dialogue by Monte Collins. Based on the "Joe Palooka" comic strip by Ham Fisher.

Cast: Joe Kirkwood, Elyse Knox, William Frawley, Stanley Clements, John Shelton, Mary Beth Hughes, Sheldon Leonard, Frank Jenks, Lyle Talbot, Jack Roper, Eddie Gribbon, Wally Vernon, Ralph Sanford, Bill Martin, "Big" Ben Moroz, Hal Fieberling, William Ruhl, Chester Clute, Douglas Fowley, Stanley Prager, Hugh Charles, Forrest Matthews, Gertrude Astor, Hal Gerard.

Gamblers stage a phony kidnapping in an effort to get boxer Joe Palooka (Joe Kirkwood) to throw a championship fight.

Running time: 64 minutes. Release date: September 19, 1948.

Working title: **A Joe Named Palooka.**

571. The Rangers Ride (western) Directed by Derwin Abrahams. Produced by Louis Gray. Screenplay by Basil Dickey.

Cast: Jimmy Wakely, Dub "Cannonball" Taylor, Virginia Belmont, Cactus Mack, Bud Taylor, Bud Osborne, Riley Hill, Marshall Reed, Steve Clark, Pierce Lyden, Boyd Stockman, Bob Woodward, Milburn Morante, Carol Henry, Don Weston, Arthur (Fiddlin') Smith, James Diehl, Jack Sparks, Louis Armstrong (not the famed musician).

An ex-Texas Ranger (Jimmy Wakely) fights to break up a private state police force which is using its authority for purposes of fleecing the ranchers.

Running time: 56 minutes. Release date: September 26, 1948.

572. The Sheriff of Medicine Bow (western) Directed by Lambert Hillyer. Produced by Barney Sarecky. Screenplay by J. Benton Cheney.

Cast: Johnny Mack Brown, Raymond Hatton, Max Terhune, Evelyn Finley, George J. Lewis, Bill Kennedy, Frank LaRue, Peter Perkins, Carol Henry, Bob Woodward, Ted Adams.

A sheriff (Johnny Mack Brown) paroles a bank robber (Raymond Hatton) whose daughter (Evelyn Finley) is having difficulty running their ranch.

Running time: 55 min. Release date: Oct. 3, 1948.

573. Outlaw Brand (western) Directed by Lambert Hillyer. Produced by Louis Gray. Screenplay by J. Benton Cheney.

Cast: Jimmy Wakely, Dub "Cannonball" Taylor, Kay Morley, Christine Larson, Bud Osborne, Leonard Penn, Nolan Leary, Tom Chatterton, John James, Boyd Stockman, Frank McCarroll, Jack Rivers, Dick Reinhart, Ray Whitley, Louis Armstrong, Jay Kirby, Eddie Majors.

254

Jimmy hires out to a rancher to capture Midnight, an outlaw stallion that has been raiding domestic herds, and is innocently entangled in a maze of nefarious events resulting from the rancher's bad luck at cards and women.

Running time: 58 minutes. Release date: October 24, 1948.

574. Smugglers' Cove (comedy) Directed by William Beaudine. Produced by Jan Grippo. Screenplay by Edmond Seward and Tim Ryan. Based on the Bluebook Magazine story "Smuggler's Cove" by Talbert Josselyn.

Cast: Leo Gorcey, Huntz Hall, Gabriel Dell, Martin Kosleck, Billy Benedict, David Gorcey, Bennie Bartlett, Paul Harvey, Amelita Ward, Jacqueline Dalya, Eddie Gribbon, Gene Stutenroth (Roth), Leonid Snegoff, John Bleifer, Andre Pola, William Ruhl, Emmett Vogan, Buddy Gorman, George Meader.

Slip Mahoney (Leo Gorcey) receives a telegram intended for another party; believing he's inherited a Long Island estate, Slip and the other Bowery Boys (Huntz Hall, Gabriel Dell, Billy Benedict, David Gorcey, Bennie Bartlett) move into the manor, unaware that it's a secret hideout for a gang of jewel smugglers.

Running time: 66 minutes. Release date: October 24, 1948.

575. Gunning for Justice (western) Directed by Ray Taylor. Produced by Barney Sarecky. Screenplay by J. Benton Cheney.

Cast: Johnny Mack Brown, Raymond Hatton, Max Terhune, Evelyn Finley, House Peters, Jr., Ted Adams, I. Stanford Jolley, Bud Osborne, Dan White, Bill Potter, Bob Woodward, Carol Henry, Boyd Stockman, Dee Cooper, Artie Ortego.

Johnny is entrusted with a map purporting to indicate the whereabouts of gold bullion hijacked en route to General Lee during the Civil War.

Running time: 55 min. Release date: Nov. 7, 1948.

576. Courtin' Trouble (western) Directed by Ford Beebe. Produced by Louis Gray. Screenplay by Ronald Davidson.

Cast: Jimmy Wakely, Dub "Cannonball" Taylor, Virginia Belmont, Leonard Penn, Marshall Reed, Steve Clark, House Peters, Jr., Frank LaRue, William Norton Bailey, Bud Osborne, Bill Hale, Bob Woodward, Carol Henry, Bill Potter, Don Weston, Louis Armstrong (not the famed musician), Fiddlin' Arthur Smith.

Jimmy jails a gunman accused of murder but is forced to release him when the witness is found dead.

Running time: 56 minutes. Release date: November 21, 1948.

577. Kidnapped (adventure) Directed by William Beaudine. Produced by Lindsley Parsons. Screenplay by W. Scott Darling. From the novel by Robert Louis Stevenson.

Cast: Roddy McDowall, Sue England, Dan O'Herlihy, Roland Winters, Jeff Corey, Houseley Stevenson, Erskine Sanford, Alex Frazer, Winefriede McDowall, Bobby Anderson, Janet Murdoch, Olaf Hytten, Erville Alderson.

David Balfour (Roddy McDowall), a young Scottish lad, goes to claim his inheritance from his uncle (Houseley Stevenson); the wicked uncle arranges for the boy to be kidnapped and shipped off into slavery.

Running time: 81 minutes. Release date: November 28, 1948.

Robert Louis Stevenson's novel was filmed before, in 1938, by 20th Century-Fox; remade in 1960 and 1971.

578. Trouble Makers (comedy) Directed by Reginald LeBorg. Produced by Jan Grippo. Screenplay by Edmond Seward, Tim Ryan and Gerald Schnitzer. Original story by Gerald Schnitzer.

Cast: Leo Gorcey, Huntz Hall, Gabriel Dell, Frankie Darro, Lionel Stander, John Ridgely, Helen Parrish, Fritz Feld, Billy Benedict, David Gorcey, Bennie Bartlett, Cliff Clark, Charles LaTorre, Bernard Gorcey, William Ruhl, David Hoffman, Buddy Gorman, John Indrisano, Maynard Holmes, Pat Moran, Herman Cantor, Charles Coleman, Kenneth Lundy.

The Bowery Boys (Leo Gorcey, Huntz Hall, Billy Benedict, David Gorcey, Bennie Bartlett), operating a sidewalk telescope, witness a murder in a nearby hotel.

Feature Films 1948

Running time: 69 minutes. Release date: December 10, 1948.

579. Hidden Danger (western) Directed by Ray Taylor. Produced by Barney Sarecky. Screenplay by J. Benton Cheney and Eliot Gibbons.

Cast: Johnny Mack Brown, Raymond Hatton, Max Terhune, Christine Larson, Myron Healey, Marshall Reed, Kenne Duncan, Edmund Cobb, Steve Clark, Milburn Morante, Carol Henry, Bill Hale, Boyd Stockman, Bill Potter.

Johnny goes after the head of the Cattleman's Association (Myron Healey), who has bilked ranchers out of their rightful share of profits.

Running time: 55 minutes. Release date: December 12, 1948.

580. Jiggs and Maggie in Court (comedy) Directed by William Beaudine and Eddie Cline. Produced by Barney Gerard. Original screenplay by Barney Gerard and Eddie Cline. Based on the King Features comic strip "Bringing Up Father" by George McManus.

Cast: Joe Yule, Renie Riano, June Harrison, Riley Hill, Tim Ryan, Robert Lowell, Pat Goldin, Danny Beck, Dick Ryan, Cliff Clark, George McManus, Jimmy Aubrey, Jean Fenwick, Frank Austin, Russell Hicks, Chester Clute, Grady Sutton, Sidney Marion, Charles Middleton, Richard R. Neill, Ken Britton, Francine Faye, Bobby Hale, Fred Kelsey, Jimmy O'Brien, Herman Cantor, Marie Harmon, Baron Lichter.

Maggie (Renie Riano) resents the inconveniences that arise from her similarity to the cartoon character in the "Bringing Up Father" comic strip, so she takes cartoonist George McManus to court.

Running time: 60 minutes. Release date: December 12, 1948.

581. The Feathered Serpent (mystery) Directed by William Beaudine. Produced by James S. Burkett. Story and screenplay by Oliver Drake. Based on the character "Charlie Chan" created by Earl Derr Biggers.

Cast: Roland Winters, Key Luke, Mantan Moreland, Victor Sen Yung, Carol Forman, Robert Livingston, Martin Garralaga, Nils Asther, Beverly Jons, George J. Lewis, Lewis Denison, Jay Silverheels.

Charlie Chan (Roland Winters) is asked to find an American scientist who disappeared in a South American jungle while searching for a lost temple.

Running time: 68 minutes. Release date: December 19, 1948.

A remake of **The Riders of the Whistling Skull** (Republic, 1937).

1949

582. Crashing Thru (western) Directed by Ray Taylor. Produced by Barney Sarecky. Screenplay by Adele Buffington.

Cast: Whip Wilson, Andy Clyde, Christine Larson, Kenne Duncan, Tristram Coffin, Virginia Carroll, Steve Darrell, Jack Richardson, Jan Bryant, Bob Woodward, Tom Quinn, Dee Cooper, George J. Lewis, Boyd Stockman.

An undercover insurance agent (Whip Wilson) witnesses the murder of a ranger; in order to capture the killer, the agent assumes the identity of the murdered man.

Running time: 58 minutes. Release date: January 9, 1949.

583. Incident (mystery) Directed by William Beaudine. Produced by Harry Lewis and John Shelton. Screenplay by Fred Niblo, Jr. and Samuel Roeca. Original story by Harry Lewis. A Master Films Production.

Cast: Warren Douglas, Jane Frazee, Robert Osterloh, Joyce Compton, Anthony Caruso, Harry Lauter, Eddie Dunn, Meyer Grace, Harry Cheshire, Lynn Millan, Robert Emmett Keane, Pierre Watkin, Ralph Dunn, John Shay.

An innocent man (Warren Douglas) is beaten up after being mistaken for a gangster; his curiosity leads him into a search to find out why.

Running time: 66 minutes. Release date: January 28, 1949.

584. Gun Runner (western) Directed by Lambert Hillyer. Produced by Louis Gray. Screenplay by J. Benton Cheney.

Cast: Jimmy Wakely, Dub "Cannonball" Taylor, Noel Neill, Mae Clarke, Kenne Duncan, Marshall Reed, Carol Henry, Bud Osborne, Steve Clark, Ted Adams, Pascale Perry, Eddie Majors, Clem Fuller, Bob Woodward, Tex Atchinson, Ray Jones, Ray Whitley.

Jimmy and Cannonball, on their way to file a homestead claim at Canon City, rescue the sheriff's daughter (Noel Neill) from a gang engaged in smuggling guns to the Indians.

Running time: 54 minutes. Release date: January 30, 1949.

585. Henry, the Rainmaker (comedy) Directed by Jean Yarbrough. Produced by Peter Scully. Screenplay by Lane Beauchamp. Story by D.D. Beauchamp. A Mayfair Production.

Cast: Raymond Walburn, Walter Catlett, William Tracy, Mary Stuart, Barbara Brown, Gary Gray, Addison Richards, Lois Austin, George Nokes, Mary Field, Robert Emmett Keane, Ruth Lee, Patty King, Edna Holland.

Henry Latham (Raymond Walburn), a civic-minded family man, charges the town's mayor (Walter Catlett) with responsibility for a long dry spell and employs a professional "rainmaker" to demonstrate what should be done in this situation.

Running time: 64 minutes. Release date: February 13, 1949.

586. Law of the West (western) Directed by Ray Taylor. Produced by Barney Sarecky. Screenplay by J. Benton Cheney.

Cast: Johnny Mack Brown, Max Terhune, Gerry Patterson, Bill Kennedy, Jack Ingram, Riley Hill, Eddie Parker, Marshall Reed, Kenne Duncan, Jack Harrison, Bud Osborne, Steve Clark, Bob Woodward, Frank Ellis.

A crooked real estate agent mistakes a Federal man (Johnny Mack Brown) for a gunman and hires him as a bodyguard.

Running time: 54 min. Release date: Feb. 20, 1949.

587. Joe Palooka in the Big Fight (comedy-drama) Directed by Cyril Endfield. Produced by Hal E. Chester. Screenplay by Stanley Prager. Based on the "Joe Palooka" comic strip by Ham Fisher.

Cast: Joe Kirkwood, Leon Errol, Lina Romay, David Bruce, George O'Hanlon, Lyle Talbot, Virginia Welles, Greg McClure, Taylor Holmes, Lou Lubin, Benny Baker, Eddie Gribbon, Harry Hayden, Ian MacDonald, Jack Roper, Frances Osborne, Frank Fenton, George Fisher.

When pugilist Joe Palooka (Joe Kirkwood) is framed for a murder, he sets out to find the real killer.

Running time: 66 minutes. Release date: March 6, 1949.

588. Gun Law Justice (western) Directed by Lambert Hillyer. Produced by Louis Gray. Screenplay by Basil Dickey.

Cast: Jimmy Wakely, Dub "Cannonball" Taylor, Jane Adams, Ray Whitley, Lee Phelps, Bud Osborne, John James, Edmund Cobb, Myron Healey, Ray Jones, Zon Murray, Tom Chatterton, I. Stanford Jolley, Carol Henry, Bob Curtis, Eddie Majors, Tex Atchinson, George Morrell, Herman Hack.

Jimmy protects a former outlaw (Lee Phelps) who wants to go straight but has been wrongfully accused of a robbery.

Running time: 55 minutes. Release date: March 13, 1949.

589. Bomba, the Jungle Boy (adventure) Directed by Ford Beebe. Produced by Walter Mirisch. Screenplay by Jack DeWitt. Based on the story "Bomba, the Jungle Boy" by Roy Rockwood. In Sepiatone.

Cast: Johnny Sheffield, Peggy Ann Garner, Onslow Stevens, Charles Irwin, Robert "Smoki" Whitfield, Martin Wilkins, Oto the monkey.

A magazine photographer (Onslow Stevens) and his daughter (Peggy Ann Garner) go on safari in the African jungle. When the girl becomes separated from her father, she is befriended and protected by Bomba (Johnny Sheffield), a white boy who grew up in the jungle.

Running time: 71 minutes. Release date: March 20, 1949.

590. Temptation Harbor (drama) Directed by Lance Comfort. Produced by Victor Skutezky. Screenplay by Rodney Ackland, Frederick Gotfurt and Victor Skutezky. From the novel "Newhaven-Dieppe" by Georges Simenon.

Cast: Robert Newton, Simone Simon, William Hartwell, Marcel Dalio, Margaret Barton, Edward Rigby, Joan Hopkins, Kathleen Harrison, Leslie Dwyer, Charles Victor, Irene Handl.

A railway signalman (Robert Newton) falls into possession of a suitcase full of stolen bank notes and goes on a spree.

Running time: 110 minutes. Release date: March 27, 1949.

An Associated British Pathe production, released in Great Britain in 1947; released in the U.S. by Monogram.

591. Trail's End (western) Directed by Lambert Hillyer. Produced by Barney Sarecky. Screenplay by J. Benton Cheney.

Cast: Johnny Mack Brown, Max Terhune, Kay Morley, Douglas Evans, Zon Murray, Myron Healey, Keith Richards, George Chesebro, William Norton Bailey, Carol Henry, Boyd Stockman, Eddie Majors.

Johnny comes to the aid of an ex-convict wrongfully accused of murdering a rancher.

Running time: 57 minutes. Release date: April 3, 1949.

592. Tuna Clipper (adventure-drama) Directed by William Beaudine. Produced by Lindsley Parsons. Screenplay by W. Scott Darling.

Cast: Roddy McDowall, Elena Verdugo, Roland Winters, Rick Vallin, Dickie Moore, Russell Simpson, Doris Kemper, Peter Mamakos, Richard Avonde, Michael Vallon.

In order to pay a debt, a young man (Roddy McDowall) leaves home, taking employment and residence with a tuna-fishing family.

Running time: 77 min. Release date: April 10, 1949.

Roddy McDowall, Elena Verdugo and Dickie Moore in "Tuna Clipper" (1949).

593. Fighting Fools (comedy) Directed by Reginald LeBorg. Produced by Jan Grippo. Story and screenplay by Edmond Seward, Gerald Schnitzer and Bert Lawrence.

Cast: Leo Gorcey, Huntz Hall, Gabriel Dell, Billy Benedict, David Gorcey, Bennie Bartlett, Frankie Darro, Lyle Talbot, Bernard Gorcey, Teddy Infuhr, Dorothy Vaughan, Evelynne Eaton, Frank Moran, Tom Kennedy, Anthony Warde, Bill Cartledge, Ben Welden, Ralph Peters, Eddie Gribbon, Marty Mason, Paul Maxey, Robert Walcott, Meyer Grace, Frank Hagney, Bert Hanlon, Bert Conway, Bud Gorman, Roland Dupree, Stanley Andrews, Johnny Duncan, Sam Hayes, Mike Pat Donovan, Joe Gray, Larry Anzalone, Johnny Kern, Al Bayne, Jack Mower, Charlie Sullivan, Jimmy O'Gatty, Gene Delmont, John Indrisano, Sammy LaMarr, Benny Goldberg, Eddie Rio, Carl Sklover, Joe Greb.

Feature Films 1949

The Bowery Boys (Leo Gorcey, Huntz Hall, Gabriel Dell, Billy Benedict, David Gorcey, Bennie Bartlett) set out to break up a crooked prizefight racket.
Running time: 69 minutes. Release date: April 17, 1949.

594. Sky Dragon (mystery) Directed by Lesley Selander. Produced by James S. Burkett. Screenplay by Oliver Drake and Clint Johnston. Story by Clint Johnston. Based on the character "Charlie Chan" created by Earl Derr Biggers.

Cast: Roland Winters, Keye Luke, Mantan Moreland, Noel Neill, Tim Ryan, Iris Adrian, Elena Verdugo, Milburn Stone, Lyle Talbot, Paul Maxey, Joel Marston, John Eldredge, Eddie Parks, Louise Franklin, Lyle Latell, George Eldredge, Bob Curtis, Emmett Vogan, Charles Jordan.

Charlie Chan (Roland Winters) investigates a murder and robbery which took place aboard a commercial plane, with the passengers, stewardesses and two pilots as suspects.
Running time: 64 min. Release date: May 1, 1949.
Working title: **Murder in the Air.**

595. Across the Rio Grande (western) Directed by Oliver Drake. Produced by Louis Gray. Screenplay by Ronald Davidson.

Cast: Jimmy Wakely, Dub "Cannonball" Taylor, Reno Browne, Riley Hill, Terry Frost, Dennis Moore, Kenne Duncan, Ted Adams, Myron Healey, Bud Osborne, John James, Bob Curtis, Carol Henry, Boyd Stockman, William Norton Bailey, Polly Burgin (Bergen), Bob Woodward, Bill Potter.

Jimmy goes after outlaws who are smuggling stolen ore across the border.
Running time: 56 minutes. Release date: May 15, 1949.

596. Mississippi Rhythm (musical) Directed by Derwin Abrahams. Produced by Lindsley Parsons. Screenplay by Gretchen Darling. Original story by Louise Rousseau.

Left to right: Elena Verdugo, Roland Winters and Noel Neill in "Sky Dragon" (1949), the final entry in Monogram's Charlie Chan series.

Cast: Jimmie Davis, Lee "Lasses" White, Veda Ann Borg, Sue England, James Flavin, Lyle Talbot, Paul Maxey, Paul Bryar, Joel Marston, Guy Beach, The Sunshine Boys.

A land agent (Jimmie Davis) learns that a crooked judge is cheating settlers by selling them dry land.

Running time: 68 minutes. Release date: May 29, 1949.

597. West of Eldorado (western) Directed by Ray Taylor. Produced by Barney Sarecky. Screenplay by Adele Buffington.

Cast: Johnny Mack Brown, Max Terhune, Reno Browne, Teddy Infuhr, Milburn Morante, Marshall Reed, William Norton Bailey, Terry Frost, Bud Osborne, Kenne Duncan, Bill Potter, Bob Woodward, Boyd Stockman, Artie Ortego.

After killing an outlaw (Kenne Duncan), Johnny becomes the guardian of his orphaned kid brother (Teddy Infuhr).

Running time: 56 minutes. Release date: June 5, 1949.

598. Leave It to Henry (comedy) Directed by Jean Yarbrough. Produced by Peter Scully. Screenplay by D.D. Beauchamp. A Mayfair Production.

Cast: Raymond Walburn, Walter Catlett, Gary Gray, Mary Stuart, Barbara Brown, Houseley Stevenson, Ida Moore, Olin Howlin, Pat Phelan, George McDonald, Maynard Holmes, Burk Symon, William Vedder, Harry Harvey, Pat Collins, William Hudson, Gertrude Astor.

Henry Latham (Raymond Walburn) induces the mayor (Walter Catlett) to join him in building a boat to be sailed, afire, down the local river past a park where a group headed by Henry's wife is celebrating the town's 100th anniversary. But when a toll bridge burns down because of the boat, Henry winds up in jail.

Running time: 57 minutes. Release date: June 12, 1949.

599. Hold That Baby! (comedy) Directed by Reginald LeBorg. Produced by Jan Grippo. Story and screenplay by Charles R. Marion and Gerald Schnitzer.

Cast: Leo Gorcey, Huntz Hall, Gabriel Dell, Frankie Darro, Anabel Shaw, Billy Benedict, David Gorcey, Bennie Bartlett, John Kellogg, Max Marx, Bernard Gorcey, Edward Gargan, Florence Auer, Meyer Grace, Judy and Jody Dunne, Ida Moore, William Ruhl, Emmett Vogan, Pierre Watkin, Torben Meyer, Fred Nurney, Francis Irvin, Lin Mayberry, William J. O'Brien, Danny Beck, Cay Forester, Herbert Patterson, John O'Connor, Harold Noflin, Roy Aversa, Buddy Gorman, Robert Cherry, Angi O. Poulos.

The Bowery Boys (Leo Gorcey, Huntz Hall, Gabriel Dell, Billy Benedict, David Gorcey, Bennie Bartlett), operators of a laundromat, find an abandoned baby who is the heir to a fortune.

Running time: 64 minutes. Release date: June 26, 1949.

600. Brand of Fear (western) Directed by Oliver Drake. Produced by Louis Gray. Screenplay by Basil Dickey.

Cast: Jimmy Wakely, Dub "Cannonball" Taylor, Gail Davis, Ray Whitley, Myron Healey, Marshall Reed, Frank McCarroll, Holly Bane, Tom London, William Norton Bailey, William Ruhl, Boyd Stockman, Dee Cooper, Bob Woodward, Bob Curtis, Bill Potter, Don Weston, Joe Galbraith, Denver Dixon (Victor Adamson).

A cowboy (Jimmy Wakely) involved with a school teacher (Gail Davis) discovers she's the daughter of an ex-convict.

Running time: 56 min. Release date: July 10, 1949.

601. Forgotten Women (drama) Directed by William Beaudine. Produced by Jeffrey Bernerd. Screenplay by W. Scott Darling. Story by Jeffrey Bernerd.

Cast: Elyse Knox, Edward Norris, Robert Shayne, Theodora Lynch, Veda Ann Borg, Noel Neill, Tim Ryan, Bill Kennedy, Warren Douglas, Selmer Jackson.

The story of three women (Elyse Knox, Theodora Lynch, Veda Ann Borg) who drown their sorrows in alcohol.

Running time: 65 minutes. Release date: July 17, 1949.

602. Shadows of the West (western) Directed by Ray Taylor. Produced by Barney Sarecky. Screenplay by Adele Buffington.

Cast: Whip Wilson, Andy Clyde, Riley Hill, Reno Browne, Bill Kennedy, Pierce Lyden, Keith Richards, William Ruhl, Ted Adams, Lee Phelps, Bert Hamilton, Bud Osborne, Donald Kerr, Billy Hammond, Clem Fuller, Carol Henry, Bob Woodward, Edmund Glover, Dee Cooper, Curt Barrett, Red Egner.

A U.S. Marshal (Whip Wilson) and his ex-sheriff friend Winks (Andy Clyde) thwart outlaws who have framed a rancher and his son for a robbery and murder.

Running time: 59 minutes. Release date: July 24, 1949.

603. Trail of the Yukon (adventure) Directed by William Beaudine. Produced by Lindsley Parsons. Screenplay by Oliver Drake. From the story "The Gold Hunters" by James Oliver Curwood.

Cast: Kirby Grant, Suzanne Dalbert, Bill Edwards, Iris Adrian, Dan Seymour, William Forrest, Anthony Warde, Maynard Holmes, Peter Mamakos, Jay Silverheels, Guy Beach, Stanley Andrews, Dick Elliott, Bill Kennedy, Harrison Hearne, Burt Wenland, Alan Bridge, Wally Walker, Chinook the Wonder Dog.

In a small Canadian town, a Mountie (Kirby Grant) exposes the local banker as being the mastermind behind a robbery.

Running time: 69 minutes. Release date: July 31, 1949.

604. Range Justice (western) Directed by Ray Taylor. Produced by Barney Sarecky. Screenplay by Ronald Davidson.

Cast: Johnny Mack Brown, Max Terhune, Felice Ingersoll, Sarah Padden, Fred Kohler, Jr., Tristram Coffin, Riley Hill, Eddie Parker, Kenne Duncan, Myron Healey, Bill Hale, Bill Potter, Bob Woodward, Bill Williams.

A cowhand (Johnny Mack Brown) infiltrates a gang of cattle rustlers so he can prevent them from taking control of a ranch.

Running time: 57 minutes. Release date: August 7, 1949.

605. Joe Palooka in the Counterpunch (comedy) Directed by Reginald LeBorg. Produced by Hal E. Chester. Original screenplay by Henry Blankfort and Cyril Endfield. Based on the "Joe Palooka" comic strip by Ham Fisher.

Cast: Joe Kirkwood, Leon Errol, Elyse Knox, Sheila Ryan, Marcel Journet, Walter Sande, Douglass Dumbrille, Ian Wolfe, Harry Lewis, Frank Sully, Eddie Gribbon, Douglas Fowley, Suni Chorre, Ralph Graves, Roland Dupree, Martin Garralaga, Gertrude Messinger, Sam

Hayes, John Hart, John Indrisano, Joe Herrera, Robert Conway.

On a trip to South America, boxer Joe Palooka (Joe Kirkwood) helps a professor deliver an Inca statue to a museum and, in the process, becomes involved with counterfeiters.

Running time: 74 minutes. Release date: August 14, 1949.

Working title: **Return Bout.**

606. **Haunted Trails** (western) Directed by Lambert Hillyer. Produced by Eddie Davis. Screenplay by Adele Buffington.

Cast: Whip Wilson, Andy Clyde, Reno Browne, Dennis Moore, I. Stanford Jolley, William Ruhl, John Merton, Mary Gordon, Steve Clark, Myron Healey, Milburn Morante, Eddie Majors, Bud Osborne, Ted Adams, Lynton Brent, Bill Potter, Jason Robards, Sr., Carl Mathews, Thornton Edwards, Chuck Roberson.

Whip goes after a gang trying to obtain their rights to a ranch by passing off Winks (Andy Clyde) as an heir.

Running time: 58 minutes. Release date: August 21, 1949.

607. **Jiggs and Maggie in Jackpot Jitters** (comedy) Directed by William Beaudine. Produced by Barney Gerard. Original screenplay by Barney Gerard and Eddie Cline. Based on the King Features comic strip "Bringing Up Father" by George McManus.

Cast: Joe Yule, Renie Riano, George McManus, Walter McCarthy, Tim Ryan, Jimmy Aubrey, Tom Kennedy, Betty Blythe, Ed East, Earle Hodgins, Willie Best, Sid Marion, Marcelle Imhof, Hank Mann, Chester Conklin, Leon Belasco, Eddie Kane, Sam Hayes, Joe Hernandez.

Maggie (Renie Riano) buys a horse so she can join an exclusive club, only to discover she is allergic to the animal.

Running time: 67 minutes. Release date: August 28, 1949.

608. **Roaring Westward** (western) Directed by Oliver

Drake. Produced by Louis Gray. Screenplay by Ronald Davidson.

Cast: Jimmy Wakely, Dub "Cannonball" Taylor, Lois Hall, Dennis Moore, Jack Ingram, Claire Whitney, Marshall Reed, Kenne Duncan, Holly Bane, Buddy Swan, Nolan Leary, Bud Osborne, Ted French, Bob Woodward, Al Haskell, Art Mix, Rudy Bowman, Tom Smith, Denver Dixon (Victor Adamson).

Jimmy tries to prove the innocence of a young man, a member of the Sheriff's Association School, who has been falsely implicated in a murder.

Running time: 58 minutes. Release date: September 15, 1949.

609. Angels in Disguise (comedy) Directed by Jean Yarbrough. Produced by Jan Grippo. Story and screenplay by Charles R. Marion, Gerald Schnitzer and Bert Lawrence.

Cast: Leo Gorcey, Huntz Hall, Gabriel Dell, Billy Benedict, David Gorcey, Bennie Bartlett, Bernard Gorcey, Edward Ryan, Mickey Knox, Jean Dean, Richard Benedict, Joseph Turkel, Ray Walker, William Forrest, Pepe Hern, Marie Blake, Roy Gordon, Jane Adams, Don Harvey, Tristram Coffin, Rory Mallison, Lee Phelps, Jack Mower, William J. O'Brien, Carl Sklover, Herbert Patterson, Dorothy Abbott, John Morgan, Tom Monroe, Harold Baker, Jack Gargan, Peter Virgo, Doretta Johnson, Wade Crosby.

The Bowery Boys (Leo Gorcey, Huntz Hall, Billy Benedict, David Gorcey, Bennie Bartlett) pose as mobsters in order to flush out the gang responsible for the death of a police officer.

Running time: 63 min. Release date: Sept. 25, 1949.

610. Black Midnight (action-drama) Directed by Oscar (Budd) Boetticher. Produced by Lindsley Parsons. Screenplay by Clint Johnston and Erna Lazarus. Original story by Clint Johnston.

Cast: Roddy McDowall, Lyn Thomas, Damian O'Flynn, Rand Brooks, Kirby Grant, Gordon Jones, Fay Baker.

A young man (Roddy McDowall) tames a wild stallion and breaks up the horse-stealing activities of a rancher's son.

Running time: 66 minutes. Release date: October 2, 1949.

611. Western Renegades (western) Directed by Wallace Fox. Produced by Eddie Davis. Screenplay by Adele Buffington.

Cast: Johnny Mack Brown, Max Terhune, Riley Hill, Jane Adams, Steve Clark, Marshall Bradford, Hugh Prosser, Marshall Reed, Constance Worth, James Harrison, Terry Frost, William Ruhl, Myron Healey, Milburn Morante, John Merton, Dee Cooper, Chuck Roberson, Bill Potter, Lane Bradford.

A U.S. Marshal (Johnny Mack Brown) infiltrates an outlaw gang in order to absolve a friend of a murder charge.

Running time: 56 minutes. Release date: October 9, 1949.

612. The Wolf Hunters (adventure) Directed by Oscar (Budd) Boetticher. Produced by Lindsley Parsons. Screenplay by W. Scott Darling. From a story by James Oliver Curwood.

Cast: Kirby Grant, Jan Clayton, Edward Norris, Helen Parrish, Charles Lang, Ted Hecht, Luther Crockett, Elizabeth Root, Chinook the Wonder Dog.

A Mountie (Kirby Grant) and his dog track down a gang of murderous fur thieves.

Running time: 70 minutes. Release date: October 30, 1949.

613. Riders of the Dusk (western) Directed by Lambert Hillyer. Produced by Eddie Davis. Screenplay by Jess Bowers (Adele Buffington) and Robert Tansey.

Cast: Whip Wilson, Andy Clyde, Reno Browne, Tristram Coffin, Marshall Reed, Myron Healey, John Merton, Holly Bane, Lee Roberts, Dee Cooper, Thornton Edwards, Ray Jones.

A U.S. Marshal (Whip Wilson) pursues a mysterious rider who is wanted for cattle rustling.

Running time: 57 minutes. Release date: November 13, 1949.

One-sheet for "Master Minds" (1949), one of the best entries in the "Bowery Boys" series.

614. Master Minds (comedy) Directed by Jean Yarbrough. Produced by Jan Grippo. Screenplay by Charles R. Marion. Additional dialogue by Bert Lawrence.

Cast: Leo Gorcey, Huntz Hall, Gabriel Dell, Alan Napier, Glenn Strange, Billy Benedict, Bennie Bartlett, David Gorcey, William Yetter, Jane Adams, Bernard Gorcey, Kit Guard, Skelton Knaggs, Whitey Roberts, Harry Tyler, Minerva Urecal, Chester Clute, Anna Chandler, Stanley Blystone, Robert Coogan, Pat Goldin, Tim Connor, Kent O'Dell.

A toothache gives Sach (Huntz Hall) the ability to read minds; a mad scientist (Alan Napier) kidnaps the hapless Bowery Boy and subjects him to a thought-transference operation, exchanging his mind with that of a man–beast (Glenn Strange).

Running time: 64 minutes. Release date: November 20, 1949.

615. Lawless Code (western) Directed by Oliver Drake. Produced by Louis Gray. Screenplay by Basil Dickey.

Cast: Jimmy Wakely, Dub "Cannonball" Taylor, Ellen Hall, Riley Hill, Tristram Coffin, Terry Frost, Myron Healey, Bud Osborne, Kenne Duncan, Bob Curtis, Steve Clark, Frank McCarroll, Beatrice Maude, Carl Deacon Moore, Michael Royal.

Jimmy comes to the aid of an innocent man wrongfully accused of murdering his uncle.

Running time: 58 minutes. Release date: December 4, 1949.

616. Bomba on Panther Island (adventure) Directed by Ford Beebe. Produced by Walter Mirisch. Screenplay by Ford Beebe. Story by Roy Rockwood.

Cast: Johnny Sheffield, Allene Roberts, Lita Baron, Bill Walker, Charles Irwin, Henry Lewis, Robert "Smoki" Whitfield.

Bomba (Johnny Sheffield) encounters a jungle expedition whose agricultural experiments are stymied by a black killer panther.

Running time: 76 minutes. Release date: December 18, 1949.

617. Range Land (western) Directed by Lambert Hillyer. Produced by Eddie Davis. Screenplay by Adele Buffington.

Cast: Whip Wilson, Andy Clyde, Reno Browne, Reed Howes, Kenne Duncan, Kermit Maynard, Steve Clark, Stanley Blystone, Leonard Penn, John (Bob) Cason, William M. Griffith, Michael Dugan, Carol Henry.

Whip and Winks (Andy Clyde) pursue stagecoach robbers responsible for the theft of a fortune in gold bars.

Running time: 56 minutes. Release date: December 25, 1949.

1950

618. Blue Grass of Kentucky (drama) Directed by William Beaudine. Produced by Jeffrey Bernerd. Original screenplay by W. Scott Darling. In Cinecolor.

Cast: Bill Williams, Jane Nigh, Ralph Morgan, Russell Hicks, Robert "Buzzy" Henry, Ted Hecht, Dick Foote, Jack Howard, Bill Terrell, Stephen S. Harrison, Pierre Watkin.

Against the background of the Kentucky Derby, a young couple (Bill Williams, Jane Nigh), from two rival families of horse breeders, falls in love.

Running time: 72 minutes. Release date: January 22, 1950.

619. Fence Riders (western) Produced and directed by Wallace Fox. Screenplay by Eliot Gibbons.

Cast: Whip Wilson, Andy Clyde, Reno Browne, Myron Healey, Riley Hill, Edward Cassidy, Terry Frost, Frank McCarroll, George DeNormand, Holly Bane, Carl Mathews, John Merton, Buck Bailey, Johnny Mack Brown (according to film historian John Cocchi, Johnny Mack Brown can be "glimpsed briefly just standing around in one scene, apparently waiting for a scene to be set up for one of his own movies.").

Whip and his pal Winks (Andy Clyde) aid a ranch owner (Reno Browne) in her fight against a gang of cattle rustlers.

Running time: 57 minutes. Release date: January 19, 1950.

620. Joe Palooka Meets Humphrey (comedy) Directed by Jean Yarbrough. Produced by Hal E. Chester. Screenplay by Henry Blankfort. Based on the "Joe Palooka" comic strip by Ham Fisher.

Cast: Joe Kirkwood, Leon Errol, Pamela Blake, Robert Coogan, Jerome Cowan, Joe Besser, Don McGuire, Donald McBride, Curt Bois, Clem Bevans, Frank Sully, Eddie Gribbon, Sam Balter.

Hoping they won't be bothered by press or profession, boxer Joe Palooka (Joe Kirkwood) and Anne Howe (Pamela Blake) head for their honeymoon destination; en route they meet Humphrey (Robert Coogan), who has been scheduled for a match with Palooka. Realizing Humphrey's sheer bulk is a menace to Joe's professional standing, Knobby Walsh (Leon Errol) poses as Lord Poole, an English fight manager.

Running time: 65 minutes. Release date: February 5, 1950.

Working title: **Honeymoon for Five.**

621. Blonde Dynamite (comedy) Directed by William Beaudine. Produced by Jan Grippo. Screenplay by Charles R. Marion.

Cast: Leo Gorcey, Huntz Hall, Adele Jergens, Gabriel Dell, Harry Lewis, Billy Benedict, David Gorcey, Buddy Gorman, Murray Alper, Bernard Gorcey, Jody Gilbert, John Harmon, Michael Ross, Lynn Davies, Beverlee Crane, Karen Randle, Stanley Andrews, Constance Purdy, Florence Auer, Tom Kennedy, Robert Emmett Keane, Dick Elliott.

The Bowery Boys (Leo Gorcey, Huntz Hall, Billy Benedict, David Gorcey, Buddy Gorman) open an escort bureau and get involved with gangsters trying to break into the bank next door.

Running time: 66 minutes. Release date: February 12, 1950.

622. West of Wyoming (western) Directed by Wallace Fox. Produced by Eddie Davis.

Cast: Johnny Mack Brown, Gail Davis, Myron Healey, Dennis Moore, Stanley Andrews, Milburn Morante, Mary Gordon, Carl Mathews, Paul Cramer, John Merton, Mike Ragan (Holly Bane), Steve Clark, Frank McCarroll, Bud Osborne.

A government agent (Johnny Mack Brown) battles a wealthy cattleman (Stanley Andrews) out to prevent settlers from claiming gold-rich territory.

Running time: 57 minutes. Release date: February 19, 1950.

623. Young Daniel Boone (western-drama) Directed by Reginald LeBorg. Produced by James S. Burkett. Screenplay by Clint Johnson and Reginald LeBorg. In Cinecolor.

Cast: David Bruce, Kristine Miller, Damian O'Flynn, Don Beddoe, Mary Treen, John Mylong, William Roy, Stanley Logan, Herbert Baish, Nip T. Strongheart, Richard Foote, Stephen S. Harrison.

Daniel Boone (David Bruce), a scout, is sent into the wilderness to locate possible survivors of an Indian massacre.

Running time: 71 minutes. Release date: March 5, 1950.

624. Over the Border (western) Produced and directed by Wallace Fox. Screenplay by J. Benton Cheney.

Cast: Johnny Mack Brown, Wendy Waldron, Myron Healey, Marshall Reed, Mike Ragan (Holly Bane), House Peters, Jr., Pierre Watkin, Hank Bell, George DeNormand, Milburn Morante, Frank Jaquet, Buck Bailey, George Sowards, Carol Henry, Frank McCarroll, Bud Osborne, Herman Hack, Ray Jones, Artie Ortego, Bob Woodward.

A Wells Fargo agent (Johnny Mack Brown) thwarts a plot to smuggle silver bars in from Mexico.

Running time: 58 minutes. Release date: March 12, 1950.

625. Killer Shark (adventure) Directed by Oscar (Budd) Boetticher. Produced by Lindsley Parsons. Original screenplay by Charles Lang.

Top: Johnny Mack Brown (left) shows Myron Healey the proper way to hold a firearm in "Over the Border" (1950). Bottom: Virginia Welles (left), Phil Brito and Sheila Ryan in "Square Dance Katy" (1950).

Cast: Roddy McDowall, Laurette Luez, Eddie Norris, Roland Winters, Rick Vallin, Douglas Fowley, Nacho Galindo, Ralf Harolde, Dick Moore, Ted Hecht, Charles Lang, Robert Espinoza, Julio Sebastian, Julian Rivero, Frank Sully, George Slocum.

A college student (Roddy McDowall) goes to a Mexican fishing village to visit his father, a shark boat operator, whom he hasn't seen in many years.

Running time: 76 minutes. Release date: March 19, 1950.

626. Square Dance Katy (musical) Directed by Jean Yarbrough. Produced by Lindsley Parsons. Screenplay by Warren Wilson.

Cast: Vera Vague, Phil Brito, Virginia Welles, Warren Douglas, Sheila Ryan, Dorothy Vaughn, Harry Cheshire, Fenton "Jonesy" Jones, Jon Riffel, Warren Jackson, Donald Kerr, Jimmie Davis and His Sunshine Band.

A soap company representative (Warren Douglas) goes hunting for talent in a rural community and meets Katy (Virginia Welles), who wants her boy friend Dodo (Phil Brito) and his hillbilly band to break into television. However, the representative is more impressed with Katy's singing and brings her to New York to star in the company's show.

Running time: 76 minutes. Release date: March 25, 1950.

627. Gunslingers (western) Produced and directed by Wallace Fox. Screenplay by Adele Buffington.

Cast: Whip Wilson, Andy Clyde, Reno Browne, Dennis Moore, Riley Hill, Sarah Padden, Hank Bell, Bill Kennedy, Steve Clark, George Chesebro, Carl Mathews, Frank McCarroll, Reed Howes, Carol Henry, George DeNormand.

In an effort to help a friend who has been wrongfully convicted on cattle rustling charges, Whip sets out to gather information on the criminal gang who framed him.

Running time: 55 minutes. Release date: April 9, 1950.

628. Mystery at the Burlesque (mystery) Directed by Val Guest. Produced by Daniel M. Angel. Screenplay by Val Guest.

Cast: Garry Marsh, Jon Pertwer, Jack Livesey, Elliot Makheen, Jimmy Edwards, Diana Decker, Donald Clive, The Windmill Theatre Company and staff.

When a dead body is found in the front row of a theater, the police put a stage troupe through their numbers as a means of determining which of the players or stage employees were in a position to fire the shot that killed the man.

Running time: 58 minutes. Release date: April 16, 1950.

An Associated British Pathe production, released in Great Britain as **Murder at the Windmill** (1949); released in the U.S. by Monogram.

629. Jiggs and Maggie Out West (comedy) Directed by William Beaudine. Produced by Barney Gerard. Screenplay by Barney Gerard and Adele Buffington. Story by Barney Gerard and Eddie Cline. Based on the King Features comic strip "Bringing Up Father" by George McManus.

Cast: Joe Yule, Renie Riano, George McManus, Tim Ryan, Jim Bannon, Riley Hill, Pat Goldin, June Harrison, Terry McGinnis, Henry "Bomber" Kulkowich (Henry Kulky), Billy Griffin, Kenne Duncan, Tom Kennedy, William Vincent.

Jiggs (Joe Yule) and Maggie (Renie Riano) head for a western ghost town, where Maggie searches for a gold treasure mentioned in her grandfather's will.

Running time: 66 minutes. Release date: April 23, 1950.

630. Six Gun Mesa (western) Directed by Wallace Fox. Produced by Eddie Davis. Screenplay by Adele Buffington.

Cast: Johnny Mack Brown, Gail Davis, Riley Hill, Leonard Penn, Marshall Reed, Steve Clark, Milburn Morante, Carl Mathews, Bud Osborne, George DeNormand, Stanley Blystone, Frank Jaquet, Artie Ortego, Merrill McCormack.

Johnny comes to the aid of a foreman (Riley Hill)

held responsible for a cattle stampede that killed several cowhands.

Running time: 56 minutes. Release date: April 30, 1950.

631. Father Makes Good (comedy) Directed by Jean Yarbrough. Produced by Peter Scully. Screenplay by D.D. Beauchamp. Based on the Good Housekeeping Magazine story "Journey at Sunrise" by D.D. Beauchamp.

Cast: Raymond Walburn, Walter Catlett, Gary Gray, Mary Stuart, Barbara Brown, Olin Howlin, Jack Kirkwood, Betty King, George Nokes, Robert Emmett Keane, Mary Field.

To show his opposition to the mayor's tax on milk, Henry Latham (Raymond Walburn) purchases a cow.

Running time: 61 minutes. Release date: May 7, 1950.

632. Lucky Losers (comedy) Directed by William Beaudine. Produced by Jan Grippo. Screenplay by Charles R. Marion. Additional dialogue by Bert Lawrence.

Cast: Leo Gorcey, Huntz Hall, Hillary Brooke, Gabriel Dell, Lyle Talbot, Billy Benedict, David Gorcey, Buddy Gorman, Bernard Gorcey, Joseph Turkel, Harry Tyler, Harry Cheshire, Frank Jenks, Douglas Evans, Wendy Waldron, Glenn Vernon, Chester Clute, Selmer Jackson, Dick Elliott, Mary Treen.

Working as Wall Street runners, Bowery Boys Slip (Leo Gorcey) and Sach (Huntz Hall) uncover evidence that an apparent suicide was actually a murder.

Running time: 69 minutes. Release date: May 14, 1950.

633. Humphrey Takes a Chance (comedy) Directed by Jean Yarbrough. Produced by Hal E. Chester. Original screenplay by Henry Blankfort. Based on the "Joe Palooka" comic strip by Ham Fisher.

Cast: Leon Errol, Joe Kirkwood, Pamela Blake, Robert Coogan, Jerome Cowan, Joe Besser, Don McGuire, Donald MacBride, Curt Bois, Clem Bevans, Frank Sully, Eddie Gribbon, Meyer Grace, Lillian Bronson, Sam Balter.

Fight promoter Knobby Walsh (Leon Errol) takes Joe Palooka (Joe Kirkwood), Joe's wife (Pamela Blake) and Humphrey (Robert Coogan) to a small town, where Knobby decides to enter Humphrey as a candidate in a mayoral election.

Running time: 74 minutes. Release date: June 4, 1950.

Also known as **Joe Palooka in Humphrey Takes a Chance.**

634. Sideshow (mystery–drama) Directed by Jean Yarbrough. Produced by William F. Broidy. Screenplay by Sam Roeca. Story by William F. Broidy.

Cast: Don McGuire, Tracey Roberts, John Abbott, Eddie Quillan, Ray Walker, Richard Foote, Jimmy Conlin, Iris Adrian, Ted Hecht, Stephen Chase, Donald Kerr, Frank Fenton, Kathy Johnson, Jack Ingram, Dale Van Sickle.

A Treasury Department agent (Don McGuire) takes a job with a carnival in order to expose a gang of jewel smugglers who are operating out of it.

Running time: 67 minutes. Release date: June 18, 1950.

635. The Lost Volcano (adventure) Directed by Ford Beebe. Produced by Walter Mirisch. Screenplay by Ford Beebe.

Cast: Johnny Sheffield, Donald Woods, Marjorie Lord, John Ridgely, Robert Lewis, Elena Verdugo, Tommy Ivo, Don Harvey, Grandon Rhodes.

Bomba (Johnny Sheffield) swings to the rescue when a zoologist's young son (Tommy Ivo) is kidnapped by two jungle guides who are seeking the location of a lost volcano reputed to overlay an ancient city.

Running time: 67 minutes. Release date: June 25, 1950.

636. Arizona Territory (western) Directed by Wallace Fox. Produced by Vincent Fennelly. Original screenplay by Adele Buffington.

Cast: Whip Wilson, Andy Clyde, Nancy Saunders,

Dennis Moore, John Merton, Carl Mathews, Carol Henry, Bud Osborne, Frank Austin, Ted Adams.

Jeff Malloy (Whip Wilson) rescues Doris Devin (Nancy Saunders), owner of a trading post, from an ambush planned by her uncle, who is trying to scare her out of the territory so he can continue his counterfeiting operations.

Running time: 56 minutes. Release date: July 2, 1950.

637. The Silk Noose (mystery) Directed by Edmond T. Greville. Produced by Edward Dryhurst. Screenplay by Richard Llewellyn, from his own play.

Cast: Carole Landis, Joseph Calleia, Derek Farr, Stanley Holloway, Nigel Patrick, Ruth Nixon, Carol Van Derman, John Slater, Leslie Bradley, Reginald Tate, Edward Rigby, John Salew, Robert Adair, Hay Petrie, Uriel Porter, Ella Retford, Brenda Hogan.

An American newspaperwoman (Carole Landis) in London decides to break up the nefarious operations of Sugiani (Joseph Calleia), a black marketeer.

Running time: 72 minutes. Release date: July 9, 1950.

An Associated British Pathe production, released in Great Britain as **Noose** (1948); released in the U.S. by Monogram.

638. A Modern Marriage (drama) Directed by Paul Landres. Produced by David Diamond. Screenplay by Sam Roeca and George Wallace Sayre.

Cast: Reed Hadley, Margaret Field, Robert Clarke, Nana Bryant, Charles Smith, Dick Elliott, Christine McIntyre, Lelah Tyler, Pattee Chapman, Frank Fenton, Edward Keane.

A doctor (Reed Hadley) from the American Institute of Family Relations is called in to find out why a young woman (Margaret Field) ran away from her husband (Robert Clarke) on their honeymoon and attempted suicide.

Running time: 66 minutes. Release date: July 10, 1950.

639. Snow Dog (adventure) Directed by Frank McDonald.

Produced by Lindsley Parsons. Screenplay by William Raynor. From the story "Tentacles of the North" by James Oliver Curwood.

Cast: Kirby Grant, Elena Verdugo, Rick Vallin, Milburn Morante, Richard Karlan, Jane Adrian, Hal Gerard, Richard Avonde, Duke York, Guy Zanette, Chinook the Wonder Dog.

A Mountie (Kirby Grant) is summoned to a Canadian trapping community after several trappers have been found dead, apparently clawed to death by a killer wolf.

Running time: 63 minutes. Release date: July 16, 1950.

640. County Fair (drama) Directed by William Beaudine. Produced by Walter Mirisch. Screenplay by W. Scott Darling. A Jeffrey Bernerd Production. In Cinecolor.

Cast: Rory Calhoun, Jane Nigh, Florence Bates, Warren Douglas, Raymond Hatton, Emory Parnell, Rory Mallison, Harry Cheshire, Milton Kibbee.

A young woman (Jane Nigh), whose mother (Florence Bates) operates a county fair hamburger stand, falls in love with a wealthy racehorse owner (Rory Calhoun).

Running time: 76 minutes. Release date: July 30, 1950.

641. Triple Trouble (comedy) Directed by Jean Yarbrough. Produced by Jan Grippo. Screenplay by Charles R. Marion. Additional dialogue by Bert Lawrence.

Cast: Leo Gorcey, Huntz Hall, Gabriel Dell, Richard Benedict, Pat Collins, Lyn Thomas, Bernard Gorcey, Paul Dubov, Billy Benedict, David Gorcey, Joseph Turkel, George Chandler, Eddie Gribbon, Jonathan Hale, Joseph Crehan, Effie Lairch, Edward Gargan, Eddie Foster, Frank Marlowe, Tom Kennedy, Lyle Talbot.

Bowery Boys Slip (Leo Gorcey) and Sach (Huntz Hall) take the rap for a warehouse robbery and are sent to prison.

Running time: 66 minutes. Release date: August 13, 1950.

642. Silver Raiders (western) Directed by Wallace Fox.

Patricia Rios (left), Andy Clyde and Virginia Herrick in "Silver Raiders" (1950).

Produced by Vincent M. Fennelly. Screenplay by Daniel B. Ullman.

Cast: Whip Wilson, Andy Clyde, Virginia Herrick, Leonard Penn, Patricia Rios, Dennis Moore, Kermit Maynard, Reed Howes, Riley Hill, Marshall Reed, George DeNormand.

An Arizona Ranger (Whip Wilson) poses as an outlaw and joins a bandit gang that steals silver in Mexico and sells it in the United States.

Running time: 55 minutes. Release date: August 20, 1950.

643. Big Timber (action-drama) Directed by Jean Yarbrough. Produced by Lindsley Parsons. Screenplay by Warren Wilson.

Cast: Roddy McDowall, Jeff Donnell, Lyn Thomas,

Gordon Jones, Tom Greenway, Ted Hecht, Robert Shayne, Lyle Talbot.

A young man (Roddy McDowall) gets a job in a lumber camp, where a jealous co-worker rigs matters to make it appear that the youth is an incompetent bungler.

Running time: 73 minutes. Release date: September 10, 1950.

Also known as **Tall Timber**.

644. Law of the Panhandle (western) Directed by Lewis Collins. Produced by Jerry Thomas. Screenplay by Joseph Poland.

Cast: Johnny Mack Brown, Jane Adams, Riley Hill, Marshall Reed, Myron Healey, Ted Adams, Lee Roberts, Carol Henry, Milburn Morante, Bob Duncan, Kermit Maynard, Boyd Stockman, George DeNormand, Tex Palmer, Ray Jones.

A U.S. Marshal (Johnny Mack Brown) helps a sheriff (Riley Hill) battle a gang of ruthless outlaws who are forcing ranchers off their property so they can buy it for future railroad sites.

Running time: 55 minutes. Release date: September 17, 1950.

645. Bomba and the Hidden City (adventure) Directed by Ford Beebe. Produced by Walter Mirisch. Screenplay by Carroll Young.

Cast: Johnny Sheffield, Sue England, Paul Guilfoyle, Robert "Smoki" Whitfield, Damian O'Flynn, Leon Belasco, Charles LaTorre.

Bomba (Johnny Sheffield) comes to the aid of a young girl (Sue England) who is sold at the slave market to an evil provincial governor.

Running time: 71 minutes. Release date: September 24, 1950.

Also known as **The Hidden City**.

646. Cherokee Uprising (western) Directed by Lewis Collins. Produced by Vincent M. Fennelly. Screenplay by Daniel B. Ullman.

Cast: Whip Wilson, Andy Clyde, Lois Hall, Iron Eyes

Cody, Sam Flint, Forrest Taylor, Marshall Reed, Chief Yowlachie, Lee Roberts, Stanley Price, Lyle Talbot, Edith Mills.

At the request of the town judge, U.S. Marshals Bob Foster (Whip Wilson) and Jake Jones (Andy Clyde) are sent to investigate a series of Indian raids.

Running time: 57 minutes. Release date: October 8, 1950.

647. Hot Rod (drama) Directed by Lewis D. Collins. Produced by Jerry Thomas. Screenplay by Daniel B. Ullman.

Cast: James Lydon, Art Baker, Gil Stratton, Jr., Gloria Winters, Myron Healey, Tommy Bond, Jean Dean, Bret Hamilton, Marshall Reed, Dennis Moore, William Vincent.

Against his father's wishes, a young man (James Lydon) converts his car into a hot rod.

Running time: 61 minutes. Release date: October 22, 1950.

648. Blues Busters (musical-comedy) Directed by William Beaudine. Produced by Jan Grippo. Screenplay by Charles R. Marion. Additional dialogue by Bert Lawrence.

Cast: Leo Gorcey, Huntz Hall, Adele Jergens, Gabriel Dell, Craig Stevens, Phyllis Coates, Bernard Gorcey, Billy Benedict, David Gorcey, Buddy Gorman, Paul Bryar, William Vincent, Matty King, Hank Mann. John Lorenz and Gloria Wood dub the singing voices for Huntz Hall and Adele Jergens.

After undergoing a tonsillectomy, Horace Debussy "Sach" Jones (Huntz Hall) discovers he has a beautiful singing voice; Slip Mahoney (Leo Gorcey) and the other Bowery Boys (Gabriel Dell, Billy Benedict, David Gorcey, Buddy Gorman) then turn Louie's Sweet Shop into a nightclub, promoting Sach as "The Bowery Thrush."

Running time: 67 minutes. Release date: October 29, 1950.

Working title: **Bowery Thrush.**

649. Joe Palooka in the Squared Circle (comedy-drama)

Gabriel Dell (left), Huntz Hall and Leo Gorcey in "Blues Busters" (1950), one of the best entries in the Bowery Boys series.

Directed by Reginald LeBorg. Produced by Hal E. Chester. Screenplay by Jan Jeffries. Original story by B.F. Melzer. Based on the "Joe Palooka" comic strip by Ham Fisher.

Cast: Joe Kirkwood, James Gleason, Lois Hall, Edgar Barrier, Myrna Dell, Robert Coogan, Dan Seymour, Charles Halton, Frank Jenks, Greg McClure, Eddie Gribbon, Robert Griffin, John Harmon, Jack Roper, Sue Carlton, William Haade, Stanley Prager, Marvin Williams, Hal Fieberling, John Merrick, Paul Bryar.

Fighter Joe Palooka (Joe Kirkwood) witnesses a gangland slaying and resolves to bring the murderers to justice.

Running time: 63 minutes. Release date: November 5, 1950.

650. Outlaw Gold (western) Directed by Wallace Fox. Produced by Vincent M. Fennelly. Screenplay by Daniel B. Ullman.

Cast: Johnny Mack Brown, Jane Adams, Myron Healey,

Milburn Morante, Marshall Reed, Hugh Prosser, Carol Henry, Bud Osborne, George DeNormand, Frank Jaquet, Carl Mathews, Ray Jones, Steve Clark, Bob Woodward, Merrill McCormack.

When a shipment of gold belonging to the Mexican government is stolen, a U.S. Ranger (Johnny Mack Brown) is sent to investigate.

Running time: 56 minutes. Release date: November 26, 1950.

Originally titled **Massacre Valley**.

651. Father's Wild Game (comedy) Directed by Herbert I. Leeds. Produced by Peter Scully. Original screenplay by D.D. Beauchamp.

Cast: Raymond Walburn, Walter Catlett, Gary Gray, Jane Darwell, Barbara Brown, M'Liss McClure, Fred Libby, George Nokes, Roscoe Ates, Ralph Sanford, Emmett Vogan, Maxine Semon, Doris Kemper, Ann Tyrell.

Balking at high meat prices, Henry Latham (Raymond Walburn) goes on a hunting trip.

Running time: 61 min. Release date: Dec. 3, 1950.

652. Outlaws of Texas (western) Directed by Thomas Carr. Produced by Vincent M. Fennelly. Screenplay by Daniel B. Ullman.

Cast: Whip Wilson, Andy Clyde, Phyllis Coates, Terry Frost, Tommy Farrell, Zon Murray, George DeNormand, Steve Carr, Stanley Price.

In an effort to track down a band of murderous stagecoach robbers, U.S. Marshals Tom (Whip Wilson) and Hungry (Andy Clyde) pose as outlaws.

Running time: 56 minutes. Release date: December 10, 1950.

653. Call of the Klondike (adventure) Directed by Frank McDonald. Produced by Lindsley Parsons and William F. Broidy. Screenplay by Charles Lang. From a story by James Oliver Curwood.

Cast: Kirby Grant, Anne Gwynne, Lynne Roberts, Tom Neal, Russell Simpson, Marc Krah, Paul Bryar, Pat Gleason, Duke York, Chinook the Wonder Dog.

A Mountie (Kirby Grant) and a young woman (Anne Gwynne) discover a gold mine while searching for her missing father.
Running time: 67 minutes. Release date: December 17, 1950.

1951

654. Sierra Passage (western) Directed by Frank McDonald. Produced by Lindsley Parsons. Screenplay by Tom W. Blackburn, Warren D. Wandberg and Sam Roeca.

Cast: Wayne Morris, Lola Albright, Lloyd Corrigan, Alan Hale, Jr., Roland Winters, Jim Bannon, Billy Gray, Paul McGuire, Richard Karlan, George Eldredge.

A star marksman (Wayne Morris) with a minstrel show seeks revenge on the man who murdered his father.
Running time: 81 minutes. Release date: January 7, 1951.

655. Colorado Ambush (western) Directed by Lewis Collins. Produced by Vincent M. Fennelly. Screenplay by Myron Healey.

Cast: Johnny Mack Brown, Myron Healey, Lois Hall, Tommy Farrell, Christine McIntyre, Lyle Talbot, Lee Roberts, Marshall Bradford, Joe McGuinn, John Hart, Roy Butler, George DeNormand.

A U.S. Ranger (Johnny Mack Brown) investigates the murders of three Wells Fargo messengers.
Running time: 51 minutes. Release date: January 14, 1951.

656. Bowery Battalion (comedy) Directed by William Beaudine. Produced by Jan Grippo. Screenplay by Charles R. Marion. Additional dialogue by Bert Lawrence.

Cast: Leo Gorcey, Huntz Hall, Virginia Hewitt, Donald MacBride, Russell Hicks, Billy Benedict, David Gorcey, Buddy Gorman, Bernard Gorcey, Selmer Jackson, John Bleifer, Al Eben, Frank Jenks, Michael Ross, Emil Sitka, Harry Lauter, William Ruhl.

The Bowery Boys (Leo Gorcey, Huntz Hall, Billy

Lola Albright and Wayne Morris in "Sierra Passage" (1951).

Benedict, David Gorcey, Buddy Gorman), privates in the army, are on the trail of spies.

Running time: 69 minutes. Release date: January 24, 1951.

657. Blue Blood (drama) Directed by Lew Landers. Produced by Ben Schwalb. Screenplay by W. Scott Darling. Suggested by the story "Dog Meat" by Peter B. Kyne. In Cinecolor.

Cast: Bill Williams, Jane Nigh, Arthur Shields, Audrey Long, Lyle Talbot, Harry Shannon, Harry V. Cheshire, William J. Tannen, Milton Kibbee.

Two girls (Jane Nigh, Audrey Long), daughters of a wealthy horse breeder, and an elderly trainer (Arthur Shields) down on his luck rescue a horse bound for the meat factory and retrain him into a racing winner.

Running time: 72 minutes. Release date: January 28, 1951.

658. Abilene Trail (western) Directed by Lewis Collins. Produced by Vincent M. Fennelly. Screenplay by Harry Fraser.

Cast: Whip Wilson, Andy Clyde, Tommy Farrell, Steve Clark, Noel Neill, Dennis Moore, Marshall Reed, Lee Roberts, Milburn Morante, Ted Adams, Bill Kennedy, Stanley Price, Lyle Talbot.

The Kansas Kid (Whip Wilson) and Sagebrush (Andy Clyde), unjustly accused as horse thieves, flee from a sheriff's posse and take jobs with a trail herd.

Running time: 54 minutes. Release date: February 4, 1951.

659. Rhythm Inn (musical) Directed by Paul Landres. Produced by Lindsley Parsons. Original screenplay by Bill Raynor.

Cast: Jane Frazee, Kirby Grant, Charles Smith, Lois Collier, Fritz Feld, Ralph Sanford, Armida, Anson Weeks and His Orchestra, Jean Ritchie, Ames and Arno, Ramon Ros, Pete Daily, Wingy Manone, Walter Gross, Ralph Peters, Matty Matlock, Joe Yukl, Budd Hatch, Barrett Deems.

After a Dixieland band pawns their instruments at a music store, the bandleader (Kirby Grant) and the singer (Jane Frazee) talk a store clerk (Charles Smith), who's an aspiring songwriter, into smuggling the instruments out each night so the band can fulfill a nightclub engagement.

Running time: 73 minutes. Release date: February 11, 1951.

Kirby Grant and Jane Frazee in "Rhythm Inn" (1951).

660. Navy Bound (drama) Directed by Paul Landres. Produced by William F. Broidy. Screenplay by Sam Roeca. From a magazine story by Talbert Josselyn.

Cast: Tom Neal, Wendy Waldron, Regis Toomey, John Abbott, Murray Alper, Paul Bryar, Harvey Parry, Ric Roman, John Compton, Stephen Harrison, Billy Bletcher, Ray Kemper.

A navy boxing champion (Tom Neal) leaves the services to help his foster father pay off the debt on his fishing boat.

Running time: 61 minutes. Release date: March 4, 1951.

661. Man from Sonora (western) Directed by Lewis Collins. Produced by Vincent M. Fennelly. Screenplay by Maurice Tombragel.

Cast: Johnny Mack Brown, Phyllis Coates, Lyle Talbot, House Peters, Jr., Lee Roberts, John Merton, Stanley Price, Dennis Moore, Ray Jones, Pierce Lyden, Sam Flint, George DeNormand.

Johnny battles a gang of outlaws responsible for the Silver Springs stagecoach robbery.

Running time: 54 minutes. Release date: March 11, 1951.

Working title: **Man from El Paso.**

662. Gypsy Fury (drama) Directed by Christian-Jaque. Produced by Lorens Marmstedt and Alf Jorgensen. Based on a novel by Viktor Rydberg. English dialogue written and directed by Romney Brent.

Cast: Viveca Lindfors, Christopher Kent, Romney Brent, Johnny Chabot, Lauritz Falk, Edvin Adolphson, Naima Wifstrand, Marta Dorff, Vibeke Falk, Rauzena.

A nobleman (Christopher Kent) forsakes his royal life to marry a beautiful gypsy (Viveca Lindfors).

Running time: 63 minutes. Release date: March 18, 1951.

A Swedish-French production, released in the U.S. by Monogram.

663. The Lion Hunters (adventure) Directed by Ford Beebe. Produced by Walter Mirisch. Screenplay by Ford Beebe.

Cast: Johnny Sheffield, Morris Ankrum, Ann B. Todd, Douglas Kennedy, Robert "Smoki" Whitfield, Robert Davis.

After a lion is shot and left to die, Bomba (Johnny Sheffield) searches for the ruthless hunters (Morris Ankrum, Douglas Kennedy), who are trapping lions in sacred territory.

Running time: 75 min. Release date: Mar. 25, 1951.

664. Canyon Raiders (western) Directed by Lewis Collins. Produced by Vincent M. Fennelly. Screenplay by Jay Gilgore.

Cast: Whip Wilson, Fuzzy Knight, Jim Bannon, Phyllis Coates, I. Stanford Jolley, Barbara Woodell, Marshall Reed, Riley Hill, Bill Kennedy.

Whip and his pals (Fuzzy Knight, Jim Bannon, Riley Hill) clash with a gang of rustlers.

Running time: 54 minutes. Release date: April 8, 1951.

665. Ghost Chasers (comedy) Directed by William Beaudine. Produced by Jan Grippo. Screenplay by Charles R. Marion. Additional dialogue by Bert Lawrence.

Cast: Leo Gorcey, Huntz Hall, Lloyd Corrigan, Lela Bliss, Jan Kayne, Phil Van Zandt, Billy Benedict, David Gorcey, Buddy Gorman, Bernard Gorcey, Robert Coogan, Michael Ross, Donald Lawton, Hal Gerard, Marshall Bradford, Argentina Brunetti, Doris Kemper, Belle Mitchell, Paul Bryar, Pat Gleason, Bob Peoples, Marjorie Eaton, Bess Flowers.

When the Bowery Boys set out to expose some phony spiritualists, a friendly ghost (Lloyd Corrigan) befriends Sach (Huntz Hall).

Running time: 69 minutes. Release date: April 29, 1951.

666. Blazing Bullets (western) Directed by Wallace Fox. Produced by Vincent M. Fennelly. Screenplay by George Daniels.

Cast: Johnny Mack Brown, Lois Hall, House Peters, Jr., Stanley Price, Dennis Moore, Edmund Cobb, Milburn Morante, Forrest Taylor, Edward Cassidy, George De-Normand, Carl Mathews.

Johnny goes to the aid of a young woman (Lois Hall) whose fiance is suspected of kidnapping her father.

Running time: 51 minutes. Release date: May 6, 1951.

Working title: **Gold Bullets.**

667. Cavalry Scout (western) Directed by Lesley Selander.

Produced by Walter Mirisch. Screenplay by Daniel B. Ullman and Thomas Blackburn. In Cinecolor.

Cast: Rod Cameron, Audrey Long, Jim Davis, James Millican, James Arness, John Doucette, William Phillips, Stephen Chase, Rory Mallison, Eddy Waller, Paul Bryar.

Kirby Frye (Rod Cameron), an army civilian scout, is on the trail of two Gatling guns and other ordnance stolen from an arsenal.

Running time: 78 minutes. Release date: May 13, 1951.

668. According to Mrs. Hoyle (drama) Directed by Jean Yarbrough. Produced by Barney Gerard. Screenplay by W. Scott Darling and Barney Gerard. Adapted from a novelette by Jean Z. Owen.

Cast: Spring Byington, Anthony Caruso, Brett King, Tanis Chandler, Stephen Chase, Robert Karnes, Tristram Coffin, James Flavin, Paul Bryar, Charles Williams, Harry Lauter, Michael Whalen, Leander de Cordova, Wilbur Mack, Frank Jaquet, Marcelle Imhof, Baron James Lichter, Joey Ray, Ted Stanhope, Don Harvey, Rory Mallison.

Mrs. Hoyle (Spring Byington), a retired school teacher, tries to reform a gang of crooks who've taken over the hotel she resides in.

Running time: 60 minutes. Release date: May 20, 1951.

669. Nevada Badmen (western) Directed by Lewis Collins. Produced by Vincent M. Fennelly. Screenplay by Joseph O'Donnell. A Frontier Pictures Production.

Cast: Whip Wilson, Fuzzy Knight, Jim Bannon, Phyllis Coates, I. Stanford Jolley, Marshall Reed, Riley Hill, Lee Roberts, Pierce Lyden, Bill Kennedy, Bud Osborne, Stanley Price, Artie Ortego, Carl Mathews.

Whip and his pals (Fuzzy Knight, Jim Bannon, Riley Hill) come to the aid of a young woman (Phyllis Coates) when a corrupt banker tries to foreclose on her ranch property, which is the site of a gold mine.

Running time: 58 minutes. Release date: May 27, 1951.

670. Casa Manana (musical) Directed by Jean Yarbrough. Produced by Lindsley Parsons. Screenplay by Bill Raynor.

Cast: Robert Clarke, Virginia Welles, Robert Karnes, Tony Roux, Carol Brewster, Paul Maxey, Jean Richey, The Rio Brothers, Eddie LeBaron and His Orchestra, Spade Cooley, Yadira Jiminez, Zaro and D'Lores, Mercer Brothers, Armando and Lita, Betty and Beverly, Olga Perez, Davis and Johnson.

A secretary (Virginia Welles) has aspirations of becoming a singer, so her boy friend (Robert Clarke) purchases a nitery, "Casa Manana," and plans to reopen it with her as the star attraction.

Running time: 73 minutes. Release date: June 10, 1951.

671. Father Takes the Air (comedy) Directed by Frank McDonald. Produced by Peter Scully. Original screenplay by D.D. Beauchamp. A Mayfair Production.

Cast: Raymond Walburn, Walter Catlett, Gary Gray, Florence Bates, Barbara Brown, M'Liss McClure, James Brown, George Nokes, Carl Milletaire, Tom Dugan, Billy Bletcher, Maxine Semon, Don Hicks, Joan Valerie, Sam Flint.

Henry Latham (Raymond Walburn) and Mayor Colton (Walter Catlett), helping Latham's daughter Barbara (M'Liss McClure) operate a flying school, become involved with a bank robber when he charters a plane.

Running time: 61 minutes. Release date: June 17, 1951.

672. Montana Desperado (western) Directed by Wallace Fox. Produced by Vincent M. Fennelly. Screenplay by Daniel B. Ullman. A Frontier Pictures Production.

Cast: Johnny Mack Brown, Virginia Herrick, Myron Healey, Marshall Reed, Steve Clark, Edmund Cobb, Lee Roberts, Carl Mathews, Ben Corbett.

A rancher (Johnny Mack Brown) tries to find out the identity of a masked killer responsible for the deaths of several other ranchers.

Running time: 51 minutes. Release date: June 24, 1951.

Myron Healey (left) prepares to clobber a stern but unsuspecting Johnny Mack Brown in this publicity shot for "Montana Desperado" (1951).

673. Yukon Manhunt (adventure) Directed by Frank McDonald. Produced by Lindsley Parsons. Screenplay by Bill Raynor. From a story by James Oliver Curwood.

Cast: Kirby Grant, Gail Davis, Margaret Field, Rand Brooks, Nelson Leigh, John Doucette, Paul McGuire, Chinook the Wonder Dog.

A Mountie (Kirby Grant) goes after the crooks who are robbing payroll messengers.

Running time: 63 minutes. Release date: July 8, 1951.

674. Stagecoach Driver (western) Directed by Lewis Collins. Produced by Vincent M. Fennelly. Screenplay by Joseph O'Donnell. A Frontier Pictures Production.

Cast: Whip Wilson, Fuzzy Knight, Jim Bannon, Gloria Winters, Lane Bradford, Barbara Allen, John Hart, Leonard Penn, Stanley Price, Marshall Reed, George DeNormand.

Running time: 52 minutes. Release date: July 15, 1951.

675. Let's Go Navy! (comedy) Directed by William Beaudine. Produced by Jan Grippo. Screenplay by Max Adams. Additional dialogue by Bert Lawrence.

Cast: Leo Gorcey, Huntz Hall, Allen Jenkins, Tom Neal, Charlita, Paul Harvey, Billy Benedict, David Gorcey, Buddy Gorman, Bernard Gorcey, Emory Parnell, Richard Benedict, Douglas Evans, Frank Jenks, Tom Kennedy, Dorothy Ford, Harry Lauter, Dave Willock, Peter Mamakos, Ray Walker, Jonathan Hale, Paul Bryar, Richard Monahan, William Lechner, George Offerman, Jr., Mike Lally, Russ Conway, Harry Strang, William Vincent, Lee Graham, Pat Gleason, George Eldredge, William Hudson, Bob Peoples, John Close, Emil Sitka, Ray Dawe, Murray Alper, Jimmy Cross, Bill Chandler, Don Gordon, Neyle Morrow, Joey Ray.

The Bowery Boys (Leo Gorcey, Huntz Hall, Billy Benedict, David Gorcey, Buddy Gorman) join the navy in an effort to track down a pair of crooks (Tom Neal, Richard Benedict).

Running time: 68 min. Release date: July 29, 1951.

676. Oklahoma Justice (western) Directed by Lewis Collins. Produced by Vincent M. Fennelly. Screenplay by Joseph O'Donnell.

Cast: Johnny Mack Brown, Jimmy Ellison, Phyllis Coates, Barbara Allen, Kenne Duncan, Lane Bradford, Marshall Reed, Zon Murray, I. Stanford Jolley, Stanley Price, Bruce Edwards, Richard Avonde, Carl Mathews, Edward Cassidy, Lyle Talbot, George DeNormand.

A U.S. Marshal (Johnny Mack Brown), posing as a bandit, infiltrates an outlaw gang operating in the Oklahoma territory.

Christine McIntyre and Whip Wilson are ready for action in "Wanted: Dead or Alive" (1951).

Running time: 56 minutes. Release date: August 19, 1951.
Working title: **Oklahoma Outlaws.**

677. Wanted: Dead or Alive (western) Directed by Thomas Carr. Produced by Vincent M. Fennelly. Screenplay by Clint Johnston. A Frontier Pictures Production.
Cast: Whip Wilson, Fuzzy Knight, Jim Bannon, Christine McIntyre, Leonard Penn, Lane Bradford, Zon Murray, Marshall Reed, Stanley Price, Ray Jones, Jack O'Shea.
Running time: 59 minutes. Release date: September 9, 1951.

678. Triple Cross (comedy-drama) Directed by Reginald LeBorg. Produced by Hal E. Chester. Screenplay by Jan Jeffries. Original story by Harold Bancroft. Based on the "Joe Palooka" comic strip by Ham Fisher.

Cast: Joe Kirkwood, James Gleason, Cathy Downs, John Emery, Steve Brodie, Don Harvey, Rufe Davis, Jimmy Wallington, Mary Young, Eddie Gribbon, Sid Tomack, Dickie LeRoy, Jimmy Lloyd, Cliff Clark, Hank Worden.

Returning from a fishing trip, Joe Palooka (Joe Kirkwood), his wife Ann (Cathy Downs) and his manager Knobby Walsh (James Gleason) are kidnapped by escaped convicts (John Emery, Steve Brodie, Don Harvey).

Running time: 60 minutes. Release date: September 16, 1951.

Also known as **Joe Palooka in Triple Cross**.

679. Whistling Hills (western) Directed by Derwin Abrahams. Produced by Vincent M. Fennelly. Screenplay by Fred Myton. A Frontier Pictures Production.

Cast: Johnny Mack Brown, Jimmy Ellison, Pamela Duncan, Noel Neill, I. Stanford Jolley, Lee Roberts, Marshall Reed, Lane Bradford, Bud Osborne, Pierce Lyden, Frank Ellis, Ray Jones, Merrill McCormack.

A cowboy (Johnny Mack Brown) and a sheriff (Jimmy Ellison) set out to round up a gang of masked outlaws who have been holding up stagecoaches.

Running time: 58 minutes. Release date: October 7, 1951.

680. Yellow Fin (action-drama) Directed by Frank McDonald. Produced by Lindsley Parsons. Screenplay by Warren D. Wandberg and Clint Johnston.

Cast: Wayne Morris, Adrian Booth, Gloria Henry, Damian O'Flynn, Gordon Jones, Paul Fierro, Nacho Galindo, Warren Douglas, Guy Zanette.

A father and son fisherman team, who have operated their own boat for years, run into a streak of bad luck which gives their craft a "jinxed" reputation.

Running time: 74 minutes. Release date: October 14, 1951.

681. Elephant Stampede (adventure) Directed by Ford Beebe. Produced by Walter Mirisch. Screenplay by Ford Beebe.

Cast: Johnny Sheffield, Donna Martell, Edith Evanson, Martin Wilkins, John Kellogg, Myron Healey, Leonard Mudie, Guy Kingsford, James Adamson, Max Thrower, James Payne.

Bomba (Johnny Sheffield) goes after two crooks (John Kellogg, Myron Healey) who are killing elephants to obtain ivory.

Running time: 71 minutes. Release date: October 28, 1951.

Also known as **Bomba and the Elephant Stampede.**

682. Lawless Cowboys (western) Directed by Lewis Collins. Produced by Vincent M. Fennelly. Screenplay by Maurice Tombragel.

Cast: Whip Wilson, Fuzzy Knight, Jim Bannon, Pamela Duncan, Lee Roberts, Lane Bradford, I. Stanford Jolley, Bruce Edwards, Marshall Reed, Ace Malloy, Stanley Price, Richard Emory.

A former Texas Ranger (Whip Wilson) is hired by the Central City Rodeo Committee to investigate a gambling syndicate believed to be fixing rodeo events.

Running time: 58 minutes. Release date: November 7, 1951.

683. Flight to Mars (science fiction) Directed by Lesley Selander. Produced by Walter Mirisch. Screenplay by Arthur Strawn. In Cinecolor.

Cast: Marguerite Chapman, Cameron Mitchell, Arthur Franz, Virginia Houston, John Litel, Morris Ankrum, Richard Gaines, Lucille Barkley, Robert H. Barrat, Edward Earle, William Forrest, Bob Peoples, Tony Marsh, Tristram Coffin, Bill Neff, Trevor Bardette, Russ Conway, Raymond Bond, Everett Glass, David Bond, Wilbur Mack, Stanley Blystone, William Bailey, Frank O'Connor.

Journeying to Mars, scientists (Cameron Mitchell, Arthur Franz, Virginia Houston, John Litel, Richard Gaines) learn of a plot to conquer the Earth.

Running time: 72 minutes. Release date: November 11, 1951.

684. Crazy Over Horses (comedy) Directed by William

300

Arthur Franz and Marguerite Chapman in "Flight to Mars" (1951).

Beaudine. Produced by Jerry Thomas. Screenplay by Tim Ryan.

Cast: Leo Gorcey, Huntz Hall, Ted de Corsia, Allen Jenkins, Gloria Saunders, Tim Ryan, Billy Benedict, David Condon (Gorcey), Bennie Bartlett, Bernard Gorcey, Russell Hicks, Peggy Wynne, Bob Peoples, Michael Ross, Perc Landers, Leo "Ukie" Sherin, Robert "Smoki" Whitfield, Sam Balter, Ray Page, Darr Smith, Wilbur Mack, Gertrude Astor, Bill Cartledge, Whitey Hughes, Delmar Thomas, Bernard Pludow, Ben Frommer.

When Sweet Shop proprietor Louie Dumbrowski (Bernard Gorcey) receives a horse as payment for a debt, the Bowery Boys (Leo Gorcey, Huntz Hall, Billy Benedict, David Condon, Bennie Bartlett) become involved with gamblers who are trying to fix a race.

301

**Phyllis Coates and Wild Bill Elliott in "The Longhorn"
(1951).**

Running time: 65 minutes. Release date: November 18, 1951.

Released in Great Britain as **Win, Place and Show.**

685. The Longhorn (western) Directed by Lewis Collins. Produced by Vincent M. Fennelly. Screenplay by Daniel B. Ullman. In Sepiatone.

Cast: Wild Bill Elliott, Myron Healey, Phyllis Coates,

John Hart, Marshall Reed, William Fawcett, Lee Roberts, Carol Henry, Zon Murray, Steve Clark, Marshall Bradford, Herman Hack, Carl Mathews, Lane Bradford.

A rancher (Wild Bill Elliott) forms a trail drive from Wyoming to Oregon.

Running time: 70 minutes. Release date: November 25, 1951.

686. Texas Lawmen (western) Directed by Lewis Collins. Produced by Vincent M. Fennelly. Screenplay by Joseph Poland.

Cast: Johnny Mack Brown, Jimmy Ellison, I. Stanford Jolley, Lee Roberts, Terry Frost, Marshall Reed, John Hart, Lyle Talbot, Pierce Lyden, Stanley Price, Lane Bradford.

A U.S. Marshal (Johnny Mack Brown) and a sheriff (Jimmy Ellison) set out to capture the sheriff's father (I. Stanford Jolley) and brother (Lee Roberts), bandits responsible for a payroll robbery.

Running time: 54 minutes. Release date: December 2, 1951.

Also known as **Lone Star Lawman.**

687. Northwest Territory (adventure) Directed by Frank McDonald. Produced by Lindsley Parsons. Screenplay by Bill Raynor. From a story by James Oliver Curwood.

Cast: Kirby Grant, Gloria Saunders, Warren Douglas, Pat Mitchell, Tristram Coffin, John Crawford, Duke York, Don Harvey, Sam Flint, Chinook the Wonder Dog.

A Mountie (Kirby Grant) and his dog track down the man who murdered an oil prospector.

Running time: 61 minutes. Release date: December 9, 1951.

688. Stage to Blue River (western) Directed by Lewis Collins. Produced by Vincent M. Fennelly. Screenplay by Joseph Poland. A Frontier Pictures Production.

Cast: Whip Wilson, Fuzzy Knight, Phyllis Coates, Lee Roberts, John Hart, Lane Bradford, Pierce Lyden, Terry Frost, I. Stanford Jolley, William Fawcett, Steve Clark, Stanley Price, Bud Osborne.

A U.S. Marshal (Whip Wilson) helps a young woman (Phyllis Coates) protect her stagecoach line from a corrupt sheriff (Pierce Lyden) who is actually the boss of an outlaw gang.
Running time: 56 minutes. Release date: December 30, 1951.

1952

689. The Steel Fist (drama) Directed by Wesley Barry. Produced by William F. Broidy. Screenplay by C.K. Kivari. Original story by Phyllis Parker.
Cast: Roddy McDowall, Kristine Miller, Harry Lauter, Rand Brooks, Byron Foulger, Kate Lawson, Murray Alper, Bob Peoples, Gil Perkins, Fred Krone.
A Russian student (Roddy McDowall) opposes the communist labor program and is forced to flee the country, with the help of an underground organization.
Running time: 73 minutes. Release date: January 6, 1952.

690. Texas City (western) Directed by Lewis Collins. Produced by Vincent M. Fennelly. Screenplay by Joseph Poland. A Silvermine Production.
Cast: Johnny Mack Brown, Jimmy Ellison, Lois Hall, Lorna Thayer, Lane Bradford, Marshall Reed, Terry Frost, Lyle Talbot, Pierce Lyden, John Hart, Bud Osborne, Stanley Price.
A U.S. Marshal (Johnny Mack Brown) tries to find out who's been providing crooks with information about secret army gold shipments.
Running time: 54 minutes. Release date: January 27, 1952.
Working title: **Ghost Town.**

691. Night Raiders (western) Directed by Howard Bretherton. Produced by Vincent M. Fennelly. Screenplay by Maurice Tombragel. A Silvermine Production.
Cast: Whip Wilson, Fuzzy Knight, Lois Hall, Tommy Farrell, Terry Frost, Lane Bradford, Marshall Reed, Steve Clark, Iron Eyes Cody, Boyd Stockman, Edward

Johnny Mack Brown delivers a blow to Lyle Talbot's chin in "Texas City" (1952).

Cassidy, Carol Henry, Forrest Taylor, Roy Butler, Stanley Price.

Federal Marshals (Whip Wilson, Tommy Farrell) are called in to investigate a series of mysterious night raids plaguing ranchers; the purpose of these raids is to force the local sheriff (Marshall Reed), who has taken part in a robbery, to reveal the hiding place of the stolen loot.

Running time: 52 minutes. Release date: February 3, 1952.

692. Fort Osage (western) Directed by Lesley Selander.

Left to right: Fuzzy Knight, Whip Wilson and Tommy Farrell in "Night Raiders" (1952).

Produced by Walter Mirisch. Story and screenplay by Daniel B. Ullman. In Cinecolor.

Cast: Rod Cameron, Jane Nigh, Morris Ankrum, Douglas Kennedy, John Ridgely, William Phipps, I. Stanford Jolley, Dorothy Adams, Francis McDonald, Myron Healey, Lane Bradford, Iron Eyes Cody, Barbara Woodell, Russ Conway.

A frontier scout (Rod Cameron), hired to head a

California-bound wagon train from Fort Osage, discovers that his bosses are the cause of an Indian uprising.

Running time: 72 minutes. Release date: February 10, 1952.

693. Aladdin and His Lamp (fantasy) Directed by Lew Landers. Produced by Walter Wanger. Screenplay by Howard Dimsdale and Millard Kaufman. In Cinecolor.

Cast: Patricia Medina, John Sands, Richard Erdman, John Dehner, Billy House, Ned Young, Noreen Nash, Rick Vallin, Charles Horvath, Sujata, Arabella.

In this Arabian Nights tale, Aladdin (John Sands), a young pickpocket in Bagdad, falls in love with Jasmine (Patricia Medina), the daughter of the Caliph, and finds a magic lamp with a mystical genie (Charles Horvath).

Running time: 67 minutes. Release date: February 24, 1952.

694. Waco (western) Directed by Lewis Collins. Produced by Vincent M. Fennelly. Screenplay by Daniel B. Ullman. In Sepiatone.

Cast: Wild Bill Elliott, Pamela Blake, I. Stanford Jolley, Rand Brooks, Richard Avonde, Stanley Andrews, Paul Pierce, Lane Bradford, Pierce Lyden, Terry Frost, Stanley Price, Michael Whalen, Ray Bennett, House Peters, Jr., Richard Paxton, Ray Jones, Edward Cassidy, Russ Whiteman.

Wild Bill Elliott is forced to become a fugitive when he's denied a fair trial after killing a crooked gambler.

Running time: 68 minutes. Release date: February 24, 1952.

695. Rodeo (action-drama) Directed by William Beaudine. Produced by Walter Mirisch. Screenplay by Charles R. Marion. In Cinecolor.

Cast: Jane Nigh, John Archer, Wallace Ford, Gary Gray, Frances Rafferty, Sarah Hayden, Frank Ferguson, Myron Healey, Fuzzy Knight, Robert Karnes, Jim Bannon, I. Stanford Jolley.

A young woman (Jane Nigh) takes over a rodeo when its promoter skips out, owing her father $1,800.

Florence Lake and Jimmy Ellison in "Man from the Black Hills" (1952).

Running time: 70 minutes. Release date: March 9, 1952.

696. Hold That Line (comedy) Directed by William Beaudine. Produced by Jerry Thomas. Screenplay by Tim Ryan and Charles R. Marion. Additional dialogue by Bert Lawrence.

Cast: Leo Gorcey, Huntz Hall, John Bromfield, Mona Knox, Veda Ann Borg, Taylor Holmes, David Condon (Gorcey), Bennie Bartlett, Bernard Gorcey, Bob Nichols, Gil Stratton, Jr., Gloria Winters, Francis Pierlot, Pierre Watkin, Byron Foulger, Paul Bryar, Bob Peoples, Tom

Hanlon, George Lewis, Al Eben, Ted Stanhope, Percival Vivian, Tom Kennedy, Bert Davidson, Marjorie Eaton, Jean Dean, Steve Wayne, Ted Jordan, George Sanders (not the Academy Award-winning actor), Marvelle Andre.

The Bowery Boys (Leo Gorcey, Huntz Hall, David Condon, Bennie Bartlett, Gil Stratton, Jr.) go to college; in a chemistry lab, Sach (Hall) concocts a strength serum that transforms him into a collegiate football star.

Running time: 64 minutes. Release date: March 23, 1952.

697. Man from the Black Hills (western) Directed by Thomas Carr. Produced by Vincent M. Fennelly. Screenplay by Joseph O'Donnell. A Silvermine Production.

Cast: Johnny Mack Brown, Jimmy Ellison, Rand Brooks, Stanley Andrews, Florence Lake, Robert Bray, I. Stanford Jolley, Lane Bradford, Denver Pyle, Stanley Price, Ray Bennett, Joel Allen, Bud Osborne, Merrill McCormack, Roy Bucko, Ralph Bucko.

Johnny helps a friend (Jimmy Ellison) unmask an imposter (Rand Brooks) who's trying to lay claim to a gold mine.

Running time: 51 minutes. Release date: March 30, 1952.

698. Jet Job (drama) Directed by William Beaudine. Produced by Ben Schwalb. Written by Charles R. Marion.

Cast: Stanley Clements, Elena Verdugo, John Litel, Bob Nichols, Tom Powers, Dorothy Adams, Todd Karns, Paul Stanton, Dave Willock, John Kellogg, Russ Conway, Steve Roberts, Arthur Space, William Forrest, William Tannen.

Rival plane companies, seeking the same army contract, cost a test pilot (Stanley Clements) his license and almost his life because of greed.

Running time: 63 minutes. Release date: April 6, 1952.

699. The Gunman (western) Directed by Lewis Collins. Produced by Vincent M. Fennelly. Screenplay by Fred Myton. A Silvermine Production.

Cast: Whip Wilson, Fuzzy Knight, Phyllis Coates, Rand Brooks, Terry Frost, Lane Bradford, I. Stanford Jolley, Gregg Barton, Russ Whiteman, Richard Avonde, Robert Bray.
Running time: 52 minutes. Release date: April 13, 1952.
Also known as **Mr. Hobo.**

700. Wild Stallion (western) Directed by Lewis Collins. Produced by Walter Mirisch. Screenplay by Daniel B. Ullman. In Cinecolor.
Cast: Ben Johnson, Edgar Buchanan, Martha Hyer, Hayden Rorke, Hugh Beaumont, Orley Lindgren, Don Haggerty, Susan Odin.
A cavalry officer (Ben Johnson) returns to the post on the day his benefactor and his pet colt are being retired, and recalls, in flashback, the events leading up to his graduation from West Point.
Running time: 70 minutes. Release date: April 27, 1952.

701. Kansas Territory (western) Directed by Lewis Collins. Produced by Vincent M. Fennelly. Screenplay by Daniel B. Ullman. In Sepiatone.
Cast: Wild Bill Elliott, Peggy Stewart, House Peters, Jr., Fuzzy Knight, Lane Bradford, I. Stanford Jolley, Lyle Talbot, Stanley Andrews, Marshall Reed, Terry Frost, John Hart, William Fawcett, Lee Roberts, Ted Adams, Pierce Lyden.
A former outlaw (Wild Bill Elliott) vows to avenge his brother's death and, to his surprise, learns that his sibling had turned renegade.
Running time: 65 min. Release date: May 4, 1952.

702. Desert Pursuit (western) Directed by George Blair. Produced by Lindsley Parsons. Screenplay by W. Scott Darling. From the novel "Starlight Canyon" by Kenneth Perkins.
Cast: Wayne Morris, Virginia Grey, Anthony Caruso, George Tobias, Emmett Lynn, Gloria Talbott, Frank Lackteen, John Doucette, Billy Wilkerson, Robert Bice.

Loaded with gold, a miner (Wayne Morris) and a lady-of-fortune (Virginia Grey) flee across Death Valley, pursued by three Arabs (Anthony Caruso, George Tobias, John Doucette) mounted on camels.
Running time: 71 minutes. Release date: May 11, 1952.

703. African Treasure (adventure) Directed by Ford Beebe. Produced by Walter Mirisch. Screenplay by Ford Beebe. Story by Roy Rockwood.
Cast: Johnny Sheffield, Laurette Luez, Arthur Space, Martin Garralaga, Lane Bradford, Leonard Mudie, Lyle Talbot, Robert "Smoki" Whitfield, James Adamson, Jack Williams, Wesley Bly, "Sugar Foot" Anderson, Woodrow Wilson (Woody) Strode.
Bomba (Johnny Sheffield) sets out to find diamond smugglers who are posing as geologists.
Running time: 70 minutes. Release date: June 8, 1952.

704. Gold Fever (western) Directed by Leslie Goodwins. Produced by John Calvert. Screenplay by Edgar B. Anderson, Jr. and Cliff Lancaster.
Cast: John Calvert, Ralph Morgan, Ann Cornell, Gene Roth, Tom Kennedy, Judd Holdren, Danny Rense, Bobby Graham, George Morrell.
An aging gold prospector (Ralph Morgan) is grubstaked by a young man (John Calvert) to work a secret mine, but bandits try to take it over.
Running time: 63 minutes. Release date: June 15, 1952.

705. Here Come the Marines (comedy) Directed by William Beaudine. Produced by Jerry Thomas. Screenplay by Tim Ryan, Charles R. Marion and Jack Crutcher.
Cast: Leo Gorcey, Huntz Hall, Hanley Stafford, Myrna Dell, Arthur Space, David Condon (Gorcey), Bennie Bartlett, Bernard Gorcey, Gil Stratton, Jr., Paul Maxey, Murray Alper, Tim Ryan, William Newell, Riley Hill, Lisa Wilson, James Flavin, Robert Coogan, Leo "Ukie" Sherin, Sammy Finn, Buck Russell, Stanley Blystone,

Chad Mallory, Perc Landers, Alan Jeffory, Bob Cudlip, Bob Peoples, William Vincent, Jack Wilson, Dick Paxton, Barbara Grey, Courtland Shepard, William Bailey, Paul Bradley.

The Bowery Boys (Leo Gorcey, Huntz Hall, David Condon, Bennie Bartlett, Gil Stratton, Jr.) are drafted into the Marines; they later tangle with Jolly Joe Johnson (Paul Maxey), the crooked owner of a gambling house.

Running time: 66 minutes. Release date: June 29, 1952.

Working title: **Bowery Leathernecks.** Released in Great Britain as **Tell It to the Marines.**

706. Wagons West (western) Directed by Ford Beebe. Produced by Vincent M. Fennelly. Screenplay by Daniel B. Ullman. In Cinecolor.

Cast: Rod Cameron, Peggie Castle, Noah Beery, Jr., Michael Chapin, Henry Brandon, Sarah Hayden, Frank Ferguson, Anne Kimbell, Wheaton Chambers, Riley Hill, Effie Laird, I. Stanford Jolley, Harry Tyler, Almira Sessions.

A wagon master (Rod Cameron), leading a wagon train westward, discovers passengers who are selling rifles to the Indians.

Running time: 70 minutes. Release date: July 6, 1952.

707. Dead Man's Trail (western) Directed by Lewis Collins. Produced by Vincent M. Fennelly. Screenplay by Joseph Poland. A Frontier Pictures Production.

Cast: Johnny Mack Brown, Jimmy Ellison, Barbara Allen, I. Stanford Jolley, Terry Frost, Lane Bradford, Gregg Barton, Richard Avonde, Dale Van Sickel, Stanley Price.

After an escaped convict is murdered by his gang, his brother (Jimmy Ellison) helps a Texas Ranger (Johnny Mack Brown) track down the outlaws.

Running time: 59 minutes. Release date: July 20, 1952.

708. Sea Tiger (mystery-drama) Directed by Frank

McDonald. Produced by William F. Broidy. Screenplay by Sam Roeca. Based on the story "Island Freighter" by Charles Yerkow.

Cast: John Archer, Marguerite Chapman, Mara Corday, Harry Lauter, Lyle Talbot, Marvin Press, Paul McGuire, Ralph Sanford, John Mylong, Sam Flint, Chad Mallory, John Reese.

After being cleared of collusion with the Japanese during World War II, a sea captain (John Archer) becomes a murder suspect.

Running time: 71 minutes. Release date: July 27, 1952.

709. Montana Incident (western) Directed by Lewis Collins. Produced by Vincent M. Fennelly. Screenplay by Daniel B. Ullman.

Cast: Whip Wilson, Noel Neill, Peggy Stewart, Rand Brooks, Hugh Prosser, William Fawcett, Terry Frost, Marshall Reed, Lyle Talbot, Russ Whiteman, Barbara Woodell, Bruce Edwards, Stanley Price.

Two railroad surveyors (Whip Wilson, Rand Brooks) help free a little Montana town from the economic strangehold of the Martin family, who want to keep homesteaders dependent on their enterprises.

Running time: 54 min. Release date: Aug. 10, 1952.

Also known as **Gunsmoke Range.**

710. The Rose Bowl Story (drama) Directed by William Beaudine. Produced by Richard Heermance. Written by Charles R. Marion. In Cinecolor.

Cast: Marshall Thompson, Vera Miles, Keith Larsen, Natalie Wood, Jim Backus, Richard Rober, Tom Harmon, Ann Doran, James Dobson, Clarence Kolb, Barbara Woodell, Bill Walsh, Nancy Thorne (the 1952 Tournament of Roses Queen) and her court (Ann Cottingham, Diana Dial, Carolyn Graves, Barbara Fisher, Sharon Ann Kelley, Marcia Long).

An ambitious college football player (Marshall Thompson), star of a Big Ten team, arrives in Pasadena for the Rose Bowl game and comes to realize that love of the sport is more important than commercial gain.

Running time: 73 minutes. Release date: August 24, 1952.

711. Yukon Gold (adventure) Directed by Frank McDonald. Produced by William F. Broidy. Screenplay by Bill Raynor. From a story by James Oliver Curwood.

Cast: Kirby Grant, Martha Hyer, Harry Lauter, Phil Van Zandt, Frances Charles, Mauritz Hugo, James Parnell, Sam Flint, I. Stanford Jolley, Chinook the Wonder Dog.

A Mountie (Kirby Grant) is on the trail of a murderer in a lawless mining settlement.

Running time: 62 min. Release date: Aug. 31, 1952.

712. Fargo (western) Directed by Lewis Collins. Produced by Vincent M. Fennelly. Screenplay by Joseph Poland and Jack DeWitt. A Silvermine Production. In Sepiatone.

Cast: Wild Bill Elliott, Phyllis Coates, Myron Healey, Fuzzy Knight, Jack Ingram, Arthur Space, Bob Wilke, Terry Frost, Robert Bray, Tim Ryan, Florence Lake, Stanley Andrews, Richard Reeves, Gene Roth.

After the murder of his rancher brother, Wild Bill Elliott returns to the Dakota territory; aided by ranchers he puts up barbed wire, starting open war on ruthless cattlemen.

Running time: 69 minutes. Release date: September 7, 1952.

713. Feudin' Fools (comedy) Directed by William Beaudine. Produced by Jerry Thomas. Screenplay by Bert Lawrence and Tim Ryan.

Cast: Leo Gorcey, Huntz Hall, Anne Kimbell, Dorothy Ford, Paul Wexler, Bennie Bartlett, David Condon (Gorcey), Bernard Gorcey, Oliver Blake, Bob Easton, O.Z. Whitehead, Lyle Talbot, Leo "Ukie" Sherin, Benny Baker, Russell Simpson, Fuzzy Knight, Arthur Space, Robert Bray, Bob Keys, Stanley Blystone.

The Bowery Boys (Leo Gorcey, Bennie Bartlett, David Condon) journey to Hogliver Hollow, Kentucky, where Sach (Huntz Hall) has inherited a farm. Once there, they get caught in the middle of a hillbilly feud.

Phyllis Coates, Wild Bill Elliott and Myron Healey in "Fargo" (1952).

Running time: 63 minutes. Release date: September 21, 1952.

714. Army Bound (action-drama) Directed by Paul Landres. Produced by Ben Schwalb. Story and screenplay by Al Martin.

Cast: Stanley Clements, Karen Sharpe, Steve Brodie, John Fontaine, Harry Hayden, Lela Bliss, Gil Stratton, Jr., Danny Welton, Mona Knox, Jean Dean, Louis Tomei, Joey Ray.

An auto racer (Stanley Clements) is drafted into the army and finds a former rival (John Fontaine) is his commanding officer.

Running time: 61 minutes. Release date: October 5, 1952.

715. Canyon Ambush (western) Directed by Lewis Collins. Produced by Vincent M. Fennelly. Screenplay by Joseph Poland. A Silvermine Production.

Cast: Johnny Mack Brown, Phyllis Coates, Lee Roberts, Dennis Moore, Hugh Prosser, Marshall Reed, Denver Pyle, Pierce Lyden, Stanley Price, Bill Koontz, Frank Ellis, Russ Whiteman, Carol Henry, George De-Normand.

A government agent (Johnny Mack Brown) helps a sheriff (Lee Roberts) expose a masked rider (Hugh Prosser), the mastermind behind a series of robberies.

Running time: 53 minutes. Release date: October 12, 1952.

Working title: **Guns Along the Border.**

716. Arctic Flight (adventure-mystery) Directed by Lew Landers. Produced by Lindsley Parsons. Screenplay by Robert Hill and George Bricker. Based on the story "Shadow of the Curtain" by Ewing Scott.

Cast: Wayne Morris, Lola Albright, Alan Hale, Jr., Carol Thurston, Phil Tead, Tom Richards, Anthony Garson, Kenneth MacDonald, Paul Bryar, Dale Van Sickel.

An Alaskan bush pilot (Wayne Morris), flying a big game hunter (Alan Hale, Jr.) in search of polar bears, discovers his passenger is really a Communist spy.

Running time: 78 minutes. Release date: October 19, 1952.

717. Behind Southern Lines (western) Directed by Thomas Carr. Produced by Wesley E. Barry. Screenplay by Melvin Levy and Maurice Tombragel.

Cast: Guy Madison, Andy Devine, Rand Brooks, Murray Alper, Jonathan Hale, Orley Lindgren, Milburn Stone, Robert Shayne, Lee Phelps, Bill Meade, Duke York.

Compiled from two episodes of the Wild Bill Hickok television series: "Behind Southern Lines" and "The Silver Mine Protection Story."

Running time: 51 minutes. Release date: November 2, 1952.

Guy Madison (left), as James Butler "Wild Bill" Hickok, and Andy Devine, as his sidekick Jingles, in "The Ghost of Crossbones Canyon" (1952). This and other Hickok westerns released by Monogram (and later, Allied Artists) were compiled from episodes of the popular Wild Bill Hickok television series (which was also known as The Adventures of Wild Bill Hickok).

718. The Ghost of Crossbones Canyon (western) Directed by Frank McDonald. Produced by Wesley E. Barry. Screenplay by Maurice Tombragel.

Cast: Guy Madison, Andy Devine, Betty Davison, John Doucette, Russell Simpson.

Compiled from two episodes of the Wild Bill Hickok television series, episode titles unknown.

Running time: 56 minutes. Release date: November 2, 1952.

719. Trail of the Arrow (western) Directed by Thomas Carr. Produced by Wesley E. Barry. Screenplay by Maurice Tombragel.

Cast: Guy Madison, Andy Devine, Wendy Waldron, Raymond Hatton, Terry Frost, Jack Reynolds, Steve Pendleton, Neyle Morrow.

Compiled from two episodes of the Wild Bill Hickok television series: "The Indian Bureau Story" and one unknown title.

Running time: 54 minutes. Release date: November 2, 1952.

720. The Yellow-Haired Kid (western) Directed by Frank McDonald. Produced by Wesley E. Barry. Screenplay by Dwight Babcock and Maurice Tombragel.

Cast: Guy Madison, Andy Devine, Alan Hale, Jr., Marcia Mae Jones, Alice Rolph, David Bruce, William Phipps, Riley Hill, Tommy Ivo, Emory Parnell.

Compiled from two episodes of the Wild Bill Hickok television series: "The Yellow-Haired Kid" and "Johnny Deuce."

Running time: 52 minutes. Release date: November 2, 1952.

721. Wyoming Roundup (western) Directed by Thomas Carr. Produced by Vincent M. Fennelly. Screenplay by Daniel B. Ullman.

Cast: Whip Wilson, Phyllis Coates, Tommy Farrell, Henry Rowland, House Peters, Jr., I. Stanford Jolley, Richard Emory, Bob Wilke, Stanley Price.

Whip and Tommy ride into Willows, Wyoming, where they become deputy marshals and clash with a local gunman (Bob Wilke).

Running time: 53 minutes. Release date: November 9, 1952.

Working title: **Hired Guns.**

722. No Holds Barred (comedy) Directed by William

Johnny Sheffield and Karen Sharpe in "Bomba and the Jungle Girl" (1952), an entry in the Bomba the Jungle Boy series, Monogram's answer to the Tarzan pictures.

Beaudine. Produced by Jerry Thomas. Screenplay by Tim Ryan, Jack Crutcher and Bert Lawrence.

Cast: Leo Gorcey, Huntz Hall, Marjorie Reynolds, Leonard Penn, Henry Kulky, David Condon (Gorcey), Bennie Bartlett, Bernard Gorcey, Hombre Montana, Murray Alper, Barbara Grey, Lisa Wilson, Nick Stewart, Sandra Gould, Ray Walker, Tim Ryan, Bob Cudlip, Mort Mills, Bill Page, John Eldredge, Meyer Grace, Jimmy Cross, Ted Christy, Pat Fraley, "Brother" Frank Jares, Leo "Ukie" Sherin, John Indrisano, Count John Maximillian Smith, Mike Ruby.

When Sach (Huntz Hall) develops superstrength in his head, Slip (Leo Gorcey) and the other Bowery Boys (David Condon, Bennie Bartlett) turn him into a championship wrestler.

Running time: 65 minutes. Release date: November 23, 1952.

723. Bomba and the Jungle Girl (adventure) Directed by Ford Beebe. Produced by Walter Mirisch. Screenplay by Ford Beebe.

Cast: Johnny Sheffield, Karen Sharpe, Walter Sande, Suzette Harbin, Martin Wilkins, Morris Buchanan, Leonard Mudie, Don Blackman, Bruce Carruther, Jack Clisby, Amanda Randolph, Roy Glenn, Bill Walker.

Bomba (Johnny Sheffield), trying to trace the skeletons of his unknown parents, learns that a native chief (Martin Wilkins) had killed them.

Running time: 70 minutes. Release date: December 7, 1952.

Also known as **Jungle Girl.**

SHORT SUBJECTS

1933/34

724. Port O' Call Novelties (series) These one-reel travelogues were produced and narrated by Deane H. Dickason.

724a. The Seventh Wonder (Release date: 12/1/33)
724b. City of the Sun (1/1/34)
724c. Love's Memorial (2/1/34)
724d. Children of the Nile (3/1/34)
724e. The Peacock Throne (4/1/34)
724f. Jungle Bound (5/1/34)
724g. The Last Resort (6/1/34)
724h. Mother Ganges (7/1/34)
724i. The First Paradise (8/1/34)
724j. Dravidian Glamor (9/1/34)
724k. Adventure Isle (10/1/34)
724l. Queen of the Indies (11/1/34)
724m. A Mediterranean Mecca (12/1/34)

1941

725. Tillie's Punctured Romance (comedy) Produced and directed by Mack Sennett. New titles by Mort Greene. Re-edited by Guy V. Thayer, Jr. Music by Dr. Edward Kleniyi.

Cast: Charlie Chaplin, Marie Dressler, Mabel Normand, Phyllis Allen, Charles Bennett, Billie Bennett, Chester Conklin, Charley Chase, Edgar Kennedy, Al St. John, Slim Summerville, Eddie Sutherland, Hank Mann, Gordon Griffith.

An abbreviated reissue of the first feature-length comedy film (which was released November 1914). A

city slicker (Chaplin) schemes to get a country girl's (Marie Dressler) money.
Running time: 38 minutes. Release date: September 23, 1941.
This Monogram edition was itself reissued in 1950 by Burwood Pictures.

1947

726. Climbing the Matterhorn (drama) Directed by Irving Allen. Photographed by Ansco Color.
A young English couple attempts to climb the Matterhorn in the Swiss Alps; after the mountaineers have an accident, the local villagers rescue them by torchlight.
Running time: 21 minutes. Release date: May 30, 1947.

1950

727. Little Rascals. In 1950 Monogram reissued 50 two-reel and 30 one-reel Our Gang comedy shorts originally produced by Hal Roach and released by Metro-Goldwyn-Mayer. Since the name "Our Gang" was sold to M-G-M, Monogram released them as "Little Rascals" comedies.

FILM TITLE INDEX

The number after each film title and year of release refers to the entry number, not the page number.

Abilene Trail (1951) 658
According to Mrs. Hoyle (1951) 668
Across the Plains (1939) 183
Across the Rio Grande (1949) 595
Adolescence see Stolen Paradise (1941) 289
Adventure Isle (1934) 724k
Adventures of Kitty O'Day (1945) 433
African Treasure (1952) 703
Air Devils see Flying Wild (1941) 260
Aladdin and His Lamp (1952) 693
Alaska (1944) 426
Allotment Wives (1945) 463
Allotment Wives, Inc. see Allotment Wives (1945) 463
Amateur Detective see Irish Luck (1939) 191
Amateur Detective see On the Spot (1940) 227
Angels' Alley (1948) 548
Angels in Disguise (1949) 609
The Ape see House of Mystery (1934) 73
The Ape (1940) 243
The Ape Man (1943) 356
Arctic Flight (1952) 716
Are These Our Parents? (1944) 408
Arizona Bound (1941) 274
Arizona Frontier (1940) 237
Arizona Ranch Hands see Ridin' the Cherokee Trail (1941) 259
Arizona Roundup (1942) 312
Arizona Stagecoach (1942) 333

Arizona Sunset see Range Renegades (1948) 557
Arizona Territory (1950) 636
Arizona Whirlwind (1944) 393
Arm of the Law (1932) 22
Army Bound (1952) 714
Army Wives (1945) 432
At the Villa Rose see House of Mystery (1941) 266
Atlantic Flight (1937) 124
Attorney for the Defense see Silent Witness (1943) 350
Aunt Emma Paints the Town see So's Your Aunt Emma! (1942) 320
The Avenger (1933) 57

Back Trail (1948) 563
Backfire see The Law Comes to Gunsight (1947) 523
Bad Man from Bodie see The Gunman from Bodie (1941) 284
Barefoot Boy (1938) 153
Beauty and the Bandit (1946) 502
Beggars in Ermine (1934) 71
Behind Prison Bars see The Outer Gate (1937) 122
Behind Southern Lines (1952) 717
Behind the Mask (1946) 479
Belle of the Bowery see Sunbonnet Sue (1945) 461
Below the Border (1942) 305
Below the Deadline (1946) 492
Betrayed see When Strangers Marry (1944) 427

323

Big Timber (1950) 643
Black Beauty (1933) 47
Black Dragons (1942) 313
Black Magic (1944) 414
Black Market Babies (1945) 462
Black Market Rustlers (1943) 369
Black Midnight (1949) 610
Blazing Barriers (1937) 117
Blazing Bullets (1951) 666
Blazing Guns (1943) 375
Block Busters (1944) 410
Blonde Dynamite (1950) 621
Blue Blood (1951) 657
Blue Grass of Kentucky (1950) 618
Blue Steel (1934) 76
Blues Busters (1950) 648
Bomba and the Elephant Stampede
  see Elephant Stampede (1951) 681
Bomba and the Hidden City (1950)
  645
Bomba and the Jungle Girl (1952)
  723
Bomba on Panther Island (1949) 616
Bomba, the Jungle Boy (1949) 589
Boot Hill Bandits (1942) 321
Border Bandits (1946) 464
Born for Glory see Torpedo Rider
  (1940) 214
Born Tough see He Couldn't Take
  It (1933) 65
Borrowed Hero (1941) 295
Bowery at Midnight (1942) 342
Bowery Battalion (1951) 656
Bowery Blitzkrieg (1941) 282
Bowery Bombshell (1946) 490
Bowery Boys see Docks of New
  York (1945) 439
Bowery Buckaroos (1947) 538
Bowery Champs (1944) 428
Bowery Leathernecks see Here
  Come the Marines (1952) 705
Bowery Thrush see Blues Busters
  (1950) 648
Boy of the Streets (1938) 135
Boys of the City (1940) 232
Boys' Reformatory (1939) 181
Brand of Fear (1949) 600
Break the News (1941) 262
Breed of the Border (1933) 45
A Bride for Henry (1937) 127

Bringing Up Father (1947) 505
Broadway to Cheyenne see From
  Broadway to Cheyenne (1932) 32
Broken Dreams (1933) 64
Bullets and Bullion see Under-
  ground Rustlers (1941) 293
Bullets and Saddles (1943) 378

Call of the Jungle (1944) 415
Call of the Klondike (1950) 653
Campus Rhythm (1943) 382
Campus Sleuth (1948) 551
Canyon Ambush (1952) 715
Canyon Raiders (1951) 664
Casa Manana (1951) 670
The Case of the Missing Brides see
  The Corpse Vanishes (1942) 322
Cavalry Scout (1951) 667
Chamber of Horrors (1940) 250
Charlie Chan in Alcatraz see Dark
  Alibi (1946) 480
Charlie Chan in Black Magie see
  Black Magic (1944) 414
Charlie Chan in Mexico see The
  Red Dragon (1946) 469
Charlie Chan in the Secret Service
  (1944) 392
Chasing Trouble (1940) 210
Cheers of the Crowd (1935) 115
Cherokee Uprising (1950) 646
The Cheyenne Kid (1940) 212
Children of the Nile (1934) 724d
China's Little Devils (1945) 446
The Chinese Cat (1944) 403
The Chinese Ring (1947) 539
The Circus Comes to Town see
  Under the Big Top (1938) 154
Cisco and the Angel see Beauty and
  the Bandit (1946) 502
The Cisco Kid Comes Through see
  The Cisco Kid Returns (1945) 436
The Cisco Kid in Old New Mexico
  see In Old New Mexico (1945) 445
The Cisco Kid Returns (1945) 436
City Limits (1934) 74
City Limits see Father Steps Out
  (1941) 275
City of the Sun (1934) 724b

Film Title Index

Clancy Street Boys (1943) 360
Climbing the Matterhorn (1947) 726
Club Paradise see Sensation Hunters (1945) 457
Code of the Rangers (1938) 144
Code of the Saddle (1947) 526
Colorado Ambush (1951) 655
The Colorado Trail see Pals of the Silver Sage (1940) 221
Come Out Fighting (1945) 455
Continental Express (1942) 311
Convict's Code (1939) 168
Cooking Up Trouble see Three of a Kind (1944) 411
The Corpse Vanished see Revenge of the Zombies (1943) 373
The Corpse Vanishes (1942) 322
Cosmo Jones — Crime Smasher see Cosmo Jones in the Crime Smasher (1943) 351
Cosmo Jones in the Crime Smasher (1943) 351
County Fair (1937) 132
County Fair (1950) 640
The County Fair (1932) 18
Courtin' Trouble (1948) 576
Covered Wagon Trails (1940) 219
Cowboy Cavalier (1948) 561
Cowboy Commandos (1943) 363
Cowboy from Sundown (1940) 223
Crashing Broadway (1933) 51
Crashing Thru (1939) 201
Crashing Thru (1949) 582
Crazy Knights (1944) 430
Crazy Over Horses (1951) 684
Crime Reporter see Criminal Investigator (1942) 341
Crime Smasher see Cosmo Jones in the Crime Smasher (1943) 351
Criminal Investigator (1942) 341
Crossed Trails (1948) 552

Dames and Dynamite see Flirting with Danger (1934) 95
Danger Ahead (1940) 208
Danger Flight (1939) 196
Danger Valley (1937) 130
Dangerous Fingers see Wanted by Scotland Yard (1939) 180
Dangerous Money (1946) 499
Dark Alibi (1946) 480
Dark Eyes of London see The Human Monster (1940) 216
Dawn on the Great Divide (1942) 348
The Dawn Rider (1935) 110
Dead Man's Shoes (1941) 255
Dead Man's Trail (1952) 707
The Deadly Game (1941) 278
Death Valley Rangers (1943) 384
Decoy (1946) 496
Desert Pursuit (1952) 702
The Desert Trail (1935) 106
Detective Kitty O'Day (1944) 402
Devil's Mate (1933) 60
The Diamond Trail (1932) 41
Dillinger (1945) 440
Divorce (1945) 452
Do Not Disturb see One Thrilling Night (1942) 326
Docks of New Orleans (1948) 549
Docks of New York (1945) 439
Dr. Paul Joseph Goebbels see Enemy of Women (1944) 424
Don't Gamble with Strangers (1946) 485
Doomed to Die (1940) 235
Double Trouble (1941) 292
Down Texas Way (1942) 324
Down the Wyoming Trail (1939) 185
Dravidian Glamor (1934) 724j
The Driftin' Kid (1941) 286
Drifting Along (1946) 468
Drifting Westward (1939) 169
Drums of the Desert (1940) 244
Dugan of the Badlands (1931) 2
Dynamite Canyon (1941) 279

East of the Bowery see Follow the Leader (1944) 404
East Side Kids (1940) 211
Elephant Stampede (1951) 681
Enemy of Women (1944) 424

The Face of Marble (1946) 467
Fall Guy (1947) 515

False Fronts see The Phantom Broadcast (1933) 46
Fame Street see Police Court (1932) 17
Farewell to Fame see Let's Go Collegiate (1941) 283
Fargo (1952) 712
Fashion Model (1945) 441
Fatal Alarm see Flames (1932) 24
Fatal Fingertips see Dark Alibi (1946) 480
The Fatal Hour (1940) 205
Father Makes Good (1950) 631
Father Steps Out (1941) 275
Father Takes the Air (1951) 671
Father's Wild Game (1950) 651
Fear (1946) 472
The Feathered Serpent (1948) 581
Federal Bullets (1937) 129
Female Fugitive (1938) 145
Fence Riders (1950) 619
Feudin' Fools (1952) 713
The Fifth Round see Tough Kid (1938) 166
The Fight for Peace (1939) 194
The Fighting Champ (1932) 39
Fighting Fools (1949) 593
Fighting Mad (1939) 197
Fighting Mad see Joe Palooka in Fighting Mad (1948) 546
The Fighting Ranger (1948) 566
The Fighting Texan see The Gentleman from Texas (1946) 482
The Fighting Texans (1933) 53
Fire Alarm see Flames (1932) 24
The First Paradise (1934) 724i
Flame of the West (1945) 449
Flames (1932) 24
Flashing Guns (1947) 527
Flight to Mars (1951) 683
Flirting with Danger (1934) 95
Flying Wild (1941) 260
Follow the Leader (1944) 404
Forbidden Trails (1941) 299
Foreign Agent (1942) 339
Forever Yours (1945) 434
Forgotten Hero see Hoosier Schoolboy (1937) 118
Forgotten Women (1931) 11
Forgotten Women (1949) 601

Fort Osage (1952) 692
The Four Just Men see The Secret Four (1940) 206
Fraternity Sweetheart see Campus Rhythm (1943) 382
Freckles Comes Home (1942) 300
Freddie Steps Out (1946) 487
French Leave (1948) 553
From Broadway to Cheyenne (1932) 32
Frontier Agent (1948) 555
Frontier Feud (1945) 459
The Fugitive (1933) 54
Fugitive Valley (1941) 277

G.I. Honeymoon (1945) 442
The Gallant Fool (1933) 48
Galloping Romeo (1933) 56
Galloping Thru (1931) 12
Gang Bullets (1938) 160
The Gang's All Here (1941) 272
Gangster's Boy (1938) 161
The Gaunt Stranger see The Phantom Strikes (1939) 199
The Gay Cavalier (1946) 475
The Gentleman from Arizona (1939) 203
Gentleman from Dixie (1941) 281
The Gentleman from Texas (1946) 482
Gentleman Joe Palooka (1946) 498
Ghost Chasers (1951) 665
Ghost City (1932) 13
Ghost Crazy see Crazy Knights (1944) 430
The Ghost Creeps see Boys of the City (1940) 232
Ghost Guns (1944) 425
The Ghost of Crossbones Canyon (1952) 718
The Ghost of John Holling see Mystery Liner (1934) 72
The Ghost Rider (1943) 358
Ghost Town see Texas City (1952) 690
Ghost Town Law (1942) 316
Ghosts in the Night see Ghosts on the Loose (1943) 367

Ghosts in the Night see Spooks Run Wild (1941) 288
Ghosts on the Loose (1943) 367
Ginger (1947) 509
The Girl from Calgary (1932) 29
Girl from Nowhere see Should a Girl Marry? (1939) 184
Girl from the Rio (1939) 188
Girl o' My Dreams (1934) 93
A Girl of the Limberlost (1934) 88
God's Country and the Man (1937) 125
Gold Bullets see Blazing Bullets (1951) 666
Gold Fever (1952) 704
The Golden Eye (1948) 568
The Golden Trail (1940) 231
The Gorilla Strikes see The Ape Man (1943) 356
Grand Street Boys see Clancy Street Boys (1943) 360
Great God Gold (1935) 105
The Guilty (1947) 516
Guilty or Not Guilty (1932) 33
Gun Law Justice (1949) 588
Gun Packer (1938) 162
Gun Runner (1949) 584
Gun Smoke (1945) 437
Gun Talk (1947) 541
The Gunman (1952) 699
The Gunman from Bodie (1941) 284
Gunning for Justice (1948) 575
Guns Along the Border see Canyon Ambush (1952) 715
Gunslingers (1950) 627
Gunsmoke Range see Montana Incident (1952) 709
Gunsmoke Trail (1938) 148
Gypsy Fury (1951) 662

Happy Landing (1934) 86
Hard Boiled Mahoney (1947) 520
Haunted House (1940) 233
The Haunted Mine (1946) 473
Haunted Ranch (1943) 354
Haunted Trails (1949) 606
He Couldn't Take It (1933) 65
He Knew Too Much see Devil's

Mate (1933) 60
He Wore a Star see The Star Packer (1934) 83
The Healer (1935) 109
Henry the Rainmaker (1949) 585
Her Bachelor Husband see What a Man! (1944) 391
Her First Romance (1940) 251
Here Come the Marines (1952) 705
Here Comes Kelly (1943) 372
Here Comes Trouble see Trouble Chasers (1945) 448
Here We Go Again see Pride of the Bowery (1941) 257
Heroes in Blue (1939) 198
The Hidden City see Bomba and the Hidden City (1950) 645
Hidden Danger (1948) 579
Hidden Enemy (1940) 207
Hidden Valley (1932) 34
High Conquest (1947) 525
High Gear see In Fast Company (1946) 486
High School Hero (1946) 495
High Tide (1947) 533
Hillbilly Blitzkrieg (1942) 331
Hired Guns see Wyoming Roundup (1952) 721
Hitler's Women see Women in Bondage (1944) 387
Hold That Baby! (1949) 599
Hold That Line (1952) 696
Honeymoon for Five see Joe Palooka Meets Humphrey (1950) 620
Honeymoon Limited (1935) 111
Honor of the Mounted (1932) 27
The Honor System see Mr. Muggs Steps Out (1943) 379
Hoosier Schoolboy (1937) 118
The Hoosier Schoolmaster (1935) 108
Hot Rhythm (1944) 399
Hot Rod (1950) 647
House of Mystery (1941) 266
The House of Mystery (1934) 73
The Human Ghost see House of Mystery (1941) 266
The Human Monster (1940) 216
Humphrey Takes a Chance (1950) 633

I Am a Criminal (1938) 164
I Escaped from the Gestapo (1943) 361
I Killed That Man (1941) 294
I Killed the Count see Who Is Guilty? (1940) 240
I Was a Criminal see The Unknown Guest (1943) 377
I Wouldn't Be in Your Shoes (1948) 556
In Fast Company (1946) 486
In Line of Duty (1931) 7
In Old New Mexico (1945) 445
In Self Defense see Perilous Waters (1948) 547
In the Night see The Gang's All Here (1941) 272
Incident (1949) 583
The Invisible Ghost (1941) 264
Irish and Proud of It see King Kelly of the U.S.A. (1934) 87
Irish Luck (1939) 191
Isle of Fury see Isle of Missing Men (1942) 334
Isle of Missing Men (1942) 334
Isle of Terror see Isle of Missing Men (1942) 334

The Jade Mask (1945) 435
Jane Eyre (1934) 84
Jet Job (1952) 698
Jiggs and Maggie in Court (1948) 580
Jiggs and Maggie in Jackpot Jitters (1949) 607
Jiggs and Maggie in Society (1947) 540
Jiggs and Maggie Out West (1950) 629
Jinx Money (1948) 560
A Joe Named Palooka see Winner Take All (1948) 570
Joe Palooka, Champ (1946) 481
Joe Palooka in Fighting Mad (1948) 546
Joe Palooka in Humphrey Takes a Chance see Humphrey Takes a Chance (1950) 633

Joe Palooka in the Big Fight (1949) 587
Joe Palooka in the Counterpunch (1949) 605
Joe Palooka in the Knockout (1947) 534
Joe Palooka in the Squared Circle (1950) 649
Joe Palooka in Triple Cross see Triple Cross (1951) 678
Joe Palooka Meets Humphrey (1950) 620
John Dillinger, Killer see Dillinger (1945) 440
Johnny Doesn't Live Here Anymore (1944) 407
Jungle Bound (1934) 724f
Jungle Bride (1933) 42
Jungle Girl see Bomba and the Jungle Girl (1952) 723
Junior Prom (1946) 478

Kansas Territory (1952) 701
Keeper of the Bees (1935) 112
Kid Dynamite (1943) 353
The Kid from Santa Fe (1940) 225
Kidnapped (1948) 577
The Kid's Last Ride (1941) 258
Killer Shark (1950) 625
Kilroy Was Here (1947) 528
King Kelly of the U.S.A. (1934) 87
King of the Bandits (1947) 537
King of the Stallions (1942) 335
King of the Zombies (1941) 268
Klondike (1932) 30
Klondike Fury (1942) 315
Klondike Victory see Klondike Fury (1942) 315
The Knockout see Joe Palooka in the Knockout (1947) 534

Lady Beware see The Thirteenth Guest (1932) 31
Lady, Let's Dance (1944) 398
Land of Fighting Men (1938) 142
Land of Hunted Men (1943) 357
Land of the Lawless (1947) 521

Film Title Index

Land of the Outlaws (1944) 419
Land of the Six Guns (1940) 224
Land of Wanted Men (1931) 10
The Last Alarm (1940) 228
The Last Resort (1934) 724g
Laughing at Danger (1940) 236
The Law Comes to Gunsight (1947)
523
Law Men (1944) 400
Law of the Jungle (1942) 306
Law of the North (1932) 25
Law of the Panhandle (1950) 644
Law of the Sea (1932) 14
Law of the Valley (1944) 423
Law of the West (1949) 586
The Law Rides Again (1943) 368
Lawless Code (1949) 615
Lawless Cowboys (1951) 682
The Lawless Frontier (1934) 94
Leave It to Henry (1949) 598
Leave It to the Irish (1944) 416
The Legion of Missing Men (1937)
121
Lena Rivers see The Sin of Lena
Rivers (1938) 163
Let's Get Tough! (1942) 325
Let's Go Collegiate (1941) 283
Let's Go Navy! (1951) 675
Li'l Louisiana Belle see Gentleman
from Dixie (1941) 281
The Lion Hunters (1951) 663
Little Devils see China's Little
Devils (1945) 446
Little MacArthurs see Let's Get
Tough! (1942) 325
Little Mobsters see Kid Dynamite
(1943) 353
Little Pal see The Healer (1935) 109
Little Rascals 727
Little Tenderfoot see Song of the
Buckaroo (1939) 167
Live Wires (1946) 465
The Living Ghost (1942) 345
Lock Your Doors see The Ape Man
(1943) 356
Lone Star Law see Lone Star Law
Men (1941) 296
Lone Star Law Men (1941) 296
Lonesome Trail (1945) 460
The Longhorn (1951) 685

Lost in the Stratosphere (1934) 91
The Lost Trail (1945) 458
The Lost Volcano (1950) 635
The Loudspeaker (1934) 79
Louisiana (1947) 536
Love's Memorial (1934) 724c
The Luck of Roaring Camp (1937)
131
Lucky Larrigan (1932) 38
Lucky Losers (1950) 632
The Lucky Texan (1934) 68
Lure of the Islands (1942) 329

Mad Lover see Enemy of Women
(1944) 424
Main Street Girl see Sensation
Hunters (1945) 457
Make a Million (1935) 114
The Man from Arizona (1932) 35
The Man from Death Valley (1931) 6
Man from El Paso see Man from
Sonora (1951) 661
Man from Headquarters (1942) 303
Man from New Mexico (1932) 19
Man from Sonora (1951) 661
Man from Texas (1939) 179
Man from the Black Hills (1952) 697
The Man from Utah (1934) 77
Man with Two Lives (1942) 314
The Mandarin Secret see Shadows
Over Chinatown (1946) 491
Manhattan Love Song (1934) 75
Man's Country (1938) 152
The Marines Are Here (1938) 150
Marked Trails (1944) 412
Mason of the Mounted (1932) 23
Massacre Valley see Outlaw Gold
(1950) 650
Master Minds (1949) 614
Maxwell Archer, Detective (1942)
304
A Mediterranean Mecca (1934) 724m
Meet Maxwell Archer see Maxwell
Archer, Detective (1942) 304
Meeting at Midnight see Black
Magic (1944) 414
Melody Parade (1943) 370
Mexicali Kid (1938) 156
Michael O'Halloran (1948) 565

329

Film Title Index

Midnight Limited (1940) 217
The Midnight Patrol (1932) 20
Million Dollar Baby (1934) 98
Million Dollar Kid (1944) 395
The Mind of Mr. Reeder see The
    Mysterious Mr. Reeder (1940) 222
The Missing Lady (1946) 493
Missing People (1940) 247
Mississippi Rhythm (1949) 596
Mr. Hex (1946) 503
Mr. Hobo see The Gunman (1952)
    699
Mr. Muggs Meets a Deadline see
    Bowery Champs (1944) 428
Mr. Muggs Rides Again (1945) 450
Mr. Muggs Steps Out (1943) 379
Mr. Wise Guy (1942) 309
Mr. Wong at Headquarters see The
    Fatal Hour (1940) 205
Mr. Wong, Detective (1938) 158
Mr. Wong in Chinatown (1939) 187
The Model Murder see Fashion
    Model (1945) 441
A Modern Marriage (1950) 638
Money Means Nothing (1934) 80
Montana Desperado (1951) 672
Montana Incident (1952) 709
The Montana Kid (1931) 5
Monte Carlo Nights (1934) 78
Moon Over Montana (1946) 470
The Moonstone (1934) 85
Mother and Son (1931) 4
Mother Ganges (1934) 724h
Murder at Malibu Beach see The
    Trap (1946) 507
Murder at the Windmill see Mystery
    at the Burlesque (1950) 628
Murder by Appointment see Murder
    by Invitation (1941) 273
Murder by Invitation (1941) 273
Murder by the Stars see The Invisi-
    ble Ghost (1941) 264
Murder in the Air see Sky Dragon
    (1949) 594
Murder in the Family see Crazy
    Knights (1944) 430
Murder in the Stratosphere see Lost
    in the Stratosphere (1934) 91
Murder on the Yukon (1940) 213
Music Man (1948) 569

Mutiny in the Big House (1939) 195
My Mother see Self Defense (1932)
    40
My Old Kentucky Home (1938) 139
The Mysterious Mr. Reeder (1940)
    222
Mysterious Mr. Wong (1935) 99
Mystery at the Burlesque (1950) 628
Mystery Liner (1934) 72
The Mystery Man (1935) 107
The Mystery of Mr. Wong (1939) 174
The Mystery of the Golden Eye see
    The Golden Eye (1948) 568
The Mystery of the 13th Guest (1943)
    380
Mystery of the Wentworth Castle
    see Doomed to Die (1940) 235
Mystery Plane (1939) 175

The Navajo Trail (1945) 431
Navy Bound (1951) 660
Navy Secrets (1939) 170
Nearly Eighteen (1943) 381
'Neath Brooklyn Bridge (1942) 344
'Neath the Arizona Skies (1934) 97
Nevada Badmen (1951) 669
News Hounds (1947) 530
Newshounds see News Hounds
    (1947) 530
Night Raiders (1952) 691
No Escape see I Escaped from the
    Gestapo (1943) 361
No Holds Barred (1952) 722
No Time for Love see One Thrilling
    Night (1942) 326
Noose see The Silk Noose (1950)
    637
Northwest Territory (1951) 687
Numbered Woman (1938) 147
Numbers of Monte Carlo see Monte
    Carlo Nights (1934) 78
The Nut Farm (1935) 104

Oh, What a Night! (1944) 418
Oklahoma Blues (1948) 550
Oklahoma Bound see Take Me

330

Film Title Index

Back to Oklahoma (1940) 248
Oklahoma Jim (1931) 8
Oklahoma Justice (1951) 676
Oklahoma Outlaws **see** Oklahoma
  Justice (1951) 676
Oklahoma Terror (1939) 192
The Old Gray Mayor **see** Smart
  Politics (1948) 542
Old Swimmin' Hole (1940) 246
Oliver Twist (1933) 44
On the Spot (1940) 227
One Thrilling Night (1942) 326
Our Gang **see** Little Rascals 727
The Outer Gate (1937) 122
Outlaw Brand (1948) 573
Outlaw Gold (1950) 650
Outlaw Trail (1944) 401
Outlaws of Stampede Pass (1943)
  376
Outlaws of Texas (1950) 652
Over the Border (1950) 624
Overland Mail (1939) 200
Overland Trails (1948) 545

The Painted Trail (1938) 140
Pals of the Silver Sage (1940) 221
Paradise Canyon (1935) 113
Paradise Isle (1937) 120
Partners of the Sunset (1948) 554
Partners of the Trail (1931) 3
Partners of the Trail (1944) 397
Party Girl **see** Sensation Hunters
  (1945) 457
The Peacock Throne (1934) 724e
Perilous Waters (1948) 547
The Phantom Broadcast (1933) 46
The Phantom Killer **see** The Invisi-
  ble Ghost (1941) 264
The Phantom Killer (1942) 337
Phantom of Chinatown (1940) 249
Phantom of the Air **see** The Phan-
  tom Broadcast (1933) 46
Phantom Ranger (1938) 149
The Phantom Strikes (1939) 199
Pioneer Days (1940) 209
The Pioneers (1941) 267
Police Bullets (1942) 336
Police Court (1932) 17
Port o' Call Novelties (series) 724

Port of Missing Girls (1938) 141
Prairie Express (1947) 535
Pride of the Army **see** War Dogs
  (1942) 343
Pride of the Bowery (1941) 257
The Private Life of Dr. Paul Joseph
  Goebbels **see** Enemy of Women
  (1944) 424
Private Nurse **see** Numbered Wo-
  man (1938) 147
Private Snuffy Smith (1942) 302
The Process Server **see** He Couldn't
  Take It (1933) 65

Queen of the Indies (1934) 724I
Queen of the Yukon (1940) 239

The Radio Star **see** The Loud-
  speaker (1934) 79
Raiders of the Border (1944) 390
Raiders of the South (1947) 511
Rainbow Over the Range (1940) 234
Rainbow Over the Rockies (1947) 513
Rainbow Ranch (1933) 55
Rainbow Valley (1935) 103
Randy Rides Alone (1934) 81
Randy Strikes Oil **see** The Fighting
  Texans (1933) 53
The Range Busters (1940) 238
Range Justice (1949) 604
Range Land (1949) 617
Range Law (1944) 406
Range Renegades (1948) 557
The Ranger's Code (1933) 58
The Rangers Ride (1948) 571
Reckless Romeos **see** Flirting with
  Danger (1934) 95
The Reckoning (1932) 16
The Red Dragon (1946) 469
The Red Hornet **see** The Chinese
  Ring (1947) 539
Redhead (1934) 92
Redhead (1941) 269
Return Bout **see** Joe Palooka in the
  Counterpunch (1949) 605
The Return of Casey Jones (1933) 49

331

Film Title Index

Return of the Ape Man (1944) 409
Revenge of the Zombies (1943) 373
Rhythm Inn (1951) 659
Rhythm of the Rio Grande (1940) 215
Rhythm Parade (1942) 347
Riders from Nowhere (1940) 226
Riders of Destiny (1933) 63
Riders of the Dawn (1937) 119
Riders of the Dawn (1945) 454
Riders of the Dusk (1949) 613
Riders of the Frontier (1939) 189
Riders of the Rio Grande see Across the Plains (1939) 183
Riders of the West (1942) 332
Ridin' Down the Trail (1947) 532
Ridin' the Cherokee Trail (1941) 259
Riding the California Trail (1947) 510
Riding the Sunset Trail (1941) 290
The Right Man see Her First Romance (1940) 251
The Right to Live see Forever Yours (1945) 434
Riot Squad (1941) 297
Road to Happiness (1941) 298
Roar of the Press (1941) 265
Roaring Westward (1949) 608
Robin Hood of Monterey (1947) 531
Rock River Renegades (1942) 310
Rocky (1948) 543
Rodeo (1952) 695
Roll, Wagons, Roll (1939) 190
Rollin' Home to Texas (1940) 253
Rollin' Westward (1939) 173
Romance of the Limberlost (1938) 151
Romance of the Rockies (1937) 134
The Rose Bowl Story (1952) 710
Rose of the Rio Grande (1938) 143
Rough Riders see Arizona Bound (1941) 274
Rubber Racketeers (1942) 328

Saddle Mountain Roundup (1941) 280
Saddle Serenade (1945) 451
The Sagebrush Trail (1933) 66

Saleslady (1938) 137
Sarge Goes to College (1947) 522
Sarong Girl (1943) 362
The Scarlet Clue (1945) 444
The Schoolmaster see The Hoosier Schoolmaster (1935) 108
Sea Tiger (1952) 708
The Secret Four (1940) 206
Self Defense (1932) 40
Sensation Hunters (1933) 61
Sensation Hunters (1945) 457
The Seventh Wonder (1933) 724a
The Shadow and the Missing Lady see The Missing Lady (1946) 493
The Shadow Behind the Mask see Behind the Mask (1946) 479
Shadow of Blackmail see Wife Wanted (1946) 501
The Shadow Returns (1946) 471
Shadows of Suspicion (1944) 420
Shadows of the Orient (1937) 123
Shadows of the Underworld (1942) 308
Shadows of the West (1949) 602
Shadows on the Range (1946) 500
Shadows Over Chinatown (1946) 491
The Shanghai Chest (1948) 562
The Shanghai Cobra (1945) 456
The Sheriff of Medicine Bow (1948) 572
She's in the Army (1942) 323
Ships of Hate (1931) 1
Shock (1934) 82
Should a Girl Marry? (1939) 184
Sideshow (1950) 634
Sierra Passage (1951) 654
Sign of the Wolf (1941) 261
The Silent Battle see Continental Express (1942) 311
Silent Witness (1943) 350
The Silk Noose (1950) 637
Silver Raiders (1950) 642
Silver Range (1946) 504
Silver Skates (1943) 355
Silver Stallion (1941) 270
Silver Trails (1948) 567
The Sin of Lena Rivers (1938) 163
Sing Sing Nights (1934) 96
Single-Handed Sanders (1932) 15

332

Film Title Index

Siren of the South Seas see Paradise Isle (1937) 120
Six-Gun Gospel (1943) 371
Six Gun Mesa (1950) 630
Six Gun Serenade (1947) 519
16 Fathoms Deep (1934) 67
16 Fathoms Deep (1948) 564
Sky Bandits (1940) 230
Sky Dragon (1949) 594
Sky Patrol (1939) 193
Sky Pilot see Mystery Plane (1939) 175
Skyway (1933) 59
Smart Alecks (1942) 330
Smart Guy (1943) 385
Smart Politics (1948) 542
Smuggler's Cove (1948) 574
Snow Dog (1950) 639
Snuffy Smith see Private Snuffy Smith (1942) 302
Snuffy Smith, the Yard Bird see Private Snuffy Smith (1942) 302
Son of the Navy (1940) 218
Song of the Buckaroo (1939) 167
Song of the Drifter (1948) 544
Song of the Range (1944) 429
Song of the Sierras (1946) 506
Song of the Wasteland (1947) 524
Sonora Stagecoach (1944) 405
So's Your Aunt Emma! (1942) 320
South of Monterey (1946) 483
South of the Rio Grande (1945) 453
Speed Brent Wins see Breed of the Border (1933) 45
The Sphinx (1933) 52
Spook Busters (1946) 494
Spooks Run Wild (1941) 288
Spotlight on Scandal see Spotlight Scandals (1943) 374
Spotlight Revue see Spotlight Scandals (1943) 374
Spotlight Scandals (1943) 374
Spring Meeting see Three Wise Brides (1942) 319
Springtime in Texas (1945) 447
Spy Train (1943) 364
Square Dance Katy (1950) 626
Stage Struck (1948) 558
Stage to Blue River (1951) 688
Stagecoach Driver (1951) 674

Stand and Deliver see Bowery Blitzkrieg (1941) 282
The Star Packer (1934) 83
Star Reporter (1939) 172
Starlight Over Texas (1938) 155
Stars Over Arizona (1937) 126
The Steel Fist (1952) 689
Stolen Paradise (1941) 289
Strange Adventure (1932) 37
The Strange Mr. Gregory (1946) 466
Strange Voyage (1946) 489
The Stranger from Pecos (1943) 365
Stranger from Santa Fe (1945) 443
Streets of New York (1939) 178
Stunt Pilot (1939) 186
A Successful Failure (1934) 89
The Sultan's Daughter (1944) 386
Sunbonnet Sue (1945) 461
Sundown on the Prairie (1939) 171
Suspense (1946) 484
Sweet Sixteen see Freddie Steps Out (1946) 487
Sweetheart of Sigma Chi (1946) 508
The Sweetheart of Sigma Chi (1933) 62
Sweethearts of the U.S.A. (1944) 396
Sweethearts on Parade see Sweethearts of the U.S.A. (1944) 396
Swing Parade of 1946 (1946) 474

Take Me Back to Oklahoma (1940) 248
Tall Timber see Big Timber (1950) 643
Telephone Operator (1937) 133
Tell It to the Marines see Here Come the Marines (1952) 705
Temptation Harbor (1949) 590
Texas City (1952) 690
The Texas Kid (1943) 383
Texas Lawmen (1951) 686
Texas Pioneers (1932) 26
Texas Terror (1935) 100
Texas to Bataan (1942) 340
Texas Trouble Shooters (1942) 327
That Gang of Mine (1940) 242
There Goes Kelly (1945) 438
They Shall Have Faith see Forever Yours (1945) 434

Film Title Index

The Thirteenth Guest (1932) 31
The Thirteenth Guest (1937) 116
This Man in Paris see Shadows of the Underworld (1942) 308
Three of a Kind (1944) 411
Three Wise Brides (1942) 319
Thunder River Feud (1942) 301
Thunderbolt (1947) 529
The Tiger Man see Voodoo Man (1944) 394
Tillie's Punctured Romance (1941) 725
Time Bomb see Spy Train (1943) 364
Tomboy (1940) 220
Tomorrow's Youth (1935) 102
Tonto Basin Outlaws (1941) 285
Top Sergeant Mulligan (1941) 287
Torpedo Raider (1940) 214
Tough Kid (1938) 166
Tower of Terror (1942) 317
The Trail Beyond (1934) 90
Trail of the Arrow (1952) 719
Trail of the Silver Spurs (1941) 254
Trail of the Yukon (1949) 603
Trail Riders (1942) 346
Trail to Mexico (1946) 488
Trailin' North (1933) 50
Trailing Danger (1947) 517
Trailing Double Trouble (1940) 245
Trail's End (1949) 591
Train 2419 see The Return of Casey Jones (1933) 49
The Trap (1946) 507
Trigger Fingers (1946) 497
Trigger Law (1944) 421
Trigger Smith (1939) 176
Triggerman (1948) 559
Triple Cross (1951) 678
Triple Threat see West of Pinto Basin (1940) 252
Triple Trouble (1950) 641
Trouble Chasers (1945) 448
Trouble Makers (1948) 578
Tumbledown Ranch in Arizona (1941) 263
Tuna Clipper (1949) 592
Two-Fisted Justice (1931) 9
Two-Fisted Justice (1943) 349
Two Gun Justice (1938) 146

Under Arizona Skies (1946) 477
Under the Big Top (1938) 154
Undercover Agent (1939) 177
Underground Rustlers (1941) 293
The Unknown Guest (1943) 377
Unsung Heroes see War Dogs (1942) 343
Up in the Air (1940) 241
The Utah Kid (1944) 417

Vacation Days (1947) 512
Valley of Fear (1947) 514
Vanishing Men (1932) 21
Violence (1947) 518
Voodoo Man (1944) 394

Waco (1952) 694
Wagons West (1952) 706
Wanderers of the West (1941) 276
Wanted by Scotland Yard (1939) 180
Wanted by the Police (1938) 157
Wanted: Dead or Alive (1951) 677
War Dogs (1942) 343
A Wave, a Wac and a Marine (1944) 422
Wayne Murder Case see Strange Adventure (1932) 37
West of Eldorado (1949) 597
West of Pinto Basin (1940) 252
West of Rainbow's End (1938) 136
West of Singapore (1933) 43
West of the Alamo (1946) 476
West of the Divide (1934) 70
West of the Law (1942) 338
West of the Rio Grande (1944) 413
West of Wyoming (1950) 622
Westbound Stage (1939) 202
Western Limited (1932) 28
Western Mail (1942) 307
Western Renegades (1949) 611
Westward Bound (1944) 388
What a Man! (1944) 391
When Strangers Marry (1944) 427
When Youth Conspires see Old Swimmin' Hole (1940) 246
Where Are Your Children? (1944) 389

334

Film Title Index

Where the Buffalo Roam (1938) 159
Where the West Begins (1938) 138
Where Trails Divide (1937) 128
Where Trails End (1942) 318
Whistling Hills (1951) 679
Who Is Guilty? (1940) 240
Widows of the Press see Roar of
  the Press (1941) 265
Wife Wanted (1946) 501
The Wild Herd see Down the
  Wyoming Trail (1939) 185
Wild Horse Canyon (1938) 165
Wild Horse Range (1940) 229
Wild Horse Stampede (1943) 359
Wild Stallion (1952) 700
Win, Place and Show see Crazy
  Over Horses (1951) 684
Wings Over the Pacific (1943) 366
Winner Take All (1948) 570
Wolf Call (1939) 182
The Wolf Hunters (1949) 612
Woman in the Case see Allotment
  Wives (1945) 463
A Woman's Man (1934) 69

Women in Bondage (1944) 387
Women Must Dress (1935) 101
Wrangler's Roost (1941) 271
Wyoming Roundup (1952) 721

Yellow Fin (1951) 680
The Yellow-Haired Kid (1952) 720
Yellow Menace see Black Dragons
  (1942) 313
You Can't Beat the Law (1943) 352
Young Blood (1932) 36
Young Daniel Boone (1950) 623
The Young Recruit see Son of the
  Navy (1940) 218
You're Out of Luck (1941) 256
Yukon Flight (1940) 204
Yukon Gold (1952) 711
Yukon Manhunt (1951) 673

Zis Boom Bah (1941) 291

335

NAME INDEX

The number after each name refers to the film entry number, not the page number.

The spelling of some names varied from film to film (i.e., Eddie Featherstone/Fetherstone, Jack Carlisle/Carlyle, Douglas/Douglass Dumbrille); these have been noted wherever possible.

Abbott, Dorothy 609
Abbott, John 328, 634, 660
Abercrombie, J. 262
Abrahams, Derwin M. 468, 473, 549, 561, 571, 596, 679
Ackland, Rodney 311
Acuff, Edward 122
Adair, Phyllis 454
Adair, Robert 240, 357, 637
Adam, Ronald 247, 266, 304
Adams, Dorothy 692, 698
Adams, Eadie 116
Adams, Ernie 43, 44, 56, 58, 126, 140, 142, 152, 156, 159, 162, 167, 171, 185, 226, 264, 314, 326, 366, 390, 409, 425, 472, 517, 523, 531
Adams, Eustace L. 67, 564
Adams, Jane 588, 609, 611, 644, 650
Adams, Ken 527, 535
Adams, Max 675
Adams, Richard 211
Adams, Ted 1, 148, 197, 201, 209, 226, 229, 230, 335, 477, 482, 497, 500, 504, 511, 514, 523, 524, 526, 527, 535, 541, 545, 552, 555, 563, 572, 575, 584, 595, 602, 606, 636, 644, 658
Adamson, Ewart 382
Adamson, James 681, 703
Adamson, John 251
Adamson, Victor see Dixon, Denver
Adolphson, Edvin 662

Adrian, Iris 294, 374, 395, 426, 515, 594, 603, 634
Adrian, Jane 639
Ahn, Philip 325, 539
Ainslee, Mary 257
The Airliners 478
Aked, Muriel 311
Alba, Maria 95, 105
Alberni, Luis 33, 52, 372, 381, 486
Albert, Eddie 489
Albertson, Frank 275, 303, 350, 509
Albright, Hardie 96, 101, 432, 435
Albright, Lola 654, 716
Albright, Wally 14
Aldana, Vida 502
Alden, Betty 104
Alderson, Charles 267
Alderson, Erville 31, 562, 577
Aldrich, Davie 83
Aldrich, Fred 486
Alexander, Ben 121, 122, 168
Alexander, Jimmy 398
Alexander, Richard (Dick) 67, 138, 159, 292, 299, 390, 494
Allen, Barbara 674, 676, 707
Allen, Barbara Jo see Vague, Vera
Allen, Bob 384
Allen, Drew 475
Allen, Eddie 416
Allen, Harry 26
Allen, Irving 484, 525, 564, 726
Allen, Joe, Jr. 499

Name Index

Allen, Joel 697
Allen, John H. 450
Allen, Judith 109, 133, 141, 166
Allen, Leigh 69
Allen, Maude 208
Allen, Phyllis 725
Allen, Ruth 508
Allwyn, Astrid 29, 65, 71, 72, 78
Alper, Murray 432, 621, 660, 675, 689, 705, 717, 722
Alsace, Gene see Camron, Rocky
Alvarado, Don 47, 143
Alvarez, Carmen 155
Alvin, John 543, 562
Alyn, Kirk 507
Ambler, Joss 262
Ames, Adrienne 57
Ames, Leon 211
Ames, Michael (Tod Andrews) 394, 409
Ames, Ramsay 422, 475, 492, 502
Ames and Arno 659
Amsterdam, Morey 353, 428
Anderson, Bobby 577
Anderson, Cap 239
Anderson, Edgar B., Jr. 704
Anderson, Rick 301
Anderson, "Sugar Foot" 703
Andor, Paul 424
Andre, Lona 91, 104
Andre, Marvelle 696
Andre, Nicolle 331
Andre, Pierre 475
Andrews, Caroline 516
Andrews, Lloyd "Arkansas Slim" 215, 221, 223, 231, 234, 237, 248, 253, 259, 267, 276, 279, 286, 290
Andrews, Robert D. 161, 178, 195, 298
Andrews, Stanley 295, 547, 549, 560, 593, 603, 621, 622, 694, 697, 701, 712
Andrews, Tod see Ames, Michael
Angel, Daniel M. 628
Angold, Edith 484
Ankrum, Morris 663, 683, 692
Anthony, Emmett 114
Anthony, Stuart 17, 86, 163
Anzalone, Larry 593
Apfel, Oscar 104, 123

Appleton, Louis B., Jr. 489
Arabella 693
Archainbaud, George 426
Archer, John 268, 336, 342, 695, 708
Argyle, John 216, 250, 317
Arledge, John 132, 147
Armando and Lita 670
Armida 370, 372, 453, 659
Armstrong, Henry 481
Armstrong, Louis 561, 571, 573, 576
Armstrong, Robert 75, 95, 107, 325, 366, 496, 515
Arness, James 667
Arnold, Edward, Jr. 117
Arnold, Jessie 233, 243
Arnt, Charles 515, 565
Arthur, George K. 44
Arthur, Louise 470
Arthur, Robert 508
Asbury, Adaline 28
The Ashburns 410
Asher, Max 51
Ashley, Herb 217
Ashlock, Jessie (Jesse) 470, 506, 524, 532
Asnis, Consuelo 567
Astell, Bettey 222
Asther, Nils 426, 581
Astor, Gertrude 28, 111, 569, 570, 598, 684
Atchinson, Tex 584, 588
Atchley, Hooper 52, 158, 174
Ates, Roscoe 223, 651
Atkin, George 255
Atwill, Lionel 52, 71
Aubrey, Jimmy 114, 121, 130, 136, 209, 224, 225, 321, 354, 503, 540, 556, 580, 607
Auer, Florence 565, 599, 621
Auer, Mischa 20
Austin, Frank 302, 331, 580, 636
Austin, Gene 404
Austin, Lois 324, 442, 507, 562, 568, 585
Aversa, Roy 599
Avonde, Richard 592, 639, 676, 694, 699, 707
Aylesworth, Doug 532
Aylmer, Felix 262

337

Name Index

Ayres, Mitch, and His Orchestra
398

Babcock, Dwight 720
Backus, Jim 710
Bacon, Irving 73, 543
Baggott, King 17
Bailer, Dorothy 394
Bailey, Buck 619, 624
Bailey, Carmen 169
Bailey, Sherwood 79
Bailey, William 683, 705
Bailey, William Norton 20, 526, 551,
  563, 567, 576, 591, 595, 597, 600
Baird, Leah 42
Baish, Herbert 623
Baker, Art 647
Baker, Benny 534, 560, 587, 713
Baker, Bob 359
Baker, Bonnie 374
Baker, Fay 610
Baker, Harold 609
Baker, Ira C. 529
Baker, Kenny 355
Baker, Silver Tip 76
Baker, Tommie 196
Bakewell, William 537
Balcon, Michael 199, 206
Baldra, Chuck 259
Baldwin, Adam 188, 331
Balfour, Betty 214
Ball, Frank 19, 56, 58, 103, 106
Ballew, Smith 468, 477
Balter, Sam 620, 633, 684
Bancroft, Harold 678
Bancroft, Henry 294
Bane, Holly (Mike Ragan) 524, 545,
  600, 608, 613, 619, 622, 624
Banks, Howard 345
Banks, Leslie 250, 255
Bannon, Jim 629, 654, 664, 669,
  674, 677, 682, 695
Banthin, Larry 22
Barclay, Joan 146, 168, 203, 260,
  309, 313, 322, 456
Barcroft, Roy 179, 189, 201, 204,
  245, 305, 338, 348, 365, 371
Bardette, Trevor 683

Barker, Reginald 85, 101, 109
Barkley, Lucille 683
Barnes, Barry K. 308
Barnes, V.L. 34
Barnett, Vince 200, 211, 232, 294,
  315, 322, 342, 350, 351, 353, 361,
  396, 416, 457, 490, 534
Baron, Lita 616; see also Isabelita
Barondess, Barbara 60
Barr, Patrick 199
Barrat, Robert H. 424, 683
Barrett, Curt 468, 482, 511, 602
Barrie, Mona 298, 348
Barrier, Edgar 543, 649
Barriner, Barry 20
Barringer, A.B. 67
Barron, Robert 485
Barry, Phyllis 85, 281
Barry, Wesley E. 156, 186, 689, 717,
  718, 719, 720
Bartell, Eddie 374
Bartlett, Bennie (Benny) 160, 353,
  360, 548, 560, 574, 578, 593, 599,
  609, 614, 684, 696, 705, 713, 722
Barton, Buzz 225
Barton, Finis 61, 64
Barton, Gregg 565, 699, 707
Barton, Kirk 423
Barton, Margaret 590
Basch, Felix 387
Baskett, James 373
Basquette, Lina 22, 143
Bates, Bill 367
Bates, Florence 640, 671
Battier, Bob 253
Baucin, Escolastico 340
Bautista, Joe 428
Baxley, Jack (John) 454, 506, 513
Baxter, Alan 295, 387
Baxter, George 96
Bayne, Al 593
Beach, Brandon 192
Beach, Guy 596, 603
Beal, John 326
Beale, Will 3
Beatty, Mary 164
Beauchamp, D.D. 585, 598, 631,
  651, 671
Beauchamp, Lane 585
Beaudine, William 326, 337, 339,

338

345, 356, 360, 367, 372, 374, 379,
380, 391, 394, 399, 402, 404, 416,
418, 420, 428, 430, 433, 441, 455,
462, 467, 485, 492, 494, 503, 520,
530, 538, 539, 548, 560, 562, 568,
574, 577, 580, 581, 583, 592, 601,
603, 607, 618, 621, 629, 632, 640,
648, 656, 665, 675, 684, 695, 696,
698, 700, 705, 710, 713, 722
Beaudine, William, Jr. 508
Beavers, Louise 261
Beck, Danny 345, 503, 520, 580, 599
Beck, John 35
Beckett, Scotty 565
Beddoe, Don 623
Bedford, Barbara 88, 102, 112
Beebe, Ford 519, 576, 589, 616, 635,
645, 663, 681, 703, 706, 723
Beebe, Marjorie 24
Beecher, Elizabeth 293, 327, 354,
357, 359, 363, 378, 384
Beery, Noah, Jr. 90, 344, 706
Beery, Noah, Sr. 7, 72, 86, 360,
379, 395, 410
Beich, Albert 382
Belasco, Leon 474, 484, 607, 645
Belden, Charles S. 466, 475, 483,
502
Belita 355, 398, 484
Bell, Frank 39
Bell, Hank 6, 15, 35, 36, 66, 76,
202, 219, 271, 285, 310, 354, 368,
624, 627
Bell, Monta 446
Bell, Rex 11, 14, 22, 32, 35, 38, 41,
51, 53, 54, 55, 348
Bell, Rodney 465
Bellamy, Ralph 109
Belmont, Virginia 535, 545, 546,
550, 571, 576
Belmore, Lionel 17, 44, 84
Benedict, Billy 360, 367, 379, 395,
404, 410, 428, 439, 450, 455, 465,
486, 490, 503, 520, 530, 538, 548,
560, 574, 578, 593, 599, 609, 614,
621, 632, 641, 648, 656, 665, 675,
684
Benedict, Richard 609, 641, 675
Benge, Wilson 57
Bennet, Spencer Gordon 183, 189,

192, 202, 223, 259, 274, 284
Bennett, Billie 725
Bennett, Bruce see Brix, Herman
Bennett, Charles 725
Bennett, Earl 522
Bennett, Edna 363
Bennett, Rafael (Raphael) 145, 449
Bennett, Ray 177, 390, 431, 437,
473, 475, 477, 694, 697
Benson, George 262
Bentham, Josephine 127
Bentley, Thomas 255
Bergen, Jerry 325
Bergen, Polly (Polly Burgin) 595
Berger, Harris 211
Berke, William 124
Berkes, John 342, 343
Berkoff, Louis 466
Bernard, Barry 392
Bernard, Joe 108, 196, 261, 556
Bernard, Sam 157, 263, 325, 330,
351
Bernerd, Jeffrey 389, 408, 434, 452,
462, 463, 467, 485, 501, 508, 531,
537, 558, 601, 618, 640
Bernhard, Jack 496, 518, 547
Bert, Margaret 551
Bertholon, George 87, 95
Bertrand, Rosemary 496
Besser, Joe 620, 633
Best, Bettie 507
Best, Deannie 562
Best, Willie 467, 469, 499, 562, 607
Bettinson, Ralph 143, 235, 249, 453
Betty and Beverly 670
Betz, Matthew 32
Bevan, Billy 82
Bevans, Clem 620, 633
Beverley, Helen 414
Bice, Robert 702
Bickford, Charles 195, 239
Bieber, Nita 530
Bigelow, Charles J. 400, 406, 413,
419, 421, 423, 425, 431, 437, 443,
458, 459, 464, 473, 497, 504, 514
Biggers, Earl Derr 392, 403, 414,
435, 444, 456, 469, 480, 491, 499,
507, 539, 549, 562, 568, 581, 594
Bill, Buffalo, Jr. 94, 97, 100, 103
Bing, Herman 75

339

Name Index

Bird, Richard 250
Birell, Tala 387
Birnes, Billy 289
Bischoff, Sam 163
Bishop, Julie 533; *see also* Wells, Jacqueline
Black, Jonathan 506
Black, Maurice 67
Blackburn, Tom W. 654, 667
Blackford, Mary 62
Blackman, Don 723
Blackmer, Sidney 105, 123, 168, 361
Blackwell, Carlyle, Jr. 439
Blackwood, Hope 312
Blaine, Doris 289
Blair, Barbara 240
Blair, George 702
Blair, Reno *see* Browne, Reno
Blair, Robert 293
Blaire, Hal 253
Blake, Gladys 407, 432, 465, 565
Blake, Larry 507, 553
Blake, Marie 382, 609
Blake, Oliver 509, 516, 713
Blake, Pamela 353, 377, 465, 558, 620, 633, 694; *see also* Pearce, Adele
Blandick, Clara 139, 220, 420
Blane, Sally 14, 16, 74, 147, 197
Blankfort, Henry 315, 328, 605, 620, 633
Bleifer, John 329, 525, 553, 564, 574, 656
Bletcher, Billy 125, 660, 671
Bliss, Lela 665, 714
Bloch, Al 265
Blore, Eric 269
Bly, Wesley 703
Blystone, Stanley 6, 12, 27, 38, 104, 169, 201, 470, 556, 614, 617, 630, 683, 705, 713
Blythe, Betty 80, 88, 115, 151, 161, 163, 287, 300, 348, 362, 374, 379, 389, 403, 439, 481, 540, 607
Boardman, True 218
Bocigon, Iris 475
Boetticher, Oscar (Budd) 610, 612, 625
Bois, Curt 553, 620, 633
Boland, Mary 434

Boles, John 298
Bommart, Jean 311
Bonanova, Fortunio 386, 469
Bond, David 683
Bond, Johnny 363, 429, 447, 524
Bond, Raymond 683
Bond, Richard 256
Bond, Tommy 647
Bond, Ward 147
Bondi, Beulah 525
Boniface, Symona 360
Bonn, Walter 278
Bonnell, Lee 540
Booth, Adrian (Lorna Gray) 241, 244, 275, 433, 441, 680
Booth, Edwina 20
Bordeaux, Francine 387
Borden, Eddie 42, 465
Borden, Leo 439
Borg, Veda Ann 236, 323, 373, 377, 385, 402, 412, 501, 596, 601, 696
Borländ, Barlowe 162
Bostock, Evelyn 85
Boswell, Connee 474
Bosworth, Hobart 18, 112
Boteler, Wade 115, 150
Botiller, Dick 73
Bouchier, Chili 222
Bovard, Mary 260
Bowen, Harry 51
Bowers, Jess *see* Buffington, Adele
Bowman, Rudy 476, 608
Boyd, Beverley 358
Boyd, Mildred 467
Boyd, William "Stage" 44
Boyland, Malcolm Stuart 426
Boyle, Jack 374, 474
Boyle, Walden 507, 556
Bracey, Sidney 64
Bradbury, Robert N. 2, 34, 45, 48, 56, 58, 63, 68, 70, 76, 77, 83, 86, 90, 94, 100, 103, 110, 119, 125, 126, 128, 130, 134, 299
Bradford, Lane 500, 504, 555, 611, 674, 676, 677, 679, 682, 685, 686, 688, 690, 691, 692, 694, 697, 699, 701, 703, 707
Bradford, Marshall 611, 655, 665, 685
Bradley, Grace 92, 261

Name Index

Bradley, Harry C. 73, 74, 102
Bradley, Leslie 637
Bradley, Paul 705
Bradshaw, Dorothy 396
Brady, Ed 8, 56, 58, 92, 119, 261, 277
Branch, Houston 43, 158, 387, 410
Brandon, Henry 235, 706
Brandt, Bernard 496, 518
Brauer, Harold 512
Bray, Robert 697, 699, 712, 713
Brayton, Margaret 507, 522
Brazee, Laurie 122
Breakston, George 89
Brecher, Egon 334
Breese, Edmund 16, 17, 91
Breitigam, Gerald 246
Brenon, Herbert 44
Brent, Evelyn 158, 350, 364, 428, 511, 531, 558, 568
Brent, Linda 305, 384
Brent, Lynton 31, 267, 284, 299, 326, 332, 338, 346, 349, 365, 371, 383, 390, 397, 406, 412, 413, 458, 459, 468, 473, 482, 606
Brent, Romney 662
Brent, Roy 375, 388
Bretherton, Howard 132, 157, 166, 170, 172, 177, 181, 191, 193, 196, 207, 210, 217, 227, 236, 241, 256, 261, 305, 316, 324, 332, 338, 347, 348, 423, 431, 437, 507, 532, 559, 691
Brewer, Jameson 553
Brewster, Carol 670
Brian, Eddie (Edwin) 211, 258
Brian, Mary 78, 361
Bricker, George 273, 306, 320, 329, 716
Bridge, Al 12, 31, 32, 47, 53, 146, 148, 258, 435, 491, 492, 603
Bridge, Lois 15
Bridges, John 359, 368, 384, 388, 401, 405, 458
Bridges, Lloyd 529, 564
Brier, A.J. "Shorty" 155, 185
Bright, John 546
Brill, Patti 465, 520, 528
Bring, Lou 398
Brinkman, Nancy 450, 451, 465, 479

Brissac, Virginia 111, 442, 444
Brito, Phil 508, 569, 626
Britton, Ken 580
Brix, Herman (Bruce Bennett) 142
Broaux, Sandra 101
Brock, Gerald 364
Brodel, Mary 185
Brodie, Steve 678, 714
Brody, Ann 80
Broidy, William F. 634, 653, 660, 689, 708, 711
Brokaw, Charles 122, 133
Bromfield, John 696
Bronson, Betty 20
Bronson, Lillian 391, 633
Bronte, Charlotte 84
Brooke, Hillary 632
Brooke, Walter 424
Brooks, Jean (Jeanne Kelly) 315, 321
Brooks, Pauline 114
Brooks, Ralph 565
Brooks, Rand 528, 610, 673, 689, 694, 697, 699, 709, 717
Brooks, Shelton 433
Brophy, Ed 474, 508
Brower, Otto 14
Brown, Barbara 585, 598, 631, 651, 671
Brown, Bernard B. 450
Brown, Charles 153, 191, 246, 461, 486, 556
Brown, Dottye D. 524, 536, 551
Brown, Gilson 135
Brown, James 671
Brown, Johnny Mack 24, 358, 365, 371, 376, 383, 390, 397, 400, 406, 413, 419, 423, 425, 431, 434, 437, 443, 449, 458, 459, 464, 468, 473, 477, 482, 497, 500, 504, 511, 514, 517, 521, 523, 526, 527, 535, 541, 545, 552, 555, 559, 563, 566, 572, 575, 579, 586, 591, 597, 604, 611, 619, 622, 624, 630, 644, 650, 655, 661, 666, 672, 676, 679, 686, 690, 697, 707, 715
Brown, Karl 24, 129, 141, 147, 153, 154, 161, 337, 356
Brown, Kenneth see Butch and Buddy
Brown, Melville 91, 92, 104

341

Name Index

Brown, Ray 72
Brown, Rowland 135
Brown, Stanley (Brad Taylor) 379, 395
Brown, Tom 325
Brown, Vera 92, 269
Browne, Lucile 100, 103
Browne, Reno (Reno Blair) 477, 482, 511, 523, 555, 595, 597, 602, 606, 613, 617, 619, 627
Brownell, John C. 104
Brownlee, Frank 106
Bruce, David 587, 623, 720
Bruce, Virginia 84
Brunetti, Argentina 533, 665
Brunn, Frederic 387
Brunner, Charles 335
Bruno, Frank 158
Bryant, Jan 500, 504, 507, 527, 561, 582
Bryant, Joyce 176, 183, 211, 242
Bryant, Nana 462, 558, 638
Bryar, Paul 272, 303, 341, 362, 491, 539, 546, 551, 556, 596, 648, 649, 653, 660, 665, 667, 668, 675, 696, 716
Buchanan, Edgar 700
Buchanan, Jack 262
Buchanan, Morris 722
Bucker, William 178
Buckley, Jack 314
Bucko, Ralph 697
Bucko, Roy 36, 697
Buffington, Adele 11, 43, 85, 112, 274, 284, 299, 305, 316, 324, 332, 338, 348, 358, 365, 371, 376, 383, 390, 431, 449, 458, 459, 468, 500, 545, 552, 582, 597, 602, 606, 611, 613, 617, 627, 629, 630, 636
Bull, Peter 255
Bunston, Herbert 85
Bupp, Tommy 88, 108, 175
Burbridge, Betty 92, 111, 413, 429, 436, 445, 470
Burger, Fairfax 472
Burgin, Polly see Bergen, Polly
Burke, Frankie 211, 232
Burke, James 74, 107, 114, 490
Burke, Kathleen 135
Burkett, James S. 386, 403, 414,

415, 435, 444, 455, 469, 480, 491, 499, 507, 539, 549, 562, 564, 568, 581, 594, 623
Burns, Dave 240
Burns, Eddie 376
Burns, Edmund 28
Burns, Fred 50, 259
Burns, Harry 269, 415
Burns, Marion 8, 61, 95, 110, 113
Burns, Neal 467
Burns, Robert (Bobby) 31, 66, 142
Burr, C.C. 20, 28
Burres, William 84
Burson, Wayne 532, 544
Burston, Janet 509
Burt, Margaret 522
Burtis, Eric 211
Burtis, James 28, 107, 112
Burton, Frederick 314
Burton, Martin 64
Bush, James 71, 374, 415
Busse, Henry, and His Orchestra 398
Bussey, C.H. "Fargo" 19
Buster, Budd 138, 144, 213, 219, 252, 285, 301, 310, 321, 340, 354, 363, 378, 447, 476, 506, 513, 514
Butch and Buddy (Billy Lenhart and Kenneth Brown) 374, 432
Butler, Jimmy 132
Butler, Roy 437, 447, 451, 460, 521, 541, 545, 655, 691
Butterworth, Charles 386
Byington, Spring 668
Byrd, Ralph 244, 558
Byron, Allan see Randall, Jack
Byron, Marion 45
Byron, Richard 408
Byron, Walter 201

Cabanne, Christy 20, 28, 80, 84, 88, 112, 457, 531, 537, 563, 567
Cabanne, William (Bill) 537, 540
Cabot, Bruce 92, 452
Cady, Frank 522
Cady, Jerry 355
Caesar, Arthur 411
Cagney, William 91, 95
Cahn, Edward L. 269

342

Name Index

Cairns, Sally 219, 335
Caldwell, Betty 560
Calhoun, Rory 640
Calkins, Johnny 452, 509
Callahan, Bill 544
Callahan, Foxy 369
Callahan, George 392, 403, 414, 415,
    433, 435, 444, 456, 469, 471, 479,
    480, 493
The Callahan Brothers and Their
    Blue Ridge Mountain Boys 447
Callam, Alex 210, 328
Calleia, Joseph 637
Callejo, Cecilia 436
Calvert, Charles 472
Calvert, John 704
Cameron, Rod 667, 692, 706
Campagna, Rita 92
Campbell, Charles 551
Campbell, Colin 82
Campbell, Evelyn 28
Campbell, Kate 13, 78
Campeau, Frank 140
Camron, Rocky (Gene Alsace) 221,
    231, 237, 248, 253, 259, 267, 274,
    276, 279, 284, 286, 290, 296, 307,
    312, 318, 401, 405
Candido, Candy 347, 382, 522, 542
Cane, Charles 546
Cannon, Ray 122
Cantor, Herman 556, 568, 578, 580
Cantrell, Early 476
Canutt, Yakima 9, 53, 63, 66, 68,
    70, 76, 77, 81, 83, 94, 97, 100, 110,
    113, 119
Cappy, George 530
Cappy Barra Harmonica Boys 542
Car-Bert Dancers 445
Card, Bob 259
Card, Ken 138
Cardwell, James 456, 472, 479, 493
Carey, Harry 141, 446
Carey, Leonard 57
Carle, Frankie, and His Orchestra
    508
Carleton, Bob 505, 515
Carlin, Jean 408, 479, 506
Carlisle (Carlyle), Jack 11, 13, 23
Carlisle, Mary 62, 93
Carlson, June 239, 455

Carlton, Sue 649
Carlyle, Jack see Carlisle, Jack
Carmen, Jean 201
Carnegie, Dale 540
Carnovsky, Morris 534
Carol, Sue 7
Carpenter, Horace B. 3, 63, 70, 76,
    128, 149, 155, 249, 253, 271, 312,
    316, 318, 405, 406, 409, 449
Carpenter, John 431, 524
Carr, Harry 532
Carr, Jack 288, 331
Carr, Mary 79, 136
Carr, Nat 35
Carr, Steve 652
Carr, Thomas 524, 526, 652, 677,
    697, 717, 721
Carr, Trem 1, 2, 3, 4, 5, 8, 9, 10, 12,
    13, 15, 18, 19, 21, 22, 23, 24, 25,
    26, 27, 32, 34, 35, 36, 38, 39, 41,
    45, 48, 55, 56, 57, 58, 75, 102,
    107, 108, 115
Carradine, John 361, 373, 394, 409,
    426, 467
Carrington, C. 20
Carro, Billy 284
Carroll, John 143, 164, 182
Carroll, Richard A. 243, 461
Carroll, Virginia 192, 545, 555, 559,
    582
Carruther, Bruce 723
Carson, Robert 337
Carson, Tony 282
Carstairs, John Paddy 304
Carter, Ben 444, 480
Carter, Cathy 537, 538
Carter, Harrison 217
Carter, Monte 92, 114
Cartledge, Bill 593, 684
Caruso, Anthony 485, 530, 583,
    668, 702
Carver, Lynne (Lynn) 423, 449, 468,
    552
Caryle, Jack 25
Cason, Bob (John) 405, 419, 425,
    437, 449, 617
Cass, Maurice 494, 525
Cassell, Wally 516
Cassidy, Edward 155, 156, 159, 165,
    176, 259, 272, 312, 378, 421, 431,

343

Name Index

497, 514, 619, 666, 676, 691, 694
Castelli, Delores 488
Castello, William 207, 210, 244, 249, 256
Castle, Don 516, 533, 556
Castle, Peggie 706
Castle, William 427
Catlett, Walter 398, 585, 598, 631, 651, 671
Cavan, Allan 31, 146, 164
Cavanaugh, Hobart 60
Cavanaugh, Paul 501
Cavendish, David 292
Cavens, Fred 45
Cawthorn, Joseph 64
Cecil, Nora 377
Cellier, Antoinette 240, 266
Chabing 539, 562
Chabot, Johnny 662
Chadwell, Wallace 505
Chadwick, Cyril 61
Chadwick, I.E. 14, 17, 24, 29, 37, 42, 44, 47, 49, 121, 122, 251, 269
Chadwick, Lee 29, 37
Chaliapin, Feodor 306
Chalton, Syd 374
Chamberlain, Cyril 308
Chambers, Wheaton 483, 488, 541, 544, 706
Chambers, Whitman 61
Chan, Frances 44
Chan, Luke 99
Chan, Spencer 539
Chandlee, Dick 360
Chandler, Anna 269, 614
Chandler, Bill 675
Chandler, Chick 347, 364, 407, 569
Chandler, Eddy (Eddie) 37, 106, 392, 409, 415
Chandler, George 334, 456, 479, 493, 641
Chandler, Lane 66, 142, 146, 421, 551
Chandler, Tanis 491, 494, 507, 564, 668
Chaney, Bill 410
Chaney, Creighton see Chaney, Lon, Jr.
Chaney, Lon, Jr. 67, 93, 564
Chang, George 136

Chapin, Michael 706
Chapin, Robert 334, 442
Chaplin, Charlie 725
Chapman, Edward 206
Chapman, Marguerite 683, 708
Chapman, Pattee 638
Charles, Frances 711
Charles, Hugh 556, 570
Charles, Robert 394, 409
Charlita 675
Charlot, Andre 370
Charters, Spencer 79, 104
Chase, Alden see Chase, Stephen
Chase, Charley 725
Chase, Stephen (Alden) 211, 232, 260, 634, 667, 668
Chatterton, Tom 573, 588
Chaves, Eduardo 155
Cheatham, Jack 486, 520
Chefe, Jack 465
Cheney, J. Benton 150, 477, 482, 504, 511, 514, 517, 521, 523, 524, 535, 541, 554, 555, 561, 563, 567, 572, 573, 575, 579, 584, 586, 591, 624
Cherkose, Eddie 428
Cheron, Andre 170
Cherrill, Virginia 65
Cherrington, Tuth 479
Cherry, Robert 373, 599
Chesebro, George 18, 38, 39, 155, 156, 167, 209, 212, 219, 224, 225, 226, 229, 252, 254, 267, 271, 280, 301, 321, 349, 363, 369, 384, 393, 524, 591, 627
Cheshire, Harry V. 564, 583, 626, 632, 640, 657
Chester, Hal E. (Hally) 211, 232, 481, 498, 534, 546, 570, 587, 605, 620, 633, 649, 678
Chevalier, Maurice 262
Chevret, Lita 205
Chew, Gloria Ann 446
Chief Many Treaties 267, 335, 368
Chief Soldani 267, 393
Chief Standing Bear 26
Chief Thunder Cloud (Thunder-cloud) 197, 213, 270, 335, 368, 401, 405
Chief Yowlachie 335, 538, 646
Chisel, Kid 440

344

Chorre, Suni 534, 605
Christian-Jaque 662
Christy, Bill 465, 479
Christy, Dorothy 22, 432, 441
Christy, Ted 722
Chuck, Kenneth 539
Churchill, Berton 57, 92, 96
Churchill, Sarah 319
Cianelli, Eduardo 440, 481
Clair, Rene 262
The Clarence Muse Singers 281
Clark, Betsy Ross 127
Clark, Cliff 578, 580, 678
Clark, Dave 278
Clark, Davidson 192, 455
Clark, Harvey 43
Clark, Jimmy 518
Clark, Judy 478, 486
Clark, Steve 119, 128, 134, 190, 202,
    224, 225, 229, 254, 263, 280, 286,
    293, 301, 310, 312, 318, 321, 327,
    333, 340, 343, 346, 348, 354, 357,
    365, 369, 378, 384, 397, 400, 406,
    412, 413, 419, 423, 425, 429, 437,
    443, 449, 458, 459, 464, 468, 477,
    482, 497, 500, 519, 521, 527, 535,
    544, 550, 552, 557, 561, 566, 571,
    576, 579, 584, 586, 606, 611, 615,
    617, 622, 627, 630, 650, 658, 672,
    685, 688, 691
Clavering, Eric 317
Clay, Henry 472
Clayton, Gilbert 22
Clayton, Jan 612
Clemens, Zeke 144
Clement, Clay 73, 147, 172, 188
Clements, Stanley 330, 344, 367,
    570, 698, 714
Clensos, Steve 257, 318
Cleveland, George 72, 73, 74, 76,
    77, 78, 83, 93, 112, 114, 135, 141,
    143, 151, 154, 178, 182, 186, 195,
    200, 207, 210, 217, 220, 233, 239,
    243, 246, 426, 461
Clevely, Hugh 304
Clifford, Gordon 113
Clifford, Jack 14, 204, 213, 230
Clifton, Elmer 201, 252, 254, 506,
    513
Cline, Edward (Eddie) 302, 505,

540, 580, 607, 629
Cline, Rusty 253
Clinton, Walter 436
Clisby, Jack 723
Clive, Colin 84
Clive, Donald 628
Clive, Iris 460, 476, 506
Close, John 675
Clute, Chester 407, 494, 534, 570,
    580, 614, 632
Clyde, Andy 582, 602, 606, 613, 617,
    619, 627, 636, 642, 646, 652, 658
Clyde, June 37, 479
Coates, Phyllis 648, 652, 661, 664,
    669, 676, 685, 688, 699, 712, 715,
    721
Cobb, Edmund 285, 358, 365, 371,
    376, 383, 390, 396, 400, 413, 423,
    429, 431, 459, 521, 527, 568, 579,
    588, 666, 672
Cody, Bill 2, 5, 8, 10, 13, 23, 25, 26
Cody, Bill, Jr. 134
Cody, Iron Eyes 8, 26, 201, 335,
    538, 646, 691, 692
Cody, J.W. 8
Cody, Joe 335
Coffin, Tristram 192, 200, 210, 215,
    223, 237, 239, 241, 252, 256, 274,
    275, 283, 285, 299, 320, 322, 336,
    348, 351, 475, 477, 482, 499, 514,
    521, 536, 562, 582, 604, 609, 613,
    615, 668, 683, 687
Coghlan, Frank, Jr. 117, 181
Cohen, Bennett R. 145, 209, 425,
    519, 531, 532, 537, 550
Cohen, Sammy 503
Coke, Edward 562
Colby, Fred 508
Coldeway, Anthony 535
Coleman, Caryl 485, 501
Coleman, Charles 82, 578
Coleman, Nancy 518
Coleman, Tom 494
Coles, Mildred 544, 563
Collier, Lois 659
Collier, William, Jr. 18
Collier, William, Sr. 89
Collins, Gene 509
Collins, Hal 478, 487, 495, 512, 522,
    542, 551

Collins, Jimmy 432
Collins, Lewis D. 59, 96, 106, 108,
114, 295, 396, 644, 646, 647, 655,
658, 661, 664, 669, 674, 676, 682,
685, 686, 688, 690, 694, 699, 700,
701, 707, 709, 712, 715
Collins, Monty (Monte) 107, 217,
233, 522, 542, 546, 551, 570
Collins, Pat 598, 641
Collins, Wilkie 85
Collyer, June 91
The Colorado Hillbillies 142
Comandini, Adele 84, 88, 251
Comfort, Lance 590
Compillo, Anita 77
Compson, Betty 33, 43, 125, 129,
141, 146, 154, 236, 264, 265, 291,
361, 520
Compton, John 660
Compton, Joyce 87, 163, 355, 479,
480, 583
Condon, David see Gorcey, David
Conger, Logan 536
Conklin, Charles "Heine" 14, 25, 63
Conklin, Chester 524, 607, 725
Conlin, James 74, 634
Conn, Maurice 136, 138, 142, 144,
146, 148, 149
Connolly, Myles 466
Connor, Tim 614
The Connor Twins 98
Conrad, Paul 549
Conway, Bert 593
Conway, Lita 245, 280
Conway, Morgan 86
Conway, Robert 546, 605
Conway, Russ 675, 683, 692, 698
Coogan, Jackie 193, 528, 553
Coogan, Robert 528, 614, 620, 633,
649, 665, 705
Cook, Clyde 43, 44, 82, 315
Cook, Elisha, Jr. 440, 481, 515
Cook, Evelyn 338
Cook, Fred 399
Cook, Tommy 565
Cook, Windy 474
Cooke, Ray 20
Cookson, Peter 402, 420, 433, 442,
472, 485
Cooley, Spade 512, 670

Coons, C.C. 297
Cooper, Bobby 489
Cooper, Clancy 492
Cooper, Dee 451, 488, 504, 511, 517,
559, 575, 582, 600, 602, 611, 613
Cooper, Dennis J. 427, 457, 472
Cooper, George 24, 35, 119, 136
Cooper, Inez 366, 510
Cooper, Jackie 135, 161, 178, 389,
528, 553
Cooper, James Fenimore 267
Cooper, Jerry 370, 399
Cooper, Tex 119, 248, 263, 271, 293,
369, 376, 426
Copeland, Nick 75
Coppel, Alec 240
Corbett, Ben 274, 316, 397, 400,
406, 412, 419, 506, 672
Corbin, Virbinia Lee 11
Cord, Robert 45, 183
Corday, Mara 708
Corday, Marcelle 463
Cordova, Fred 531
Corey, Jeff 577
Corey, Jim 119, 134, 176, 271, 285,
354
Corio, Ann 362, 386, 415
Cornell, Ann 704
Cornell, Lillian 396
Corrado, Gino 6, 95, 113, 143, 360
Corrigan, Lloyd 654, 665
Corrigan, Ray "Crash" 238, 245,
252, 254, 258, 263, 271, 277, 280,
285, 293, 301, 310, 321, 327, 333,
357, 363, 369, 378
Cortez, Ricardo 294, 328
Corthell, Herbert 117, 173
Cosbey, Ronnie 150
Costello, Don 467, 547
Costello, Lou 422
Costello, Pat 282, 288, 322, 325,
342, 395
Costello, William (Willy) 141, 157,
265
Cottingham, Ann 710
Courtney, Alex 82
Courtney, Inez 116
Covington, Bruce 47
Cowan, Jerome 442, 452, 620, 633
Cowen, William 44

Name Index

Cox, Buddy 186
Cox, Victor 458, 521
Coxen, Ed 119, 136, 185
Coyle, John T. 385
Crabbe, Larry "Buster" 62
Craig, Catherine 235, 364
Craig, Nell 441
Cramer, Paul 622
Cramer, Richard (Dick) 7, 128, 140, 149, 209, 237, 245, 252, 292, 293, 301, 310, 321, 327, 333, 346, 349
Crane, Betty Mae 93
Crane, Beverly (Beverlee) 93, 621
Crane, Frank Hall 23, 97
Cravat, Noel 297
Craven, Frank 74, 434
Craven, James 263
Crawford, John 687
Crawford, Kathryn 59
Crehan, Joseph 170, 172, 414, 471, 479, 499, 536, 641
Creighton, Patsy 432
Criner, Laurence 268, 272, 306
Cripps, Kernan 271, 444
Crockett, Luther 612
Croft, Peter 199
Cromwell, Richard 297, 351
Crosby, Lou 479
Crosby, Wade 261, 548, 609
Cross, Albert 42
Cross, Jimmy 675, 722
Crowley, William X. 374, 379, 391, 404
Crutcher, Jack 705, 722
Cudlip, Bob 705, 722
Cummings, Dwight 16
Cunningham, Cecile 75
Curran, Thomas 13, 198
Currie, Louise 292, 356, 394, 395, 539
Currier, Mary 409
Curtis, Bob 588, 594, 595, 600, 615
Curtis, Clarrisa 221
Curtis, Don 248, 343
Curtis, Jo Ann 443
Curtis, Joan 318, 399
Curtis, John 346, 349
Curwood, James Oliver 90, 348, 603, 612, 639, 653, 673, 687, 711

Curzon, George 222
Cutler, Lester 396

Dae, Frank 485
Daggett, Rae 32
Dahl, Ted, and His Orchestra 93
Daily, Pete 659
Dalbert, Suzanne 603
D'Albrook, Sidney 116
Dale, Suzan 215
Dale, Virginia 515, 549
Daley, Jack 195, 239, 274, 324, 338, 358, 371
Dalio, Marcel 590
Dalkhart, Elynore 105
Daly, Mark 262
Dalya, Jacqueline 380, 574
Damino, Salvatore 155
Dane, Patricia 546
Daniel, Roger 251
Daniels, George 666
Daniels, Harold 278
D'Antonio, Carmen 520
D'Arcy, Roy 32, 121
Darcy, Sheila 191, 263
Dare, Helena 540
Dare, Irene 355
Darling, Gretchen 596
Darling, Jean 84
Darling, W. Scott 124, 133, 135, 174, 186, 187, 205, 536, 539, 549, 562, 568, 577, 592, 601, 612, 618, 640, 657, 668, 701
Darmour, Larry 123
Darmour, Roy 385
Darrell, Steve 485, 514, 517, 535, 545, 554, 556, 561, 582
Darro, Frankie 157, 166, 181, 191, 210, 227, 236, 241, 256, 272, 283, 478, 487, 495, 512, 522, 542, 548, 578, 593, 599
Darrow, John 78
D'Arvil, Yola 78
Darwell, Jane 65, 102, 651
Datig, Fred, Jr. 508
Davenport, Harry 137
Davido, Raquel 139
Davidson, Bert 696

Davidson, John 85, 403, 415
Davidson, Ronald 557, 559, 561,
566, 576, 595, 604, 608
Davidson, William 31, 33, 120, 440
Davies, Lynn 621
Davis, Charles (Chuck) 155, 185
Davis, Dix 246
Davis, Eddie 416, 606, 611, 613, 617,
622, 630
Davis, Gail 600, 622, 630, 673
Davis, Jim 268, 667
Davis, Jimmie 536, 596, 626
Davis, Joel 349
Davis, Johnny "Scat" 362
Davis, Lew 520
Davis, Martha 542
Davis, Murray 478, 487
Davis, Owen, Jr. 131
Davis, Robert 663
Davis, Rufe 678
Davis, Tim 119
Davis, William "Wee Willie" 490
Davis and Johnson 670
Davison, Betty 718
Daw, Evelyn 221
Dawe, Ray 675
Dawn, Sugar 221, 231, 276, 279,
290, 296, 312
Dawson, John (Jon) 376, 380, 385
Day, Donna 445
Day, Esther Lynd 71
Day, Johnny 186, 193
Day, Marceline 22, 32
Dean, Eddie 231, 253, 254, 333
Dean, Jean 609, 647, 696, 714
Dean, Jimmie 429, 451
Dean, Jo Ann 355
Dean, Priscilla 14, 30
Deane, Shirley 177
Dearing, Sayre 175, 485
DeBeck, Billy 302, 331
de Brulier, Nigel 195
de Bussman, Harriet 101
Decker, Diana 628
DeCordoba, Pedro 445, 531
de Cordova, Leander 668
de Corsia, Ted 684
Deems, Barrett 659
DeGrey, Sidney 71
Dehner, John 693

Dekker, Albert 484
de la Brosse, Marcel 486
De LaCruz, Joe 34
De La Motte, Marguerite 69
Delevanti, Cyril 435, 471
Deliso, James 295
Dell, Claudia 33, 127, 374, 414, 415
Dell, Gabriel 309, 325, 330, 344,
353, 379, 395, 404, 410, 428, 455,
494, 503, 520, 530, 538, 548, 560,
574, 578, 593, 599, 609, 614, 621,
632, 641, 648
Dell, Myrna 393, 649, 705
Delmont, Gene 593
DeLoue, Carl 9
Del Rio, Dora 488
del Rosario, Rosa 464
Del Ruth, Hampton 37
DeMain, Gordon (G.D. Wood) 1, 4,
5, 8, 9, 11, 12, 15, 27, 38, 49, 51,
53, 54, 55, 60, 68, 71, 72, 94, 335
DeMario, Donna 531
de Marney, Terence 240
Dembrosi, Willia 553
DeMond, Albert E. 52, 59, 61, 62,
73, 79, 91, 95, 420
Demourelle, Vic, Jr. 179
Denison, Leslie 499, 581
Dennison, Jo Carroll 493
DeNormand, George 338, 358, 360,
423, 619, 624, 627, 630, 642, 644,
650, 652, 655, 661, 666, 674, 676,
715
DePina, Albert 481
Depp, Harry 208, 337, 345, 414,
438, 441, 445
DeRita, Joe 495
Derr, E.B. 132, 139, 145, 147, 153,
160, 164, 168, 172, 177, 188
Deslys, Kay 273, 451
Desmond, Patrick 517
Desmond, William 8
Devereaux, Helen 444
DeVillard, Joe 416
Devine, Andy 717, 718, 719, 720
Devine, George 311
Devlin, Joe 396, 456, 505
Dew, Eddie 371
Dewhurst, Dorothy 222
DeWit, Jacqueline 414

Name Index

DeWitt, Jack 536, 543, 589, 712
Dial, Diana 710
Diamond, David 638
Diamond, Leo, and His Harmon-
  aires 434
Dickason, Deane H. 724
Dickens, Charles 44
Dickerson, Dudley 295, 353, 499
Dickey, Basil 571, 588, 600, 615
Dickinson, Dick 21, 23, 34, 50, 54,
  58, 70, 106, 458
Diehl, James 571
Dietz, Jack 302, 309, 313, 322, 325,
  330, 342, 344, 353, 356, 360, 367,
  374, 379, 394, 395, 404, 409, 410,
  411, 428, 430, 439, 448, 450, 454
Dillard, Art 103, 148, 267
Dillard, Bert 100, 103, 110
Dillon, John Webb 41
Dilson, Clyde 241
Dilson, John H. 115, 208, 249, 275
Dimsdale, Howard 345, 693
Dinehart, Alan 407, 418, 422
Dix, Billy 476, 488, 504, 506, 511, 513
Dixon, Denver (Victor Adamson)
  130, 155, 159, 190, 209, 231, 285,
  363, 470, 600, 608
Dixon, Peter 185
Dmytryk, Edward 251
Dobbs, George 295, 314
Dobson, James 710
Dodd, Jimmy 302, 331
Dolciame, Ray 556
Dominguez, Joe 23
Donlan, James 57
Donne, Carol 518
Donnell, Jeff 643
Donovan, Mike Pat 409, 486, 505,
  560, 593
Dooley, Billy 150
Doran, Ann 309, 710
Doran, Mary 96
Dore, Adrienne 31
Dore, Nadine 25, 37
Dorff, Marta 662
Dorr, Lester 208, 320, 420, 424,
  435, 471, 490
D'Orsay, Fifi 29
Dorsey, Jimmy, and His Orchestra
  569

Dostoevski, Fyodor 472
Doucette, John 556, 667, 673, 702,
  718
Douglas, Alan 499
Douglas, Donald 65, 69, 466
Douglas, Earl 165, 185, 201, 204,
  208, 213, 215, 284, 290
Douglas, Thomas 33, 43
Douglas, Wallace 262
Douglas, Warren 492, 525, 539, 583,
  601, 626, 640, 680, 687
Downs, Cathy 678
Downs, Johnny 269, 300, 382, 391,
  434
Doyle, Maxine 107
Drake, Claudia 382, 424, 465, 467,
  482
Drake, Dona 399
Drake, Oliver 245, 274, 277, 299,
  333, 447, 451, 454, 460, 470, 476,
  488, 506, 509, 513, 581, 594, 595,
  600, 603, 608, 615
Drake, Pauline 205
Dreifuss, Arthur 362, 370, 381, 382,
  386, 478, 487, 495, 512
Dresden, Curley 146, 162, 388
Dresser, Louise 88
Dressler, Marie 725
Drew, Lowell 162
Drexel, Nancy 23
Dryhurst, Edward 637
Dubov, Paul 641
DuBrey, Claire 84, 418, 553
Dudgeon, Elspeth 85
Duff, Warren B. 163
Duffy, Albert 265
Duffy, Jack 100
Duffy, Jesse 189
Dugan, Michael 617
Dugan, Tom 59, 62, 69, 93, 471,
  505, 671
Dumbrille, Douglas (Douglass) 449,
  494, 605
Dumont, Margaret 347
Dunbar, David 82
Duncan, Arletta 39, 48
Duncan, Bob 436, 449, 451, 470,
  506, 644
Duncan, Bud 302, 331
Duncan, John (Johnny) 360, 380,

382, 395, 450, 455, 593
Duncan, Julie 277, 327, 354, 378
Duncan, Kenne 179, 190, 202, 212,
    213, 219, 224, 225, 230, 245, 278,
    279, 290, 314, 340, 346, 359, 375,
    470, 579, 582, 584, 586, 595, 597,
    604, 608, 615, 617, 629, 676
Duncan, Kenne, Jr. 526
Duncan, Pamela 679, 682
Dunham, Phil 54, 55, 202, 252
Dunlap, Scott R. 131, 150, 169, 187,
    246, 265, 274, 284, 298, 299, 305,
    316, 324, 332, 338, 348, 358, 365,
    371, 376, 383, 390, 397, 398, 418,
    449, 461, 468, 475, 477, 482, 483,
    500, 502, 510, 511
Dunn, Eddie 490, 583
Dunn, Emma 112, 408
Dunn, James 218, 345, 416
Dunn, Ralph 147, 493, 530, 560,
    568, 583
Dunn, Tay 430
Dunne, Carole 481, 496
Dunne, Jody 599
Dunne, Judy 599
Dupree, Roland 291, 593, 605
Duran, Edna 169
Durand, David 178, 181, 211, 353,
    379, 395, 404
Durfee, Minta 253
Durkin, Grace 116
Durkin, James 60
Durlam, Arthur 321
Durlam, George Arthur 3, 5, 6, 7,
    8, 9
D'Usseau, Leon 29
Duval, Juan 215, 488
Dwire, Earl 2, 23, 27, 32, 54, 56,
    63, 66, 68, 70, 76, 77, 81, 83, 90,
    94, 97, 113, 119, 126, 130, 134, 146
Dwyer, Leslie 590
Dwyer, Marlo 251, 314
Dyer, William 66

Eagles, James (Jimmy) 31, 140
Earle, Edward 11, 150, 164, 402, 414,
    445, 480, 683
Earle, Madelyn 101

Early, Pearl 447
East, Ed 607
Easton, Bob 713
Eaton, Charles 199
Eaton, Evelyn (Evelynne) 389, 417,
    463, 593
Eaton, Marjorie 665, 696
Eavers, Ann 336
Eben, Al 656, 696
Eburne, Maude 168, 177
Echevirria, Gerald 510
Eddy, Helen Jerome 88, 112
Edwards, Allan 101
Edwards, Bill 603
Edwards, Bruce 492, 499, 676, 682,
    709
Edwards, Fred 567
Edwards, Henry 319, 522
Edwards, Jack 211
Edwards, Jimmy 628
Edwards, Sam 211, 328
Edwards, Sarah 389
Edwards, Thornton 270, 468, 531,
    539, 606, 613
Edwards, Weston 97
Eggenton, Joseph 313
Eggleston, Edward 108, 118
Egner, Red 602
Eilers, Sally 422
Einstein, Harry see Parkyakarkus
Elder, Ray 419, 443
Eldredge, George 248, 322, 342,
    345, 401, 405, 409, 421, 429, 438,
    465, 480, 486, 492, 551, 560, 562,
    594, 654, 675
Eldredge, John 465, 474, 480, 548,
    560, 594, 722
Elliot, George F. 129
Elliot, Kathleen 126, 136
Elliott, Bill (Wild Bill Elliott) 135,
    685, 694, 701, 712
Elliott, Dick 241, 287, 303, 427, 433,
    440, 495, 499, 509, 603, 621, 632,
    638
Elliott, Edythe 495, 509, 512
Elliott, Gordon see Elliott, Bill
Elliott, John 2, 4, 5, 8, 9, 12, 15, 21,
    26, 32, 34, 35, 38, 48, 114, 258,
    263, 280, 293, 310, 349, 392, 470,
    530, 548, 556

Name Index

Elliott, Lillian 157, 166, 181, 191, 198, 210, 227, 236, 298
Elliott, Robert 20, 40, 49, 184
Elliott, Wild Bill *see* Elliott, Bill
Ellis, Frank 103, 106, 134, 171, 190, 202, 219, 254, 258, 263, 271, 310, 327, 333, 337, 340, 346, 349, 369, 375, 388, 393, 401, 405, 437, 586, 679, 715
Ellis, Lloyd 536
Ellis, Paul 101
Ellis, Robert 32, 52, 88
Ellison, James (Jimmy) 398, 407, 676, 679, 686, 690, 697, 707
Ellison, Stanley 519, 532
Elston, Allan Vaughan 120
Emerson, Baron 269
Emerson, Edward 438
Emery, John 678
Emmett, Fern 74, 100, 103, 207, 336, 407
Emmett, Jay 42
Emmett, Robert *see* Tansey, Robert Emmett
Emory, Richard 682, 721
Endfield, Cyril 481, 498, 503, 520, 587, 605
England, Sue 577, 596, 645
Englander, Margaret 381
Erdman, Richard 693
Ernst, Paul 353
Errol, Leon 481, 498, 534, 546, 587, 605, 620, 633
Erskine, Laurie York 197, 201, 204, 208, 213, 230
Erwin, Billy 86
Espinoza, Robert 625
Evans, Charles 478
Evans, Clifford 266
Evans, Douglas 527, 541, 552, 561, 565, 591, 632, 675
Evans, Herbert 161, 505, 540
Evans, Jack 226
Evans, Muriel 190, 202
Evanson, Edith 435, 485, 681
Everton, Paul 295

Fain, Matty 116, 123, 129, 135, 141, 153, 157, 265, 463, 556
Fairbanks, Lucile 315
Faire, Virginia Brown 70
Fairlie, Gerald 214
Falk, Lauritz 662
Falk, Vibeke 662
Falkenberg, Jinx 167
Fallows, Ruth 137
Farley, James 211, 445
Farley, Lesley 540
Farnum, Franklyn (Franklin) 8, 86, 134, 296
Farnum, William 14
Farr, Derek 637
Farrar, James 223
Farrell, Charles 278
Farrell, M.J. 319
Farrell, Tommy 652, 655, 658, 691, 721
Farrell, Vessie 109
Fauntelle, Dian 549
Faust, Tom 444, 520
Fawcett, William 685, 688, 701, 709
Fay, Dorothy 167, 171, 173, 234
Fay, Frank 374
Fay, Jimmy 98
Faye, Francine 580
Faye, Gladys 322
Faylen, Frank 275, 283, 287, 355, 377, 380
Fazan, W. 262
Featherstone (Fetherstone), Eddie 29, 47, 86, 123
Feld, Fritz 498, 578, 659
Feldary, Eric 525, 564
Felker, Barbara 335
Felker, Tex 245
Fellowes, Rockcliffe 46
Fellows, Edith 84, 112, 251, 341
Fennelly, Vincent M. 636, 642, 646, 650, 652, 655, 658, 661, 664, 666, 669, 672, 674, 676, 677, 679, 682, 685, 686, 688, 690, 691, 694, 697, 699, 701, 706, 707, 709, 712, 715, 721
Fenner, Walter 456
Fensler, Norman 50
Fenton, Frank 587, 634, 638

351

Fenwick, Jean 452, 580
Ferguson, Al 106, 280, 340, 384, 388, 401, 405
Ferguson, Frank 695, 706
Fetherstone, Eddie *see* Featherstone, Eddie
Feusier, Norman 41
Fieberling, Hal 570, 649
Field, Alexander 216
Field, Margaret 638, 673
Field, Mary 186, 275, 485, 536, 585, 631
Fields, George 542, 551
Fields, Jerry 436
Fields, Leonard 60, 75, 87, 294
Fields, Stanley 65
Fierro, Paul 680
Figarola, Raul 67
Filauri, Antonio 298, 537
Fillmore, Clyde 489
Filmer, Joy 111
Filmer, June 111
Fimberg, Hal 422
Fine, Larry 474
Finkle, Robert 271, 277
Finley, Evelyn 237, 279, 346, 363, 369, 425, 572, 575
Finn, Sammy 705
Finn, Tate 107
Finney, Edward 155, 159, 167, 171, 173, 179, 185, 189, 190, 202, 215, 221, 223, 231, 234, 237, 248, 253, 259, 267, 270, 281, 297, 335
Fio Rito, Ted, and His Orchestra 62, 347, 355, 370
Fisher, Barbara 710
Fisher, Freddie "Schnickelfritz," and His Orchestra 386
Fisher, George 587
Fisher, Ham 481, 498, 534, 546, 570, 587, 605, 620, 633, 649, 678
Fisher, Herbert 289
Fisher, Steve 170, 556
Fiske, Robert 147, 164, 211, 313, 383
Fitzroy, Roy 18
Fix, Paul 52, 57, 60, 106, 172, 265, 377
Flaherty, Pat 133, 168, 217
Flato, Richard 525
Flavin, James 187, 191, 456, 493, 534, 596, 668, 705
Flint, Helen 75
Flint, Sam 60, 64, 298, 365, 376, 403, 478, 646, 661, 671, 687, 708, 711
The Florentine Gardens Revue 347
Flores, Iris 475, 483
Flores, Tony 253
Flowers, Bess 665
Fodor, Ladislaus 334
Foley, Red, and His Saddle Pals 267
Fong, Benson 392, 403, 444, 456, 469, 481
Fontaine, John 174
Foo, Lee Tong 174, 187, 539, 568
Foote, Bradbury 398
Boote, Richard (Dick) 618, 623, 634
Forbes, Mary 82, 315
Forbes, Ralph 46, 57, 82, 121, 387
Ford, Dorothy 675, 713
Ford, Francis 428, 533
Ford, Judith 144
Ford, Wallace 69, 80, 99, 104, 265, 273, 356, 695
Forde, Walter 199, 206, 214
Foreman, Carl 288, 347
Foreman, Jean 347
Forester, C.S. 214
Forester, Cay 375, 429, 492, 518, 599
Forman, Carol 549, 581
Forrest, Hal 175, 186, 193, 196
Forrest, William 433, 522, 603, 609, 683, 698
Forte, Joe 528
Foster, Alan 451, 455, 462
Foster, Bennett 449
Foster, Eddie 195, 265, 282, 641
Foster, Helen 13, 36, 38
Foster, John 202
Foster, Norman 108
Foster, Preston 60, 61
Foulger, Byron 131, 164, 188, 298, 303, 424, 433, 457, 520, 539, 689, 696
Fowler, Art "Dustbowl" 285, 400, 406, 413, 419
Fowler, J.C. 20
Fowley, Douglas 309, 320, 402, 424, 468, 486, 495, 515, 532, 549, 570, 605, 625

Name Index

Fox, Bebe 381
Fox, Wallace 3, 156, 162, 282, 322,
    325, 330, 342, 344, 353, 358, 376,
    395, 410, 429, 439, 450, 611, 619,
    622, 624, 627, 630, 636, 642, 650,
    666, 672
Foy, Charles 195
Foy, Mary 73
Foze, Earle 20
Fraley, Pat 722
Frambes, William 465, 505
Francis, Alec B. 44
Francis, Eugene 232, 242, 257, 260
Francis, Kay 452, 463, 501
Francis, Noel 24, 79
Francis, Olin 146, 189, 248, 253
Francis, Wilma 289, 295
Franey, Billy 83
Frank, W.R. 424
Franklin, Irene 117
Franklin, Louise 594
Franklin, Paul B. 59
Franks, Anne 387
Franks, Jerry 461
Franz, Arthur 683
Fraser, Harry 5, 8, 10, 13, 16, 21,
    23, 25, 26, 27, 32, 35, 41, 45, 48,
    49, 50, 54, 55, 56, 58, 81, 97, 332,
    658
Frawley, William 570
Frazee, Jane 583, 659
Frazer, Alex 577
Frazer, Robert 22, 78, 90, 170, 189,
    201, 265, 284, 313, 348, 365, 397,
    400
Frederick, Pauline 40
Freeto, Ralph 536
French, Charles K. 128
French, Lloyd 302
French, Ted 447, 476, 532, 608
Frick and Frack 355, 398
Friedkin, Joel 228
Friend, Joel 396
Fries, Otto 107
Frommer, Ben 684
Frost, Terry 438, 447, 459, 462, 464,
    468, 470, 473, 482, 483, 488, 500,
    504, 512, 595, 597, 611, 615, 619,
    652, 686, 688, 690, 691, 694, 699,
    701, 707, 709, 712, 719

Frye, Dwight 37, 230
Frye, Kathy 552
Fuller, Clem 584, 602
Fuller, Dale 73
Fulton, Maude 64
Fung, Willie 40, 280
Furness, Betty 71, 112
Fyffe, Will 222, 247

Gaffney, Marjorie 222
Gahan, Oscar 119, 128, 130, 148
Gaines, Richard 683
Galbert, Van 55
Galbraith, Joe 600
Gale, Joan 104
Galindo, Nacho 475, 625, 680
Gallagher, Skeets 291
Gallaudet, John 462, 491, 501, 536,
    549, 558
Gallian, Gerri 551
Galliard, Slim, Trio 508
Galloway, Morgan 163
Gan, Chester 99, 174, 202, 221
Garber, Jan, and His Orchestra 396
Garcia, Joe 138, 200, 378
Gardner, Ava 367
Gardner, Jack 278, 391
Gargan, Edward 402, 479, 599, 641
Gargan, Jack 609
Garner, Peggy Ann 589
Garon, Pauline 46, 91
Garralaga, Martin 143, 155, 215,
    436, 445, 453, 475, 483, 489, 502,
    510, 581, 605, 703
Garrett, Gary 514, 517, 521, 523,
    524, 526, 527, 535, 544
Garrett, Roy 557
Garrick, Gene 547
Garson, Anthony 716
Gasnier, Louis 213, 289
Gates, Harvey Harris 18, 131, 170,
    291, 309, 313, 322, 325, 330, 334,
    360, 439, 450, 452, 463, 485, 492
Gay, Betsy 175
Gaze, Gwen 252, 271, 293, 349
Geary, Bud 477
Gee, Frederick 284
Gee, Parker 462

Gehrung, Jean 67
Geise, Sugar 347, 372
Geldert, Clarence 42
George, Richard 317
Geraghty, Carmelita 11
Gerald, Helen 475, 507
Gerard, Barney 505, 540, 580, 607, 629, 668
Gerard, Hal 570, 639, 665
Gerard, Harold 281
Gerard, Paul 461
Gering, Walter 351
Gest, Inna see Guest, Ina
Gibbons, Eliot 526, 579, 619
Gibson, Curley 526
Gibson, Harry "The Hipster" 478
Gibson, Hoot 359, 368, 375, 384, 388, 393, 401, 405, 412, 417, 421
Gibson, Jack 535
Gibson, Judith 396, 409
Gibson, Julie 538
Gibson, Tom 212, 219, 224
Gibson, Walter B. see Grant, Maxwell
Gierman, Fred 278
Gilbert, Billy 309, 374, 411, 430, 448
Gilbert, Helen 334, 411
Gilbert, Jody 621
Gilbert, Robert L. 506, 513
Gilbreath, John 438
Gilgore, Jay 664
Gill, Gwenllian 82
Gilliat, Sidney 199
Gillie, Jean 496
Gillingwater, Claude 57, 59, 74
Gillis, Ann 344, 422, 508
Gilman, Jack 161, 410
Girard, Joseph 170, 201
Giraud, Octavio 169
Glasman, Kubec 137
Glass, Everett 683
Glassmire, Gus 345
Gleason, James 649, 678
Gleason, Lucile 89, 323
Gleason, Pat 150, 272, 294, 328, 336, 402, 438, 451, 455, 465, 653, 665, 675
Gleason, Russell 177
Glenn, Roy 723
Glennon, Bert 7

Glover, Edmund 602
Godfrey, Renee 553
Godfrey, Samuel 73
Goetz, Charles E. 203
Goldberg, Benny 593
Golden, Mildred 4
Goldin, Pat 505, 522, 528, 537, 540, 580, 614, 629
Goldsmith, I. 240
Goldsmith, Ken 118, 137
Goldstone, Phil 230
Gollard, Jerome T. 560
Gombell, Minna 101, 407, 461
Gomez, Augie 274, 354, 363
Gomez, Jerry 155
Gonatos, John 564
Good, John 525
Goodale, Spud 447
Goodman, Harold 280
Goodman, Terry 530
Goodrich, John 109, 113
Goodsell, Major 62
Goodwin, Harold 485
Goodwin, John 57
Goodwins, Leslie 355, 704
Gorcey, Bernard 313, 342, 360, 404, 410, 428, 439, 450, 465, 486, 490, 494, 503, 520, 530, 538, 560, 578, 593, 599, 609, 614, 621, 632, 641, 648, 656, 665, 675, 684, 696, 705, 713, 722
Gorcey, David (David Condon) 232, 242, 257, 260, 282, 288, 309, 325, 330, 486, 490, 494, 503, 520, 530, 538, 548, 560, 574, 578, 593, 599, 609, 614, 621, 632, 641, 648, 656, 665, 675, 684, 696, 705, 713, 722
Gorcey, Kay Marvis 353, 367, 379
Gorcey, Leo 232, 242, 257, 260, 282, 288, 309, 325, 330, 344, 353, 360, 367, 379, 395, 404, 410, 428, 439, 450, 455, 465, 486, 490, 494, 503, 520, 530, 538, 548, 560, 574, 578, 593, 599, 609, 614, 621, 632, 641, 648, 656, 665, 675, 684, 696, 705, 713, 722
Gordon, Dick 414
Gordon, Don 675
Gordon, Gavin 47, 101, 273, 294
Gordon, Hall 262

Name Index

Gordon, Huntley 32, 161, 187, 249
Gordon, Mary 228, 295, 297, 362, 372, 385, 395, 404, 452, 486, 491, 548, 606, 622
Gordon, Richard 445
Gordon, Roy 456, 565, 609
Gordon, Vera 345
Gorer, Mildred 139
Gorman, Bud 379, 395, 404, 428, 439, 450, 455, 490, 530, 548, 574, 578, 593, 599, 621, 632, 648, 656, 665, 675
Gorst, Derek 222
Gotfurt, Frederick 590
Gottschalk, Ferdinand 87, 96
Gould, Dave 347
Gould, Gretta 84
Gould, Sandra 722
Gould, William 118, 158, 161, 502, 518
Gowland, Gibson 10
Goya, Mona 308
Grace, Meyer 455, 503, 530, 548, 583, 593, 599, 633, 722
Graff, Wilton 525
Graham, Bobby 704
Graham, Frank 351
Graham, Lee 675
Graham, Morland 317
Graham, Sheilah 540
Granger, Dorothy 65, 407, 435, 491, 565
Granlund, Nils T. 347
Grandstedt, Greta 133, 361
Grant, Kirby 365, 400, 603, 610, 612, 639, 653, 659, 673, 687, 711
Grant, Lawrence 345
Grant, Maxwell (Walter B. Gibson) 471, 479, 493
Grant, Wylie 183
Granville, Bonita 484, 516
Granville, Marcelle 510
Grapewin, Charles 79
Graves, Carolyn 710
Graves, Ralph 605
Gray, Arnold 46, 104
Gray, Beatrice 417, 421, 443
Gray, Billy 654
Gray, Gary 585, 597, 631, 651, 671, 695

Gray, Geneva 541, 546, 548
Gray, Geraldine 334
Gray, Joe 503, 593
Gray, Lorna see Booth, Adrian
Gray, Louis 544, 550, 552, 554, 557, 561, 567, 571, 573, 576, 584, 588, 595, 600, 608, 615
Gray, Roger 153
Greb, Joe 593
Green, Billy 461
Green, Harry 69
Greene, Angela 537
Greene, Harrison 75, 127
Greene, Joseph J. 386
Greene, Mort 725
Greenway, Tom 643
Greig, Robert 395
Greville, Arthur 120, 137
Greville, Edmond T. 637
Grey, Barbara 705, 722
Grey, Jack 302
Grey, Virginia 702
Gribbon, Eddie 379, 503, 534, 546, 570, 574, 587, 593, 605, 620, 633, 641, 649, 678
Griffies, Ethel 84
Griffin, Billy 629
Griffin, Robert 649
Griffith, Billy 283
Griffith, Gordon 725
Griffith, William M. 617
Grippo, Jan 465, 486, 490, 494, 503, 520, 530, 538, 548, 560, 574, 578, 593, 599, 609, 614, 621, 632, 641, 648, 656, 665, 675
Grisson, Jimmy 551
Gross, Edward 302, 331
Gross, Stephen 71
Gross, Walter 659
Groves, Florence 180
The Guadalajara Trio 453, 488
Guard, Kit 9, 18, 24, 31, 39, 123, 138, 144, 148, 614
Guest, Ina 231, 232, 352, 371
Guest, Val 628
Guhl, George 273
Guilfoyle, Paul 508, 645
Gulliver, Dorothy 434
Gunn, Gilbert 250
Gurie, Sigrid 424

Name Index

Guthrie, Danny 432
Guttman, Henry 366
Gwynne, Anne 472, 653
Gynt, Greta 216

Haade, William 133, 565, 649
Haas, Gene 253
Hack, Herman 81, 94, 103, 113, 144, 149, 226, 271, 588, 624, 685
Hackathorne, George 40
Hackel, A.W. 273, 295, 314, 326, 337, 345, 420
Hackett, Karl 149, 155, 159, 171, 204, 213, 238, 248, 267, 307, 337, 384, 388, 393, 405
Hadden, Pauline 223
Hadley, Reed 145, 638
Hafka, Hans 225
Haggerty, Don 700
Hagney, Frank 119, 593
Haines, Connie 422
Haines, Donald 211, 232, 242, 257, 260, 282, 288
Haines, Rob 565
Hale, Alan, Jr. 508, 522, 569, 654, 716, 720
Hale, Bill 541, 555, 576, 579, 604
Hale, Bobby 580
Hale, Creighton 61
Hale, Jonathan 442, 452, 463, 466, 501, 543, 565, 641, 675, 717
Hale, Sonnie 199
Haley, Earl 203
Haliatt, May 216
Hall, Alfred 292
Hall, Charles 275, 287, 303, 341, 356
Hall, Doncho 302
Hall, Ellen 376, 390, 394, 406, 615
Hall, Henry 7, 31, 55, 66, 106, 233, 243, 353, 356, 394, 405, 435, 524, 552
Hall, Huntz 282, 288, 291, 309, 325, 330, 344, 353, 360, 367, 379, 395, 404, 410, 428, 439, 450, 455, 465, 486, 490, 503, 520, 530, 538, 548, 560, 574, 578, 593, 599, 609, 614, 621, 632, 641, 648, 656, 665, 675,

684, 696, 705, 713, 722
Hall, Lois 608, 646, 649, 655, 666, 690, 691
Hall, Norman S. 95, 121, 181
Hall, Ruth 49
Hall, Sherry 471
The Hall Johnson Choir 139
Haller, Ray 34
Halliday, John 69
Halligan, William 339
Halls, Ethyl 565
Halperin, Edward 204, 208, 230
Halton, Charles 424, 649
Hamberger, Art 292
Hambling, Arthur 199, 206, 266
Hamilton, Bert 602
Hamilton, Bret 647
Hamilton, Hale 47
Hamilton, John 158, 205, 294, 295, 337, 364, 420, 430, 432, 511, 518, 530
Hamilton, Mahlon 28
Hamilton, Neil 111, 112, 427
Hammar, Fay 101
Hammond, Bill 454, 602
Hammond, Victor 402, 412, 417, 421, 433, 441, 453, 486, 490
Handl, Irene 590
Hanley, Jimmy 214
Hanlon, Bert 593
Hanlon, Tom 696
Hannon, Chuck 119, 126, 130, 155, 179, 190, 202, 215, 223, 231, 237, 248, 263, 267, 271, 318, 359, 419, 437, 519, 526
Hanray, Laurence 247
Hansen, Juanita 61
Hansen, Speed 154
Harbin, Suzette 723
Harding, Lyn 247
Harker, Charmienne 539
Harlan (Harland), Kenneth 120, 137, 235, 257, 313, 315, 322, 337, 339, 350, 352, 359, 368, 370, 384
Harlan, Otis 87, 108
Harland, Kenneth see Harlan, Kenneth
Harmon, John 278, 492, 499, 515, 536, 621, 649
Harmon, Marie 447, 479, 580
Harmon, Tom 508, 710

356

Harolde, Ralf 98, 105, 177, 294, 625
Harper, Patricia 369
Harr, Silver 378
Harrigan, William 129
Harris, Ray S. 331
Harris, Roy *see* Hill, Ripley
Harrison, Jack 586
Harrison, James 611
Harrison, June 505, 521, 540, 580, 629
Harrison, Kathleen 240, 590
Harrison, Lottie 374, 379
Harrison, Rex 311
Harrison, Stephen S. 618, 623, 660
Hart, Eddie 228
Hart, Gordon 147
Hart, John 512, 605, 655, 674, 685, 686, 688, 690, 701
Hart, Louis 437, 443
Hart, Margie 329
Harte, Bret 131
Hartman, Edmund 467
Hartwell, Willia 590
Harvey, Don 609, 635, 668, 678, 687
Harvey, Harry 140, 152, 154, 173, 196, 221, 253, 320, 398, 598
Harvey, Paul 486, 574, 675
Harvey, Slim 333
Harwin, Dixon R. 278, 292
Haskell, Al 271, 608
Hatch, Budd 659
Hatton, Raymond 274, 284, 299, 305, 316, 324, 332, 338, 348, 358, 365, 371, 376, 383, 390, 397, 400, 406, 413, 419, 423, 425, 431, 437, 443, 449, 458, 459, 461, 464, 468, 473, 477, 482, 497, 500, 504, 511, 514, 517, 521, 523, 526, 527, 535, 541, 545, 552, 555, 559, 563, 566, 572, 575, 579, 640, 719
Havens, George 258
Havelock Allan, Anthony 308, 311
Havier, J. Alex 366, 415
Hawks, Frank 30
Hawthorne, Beverly 465
Hayden, Harry 137, 377, 549, 587, 714
Hayden, Sarah 695, 706
Hayes, Bernadene 139, 198, 278, 485
Hayes, Edgar 501

Hayes, George 222, 262
Hayes, George "Gabby" 30, 32, 34, 39, 40, 45, 46, 48, 49, 50, 51, 52, 53, 54, 56, 58, 59, 60, 63, 68, 70, 71, 72, 73, 74, 76, 77, 78, 81, 83, 94, 97, 100, 103, 108, 111
Hayes, Grace 291
Hayes (Heyes), Herbert 382, 395, 402
Hayes, Peter Lind 291
Hayes, Sam 593, 605, 607
Hayward, Lydia 247
Hazard, Jayne 430, 462
Head, Betty Lou 476
Healey, Myron 579, 588, 591, 595, 600, 604, 606, 611, 613, 615, 619, 622, 624, 644, 647, 650, 655, 672, 681, 685, 692, 695, 712
Healey, Steve 536
Healy, Mary 291
Hearn, Edward 219
Hearne, Harrison 603
Hecht, Ted 510, 612, 618, 625, 634, 643
Heckelmann, Charles N. 459
Heermance, Richard 710
Heifetz, L.E. 123
Henderson, Dell 107, 424
Henderson, Ray 226
Hendricks, Jack 451, 517, 519, 526, 535
Henley, Althea 46
Henley, Jack 288, 291, 302, 309
Henry, Bill (William) 315, 328, 361, 362, 381, 387
Henry, Carol 365, 541, 561, 563, 571, 572, 575, 576, 579, 584, 588, 591, 595, 602, 617, 624, 627, 636, 644, 650, 685, 691, 715
Henry, Charlotte 108, 125, 163, 282, 323
Henry, Gloria 680
Henry, Hank 478
Henry, Louise 199
Henry, O. 436, 445, 453, 475, 483, 502, 510, 531, 537
Henry, Robert "Buzzy" 411, 618
Herbert, Bryan 180, 216
Herbert, Holmes 174, 182
Herbert, Slim 536
Herbert, Tom 126, 278, 410, 420

Name Index

Herbuveaux, James 99
Herman, Al 155, 159, 167, 171, 173, 179, 185, 190, 215, 221, 231, 234, 237, 248, 253, 267, 281
Hern, Pepe 609
Hernandez, Joe 281, 607
Herrera, Joe 605
Herrick, Robert 109
Herrick, Virginia 642, 672
Hervey, Irene 111
Hewitt, Virginia 656
Heyburn, Weldon 43, 116, 124, 137, 184, 269, 310, 375, 384, 388, 403
Heyes, Herbert *see* Hayes, Herbert
Heywood, Eddie, and His Orchestra 478
Hiatt, Ruth 292
Hickman, Darryl 261
Hickman, George 505
Hickman, Howard 72, 147, 168
Hicks, Don 671
Hicks, Russell 111, 474, 480, 536, 562, 580, 618, 656, 684
Higgins, Howard 87
Higgins, Kenneth 367
Hignett, H.R. 262
Hill, Albert, Jr. 181
Hill, Doris 5, 50, 51, 56, 58
Hill, Peter Murray 266
Hill, Riley (Roy Harris) 327, 333, 425, 431, 437, 449, 458, 464, 473, 477, 497, 526, 527, 555, 557, 571, 580, 586, 595, 602, 604, 611, 615, 619, 627, 629, 630, 642, 644, 664, 669, 705, 706, 720
Hill, Robert (Bob) 140, 152, 165, 169, 200, 211, 260, 276, 367, 410, 716
Hilliard, Ernest 95
Hillie, Verna 73, 83, 90
Hillyer, Lambert 139, 160, 168, 184, 188, 365, 371, 383, 385, 397, 400, 406, 413, 419, 425, 443, 449, 453, 458, 459, 464, 477, 482, 497, 500, 504, 511, 514, 517, 521, 523, 527, 535, 541, 544, 545, 550, 552, 554, 555, 557, 566, 572, 573, 584, 588, 591, 606, 613, 617
Hinds, Samuel S. 547
Hirliman, George A. 289
Hirsch, Ray 251

Hoag, Robert 253
Hobbes, Haliwell 379
Hobbs, Peter E. 304
Hobson, Valerie 308, 311
Hodges, Joy 236
Hodges, Larry 289
Hodges, Ralph 381
Hodgins, Earle 113, 153, 238, 442, 465, 607
Hoefley, Jackie 55
Hoerl, Arthur 20, 22, 31, 33, 37, 289, 327, 333, 340, 354, 362, 378, 380, 479
Hoerner, Marjorie 508
Hoffman, David 578
Hoffman, Gertrude 243, 327
Hoffman, Joseph 314, 326, 345
Hoffman, M.H. 31, 43
Hoffman, Max, Jr. 303, 313
Hoffman, Otto 18
Hoffman, Renaus 157
Hogan, Brenda 637
Hogan, Michael 214, 222
Holcombe, Herbert 149
Holden, Gloria 547
Holden, Harry 82
Holden, Judd 704
Holland, Edna M. 461, 480, 585
Holland, John 241, 249, 265, 281
Holles, Anthony 247
Holliday, Nan 419
Holloway, Stanley 637
Holloway, Sterling 93, 287
Hollywood, Jimmy 374
Holman, Harry 44, 60, 98, 115, 294, 391
Holmes, Brown 57
Holmes, George 480, 563
Holmes, J. Merrill 239, 332
Holmes, Jack 263, 271, 280, 301, 327
Holmes, Mary J. 163
Holmes, Maynard 287, 303, 578, 598, 603
Holmes, Taylor 587, 696
Holt, Andrew 489
Holt, David 82, 508
Holt, Jennifer 401, 431, 437, 458, 470, 497, 557
Holton, Red 476
Holtz, Tenen 80

Name Index

Homans, Robert 116, 272, 352, 432, 444, 455
Hoo, Hayward Soo 446
Hoopes, Ralph 229
Hoose, Fred 211, 270, 276, 279, 286, 290, 296, 312, 318, 368
Hoover, Hyram 86
Hope, Anna 342
Hope, Jim 374
Hopkins, Elizabeth 261
Hopkins, Joan 590
Hopton, Russell 89, 115, 195
Horne, Dave 250
Horne, Jimmy, Jr. 563
Horvath, Charles 693
Hoshelle, Marjorie 462, 466, 469, 479
House, Billy 534, 693
Housman, Arthur 138, 170
Houston, George 236
Houston, Norman 67, 78, 105, 107, 114
Houston, Virginia 683
Howard, Anne 49, 51, 53, 84
Howard, Boothe 57, 72
Howard, Jack 618
Howard, Jerry "Curly" 474
Howard, John 334
Howard, Moe 474
Howard, Shemp 411, 430, 448
Howard, William K. 315
Howatt, Nina 99
Howell, Cliff 166
Howell, Kenneth 257
Howell, Virginia 172
Howes, Reed 90, 110, 113, 136, 176, 190, 202, 212, 277, 285, 296, 348, 359, 477, 617, 627, 642
Howlin, Olin 598, 631
Hoyt, Arthur 104
Hoyt, Harry O. 19, 42, 121
Hubbard, Jon 546
Hudd, Walter 255
Hudson, Rochelle 328
Hudson, William 598, 675
Hughes, Carol 287, 469, 481
Hughes, Harlie 566
Hughes, Llewellyn 154
Hughes, Lloyd 1, 111, 147
Hughes, Mary Beth 370, 570

Hughes, Whitey 684
Hugo, Mauritz 157, 341, 351, 373, 376, 412, 417, 711
Hull, Henry 120, 127, 172, 184, 188, 201, 204, 207, 228, 282
Humbert, George 92, 232
Humphrey, William J. 37
Hunt, Eleanor 76, 289
Hunt, Marsha 172
Hunt, Martita 266
Hunter, Kim 427
Hunter, Nita 543
Hunter, Ross 508
Hunter, William (Bill) 132, 364
Huntington, Laurence (Lawrence) 240, 317
Hurst, Brandon 73, 261, 298
Hurst, Paul 31, 52, 102, 121
Hurst, Vida 111
Hutchinson, Harry 250
Hyer, Martha 700, 711
Hyers, Frank 546
Hyland, Dick Irving 528
Hyland, Frances 31, 33, 69, 80
Hymer, Warren 133, 309, 320, 323, 326, 329, 336, 337, 361, 364, 498
Hytten, Olaf 72, 80, 82, 84, 85, 402, 416, 418, 562, 577

Imhof, Marcelle 540, 607, 668
Ince, John 31, 100, 104, 350, 391, 458
Ince, Ralph 14, 18
Indrisano, John 465, 486, 503, 546, 578, 593, 605, 722
Infuhr, Teddy 593, 597
Ingersoll, Felice 604
Ingram, Jack 144, 146, 148, 185, 272, 296, 312, 314, 333, 397, 406, 421, 425, 443, 449, 451, 459, 470, 476, 586, 608, 634, 712
Ingraham, Lloyd 67, 100, 103, 119, 162, 257, 375, 380, 397, 399, 406, 413, 447, 459
Iron Eyes see Cody, Iron Eyes
Irvin, Billy 79
Irvin, Francis 599
Irving, George 33, 75

Irving, Richard 518, 540
Irwin, Boyd 193, 537, 549
Irwin, Charles 85, 182, 589, 616
Irwin, Patrick 216
Isabelita 495; *see also* Baron, Lita
Ivo, Tommy 635, 720

Jackson, Selmer 116, 129, 161, 177, 218, 243, 298, 352, 434, 462, 463, 499, 522, 558, 601, 632, 656
Jackson, Thomas E. 16, 57, 467, 516
Jackson, Warren 284, 426, 626
Jacobs, Harrison 164, 385
Jacoby, Michael (Michel) 235, 408, 467, 508
Jaffe, Carl 311
Jagger, Dean 361, 426, 427
James, Alan (Alvin J. Neitz) 136, 142, 146, 176, 359, 368, 401
James, Claire 394, 451, 512
James, John (Johnny) 273, 451, 454, 460, 524, 532, 557, 573, 588, 595
James, Walter 17
Janney, Leon 17, 289
Janney, William 89
Jannsen, Else 440
Janssen, Eilene 432
Jaquet, Frank 269, 292, 414, 428, 445, 450, 624, 630, 650, 668
Jares, "Brother" Frank 722
Jarvis, Nina 255
Jason, Will 522, 542, 551, 569
Jeffory, Alan 705
Jeffreys, Anne 440
Jeffries, Jan 649, 678
Jeffries, Jim 20
Jenkins, Allen 675, 684
Jenkins, Meg 312
Jenks, Frank 442, 528, 570, 632, 649, 656, 675
Jenks, Si 6, 8, 9, 12, 40, 63, 67, 359
Jennings, Maxine 158
Jergens, Adele 621, 648
Jerome, Jerry 331
Jeske, George 20, 341
Jewell, Hollis 151
Jewell, Isabel 361, 457, 565
Jiminez, Soledad 188, 453

Jiminez, Yadira 670
Johns, John 49
Johnson, Anne 101
Johnson, Ben 700
Johnson, Doretta 609
Johnson, Edna 345
Johnson, Erskine 424
Johnson, Howard 424
Johnson, Kathy 634
Johnson, Linda 473
Johnson, Marion Page 442
Johnson, Noble 520
Johnson, Raymond K. 212, 219, 224, 225, 226, 229
Johnson, Robert Lee 118
Johnson, Hall, Choir 139
Johnston, Agnes Christine 558
Johnston, Clint 594, 610, 623, 677, 680
Jolly, I. Stanford 205, 210, 217, 253, 254, 274, 281, 312, 313, 321, 348, 359, 391, 415, 444, 447, 448, 450, 464, 504, 521, 535, 550, 566, 575, 588, 606, 664, 669, 676, 679, 682, 686, 688, 692, 694, 695, 697, 699, 701, 706, 707, 711, 721
Jolley, Normand 526
Jones, Ben 506
Jones, Buck 274, 284, 299, 305, 316, 324, 332, 338, 348
Jones, Dickie 142, 193
Jones, Fenton "Jonesy" 626
Jones, Gordon 241, 610, 643, 680
Jones, Griffith 206
Jones, Grover 218
Jones, Harry O. *see* Fraser, Harry
Jones, Haywood 549
Jones, Jack 110
Jones, Jane 141
Jones, Marcia Mae 153, 220, 233, 246, 272, 283, 720
Jones, Ray 136, 271, 348, 363, 400, 459, 464, 470, 473, 476, 477, 497, 506, 511, 524, 526, 527, 584, 588, 613, 624, 644, 650, 661, 677, 679, 694
Jons, Beverly 532, 565, 581
Jordan, Bobby 232, 257, 260, 282, 288, 309, 325, 330, 344, 353, 360, 367, 428, 465, 486, 490, 494, 503,

Name Index

520, 530, 538
Jordan, Charles 242, 336, 341, 351, 352, 356, 362, 372, 414, 418, 428, 438, 444, 491, 594
Jordan, Louis, and His Tympany Five 474
Jordan, Ted 696
Jorgensen, Alf 662
Jorman, Mildred 551
Jory, Victor 377
Joseph, Edmund 101
Josselyn, Talbert 574, 660
Journet, Marcel 605
Joy, Leatrice 246
Joy, Liya (Joyzelle) 73
Joyce, Jean 166, 189, 200
Judd, Forest 492, 564
Judd, John 383
Judels, Charles 353, 461
Judge, Arline 61, 98, 99, 306, 442
Judge, Naomi 35, 36

Kaaren, Suzanne 101, 149, 265
Kafka, John 407
Kamel, George 352, 366
Kandel, Aben 525
Kane, Edward (Eddie) 11, 18, 20, 28, 98, 172, 261, 291, 292, 295, 342, 607
Kane, Michael 89
Kane, Whitford 534
Kann, George E. 143
Karina, Sandra 141
Karlan, Richard 639, 654
Karloff, Boris 158, 174, 187, 205, 235, 243
Karlson, Phil (Philip N. Karlstein) 422, 438, 442, 456, 465, 474, 479, 480, 490, 493, 501, 528, 536, 543
Karlstein, Philip N. see Karlson, Phil
Karnes, Robert 668, 670, 695
Karns, Roscoe 298
Karns, Todd 698
Kasper, Ann 101
Katzman, Sam 211, 232, 242, 257, 260, 264, 282, 288, 291, 309, 313, 322, 325, 330, 342, 344, 353, 356,

360, 367, 374, 379, 394, 395, 404, 409, 410, 411, 428, 430, 439, 448, 450, 454, 478, 487, 495, 512
Kauffman, Irwin 522
Kaufman, Joseph 457, 471, 479, 493
Kaufman, Millard 693
Kauss, Gina 334
Kavanaugh, Frances 279, 286, 290, 296, 307, 312, 318, 346, 359, 368, 375, 384, 388, 393, 401, 405, 446, 451
Kaye, Gayle (Gail) 71, 84
Kaye, Leo 530
Kayne, Jan 665
Keane, Edward 198, 207, 217, 314, 361, 427, 441, 638
Keane, Raymond 21
Keane, Robert Emmett 465, 466, 469, 471, 530, 548, 583, 585, 621, 631
Keays, Vernon 417, 421
Keckly, Jane 74
Keefe, Cornelius 72, 139
Keefer, Phil 97
Keeler, Harry Stephen 96, 99
Keene, Tom 125, 128, 134, 140, 276, 279, 286, 290, 296, 307, 312, 318
Keener, Hazel 242, 273
Keith, Donald 22
Keith, Ian 359, 361, 372, 393, 403, 428, 503
Kellard, Robert 281, 303
Kellard, Roy 249
Kelley, Albert 42
Kelley, P.J. 288
Kelley, Sharon Ann 710
Kellogg, Bruce 491, 568
Kellogg, John 599, 681, 698
Kellogg, William 245
Kelly, Jeanne see Brooks, Jean
Kelly, John 145
Kelly, Judy 255
Kelly, Kitty 69
Kelly, Lew 166, 342
Kelly, Nancy 387
Kelly, Paul 29, 446, 463
Kelsey, Fred 264, 428, 455, 466, 505, 580
Kelso, Edmond 171, 190, 241, 256, 259, 261, 268, 272, 283, 287, 300,

320, 329, 336, 341, 373, 438, 474
Kemper, Doris 592, 651, 665
Kemper, Ray 660
Kendal, Victor 306
Kendall, Cyrus 401, 403, 422, 436, 439, 546, 547
Kennedy, Bill 485, 530, 545, 556, 559, 572, 586, 601, 602, 603, 627, 658, 664, 669
Kennedy, Dawn 490
Kennedy, Douglas 663, 692
Kennedy, Edgar 80, 87, 95, 302, 331, 351, 725
Kennedy, Jack 59, 65, 67, 151, 161, 164, 205, 243
Kennedy, Tom 505, 560, 593, 607, 621, 629, 641, 675, 696, 704
Kenney, Jack 272
Kent, Barbara 40, 44
Kent, Christopher 662
Kent, Crauford 28, 31
Kent, Dorothea 208, 432, 479, 493
Kent, Julia 510
Kent, Kenneth 266
Kent, Robert 157, 160, 168, 391, 399, 481
Kent, Travis 531
The Kentucky Jubilee Singers 163
Kenyon, Gwen 303, 320, 322, 351, 362, 392, 445
Kerby, Marion 251, 263
Kern, Johnny 593
Kerr, Donald 160, 210, 253, 265, 297, 438, 467, 556, 602, 626, 634
Kerr, Geoffrey 262
Kerrigan, J.M. 177
Kerry, Daniel 489
Keyes, Peggy 119
Keyes (Keys), Stephen 419, 476
Keys, Bob 713
Keys, Stephen see Keyes, Stephen
Kibbee, Guy 498
Kibbee, Milton 176, 242, 427, 444, 450, 455, 478, 487, 495, 512, 640, 657
Kieffer, Philip 67
Kilian, Mike 547
Kilian, Victor 168, 440
Kilpatrick, Reid 424, 444, 452, 546
Kimbell, Anne 706, 713

King, Betty 631
King, Brett 668
King, Bruce 238
King, Charles 13, 21, 27, 35, 36, 39, 51, 125, 130, 131, 149, 152, 155, 159, 162, 165, 167, 171, 179, 185, 189, 195, 212, 218, 226, 229, 265, 284, 295, 296, 299, 305, 316, 318, 321, 332, 333, 346, 349, 354, 357, 358, 365, 375, 376, 383, 384, 393, 401, 405, 419, 423, 431, 459, 532, 550
King, Charles, Jr. 173
King, Claude 85
King, Franklin 294, 407, 427, 440, 484
King, Henry, and His Orchestra 374, 396
King, Jack 284
King, John 203, 217, 238, 245, 252, 254, 258, 263, 271, 277, 280, 285, 293, 301, 306, 310, 321, 327, 333, 340, 346, 349, 354
King, Louis 17, 18, 22
King, Matty 648
King, Maurice 294, 315, 328, 361, 377, 407, 427, 440, 484
King, Max M. 339, 350, 364
King, Nancy Louise 245
King, Patty 585
King, Pee Wee, and His Golden West Cowboys 449
King, Walter Woolf 330
Kingdon, Edith 84
Kingsford, Guy 292, 306, 340, 681
Kinnell, Murray 57
Kippen, Manart 331
Kirby, George 314, 356
Kirby, Jay 554, 573
Kirk, Joe 288, 309, 330, 396
Kirk, Michael 361
Kirkland, Alexander 47
Kirkwood, Jack 631
Kirkwood, James 163
Kirkwood, Joe (Jr.) 481, 498, 534, 546, 570, 587, 605, 620, 633, 649, 678
Kissinger, Miriam 499, 507
Kivari, C.K. 689
Klein, Robert 31

Name Index

Kleniyi, Edward 725
Knaggs, Skelton 614
Knapp, Evalyn 157, 265
Knapp, Jack 150
Knight, Fuzzy 132, 138, 664, 669,
   674, 677, 682, 688, 691, 695, 699,
   701, 712, 713
Knight, June 262
Knight, Vic 536
Knowlden, Marilyn 153
Knox, Alexander 199
Knox, Elyse 422, 432, 481, 498, 508,
   534, 546, 556, 570, 601, 605
Knox, Mickey 608
Knox, Mona 696, 714
Knudsen, Peggy 547
Koenig, Mendie 439, 450, 455
Kohler, Fred, Jr. 108, 307, 604
Kolb, Clarence 710
Kolker, Henry 96, 107, 111, 362
Koontz, Bill 715
Kornman, Mary 106, 164, 227
Kortman, Robert 54, 55, 67, 131,
   136, 140, 227, 413
Kosleck, Martin 574
Krafft, John W. 98, 107, 116, 133,
   164, 168, 236, 303, 339, 385
Krah, Marc 653
Krasne, Philip N. 197, 201, 204, 208,
   213, 362, 386, 392, 403, 414, 415,
   429, 436, 445, 453
Kreuger, Knud 278
Krone, Fred 689
Krueger, Lorraine 362
Kruger, Otto 463
Krupa, Gene, and His Orchestra 542
Krusada, Carl 225, 226, 229
Kuhn, Mickey 525
Kulkowich, Henry "Bomber" *see*
   Kulky, Henry
Kulky, Henry (Henry "Bomber"
   Kulkowich) 629, 722
Kyne, Peter B. 40, 657

Labarr, Marta 262, 304
Lackey, William T. 30, 40, 46, 59,
   62, 65, 71, 74, 79, 88, 91, 93, 104,
   112, 154, 158, 161, 170, 174, 178,

205, 220, 233, 243, 372
Lackteen, Frank 10, 26, 702
Lacy, Adele 21
Ladd, Alan 251
Laidlaw, Ethan 2
Lairch, Effie 641
Laird, Effie 706
Lake, Alice 59
Lake, Arthur 93, 564
Lake, Florence 62, 697, 712
Lally, Mike 675
LaMal (LeMal), Isabel (Isobel,
   Isabelle) 31, 160, 273, 337
LaMarr, Sammy 593
Lamb, Ande 336, 343, 404, 448
Lambie, Jack 124
Lamont, Charles 102
Lamont, Larry 41
Lancaster, Cliff 704
Lancaster, Iris 90
Landers, Lew 448, 657, 693, 716
Landers, Perc 684, 705
Landis, Carole 637
Landon, Harold 253
Landon, Lois 314
Landres, Paul 638, 659, 660, 714
Lane, Charles 536
Lane, Lenita 101
Lane, Nora 203
Lane, Richard 422, 498
Lane, Vicky 436
Lang, Charles 612, 625, 653
Lang, June 269, 278, 411
Lang, Karin 418
Lang, Melvin 235, 239
Langdon, Harry 292, 374, 399, 410
Lange, Elaine 499
Lantz, Lois 518
LaPlanche, Rosemary 548
Largay, Raymond 536
Larkin, John 47, 163
LaRoux, Carmen 106, 155
Larsen, Keith 710
Larson, Bobby 385
Larson, Christine 554, 566, 567,
   573, 579, 582
Larson, Eba 295
LaRue, Frank 14, 53, 130, 136, 144,
   156, 167, 171, 185, 190, 202, 224,
   231, 237, 238, 284, 346, 413, 425,

458, 459, 464, 473, 475, 477, 482, 504, 511, 523, 527, 535, 541, 544, 550, 552, 555, 557, 572, 576
LaRue, Jack 154, 281, 352, 368, 385, 386, 404, 416, 531
Lasky, Jesse, Jr. 92
Laszlo, Alexander 481
LaTorre, Charles 578, 645
Latorre, Don 135
Lattel (Latell), Lyle 339, 594
Laurenz, John 389, 445
Lauter, Harry 583, 656, 668, 675, 689, 708, 711
LaVerne, Lucille 37
Lawrence, Bert 593, 609, 614, 632, 641, 648, 656, 665, 675, 696, 713, 722
Lawrence, Bill 309
Lawrence, Del 267
Lawrence, Marc 344, 440, 534
Lawson, Bobby 185
Lawson, Eleanor 314
Lawson, Kate 689
Lawson, Wilfred 199, 255, 317
Lawton, Donald 665
Lawton, Frank 206
Lazarus, Erna 124, 478, 565, 610
Leary, Nolan 573, 608
Lease, Rex 142, 144, 285, 354, 446
Leavitt, Douglas 382
Leavitt, Norman 569
LeBaron, Eddie, and His Orchestra 398, 670
Lebedeff, Ivan 124, 174, 329, 339, 408, 418
LeBessoniere, Erin 33
LeBorg, Reginald 481, 515, 534, 546, 570, 578, 593, 599, 605, 623, 649, 678
Lechner, William 675
Lederman, Ross 411
Lee, Allan 51
Lee, Anna 206, 525
Lee, Billy 298, 343
Lee, Connie 291
Lee, Dixie 75
Lee, Dorothy 265
Lee, Etta 99
Lee, Gwen 32
Lee, Leon 16, 22

Lee, Norman 180, 250
Lee, Phyllis 64
Lee, Ruth 355, 442, 452, 585
Lee Tong Fu 174, 187, 539, 568
Leeds, Herbert I. 651
Lefeaux, Charles 262
Leffingwell, Tom 466
le Guriadec, Lois 262
Leiber, Fritz 436, 525
Leigh, Frank 121, 409
Leigh, Nelson 548, 673
Leighton, Lillian 52
LeMal, Isabel (Isobel, Isabelle) see LaMal, Isabel
Lender, Mary Lou 132, 147
Lenhart, Billy see Butch and Buddy
Leonard, Jack 233
Leonard, Murray 546
Leonard, Sheldon 490, 496, 518, 560, 570
Leong, James B. 99, 123
Leopold, Ethelreda 394
LeRoy, Dickie 678
LeSaint, Edward 64, 102
Leslie, Edith 540
Leslie, Maxine 189, 200, 227, 236, 265, 323, 351
Lesser, Julian 565
Lessey, George 392
Lester, Susan 432
Lester, Vickie 256
Letz, Mike 417
Levering, Joseph 189
Levy, Joel, Jr. 432
Levy, Melvin 717
Lewis, Catherine 292
Lewis, Cullen see Collins, Lewis D.
Lewis, George J. 337, 383, 392, 418, 420, 453, 483, 493, 502, 549, 550, 567, 572, 581, 582, 696
Lewis, Harry 583, 605, 621
Lewis, Henry 616
Lewis, Joseph H. 232, 242, 257, 264
Lewis, Maxine 211
Lewis, Ralph S. 72, 412, 416, 417, 420, 421, 432, 435, 440, 442, 546
Lewis, Rivers 519, 524
Lewis, Robert 635
Lewis, Sybil 373
Lewis, Vera 494

Name Index

Lexy, Edward 308
Libaire, Dorothy 108
Libby, Fred 651
Lichter, Baron James 580, 668
Light, Robert 101
Linaker, Kay 122, 164, 188, 207, 343
Lincoln, Carlyn 19
Linda, Hala 121
Linden, Doris 302, 331
Linden, Eric 151
Linden, Judith 251
Lindfors, Viveca 662
Lindgren, Orley 700, 717
Lindsay, Les 35
Lindsay, Margaret 43, 426, 536
Lingham, Tom 83
Linn, Ralph 387, 438
Lipson, Jack "Tiny" 440
Litel, John 389, 516, 683, 698
Little Angelo *see* Rossitto, Angelo
Little Rascals (Our Gang) 727
Littlefield, Lucien 59, 175, 331, 350, 356, 398, 560
Littlefield, Ralph 394
Littleton, Scott 329, 364
Lively, William 211, 232, 242, 557
Livesey, Jack 628
Livingston, Robert 581
Llewellyn, Richard 637
Lloyd, Doris 44
Lloyd, George 158
Lloyd, Jimmy 678
Lloyd, Rollo 107, 303
Loder, John 304, 311
Loff, Jeanette 98
Loft, Arthur 160, 392, 416, 456
Logan, Clarence 225
Logan, James E. 527
Logan, Stanley 623
Logue, Charles 47, 96, 108, 114, 150
London, Jack 182, 239, 261, 426
London, Tom 27, 31, 34, 54, 140, 149, 167, 173, 179, 190, 202, 225, 226, 229, 245, 276, 277, 279, 290, 293, 316, 324, 332, 359, 365, 545, 600
Long, Audrey 547, 558, 657, 667
Long, Jack 19, 23
Long, Lotus 96, 99, 174, 187, 249
Long, Marcia 710

Long, Walter 140, 152, 165, 197, 270
Longden, John 199, 317
Lono, James 366
Loo, Bessie 187
Loo, Richard 174, 187, 235, 568
Lorber, Steve 234
Lorch, Theodore 27, 35, 47, 48, 54, 76, 99
Lord, Del 486
Lord, Marjorie 635
Lorenz, John 648
Lorimer, Louise 161
Loring, Teala 462, 463, 480, 490, 501, 510, 515, 520
Loudermilk, Romaine, and His Ranch House Cowboys 234
Louie, Ducky 446
Louis, Joe 481
Louise Massey's Westerners 159
Love, Montagu 366
Lowe, Edmund 315, 418, 440, 466
Lowe, Sherman L. 41, 121, 201, 335, 396
Lowell, Robert 556, 580
Lowery, Robert 323, 329, 341, 347, 348, 373, 382, 399, 441, 457
Lowry, Ed 73
Lubin, Arthur 89, 105, 111
Lubin, Lou 427, 440, 587
Luby, S. Roy 238, 245, 252, 254, 258, 263, 271, 277, 280, 285, 293, 301, 310, 321, 327, 333, 343, 357, 363, 369
Lucas, Wilfred 20, 38, 45, 52
Ludwig, Edward 69
Luez, Laurette 625, 703
Lufkin, Sam 107
Luft, Sidney 528, 553
Lugosi, Bela 99, 216, 264, 288, 313, 322, 342, 356, 367, 394, 409
Luke, Edwin 435
Luke, Keye 249, 272, 282, 283, 581, 594
Lundy, Kenneth 578
Lunge, Romilly 222, 250
Lyden, Pierce 413, 421, 449, 482, 497, 500, 511, 514, 519, 524, 545, 552, 563, 567, 571, 602, 661, 669, 679, 686, 688, 690, 694, 701, 715
Lydon, James 647

Name Index

Lyle, Clinton 71
Lyman, Abe, and His Orchestra 478, 522
Lynch, Gilda 289
Lynch, Roland 223, 231, 234
Lynch, Theodora 601
Lynn, Emmett 368, 375, 702
Lynn, Hilary 389, 408
Lynn, Peter George 175, 182, 187, 244
Lynn, Rita 503
Lynne, Betty 180
Lynwood, Burt 123
Lyon, Ben 240
Lytton, Bart 364
Lytton, J.C. 550, 554

MacBride, Donald 534, 542, 551, 560, 620, 633, 656
McCall, Jonathan 488
McCarey, Ray 93, 107
McCarroll, Frank 144, 219, 263, 271, 277, 286, 293, 357, 449, 451, 458, 460, 497, 573, 600, 615, 619, 622, 624, 627
McCarthy, John P. 1, 4, 19, 38, 39, 48, 49, 50, 51, 390, 412, 436
McCarthy, Mary C. 191, 210
McCarthy, Walter 607
McClean, Malcolm 465
McClung, Bob 181
McClure, Greg 587, 649
McClure, M'Liss 651, 671
McCollum, Warren 181, 192
McCormack (McCormick), Merrill 125, 130, 189, 195, 200, 305, 321, 630, 650, 679, 697
McCoy, Tim 136, 144, 146, 149, 274, 284, 299, 305, 316, 324, 332, 338
McCracken, Robert C. 546
McCulley, Johnston 143, 376, 390, 453
McDaniel, Hattie 91
McDaniel, Sam 440, 481
McDaniels, Etta 391
McDermott, Hugh 319
MacDonald, David 308

McDonald, Francis 7, 27, 34, 89, 453, 692
McDonald, Frank 553, 639, 653, 654, 671, 673, 680, 687, 708, 711, 718, 720
McDonald, George 598
McDonald, Ian 564, 587
MacDonald, J. Farrell 31, 109, 123, 132, 139, 147, 160, 203, 228, 302, 326, 337, 342, 345, 356, 360, 404, 420
MacDonald, Kenneth 371, 413, 458, 555, 716
McDonald, Rusty 447
McDonald, Wallace 22
McDougall, Roger 308
McDowall, Roddy 543, 577, 592, 610, 625, 643, 689
McDowall, Winefriede 577
McDowell, Claire 369, 408
McDowell, Nelson 23, 44, 110, 179, 189, 190, 202, 209, 226
McElroy, Bob 526, 535, 541
MacFadden, Hamilton 121
McFarland, Spanky 361
MacFarlane, Bruce 228
McGavin, Darren 472
McGee, Gordon 23
McGee, Pat R. 464
McGinnis, Terry 629
McGlynn, Frank 91
McGowan, John P. 138
McGowan, Robert 220, 233, 246
McGrail, Walter 136, 332
MacGrath, Leueen 304
McGuinn, Joe 221, 655
McGuire, Don 620, 633, 634
McGuire, John 264
McGuire, Paul 654, 673, 708
McGuire, William Anthony 80
McHugh, Jack 181
McHugh, Kitty 139
McHugh, Matt 91
McIntosh, Burr 62
McIntyre, Christine 284, 299, 303, 310, 332, 348, 365, 397, 413, 459, 470, 482, 514, 521, 530, 541, 638, 655, 677
Mack, Betty 3, 6, 12, 53
Mack, Billy 422

Name Index

Mack, Cactus 376, 488, 497, 500, 504, 511, 514, 517, 519, 521, 541, 557, 571
Mack, Helen 452
Mack, Jack 92
Mack, Roy 331
Mack, Tommy 542
Mack, Wilbur 79, 98, 158, 166, 235, 242, 265, 420, 558, 668, 683, 684
Mackay, Barry 214
McKay, Wanda 267, 326, 342, 361, 373, 385, 391, 394, 416, 438, 457, 528, 540, 558, 560, 568
McKee, Lafe 3, 19, 30, 36, 39, 40, 53, 56, 63, 70, 76, 77, 103, 106, 112, 209, 219
McKee, Pat 394
MacKeller, Helen 129, 153
McKenzie, Bob 35, 125, 126, 131, 248, 359
McKenzie, Ella 119
McKinney, Florine 117
McKinney, Mira Mae 292, 478
MacKinnon, Allan 308
MacLane, Barton 195
MacLaren, Mary 46, 147, 371, 459, 552
McLarnin, Jimmy 481
McLaughlin, Gibb 262
McLean, Bill 546
McLeod, Catherine 434
McMahon, Horace 546
McManus, George 505, 540, 580, 607, 629
McMurphy, Charles 423
McNally, James 215
McNaughton, Gus 240
Macollum, Barry 373
MacPhail, Angus 206
MacPherson, Harry 155
McQuarrie, Murdock 316
McTaggart, Bud 320, 338
McVea, Jack, and His Orchestra 522
McVeigh, Pat 302
McVey, Paul 249, 345, 352, 355, 380, 385
McWade, Marguerite 3
McWade, Robert 109
Madame Sul-Te-Wan 268, 373
Madison, Guy 717, 718, 719, 720

Madison, Noel 43
Main, Marjorie 135, 151, 154
Maitland, Ruth 266
Majors, Betty 476
Majors, Eddie 460, 470, 476, 573, 584, 588, 591, 606
Makeham, Elliott 206
Makheen, Elliot 628
Mallalieu, Aubrey 240, 250
Mallinson, Rory see Mallison, Rory
Mallison, Rory 537, 549, 556, 609, 640, 667, 668
Mallory, Boots 96
Mallory, Chad 705, 708
Malloy, Ace 682
Malo, Gina 250
Malvern, Paul 50, 51, 53, 54, 56, 58, 63, 66, 68, 70, 72, 73, 76, 77, 78, 81, 83, 85, 86, 90, 94, 96, 97, 100, 103, 106, 110, 113, 175, 182, 186, 193, 196, 235, 239, 244, 249, 261
Mamakos, Peter 592, 603, 675
Mandy, Jerry 232
Mangean, Teddy 331
Mann, Hank 104, 607, 648, 725
Manners, David 85
Manners, Marjorie 340
Manners, Sheila 10, 26
Manning, Knox 503
Manning, Robert 15, 21
Manone, Wingy 522, 659
Mapes, Ted 285, 301, 305, 327, 357, 397, 400, 449, 459, 468, 477
Marcelle, Lou 556
March, Nadine 180
Marcus, James 10, 21, 23, 35, 90
Maren, Jerry 407
Marin, Edward L. 57, 62
Marion, Charles R. 288, 347, 362, 370, 372, 380, 382, 385, 399, 599, 609, 614, 621, 632, 641, 648, 656, 665, 695, 696, 698, 705, 710
Marion, Sidney 580, 607
Marion-Crawford, Howard 214
Mark, Michael 481, 546
Marlowe, Frank 465, 480, 486, 510, 641
Marlowe, Jerry 295
Marmstedt, Lorens 662
Marquis, Margaret 139

367

Name Index

Marsh, Garry (Gary) 206, 262, 308, 628
Marsh, Joan 336, 379, 404
Marsh, Marian 88, 273, 281
Marsh, Tony 683
Marshall, Anthony 378
Marshall, Billy 361
Marshall, Charles "Red" 422
Marshall, Trudy 534
Marshall, Tully 30
Marston, Joel 594, 596
Martell, Donna 681
Martin, Al 228, 260, 264, 714
Martin, Bill 570
Martin, Chris-Pin 386, 531, 537
Martin, George 221
Martin, Helen 264
Martin, Jimmie 443, 519, 544
Martin, Marion 396
Martinez, Agapito 554, 557
Marvin, Frankie 447
Marvis, Kay see Gorcey, Kay Marvis
Marx, Max 166, 599
Marx, Neyle 389, 436
Mason, A.E.W. 266
Mason, Elliot 262
Mason, Herbert 311
Mason, James 128
Mason, Jean 1
Mason, LeRoy 23, 26, 92, 100, 103, 107, 140, 193, 238, 270, 307, 375
Mason, Louis 562
Mason, Marty 593
Massey, Curt 159
Massey, Louise, Westerners 159
Masters, Howard 316
Mathews, Al 525, 528, 564
Mathews, Carl (Duke) 219, 224, 225, 226, 229, 238, 245, 252, 254, 258, 263, 271, 277, 280, 285, 293, 301, 310, 321, 327, 333, 340, 349, 354, 369, 378, 429, 436, 451, 458, 535, 541, 544, 545, 554, 557, 606, 619, 622, 627, 630, 636, 650, 666, 669, 672, 676, 685
Mathews, Horace 506
Mathews, Lester 164, 184
Matlock, Matty 659
Matthews, Forrest 488, 549, 559, 570

Maude, Beatrice 615
Maxey, Paul 275, 283, 492, 593, 594, 596, 670, 705
Maxwell, Edith 29, 72, 105
Maxwell, John 275, 295, 303, 355, 426
May, Joe 407
Mayberry, Lin 599
Maynard, Ken 359, 368, 375, 384, 388, 393
Maynard, Kermit 238, 254, 310, 327, 332, 333, 346, 349, 365, 383, 390, 477, 523, 532, 617, 642, 644
Mayo, Frank 466
Mayo, George 69
Mazurki, Mike 465
Meacham, Charles 31
Meade, Bill 717
Meade, Lawrence 289
Meader, George 424, 574
Meadows, Denny see Moore, Dennis
Means, Grant 564
Medina, Patricia 693
Meehan, Elizabeth 44
Meehan, Lew 106
Meeker, George 186, 439, 450, 455, 462, 469, 492, 567
Mehaffey, Blanche 2
Meilsey, Fred 289
Melford, Frank 565
Meller, Robert 102
Melton, Frank 275, 313
Melton, Sidney 528
Melzer, B.F. 649
Menzies, Tommie 548
Mercer, Beryl 11, 64, 84, 163
Mercer Brothers 670
Mercier, Louis 525
Merkel, Una 396
Merriam, Charlotte 57, 64
Merrick, Doris 457
Merrick, John 649
Merrill, Dick 124
Merrill, Walter 157
Merritt, George 180, 199, 206, 304
Merton, John 129, 142, 145, 146, 148, 149, 159, 160, 221, 234, 239, 284, 321, 357, 363, 368, 369, 378, 413, 419, 425, 443, 449, 464, 473,

475, 500, 511, 568, 606, 611, 613, 619, 622, 636, 661
Merton, Roger 190, 231, 234
Meserow, Albert J. 105
Messinger, Gertrude 34, 605
Metcalf, Bradley 118, 161
Methot, Mayo 147, 184
Meyer, Torben 599
Michael, Gertrude 387, 389, 463
Michel, Jacques Max 308
Michelsen, Jerry 424
Michelson, Esther 556
Middlemass, Robert 315
Middleton, Charles 1, 494, 580
Middleton, Guy 262
Mikeler, Eugene 398
Miles, Arthur 430, 494
Miles, Betty 221, 259, 276, 286, 290, 296, 359, 368, 388, 405
Miles, Vera 710
Miljan, John 102, 278, 297, 341, 547
Millakowsky, Herman 387
Millan, Lynn 583
Millen, James Knox 109
Miller, Carl 46
Miller, Charles 249, 418
Miller, Fred 549
Miller, Herb, and His Orchestra 374
Miller, Kristine 623, 689
Miller, Lorraine 460
Miller, Marion 353
Miller, Mollie 536
Miller, Ray 342, 353, 356
Miller, Sidney 178, 309, 372, 399, 438
Miller, Walter 13
Milletaire, Carl 671
Millett, Arthur 18, 27, 28, 34
Millfield, Charles 494
Millican, James 667
Mills, Edith 646
Mills, Edwin (Eddie) 360, 377
Mills, Joe 9
Mills, John 214
Mills, Mort 722
Mills, Warren 478, 487, 495, 512, 522, 542, 551
The Mills Brothers 347
Milne, Peter 398, 533

Minjir, Harold 61
Mintz, Sam 569
Mirisch, Walter 515, 556, 589, 616, 635, 640, 645, 663, 667, 681, 683, 692, 695, 700, 703, 723
Mischel, Joseph 465
Mist-A-Shot 281
Mitchell, Belle 478, 495, 512, 665
Mitchell, Bruce 73
Mitchell, Cameron 683
Mitchell, Charlie 536
Mitchell, Frank 215
Mitchell, Howard 191
Mitchell, Irving 272, 313, 320, 336
Mitchell, Pat 687
Mitchum, Robert 407, 427
Mix, Art 36, 66, 219, 231, 376, 470, 608
Moehring, Kansas 324, 376, 419, 437, 517, 555
Molieri, Lillian 453
Mollison, Henry 127
Monahan, Richard 675
Mong, William V. 22, 37, 108
Monroe, Tom 609
Montana, Hombre 722
Montgomery, Doreen 266
Montgomery, Jack 219
Montgomery, R. 250
Montoya, Alex 488, 502, 510, 531
Mooney, Martin 177, 195, 309, 339, 350, 361, 486
Moore, Carl Deacon 615
Moore, Clayton 313
Moore, Dennis (Denny Meadows) 110, 165, 176, 183, 188, 191, 195, 196, 200, 211, 232, 234, 260, 265, 274, 282, 288, 305, 332, 348, 357, 363, 369, 378, 413, 429, 447, 459, 513, 555, 557, 595, 606, 608, 622, 627, 636, 642, 647, 658, 661, 666, 715
Moore, Dickie 44, 102, 564, 592, 625
Moore, Ida 598, 599
Moore, Vin 95, 115
Moraine, Lyle 129, 141
Moran, Frank 332, 367, 409, 593
Moran, Jackie 153, 220, 233, 246, 272, 283, 438, 478, 487, 495

Name Index

Moran, Lee 111
Moran, Pat 578
Moran, Patsy 223, 231, 339, 344, 379, 395, 439, 448, 455, 544
Morante, Milburn 254, 321, 332, 348, 358, 365, 371, 376, 458, 468, 524, 532, 545, 550, 552, 557, 561, 566, 571, 579, 597, 606, 611, 622, 624, 630, 639, 644, 650, 658, 666
Moreland, Alexandria 251
Moreland, Mantan 189, 191, 210, 227, 236, 241, 244, 256, 261, 268, 272, 283, 300, 306, 337, 338, 351, 362, 370, 373, 392, 403, 414, 435, 444, 456, 480, 491, 507, 539, 549, 562, 568, 581, 594
Moreno, Antonio 143
Morgan, Byron 196
Morgan, Frank 522
Morgan, Gene 218, 220
Morgan, John 50, 609
Morgan, Ralph 88, 122, 153, 315, 424, 462, 618, 704
Morgan, Loumell, Trio 370
Morgan, Russ, and His Orchestra 522
Moriarity, Pat 195
Morison, Patricia 355, 389
Morley, Karen 109, 591
Morley, Kay 519, 526, 573
Moro, Nick 312, 318
Moroz, "Big" Ben 570
Morrell, George 51, 68, 148, 149, 258, 332, 348, 358, 365, 400, 406, 412, 417, 419, 421, 423, 425, 458, 497, 504, 511, 563, 588, 704
Morris, George 462
Morris, Johnnie (Johnny) 153, 203, 239
Morris, Wayne 654, 680, 702, 716
Morrison, Chuck 231, 234
Morrison, "Sunshine Sammy" 232, 242, 257, 260, 282, 288, 309, 325, 330, 344, 353, 360, 367, 404
Morrow, Neyle 675, 719
Morse, Terry 491, 499
Morton, Charles 186
Morton, Danny 534
Morton, James C. 73
Moscov, George V. 427

Moss, William 472
Moustafa, Amira 499
Movey, Paul 364
Movita 120, 143, 182, 188, 317
Mowbray, Alan 334, 461
Mower, Jack 20, 546, 593, 609
Mudie, Leonard 444, 485, 681, 703, 723
Muir, Esther 289
Mulhall, Jack 264, 280, 282, 294, 303, 309, 339, 344, 350, 353, 356, 367
Mullahy, Donn 157, 282
Murdoch, Janet 577
Murdock, Perry 36, 45, 48, 51, 113
Murphy, Edna 11
Murphy, Horace 126, 155, 159, 167, 171, 173, 185, 197, 238, 274, 446, 454, 460
Murphy, Joseph P. 225
Murphy, Ralph 461
Murray, Arthur 540
Murray, Charles, Jr. 368, 393, 405, 410
Murray, Hugh 552
Murray, James 7, 16
Murray, John T. 105, 160
Murray, Zon 460, 506, 513, 523, 526, 541, 550, 552, 588, 591, 652, 676, 677, 685
Muse, Clarence 163, 242, 264, 281, 534
Musgrove, Gertrude 262
The Musical Tornadoes 171
Mycroft, Walter C. 255, 319
Myers, Harry 37
Mylong, John 623, 708
Myton, Fred 146, 148, 173, 281, 679, 699

Nagel, Anne 118, 127, 137, 154, 160, 168, 184, 387, 507
Nagel, Conrad 434, 558
Naish, J. Carrol 57
Napier, Alan 206, 525, 614
Napier, Elmer 436, 437, 451
Narisco, Grazia 569
Nash, George 35, 44, 46, 48, 49, 53,

54, 55, 56, 58, 67, 72, 74, 76
Nash, Noreen 693
Nataro, James 479
Natteford, Jack 292
Nazarro, Cliff 331, 347, 498
Neal, Tom 287, 326, 342, 653, 660, 675
Nedell, Bernard 463
Neff, Bill 683
Negley, Howard 507, 549
Neill, Noel 408, 478, 487, 495, 512, 522, 542, 551, 569, 584, 594, 601, 658, 679, 709
Neill, Richard R. 580
Neise, George 343
Neitz, Alvin J. see James, Alan
Nelson, Billy 440
Nelson, Bobbie (Bobby) 9, 44, 100
Nesbitt, Cathleen 250
Nesmith, Otila (Ottola) 251, 278
Neumann, Kurt 377
Neville, John T. 58, 132, 139, 145, 147, 153, 160, 172, 188, 244
Newbury, Gayl 184
Newell, William 490, 705
Newfield, Sam 144, 148, 149, 197
Newill, James 197, 201, 204, 208, 213, 230
Newman, Sam 562
Newton, Robert 590
Newton, Theodore 52
Niblo, Fred, Jr. 583
Nichols, Bob 696, 698
Nigh, Jane 618, 640, 657, 692, 695
Nigh, William 65, 72, 73, 74, 78, 99, 116, 118, 124, 127, 135, 143, 145, 151, 158, 161, 164, 174, 178, 187, 195, 205, 218, 235, 243, 291, 309, 313, 389, 408, 434, 452, 463, 475, 483, 502, 510, 556, 558
Nixon, Ruth 637
Noflin, Harold 599
Nokes, George 585, 631, 651, 671
Nolan, Bruce 259
Nolan, Mary 20
Nolbandov, Sergei 206
Nolte, William L. 19, 171, 349, 357
Noone, Jimmy, and His Orchestra 410
Norcross, Van 373

Norman, Jack see Willis, Norman
Normand, Jack 360
Normand, Mabel 725
Norris, Edward 314, 352, 366, 386, 496, 601, 612, 625
Norris, Jay 546
Norris, Margaret 15
The Northwesterners 155, 185
Norton, Edgar 408
Norton, Jack 426, 441, 444, 466, 491, 505
Nosler, Lloyd 6, 12, 15, 110
Nosseck, Max 440
Nova, Lou 481
Novarro, Estrelita 173
Novis, Donald 396
Nugent, Edward (Eddie) 88, 91, 93
Nurney, Fred 599

Oakland, Vivian 80
Oakman, Wheeler 33, 142, 144, 182, 195, 292, 320, 342, 353, 356, 367, 391, 411, 428, 448
O'Brien, Billy 70
O'Brien, Dave 152, 155, 159, 167, 169, 173, 176, 195, 197, 201, 204, 208, 211, 213, 218, 223, 225, 230, 232, 239, 242, 260, 273, 278, 288, 292, 299, 324, 335, 342, 344
O'Brien, Jimmy 580
O'Brien, William J. 599, 609
O'Bryne, Robert 514
O'Connell, Arthur 303, 306
O'Connor, Frank 265, 683
O'Connor, John 599
O'Connor, Maureen 135
O'Connor, Robert Emmett 22, 99, 135
O'Day, Nell 333
O'Dell, Doyle 267, 277
O'Dell, Kent 614
Odin, Susan 700
O'Donnell, Gene 236, 239, 243, 256, 275, 283, 295, 320, 336
O'Donnell, Jack 203
O'Donnell, Joseph 142, 149, 419, 423, 669, 674, 676, 697
Offerman, George, Jr. 181, 542, 675

Name Index

O'Flynn, Damian 362, 610, 623, 645, 680
O'Gatty, Jimmy 593
O'Hanlon, George 341, 381, 587
O. Henry see Henry, O.
Ohman, Phil, and His Orchestra 396
O'Herlihy, Dan 577
Oliver, Barry 20
Oliver, Charles 308
Oliver, Gordon 150
Olsen, Larry 452
Olson, Ole 197
O'Malley, Pat 16, 30, 182, 186, 520
O'Neil, Sally 67
O'Neill, Jean 151
O'Neill, Kitty 334
Oppenheim, E. Phillips 78
Orkow, B. Harrison 426, 432
Orlando, Don 134
Ornitz, Sam 446
Orosco, Henry 489
Ortego, Artie 8, 12, 68, 70, 76, 77, 81, 83, 90, 94, 97, 106, 274, 348, 358, 363, 365, 376, 445, 475, 482, 502, 506, 511, 517, 523, 535, 545, 552, 575, 597, 624, 630, 669
Orth, Marion 89, 96, 120, 137, 151, 154, 207, 218, 220, 418
Ortiz, Manuel 481
Orton, J.O.C. 214
Osborne, Bud 41, 128, 130, 140, 152, 156, 183, 209, 223, 224, 252, 293, 305, 332, 338, 344, 346, 348, 354, 358, 365, 371, 383, 400, 401, 405, 406, 412, 413, 417, 421, 429, 431, 436, 443, 445, 449, 464, 474, 517, 519, 526, 538, 544, 552, 561, 567, 571, 573, 575, 576, 584, 586, 588, 595, 597, 602, 606, 608, 615, 622, 624, 630, 636, 650, 669, 679, 688, 690, 697
Osborne, Frances 587
Osborne, Vivienne 46
Osborne, Will, and His Orchestra 474
Oscar, Henry 255
Oscar, John 6
O'Shea, Jack 527, 537, 538, 677
O'Shea, Michael 518

O'Shea, Oscar 147, 177
Osterloh, Robert 583
Oswald, Richard 334
Otto, Henry 60
Our Gang see Little Rascals
Overman, Jack 442, 493, 515, 546
Owen, Arthur E. 216
Owen, Cary 493
Owen, Jean Z. 668
Owen, Michael 450
Owsley, Monroe 82

Packer, Netta 516
Padden, Sarah 108, 151, 184, 218, 273, 302, 332, 406, 425, 454, 481, 534, 546, 604, 627
Padula, Margaret 353
Page, Addison 92
Page, Anita 42
Page, Bill 722
Page, Bradley 104, 115, 300, 334, 343, 350
Page, Paul 46
Page, Ray 684
Page, Roberta 115
Paia, Hawksha 366
Paiva, Nestor 457, 472, 531, 548
Pallette, Eugene 484
Palma, Joe 512
Palmer, Andraia 302
Palmer, J.L. 28
Palmer, Jasper 460, 506, 513, 537
Palmer, Lilli 250
Palmer, Tex 51, 68, 70, 81, 83, 113, 126, 130, 134, 155, 212, 225, 229, 231, 258, 263, 271, 280, 285, 293, 301, 307, 310, 312, 318, 321, 340, 346, 349, 354, 359, 401, 407, 644
Pangborn, Franklin 75, 87, 102
Panzer, Paul 5
Pardee, Doc 203
Park, Post 267, 532, 545
Parker, Bonnie Jean 517
Parker, Cecilia 54, 55, 63
Parker, Edward (Eddie) 68, 83, 90, 94, 97, 103, 125, 443, 449, 458, 459, 467, 504, 511, 514, 517, 566, 586, 604

Name Index

Parker, Edwin 196
Parker, Franklin 62, 65
Parker, Fred 221
Parker, Jean 151, 218, 265, 402, 418, 433
Parker, Jefferson 105
Parker, Norton S. 193
Parker, Phyllis 689
Parks, Eddie 374, 525, 594
Parkyakarkus (Harry Einstein) 396
Parnell, Emory 377, 518, 640, 675, 720
Parnell, James 711
Parrish, Enid 146
Parrish, Gigi 88, 93, 112
Parrish, Helen 380, 578, 612
Parry, Harvey 660
Parsons, Edwin C. 117, 150, 196
Parsons, Lindsley 66, 77, 81, 90, 103, 106, 113, 157, 166, 181, 192, 236, 241, 256, 268, 272, 275, 283, 287, 300, 303, 306, 320, 329, 336, 341, 351, 352, 355, 366, 370, 373, 380, 381, 382, 399, 402, 416, 426, 432, 433, 442, 465, 472, 474, 486, 492, 509, 536, 543, 577, 592, 596, 603, 610, 612, 625, 626, 639, 643, 653, 654, 659, 670, 673, 680, 687, 702, 716
Parsons, Milton 480, 490, 562
Patch, Wally 222, 262
Paton, Wally 146, 261
Patrick, Gail 46, 387
Patrick, Nigel 637
Patterson, Gerry 586
Patterson, Herbert 599, 609
Patterson, Pat 447
Patterson, Shirley (Shawn Smith) 383
Pauiloa, Satini 366
Paul, Johnny 451
Paul, Les 522
Paul, Russell 134
Pavelec, Teddy 520, 546
Pawley, Edward 118, 151
Pawley, William 204, 230
Paxton, Dick 542, 548, 694, 705
Paylow, Clark 363
Payne, James 681
Payson, Blanche 367

Pearce, Adele 188; *see also* Blake, Pamela
Pearson, Ford 536
Peil, Edward, Sr. 76, 77, 98, 99, 144, 171, 277, 285, 293, 313, 332, 339, 514
Pembroke, George 223, 228, 260, 264, 294, 313
Pembroke, Scott 133
Pendleton, Nat 287
Pendleton, Steve 719
Penn, Clifford 515
Penn, Leonard 495, 554, 573, 576, 617, 630, 642, 674, 677, 722
Pennick, Jack 59
Penrose, Charles 216
Peoples, Bob 665, 675, 683, 684, 689, 696, 705
Pepper, Barbara 326
Pepper, Buddy 178
Peralta, Gabriel 475
Percival, Walter 33
Perez, Olga 670
Perkins, Gil 689
Perkins, Kenneth 702
Perkins, Peter 566, 572
Peroix, Elizabeth 424
Perrin, Jack 224, 240, 252, 500
Perrins, Leslie 180
Perry, Bob 440
Perry, Jack 69
Perry, John 319
Perry, Pascale 48, 584
Pertwee, Roland 206
Pertwer, Jon 628
Peters, George 545
Peters, House, Jr. 575, 576, 624, 661, 666, 694, 701, 721
Peters, John 175, 193
Peters, Ralph 138, 152, 157, 166, 192, 236, 256, 414, 593, 659
Petrie, Hay 637
Phelan, Pat 598
Phelps, Buster 64, 71
Phelps, Lee 145, 332, 343, 486, 565, 588, 602, 609, 717
Phelps, Tex 68, 81, 97, 110
The Phelps Brothers 138
Phillips, Charles 253
Phillips, Eddie 31, 37, 129, 327

Name Index

Phillips, Herbert O. 424
Phillips, Norman 528
Phillips, Paul 411
Phillips, William 667
Phipps, William 692, 720
Pichel, Irving 44
Pickard, Dad 454
Pierce, Jack 231
Pierce, Jim 234, 237
Pierce, Paul 694
Pierlot, Francis 472, 696
Piersall, Richard 226
Pierson, Carl 113
Pierson, GeGe 382
Pigott, Tempe 44, 181
Pilbeam, Nova 319
Piltz, George 120
Pittard, Bob 265
Pitts, Zasu 320
Pludow, Bernard 684
Plummer, Rose 248, 378
Plympton, George 245, 257, 448
Pola, Andre 574
Poland, Joseph 644, 686, 688, 690,
    707, 712, 715
Pollard, Daphne 353
Pollard, Snub 20, 155, 159, 167, 213,
    342, 344, 353, 563
Pomeroy, Roy J. 82
Pope, Gloria 439
Porcasi, Paul 60, 65, 98, 298, 399
Porter, Uriel 637
Porter, William Sidney see Henry,
    O.
Portia, Rosemary 288
Post, Charles A. 15
Post, Guy Bates 117
Potter, Bill 575, 576, 579, 595, 597,
    600, 604, 606, 611
Poulos, Angi O. 599
Powers, Tom 698
Prager, Stanley 498, 570, 587, 649
Pratt, Gil 25
Pratt, Purnell 62
Preisser, June 478, 487, 495, 512,
    522, 542, 551, 569
Presnell, Robert, Sr. 516, 533
Press, Marvin 708
Pressel, Frederick 410
Preston, Joey 551

Price, Hal (Harry) 58, 63, 66, 70,
    126, 128, 130, 144, 148, 179, 183,
    200, 237, 259, 274, 299, 301, 312,
    343, 349, 369, 376, 388, 397, 400,
    401, 405, 406, 413, 423, 443, 449
Price, Nancy 255
Price, Stanley 231, 276, 279, 286,
    296, 333, 369, 383, 390, 406, 459,
    486, 646, 652, 658, 661, 666, 669,
    674, 676, 677, 682, 686, 688, 690,
    691, 694, 697, 707, 709, 715, 721
Pring, Gerald 216
Pringle, Aileen (Eileen) 17, 84, 422
Printzlau, Olga 64
Prival, Lucien 28, 52, 158
Prosser, Hugh 406, 413, 419, 429,
    433, 440, 512, 650, 709
Prouty, Jed 59, 265, 275
Pryor, Roger 320, 330, 436
Puglia, Frank 153, 205
Puig, Eva 305, 436
Punay, Rito 499
Purcell, Dick 166, 178, 191, 198, 268,
    337, 380, 416
Purdell, Reginald 247
Purdy, Constance 540, 621
Pyle, Denver 697, 715

Qualen, John 525, 564
Quigley, Charles 198
Quigley, Rita 297, 387, 507
Quillan, Eddie 370, 372, 457, 634
Quillan, John 115
Quine, Richard 84
Quinn, Louis 528
Quinn, Thomas R. 18, 419, 423,
    425, 431, 443, 449, 464, 582
Quon, Marianne 392

The Radio Rogues 374
Rafferty, Frances 695
Ragan, Mike see Bane, Holly
Raison, Milton 177, 188, 213, 263,
    386
Raker, Lorin 79, 87, 104, 111
Ralston, Esther 47, 123

Name Index

Rambeau, Marjorie 418, 432
Ramos, Bobby, and His Band 484
Ramsey, George 547
Ramsey, Quen 263
Randall, Addison 117
Randall, Jack 119, 126, 130, 138,
  142, 148, 152, 156, 162, 165, 169,
  176, 183, 192, 200, 209, 212, 219,
  224, 225, 226, 229, 361
Randall, Lorraine 128
Randall, Rebel 471
Randle, Karen 621
Randolph, Amanda 723
Randolph, Jane 486
Randolph, Lillian 281
Rankia, Doris 137
Rankin, Arthur 50
Rasch, Buck see Rasch, Wilson
Rasch, Wilson (Buck) 155, 185
Rathmell, John 155, 167, 197, 238,
  293
Rau, Neil 434
Rauzena 662
Rawlins, John 565
Rawlinson, Herbert 154, 260, 281,
  294, 297, 330, 339, 343, 351, 389
Ray, Albert 31, 33, 43
Ray, Allan 467
Ray, Joey 668, 675, 714
Ray, Marcelle 233
Ray, Nicholas 474
Ray, Phil 180, 250
Ray, Sonny 44
Raymond, Jack 222, 247, 344
Raymond, Robin 408
Raynor, William (Bill) 639, 659,
  670, 673, 687
Rea, Gennaro 136, 138
Redwing, Rodd 405
Reece, Ruth 203
Reed, Barbara 328, 471, 479, 493,
  509
Reed, Donald 86
Reed, Luther 62
Reed, Marshall 383, 397, 400, 406,
  423, 425, 437, 468, 473, 482, 500,
  511, 517, 521, 524, 535, 544, 545,
  554, 559, 563, 566, 571, 576, 579,
  584, 586, 597, 600, 608, 613, 624,
  630, 642, 644, 646, 647, 650, 658,
  664, 669, 672, 674, 676, 677, 679,
  682, 685, 686, 690, 691, 701, 709,
  715
Rees, Lanny 523
Rees, Sonny 545
Reese, John 708
Reese, Joy 439
Reeve, Alice Means 407
Reeves, Richard 712
Regan, Phil 461, 474, 508
Regas, George 67, 121
Regas, Pedro 9, 453
Reich, Albert 352
Reicher, Frank 435, 466, 471, 518,
  546
Reid, Dorothy (Mrs. Wallace Reid)
  92, 101, 111, 120, 127, 220, 227,
  233, 244, 246, 269
Reid, Wallace, Jr. 108
Reid, Mrs. Wallace see Reid,
  Dorothy
Reinhardt, John 317, 533
Reinhart, Dick 516, 524, 532, 544,
  573
Remington, Colt 552
Renaldo, Duncan 143, 436, 445, 453
Renaldo, Tito 453
Rennie, Michael 317
Rense, Danny 704
Repp, Ed Earl 371
Retford, Ella 637
Revier, Dorothy 22
Rey, Rosa 467
Reynolds, Craig 145, 164, 170, 174,
  203, 205, 218, 452
Reynolds, Jack 719
Reynolds, Margorie 152, 175, 178,
  186, 187, 193, 196, 205, 210, 217,
  235, 241, 287, 722
Rhoads, Nell 101
Rhodes, Grandon 635
Riano, Renie 505, 540, 580, 607,
  629
Rice, Florence 295, 325
Rice, Jack 398
Rich, Dick 208, 328
Rich, Frances 31, 41
Rich, Freddie, and His Orchestra
  422
Rich, Irene 239

Name Index

Richards, Addison 314, 343, 380, 385, 389, 408, 452, 455, 456, 462, 485, 585
Richards, Frances 314, 345
Richards, Grant 139
Richards, Keith 591, 602
Richards, Tom 716
Richardson, Jack 10, 19, 582
Richey, Jean 670
Richmond, Grant 154
Richmond, Kane 462, 471, 479, 485, 493, 558
Richmond, Ted 323
Richmond, Warner 86, 119, 126, 128, 129, 165, 176, 197, 215, 221, 231, 234, 401
Ricketts, Shirley (Shirley Jane Rickey) 97
Rickey, Shirley Jane see Ricketts, Shirley
Ricks, Archie 51, 70, 110, 226
Ridgely, John 578, 635, 692
Ridgeway, Fritzi 73
Riebe, Loren 144
Riffel, Jon 626
Rigby, Edward 590, 637
Riley, Mike, and His Orchestra 353
Rilla, Walter 266
Rima, Carlo 262
Ring, Cyril 370, 380, 399
Rio, Eddie 593
The Rio Brothers 670
Riordan, Marjorie 483
Rios, Patricia 642
Ripps, Don 542
Ritchie, Jean 659
Ritter, Tex 155, 159, 167, 171, 173, 179, 185, 189, 190, 202, 215, 221, 223, 231, 234, 237, 248, 253, 259, 267
Rivero, Julian 2, 38, 169, 488, 531, 547, 625
Rivers, Jack 460, 470, 476, 488, 506, 519, 524, 554, 573
Roach, Bert 493, 496
Roach, Margaret 226
Robards, Jason (Sr.) 30, 37, 60, 175, 186, 193, 196, 205, 606
Robbins, Gale 503
Rober, Richard 710

Roberson, Chuck 606, 611
Roberts, Allene 565, 616
Roberts, Ben 295
Roberts, C.E. 28
Roberts, Charles 53
Roberts, Desmond 84
Roberts, Florence 104
Roberts, J.H. 250
Roberts, Jeanie 93
Roberts, Lee 384, 523, 613, 644, 646, 655, 658, 661, 669, 672, 679, 682, 685, 686, 688, 701, 715
Roberts, Lynne 653
Roberts, Ralph 304
Roberts, Stanley 136, 138, 142, 144, 149
Roberts, Stephen (Steve) 364, 424, 698
Roberts, Ted 701
Roberts, Thayer 539, 540
Roberts, Tracey 634
Roberts, Whitey 614
Robertson, Guy 87
Robertson, Willard 98
Robins, Sam 282, 309, 322
Robinson, Dewey 170, 230, 328, 334, 344, 403, 426, 427, 438, 440, 441, 462, 474, 479, 493, 503, 546, 548
Roc, Patricia 199, 247
Roche, Aurora 445
Rochelle, Claire 225
Rockwell Jack 68, 94, 97, 126, 305, 400, 413, 443, 449, 459, 468, 477, 482, 527
Rockwood, Roy 589, 616, 703
Rocquemore, Henry 36, 39, 45, 51, 74, 100, 103, 148, 153, 233
Rodriquez, Mike J. 215
Roeca, Samuel 583, 634, 638, 654, 660, 708
Rogell, Sid 52
Rogers, Charles 292
Rogers, Ginger 31
Rogers, Jean 466
Rogers, John 84, 426
Rogers, Kent 178
Rogers, Ruth 179
Roland, Gilbert 334, 475, 483, 502, 510, 525, 531, 537

Name Index

Rolfe, Charles 317
Rolph, Alice 720
Romaine, Ruth 79, 86
Roman, Ric 660
Romanoff, Constantine 1, 67
Romas, Charles 126
Romay, Lina 587
Romm, Harry A. 474
Rooney, Ann 487, 495
Rooney, Mickey 109, 118
Rooney, Pat 3
Root, Elizabeth 612
Roper, Jack 259, 546, 570, 587, 649
Ropes, Bradford 461
Rorke, Hayden 700
Ros, Ramon 370, 659
Roscoe, Alan 37
Rose, Stan 551
Rosen, Phil 30, 36, 40, 46, 47, 52,
    60, 71, 150, 163, 239, 249, 265,
    273, 278, 288, 294, 298, 314, 352,
    366, 392, 403, 409, 414, 415, 432,
    435, 444, 445, 466, 469, 471
Rosenbloom, Maxie 330, 372, 411,
    430, 448
Rosener, George 197
Rosenwald, Francis 547
Rosing, Bodil 87
Rosner, Gezade 525
Ross, Ann 8, 26
Ross, David 194
Ross, Michael 621, 656, 665, 684
Rossitto, Angelo 187, 288, 322
Roth, Gene (Gene Stutenroth) 386,
    392, 424, 456, 503, 574, 704, 712
Roth, John 366
Roubert, Matty 132, 514
Rousseau, Louise 454, 460, 476, 596
Roux, Tony 670
Rowan, Don 157, 166, 192
Rowland, Henry 721
Roy, William 623
Royal, Charles Francis 123
Royal, Michael 615
Royce, Frosty 369
Royle, William 187, 195, 213, 218
Rub, Christian 515
Rubien, A.J. 442
Rubin, Benny 197, 291, 292, 309
Rubin, Jack 553

Rubin, Stanley 496, 518, 570
Rubini, Jan 360
Ruby, Mike 722
Rudley, Herbert 496
Ruhl, William 166, 428, 433, 456,
    465, 480, 486, 490, 492, 503, 520,
    535, 543, 544, 548, 555, 556, 560,
    561, 562, 570, 574, 578, 599, 600,
    602, 606, 611, 656
Ruick, Mel 303
Ruloff, Follette and Lunard 370
Rush, Dick 418
Rush, Jerry 381
Russell, Buck 705
Russell, Elizabeth 320, 322
Russell, Henry 465
Ruth, Mary 167, 281, 297
Ruth, Phyllis 229
Rutherford, Jack 189, 245, 253
Ruthuen, Madeline 82
Ryan, Dick 282, 309, 330, 505, 540,
    580
Ryan, Edmond 216
Ryan, Edward 609
Ryan, Irene 362, 370, 386, 399
Ryan, Sheila 605, 626
Ryan, Tim 362, 370, 380, 386, 399,
    402, 416, 420, 430, 433, 441, 442,
    465, 474, 480, 486, 490, 494, 501,
    505, 520, 530, 538, 540, 548, 560,
    562, 568, 574, 578, 580, 594, 601,
    607, 629, 684, 696, 705, 712, 713,
    722
Rydberg, Viktor 662
Ryland, Cecilia 27
Ryland, George H. 533
Ryter, Frederick 19

Sachs, Beryl 374, 379, 391, 404
The Saddle Pals 460, 476, 488, 524
St. Clair, Arthur 335, 396
St. Clair, Maurice 398, 434, 439
St. John, Adela Rogers 69
St. John, Al ("Fuzzy") 17, 25, 63,
    148, 192, 213, 725
St. Leo, Leonard 468, 473
St. Maur, Adele 64
St. Polis, John 120, 137, 149, 158,
    163, 181, 227, 233

377

Sais, Marin 189, 229
Sale, Virginia 44, 427
Salew, John 311, 637
Sande, Walter 300, 547, 605, 723
Sanders, George 696
Sanders, Sherman 538
Sands, John 693
Sanford, Erskine 424, 577
Sanford, Ralph 177, 396, 432, 433, 438, 553, 570, 651, 659, 708
Sanford, Stanley J. "Tiny" 31, 55
Santley, Fred 292
Santley, Joseph 79, 98
Sarecky, Barney A. 356, 391, 517, 519, 521, 523, 524, 526, 527, 535, 541, 545, 555, 559, 563, 566, 572, 575, 579, 582, 586, 591, 597, 602, 604
Sargent, Lewis (Louis) 19, 51
Sauber, Harry 102
Saunders, Gloria 684, 687
Saunders, Nancy 636
Savitt, Jan, and His Orchestra 495
Sawyer, Joe 481
Saylor, Syd 14, 104, 295
Sayre, George Wallace 366, 381, 389, 426, 434, 456, 462, 543, 558, 638
Sayre, Jeffrey 195
Scannell, Frank 420, 528
Scardon, Paul 546, 562
Schaefer, Armand 53, 66, 67
Schary, Dore (Jeb) 65, 372, 465
Schenz, Judy 486
Schnitzer, Gerald 322, 342, 353, 548, 560, 578, 593, 599, 609
Schofield, Paul 61, 175
Schrock, Raymond 486, 491
Schumm, Hanz 339
Schwabacher, Leslie 364
Schwalb, Ben 657, 698, 714
Scobee, Merle 155, 185
Scobee, Ray 155, 185
Scott, Bob 565
Scott, Dick 416, 426
Scott, Ewing 716
Scott, Randolph 64
Scotto, Aubrey 117
Scully, Peter 585, 598, 631, 651, 671
Seal, Peter 367

Searl, Jackie 49
Sebastian, Dorothy 1
Sebastian, Julio 625
Sedan, Rolfe 154, 236
Sedden, Margaret 49
Sedley, Harry 35
Seeley, Kay 311
Seidel, Tom 276, 290, 312, 314, 318, 358
Seider, Frank 7
Seiler, Conrad 269
Sekely, Steve 373, 387
Selander, Lesley 594, 667, 683, 692
Sell, Bernard 430
Selwynne, Clarissa 84
Semels, Harry 36, 200
Semon, Maxine 651, 671
Sennett, Mack 725
Sepulveda, Carl 357, 363, 369, 429, 506, 513, 521, 554
Sergeant, Charles 185
Seroff, Muni 392, 415
Sessions, Almira 472, 706
Seward, Edmond 486, 490, 494, 520, 530, 538, 548, 560, 574, 578, 593
Sewell, Allen B. 412
Sewell, Anna 47
Seymour, Dan 520, 603, 649
Shade, Jamesson 417
Shamberg, Bernard D. 546
Shannon, Harry 657
Shannon, Peggy 60
Sharland, Reginald 82
Sharpe, David 128, 152, 219, 270, 340, 346, 349, 354
Sharpe, Karen 714, 723
Shaw, Al 208
Shaw, Anabel 533, 599
Shaw, Anthony 308
Shaw, Charles 289
Shaw, Danny 355
Shaw, Janet 256, 407, 444, 480
Shaw, Montague (C. Montague Shaw) 82, 306
Shay, John 496, 556, 562, 583
Shayne, Robert 467, 479, 501, 601, 643, 717
Shea, Gloria 80, 89, 102, 105
Shea, Jack 546

Sheehan, John 73, 182, 556
Sheffield, Johnny 589, 616, 635, 645, 663, 681, 703, 723
Sheffield, Reginald 3, 145
Sheldon, Barbara 68
Sheldon, Jerry 284, 299
Sheldon, Julie 251
Sheldon, Kathryn 147, 181, 274, 275
Sheldon, Mary 396
Sheldon, Norman 470
Sheldon, Sidney 295, 323
Shelton, Bob 454
Shelton, John 339, 570, 583
Shepard, Courtland 705
Sheridan, Frank 198
Sheridan, James 110, 119, 125, 128, 169, 183, 200, 276, 286, 290, 296, 307, 318; *see also* Tansey, Sherry
Sheridan, Paul 308
Sherin, Leo "Ukie" 684, 705, 713, 722
Sherlock, Charles 444
Sherman, Edward 422
Shermatova, Shuma 126
The Sherrill Sisters 404
Sherwood, Bobby 551
Sherwood, Gail 543
Sherwood, Lydia 206
Shields, Arthur 657
Shields, Frank 118
Shilling, Marion 11, 18, 112
Shiner, Ronald 222, 240, 247
Shirk, Adam Hull 73, 243
Short, Dorothy 159, 165, 254, 288
Short, Lew 25
Shrum, Cal, and His Rhythm Rangers 253, 458
Shrum, Walt 253
Shubert, Nancy 66
Shuford, Andy 2, 5, 8, 10, 13, 23, 25, 26
Shumway, Lee 93, 98, 99, 273
Shumway, Walter 13, 271
Silverheels, Jay 512, 581, 603
Silverstein, David 60, 75, 87, 184, 294
Sim, Alastair 308
Simenon, Georges 590
Simmons, Michael L. 351
Simon, Simone 407, 590

Simpson, Gertrude 42, 86
Simpson, Russell 24, 67, 108, 120, 163, 538, 592, 653, 713, 718
Sinclair, Betty 330, 344, 428, 430, 439, 450, 455
Sinclair, Edward 317
Sinclair, Hugh 206
Siodmak, Curt (Kurt) 243
Sistrom, William 304
Sitka, Emil 546, 656, 675
The Six-Bar Cowboys 138
Skinner, Fred 399
Sklover, Carl 593, 609
Skutezky, Victor 590
Sky Eagle, George 335
Slack, Freddie, and His Orchestra 495
Slater, John 637
Slavin, Brad 470, 488, 506, 532
Sleeper, Martha 64, 102, 105
Sloan, Tod 20
Slocum, George 625
Sloey, Al 451
Smalley, Phillips 31
Smith, Arthur "Fiddlin'" 454, 460, 470, 476, 488, 519, 544, 550, 554, 557, 571, 576
Smith, Capt. Art 23
Smith, Capt. Verner L. 34
Smith, Charles 638, 659
Smith, Count John Maximillian 722
Smith, Darr 684
Smith, Evelynne 546
Smith, Georgann 396
Smith, Gerald O. 461
Smith, Jack C. 134, 267, 297
Smith, Jerry 252
Smith, Maime 289
Smith, Paul Gerard 398, 418
Smith, Robert 181
Smith, Roberta 410
Smith, Sharon 436
Smith, Sir C. Aubrey 434, 525
Smith, Tom 460, 608
Smith, Wonderful 287
Snegoff, Leonid 574
Snell, Earle 252, 254, 258, 271, 280, 285, 295, 301, 310, 411, 420, 428, 454, 470
Snowden, Eric 82

Name Index

Snyder, Billy 256, 542, 551
Soderling, Walter 486
Sorell, George 170
Sotello, Demas (Dimas) 437, 502
Sothern, Hugh 314
Southern, Eve 14
Southern, Jean 185
Southworth, Tommy 234
Sowards, George 624
Space, Arthur 297, 698, 703, 705, 712, 713
Sparks, Jack 571
Spaulding, George L. 539, 568
Spears, Jack 451
Spellman, Martin 164, 178, 218
Spence, Ralph 79
Spencer, Dean 127, 169, 183
Stacey, Patricia 268
Stacy, Jess 522
Stafford, Bess 92
Stafford, Hanley 705
Stamp-Taylor, Enid 319
Stander, Lionel 498, 578
Standing, Joan 84
Stanhope, Ted 295, 416, 668, 696
Stanley, Louise 142, 148, 162, 204, 212, 224, 230
Stanton, Paul 698
Starling, Pat 513
Starr, Sally 62
Starrett, Charles 42, 49, 62, 114
Staub, Ralph 204, 208, 230
Stedman, Myrtle 30, 71
Steel, Charles Q 247
Steele, Bob 34, 36, 39, 45, 48, 50, 56, 58, 373, 384, 388, 393, 401, 405, 412, 417, 421
Steele, Tom 340
Steers, Larry 546, 549
Stefani, Joseph 230
Stelita 155
Stelling, William 235
Stephens, Frank 420, 549
Stephens, Marvin 220, 300
Stephenson, James 180
Sterling, Alura 479
Sterling, Ann 428
Stevens, Cedric 436, 441
Stevens, Charles 412, 453, 464
Stevens, Craig 648

Stevens, Frank 442
Stevens, Onslow 589
Stevenson, Houseley 577, 598
Stevenson, Lew 99
Stevenson, Robert Louis 577
Stewart, Athole 206, 240, 262, 304
Stewart, Donald 318, 359, 393
Stewart, Eleanor 128, 140, 156
Stewart, Freddie 478, 487, 495, 512, 522, 536, 542, 551, 569
Stewart, George 355
Stewart, James 529
Stewart, Jerry 72
Stewart, Nick 722
Stewart, Peggy 701, 709
Stockdale, Carl 78
Stockman, Boyd 526, 535, 541, 545, 552, 554, 555, 571, 573, 575, 579, 582, 591, 595, 597, 600, 644, 691
Stoker, H.G. 214
Stone, Al 395
Stone, Arthur 98
Stone, Bobby 161, 178, 257, 260, 282, 309, 325, 330, 344, 353, 367, 379, 395, 404
Stone, Butch 542
Stone, Cliffie 544
Stone, George E. 65, 98, 114, 484
Stone, Milburn 116, 117, 124, 129, 141, 175, 186, 193, 196, 197, 201, 210, 328, 336, 350, 352, 594, 717
Stone, Paula 124
Storm, Gale 283, 300, 329, 330, 339, 347, 351, 373, 381, 382, 389, 434, 442, 461, 474
Storm, Jerry 41, 55
Stossel, Ludwig 255, 440
Strand, Jimmy 379, 395, 404, 408, 410, 428
Strang, Harry 146, 148, 149, 168, 565, 675
Strange, Glenn 83, 130, 140, 148, 162, 183, 192, 200, 209, 215, 219, 221, 223, 224, 258, 277, 286, 296, 299, 307, 321, 324, 327, 354, 359, 369, 378, 384, 405, 426, 502, 567, 614
Stratton, Gil, Jr. 647, 696, 705, 714
Stratton-Porter, Gene 88, 112, 151, 251, 300, 565

Strawn, Arthur 683
Street, Juanita 171
Street, Robert 295
Strode, Woodrow (Woody) Wilson 703
Strohbach, William 412, 417, 438, 441
Strong, Johnny 472
Strongheart, Nip T. 623
Strueby, Katherine 304
Stuart, Gloria 424
Stuart, Mary 585, 598, 631
Stuart, Nick 257, 379
Stuart, Sally 180
Stutenroth, Gene see Roth, Gene
Suedo, Julie 216
Sues, Leonard 291
Sujata 693
Sul-Te-Wan, Madame 268, 373
Sullivan, Barry 484
Sullivan, Charlie 465, 562, 593
Sullivan, Elliott 314
Sullivan, Francis L. 206
Sullivan, John Maurice 72
Sullivan, Wallace 364
Sully, Frank 283, 605, 620, 625, 633
Summers, Walter 216, 266
Summerville, Slim 725
The Sunshine Boys 596
The Sunshine Girls 429, 460
The Sunshine Serenaders 536
Sutherland, Eddie 725
Sutherland, Sidney 452, 463, 501
Sutton, Grady 62, 407, 580
Sutton, Kay 236, 256
Swain, Mack 20
Swan, Buddy 233, 608
Sydney, Basil 206, 319
Symon, Burk 598

Taggart, Ben 336
Talbot, Lyle 30, 31, 323, 408, 570, 587, 593, 594, 596, 632, 641, 643, 646, 655, 657, 658, 661, 676, 686, 690, 701, 703, 708, 709, 713
Talbott, Gloria 702
Taliaferro, Hal see Wales, Wally
Tamblyn, Eddie 62, 80

Tannen, William J. 657, 698
Tanner, Julius 196
Tansey, Robert (Robert Emmett) 113, 119, 125, 126, 128, 130, 134, 136, 140, 148, 152, 156, 159, 162, 165, 169, 176, 179, 183, 200, 202, 215, 221, 223, 231, 234, 237, 248, 253, 270, 276, 279, 286, 290, 296, 307, 312, 318, 340, 346, 349, 354, 359, 368, 375, 384, 388, 393, 401, 405, 613
Tansey, Sherry 126, 136, 148, 149, 152, 155, 156, 162, 165, 176, 179, 223, 231, 248, 312; see also Sheridan, James
Tarloff, Frank 382
Tate, Reginald 637
Taylor, Al 13
Taylor, Bud 571
Taylor, Charles T. 14
Taylor, Donald Dexter 469
Taylor, Dub "Cannonball" 532, 544, 550, 554, 557, 561, 567, 571, 573, 576, 584, 588, 595, 600, 608, 615
Taylor, Eddie 454
Taylor, Estelle 28
Taylor, Ferris 485, 505, 549
Taylor, Forrest 63, 119, 126, 128, 131, 140, 152, 162, 176, 189, 212, 215, 225, 229, 231, 232, 245, 259, 260, 271, 293, 333, 335, 346, 357, 378, 384, 396, 405, 406, 489, 568, 646, 666, 691
Taylor, Harry 551
Taylor, Kent 426
Taylor, Matt 298
Taylor, Ray 575, 579, 582, 586, 597, 602, 604
Taylor, Scott 540
Taylor, Steve 465
Tead, Phil 716
Teal, Ray 489, 493, 556
Tearle, Conway 96
Temple, Brooks 454
Tenbrook, Harry 31
The Tennessee Ramblers 259
Terhune, Max 238, 245, 252, 254, 258, 263, 271, 277, 280, 285, 293, 301, 310, 321, 327, 333, 340, 346, 349, 354, 357, 363, 369, 378, 572,

575, 579, 586, 591, 597, 604, 611
Terrell, Bill 618
Terrell, Kenneth 429, 445
Terriss, Ellaline 206
Terry, Bob 155, 159, 167, 185, 204, 208, 230
Terry, Richard (Dick) 242, 249, 295
Terry, Sheila 52, 94, 97
Terry, William 407
Thane, Dirk 252
Thayer, Guy V., Jr. 725
Thayer, Lorna 690
Thiele, William 467
Thimig, Helene 525
Thomas, Delmar 684
Thomas, Faith 310
Thomas, Jacqueline 558
Thomas, Jameson 40, 69, 71, 84, 85, 89, 96
Thomas, Jerry 644, 647, 684, 696, 705, 713, 722
Thomas, Lyn 610, 641, 643
Thompson, Cotton 524
Thompson, Gib 536
Thompson, Jimmy 536
Thompson, Kenneth 42
Thompson, Marshall 710
Thompson, Nick 263
Thorne, Nancy 710
Thorne, William L. 5, 11, 21, 25
Thorpe, Jim 237, 401
Thorpe, Richard 11
The Three Stooges 474
Thrower, Max 681
Thurston, Carol 716
Tibbetts, Martha 145
Tierney, Lawrence 440
Tilbury, Zeffie 72, 101, 129
Timm, Lee 19
Tinling, James 351
Tobias, George 702
Todd, Ann B. 663
Todd, Thelma 30
Toler, Sidney 392, 403, 414, 435, 444, 456, 469, 480, 491, 499, 507
Tomack, Sid 678
Tombes, Andrew 442
Tombragel, Maurice 661, 682, 691, 717, 718, 719, 720
Tomei, Louis 714

Tong, Kam 328
Toomey, Regis 20, 37, 92, 105, 123, 516, 533, 556, 660
Toones, Fred "Snowflake" 15, 18, 22, 37, 154, 354, 357, 364, 380
Torrence, David 84
Tors, Ivan 492
Totman, Wellyn 1, 4, 11, 12, 13, 21, 26, 32, 34, 35, 36, 38, 39, 51, 53, 72, 157, 166, 181, 278
Tracy, Lee 533
Tracy, Roy 289
Tracy, William 585
Trail, Armitage 31, 380
Trampe, Ray 181
Travell, George 339
Travis, June 150
Travis, Richard 364
Treadway, Charlotte 145, 420
Treadwell, Laura 505, 537, 556
Tree, Dorothy 174
Treen, Mary 474, 623, 632
Trent, Jean 307
Trent, John 175, 186, 193, 196
Trent, Philip 273
Troll, Max 525, 564
Trowbridge, Charles 160, 205, 469, 485, 558
Tryon, Glenn 400
Tucker, Harland (Harlan) 46, 265, 298
Tucker, Richard 24, 80, 89, 96, 188
Tucker, Robert 178
Tupper, Tristram 30, 40, 46, 57, 71, 91, 315
Turich, Felipe 531
Turich, Rosa 143, 155, 483, 502, 510, 538
Turkel, Joseph 609, 632, 641
Turner, Anita 466
Turner, Eugene 355
Turner, Maidel 80
Turner, Raymond 162
Tuttle, Bud 293
Tuttle, Burt R. 97
Tuttle, Frank 484
Tuttle, Wesley, and His Texas Stars 429, 454, 506, 513
Tyler, Harry 522, 542, 614, 632, 706
Tyler, Lela (Lelah) 392, 638

Name Index

Tyler, Tom 3, 6, 9, 12, 15, 19, 21, 27, 568
Tyrell, Ann 651
Tyson, Hilda 84

Ullman, Daniel B. 642, 646, 647, 650, 652, 667, 672, 685, 692, 694, 700, 701, 706, 709, 721
Ullman, James Ramsey 525
Ulmer, Edgar G. 361
The University of Arizona Glee Club 263
Urecal, Minerva 232, 273, 282, 322, 345, 353, 356, 367, 410, 430, 450, 457, 507, 525, 538, 614
Usher, Guy 95, 107, 114, 135, 151, 182, 187, 208, 235, 236, 239, 268, 295

Vague, Vera (Barbara Jo Allen) 626
Valdes, Miguelito 484
Valentine, John 441, 442
Valerie, Joan 671
Vallin, Rick 335, 360, 367, 381, 385, 432, 499, 592, 625, 693
Vallon, Michael 592
Vance, Lucille 342
Van Derman, Carol 637
Van Every, Billee (Bill) 69, 78
Van Horn, Emil 356
Van Sickle, Dale 634, 707, 716
Van Zandt, Phil 377, 415, 481, 485, 492, 496, 562, 665, 711
Varno, Roland 387
Vaughan, Alberta 81
Vaughan, Dorothy see Vaughn, Dorothy
Vaughn (Vaughan), Dorothy 118, 243, 246, 556, 593, 626
Vaughn, William 278, 318
Vecki, Isabelle 37
Vedder, William H. 560, 598
Velasco, Fred 155
Venable, Evelyn 139, 145
Venuti, Joe 522
Verdugo, Elena 489, 592, 594, 635, 639, 698

Vernon, Dorothy 226
Vernon, Glenn 632
Vernon, Wally 546, 570
Verschleiser, Ben 60, 64, 69, 80, 84, 98
Victor, Charles 590
Victor, Henry 268
Vidor, Charles 61
Vignola, Robert 64
Vigran, Herbert 273, 546
Vilirea, Julia 464
Villarias, Carlos 155
Villegas, Lucio 464
Vincent, Louis 141
Vincent, Russ 481
Vincent, William 629, 647, 648, 675, 705
Vine, William 361
Vinson, Helen 408
Vinton, Arthur 57, 59
Virgo, Peter 609
Vivian, Percival 696
Vlahos, John 271, 277, 280, 285, 293, 301, 310, 343
Vogan, Emmett (Jr.) 145, 351, 372, 379, 398, 408, 471, 474, 490, 499, 508, 530, 549, 574, 594, 599, 651
von Brincken, William 87, 95, 156, 170, 207
Von Eltz, Theodore 40, 246
von Morhart, Hans 278
von Seyffertitz, Gustav 72, 85
Vosburgh, John 28
Vosper, John 525
Vuolo, Tito 556

Wadsworth, Henry 355
Waggenheim, Charles 361
Waggner, George (Joseph West) 62, 65, 74, 93, 104, 112, 115, 175, 182, 186, 192, 193, 205, 218, 227, 236, 239, 244, 249, 275, 508
Wagner, William 84
Wainer, Lee 528
Wakely, Jimmy 245, 429, 446, 447, 451, 454, 460, 470, 476, 488, 506, 513, 519, 524, 532, 544, 550, 554,

557, 561, 567, 571, 573, 576, 584, 588, 595, 600, 608, 615
Walburn, Raymond 585, 598, 631, 651, 671
Walcott, Robert 593
Wald, Jerry, and His Orchestra 512, 522
Waldo, Janet 270
Waldridge, Harold 60, 75
Waldron, Wendy 624, 632, 660, 719
Wales, Ethel 30, 31
Wales, Wally (Hal Taliaferro) 53, 66, 189, 447
Walker, Bill 556, 568, 616, 723
Walker, Cheryl 210
Walker, Gertrude 361
Walker, Nella 61
Walker, Ray 59, 60, 65, 74, 79, 86, 98, 150, 377, 480, 609, 634, 675, 722
Walker, Robert 19, 209
Walker, Syd 240
Walker, Terry 129, 248, 264, 394
Walker, Wally 509, 549, 556, 603
Wall, Geraldine 414
Wallace, Beryl 134, 424
Wallace, Bryan 222
Wallace, Edgar 72, 199, 206, 216, 222, 247, 250
Wallace, John 131
Wallace, Morgan 147, 160, 172, 174
Wallace, Regina 525
Waller, Eddy 536, 667
Walling, William 9
Wallington, Jimmy 678
Walsh, Arthur 522
Walsh, George 47, 49
Walsh, Kay 222, 247
Walsh, Percy 214
Walter, Wilfred 216
Walters, Luana 53, 138, 238, 258, 274, 322, 324
Walthall, Henry B. 17, 30, 40, 71, 88
Walton, Douglas 82, 525, 533
Walton, Fred 85
Wandberg, Warren D. 654, 680
Wang, Richard 539
Wanger, Walter 693

Ward, Amelita 360, 455, 574
Ward, Blackjack 148
Ward, Michael Joseph 454
Warde, Anthony 314, 350, 361, 389, 403, 408, 420, 436, 438, 463, 480, 533, 537, 558, 593, 603
Ware, Irene 87, 115
Ware, Leon 547
Ware, Virginia 452
Waring, Leslie 222
Warner, H.B. 387, 424, 498
Warner, Jerry 505, 515, 538
Warren, Bruce 4, 109
Warren, C. Denier 262
Warren, Fred 99
Warren, Gloria 485, 499
Warren, Janet 435, 456
Warren, Julie 198
Warren, Phil 432
Warwick, John 222
Warwick, Robert 29, 161, 227
Washburn, Bryant 16, 22, 60, 193, 343, 352, 368, 404
Watkin, Pierre 120, 418, 420, 429, 439, 450, 463, 471, 479, 493, 495, 518, 520, 562, 583, 599, 618, 624, 696
Watson, Henrietta 206
Watson, William 198
Waxman, Max 284
Wayne, Frank 179
Wayne, John 63, 66, 68, 70, 76, 77, 81, 83, 90, 94, 97, 100, 103, 106, 110, 113
Wayne, Steve 696
Weaver, Marjorie 420, 441
Webb, Harry S. 209, 212, 219, 224, 225, 226, 229
Weeks, Anson, and His Orchestra 370, 659
Weeks, Barbara 9
Weeks, George W. 238, 245, 252, 254, 258, 263, 271, 277, 280, 285, 293, 301, 310, 321, 327, 333, 340, 343, 346, 349, 354, 357, 363, 369, 378
Weil, Richard, Jr. 442
Weisberg, Brenda 166
Welch, Niles 102
Welden, Ben 181, 503, 560, 593

Name Index

Welles, Virginia 587, 626, 670
Wells, Betty 344
Wells, Bill 231
Wells, Jacqueline (Julie Bishop) 79, 86, 251
Welsh, Robert 61
Welton, Danny 714
Wenland, Burt 603
Wentworth, Martha 282, 360
Werbiseck, Gesila 317
Weske, J. Victor 317
Wessel, Dick 486
West, Billy 41
West, Joseph see Waggner, George
West, Wally 106, 128, 149, 171, 215, 223, 286, 369, 384, 482
West, William 228, 260, 292
Westman, Nydia 75
Weston, Cecil 349
Weston, Don 488, 532, 550, 554, 557, 561, 571, 576, 600
Wexler, Paul 713
Whalen, Michael 261, 668, 694
Wheat, Lawrence 79
Whipper, Leigh 268
Whitaker, Charles "Slim" 19, 66, 148, 173, 192, 274, 280, 333
White, Alice 133
White, Dan 375, 376, 388, 393, 394, 417, 459, 556, 575
White, Jack 382
White, Lee "Lasses" 377, 426, 427, 429, 440, 445, 447, 451, 454, 460, 470, 476, 488, 506, 509, 513, 519, 524, 536, 568, 596
White, Paul 135, 139
White, Thelma 157, 364, 428
White Eagle 8
Whiteford, John "Blackie" 19, 23, 51, 70, 134, 159
Whitehead, Joe 435
Whitehead, O.Z. 713
Whiteman, Russ 530, 694, 699, 709, 715
Whitfield, Raoul 432
Whitfield, Robert "Smoki" 589, 616, 645, 663, 684, 703
Whitley, Crane 418
Whitley, Ray 138, 476, 554, 573, 584, 588, 600

Whitlock, Lloyd 1, 41, 68, 70, 94
Whitman, Alan 242
Whitman, Gayne 337
Whitman, Phil 29, 37
Whitney, Claire 427, 442, 473, 543, 561, 608
Whitney, Eve 510
Whitney, Gene 102
Whitney, Peter 518
Whitten, Marguerite 268, 283
Wifstrand, Naima 662
Wilcox, Art, and His Arizona Rangers 237
Wilcox, Vivian 341
Wilde, Lois 130
Wilding, Michael 319
Wiley, Hugh 158, 174, 187, 205, 235, 249
Wiley, Jan 285, 291, 301, 341, 345, 347, 348, 400, 433, 436, 438, 492
Wilhelm, Wolfgang 311
Wilke, Bob 712, 721
Wilkerson, Bill (Billy) 335, 538, 702
Wilkerson, Guy 288
Wilkins, June 209
Wilkins, Martin 306, 589, 681, 723
Willat, Irvin 131
William, Warren 472
Williams, Bill 604, 618, 657
Williams, C.B. 198, 207, 217
Williams, Charles 362, 389, 396, 668
Williams, D.J. 262
Williams, Guinn "Big Boy" 46, 150, 309, 329
Williams, Hugh 216
Williams, Jack 703
Williams, Mack 253
Williams, Marvin 649
Williams, Roger 144, 182
Williams, Sydney 347
Williams, T.R. 198, 207, 217, 228
Willing, Foy, and His Riders of the Purple Sage 451
Willingham, Willard 523
Willis, Matt 434, 489
Willis, Nolan 189, 190, 192, 202, 259
Willis, Norman (Jack Norman) 168, 345, 361, 445, 538
Willmering, Bill 504
Willock, Dave 675, 698

Willow Bird 335, 393
Wills, Bob, and His Texas Playboys 248
Wills, Walter 196
Wilsey, Jay *see* Bill, Buffalo, Jr.
Wilson, Charles 505
Wilson, Clarence 89
Wilson, Jack 705
Wilson, Lisa 705, 722
Wilson, Marie 323
Wilson, Max 551
Wilson, Warren 626, 643
Wilson, Whip 567, 582, 602, 606, 613, 617, 619, 627, 636, 642, 646, 652, 658, 664, 669, 674, 677, 682, 688, 691, 699, 709, 721
Wilton, Eric 549
Wilton, Robb 262
The Windmill Theatre Company 628
Windsor, Claire 40, 153
Windsor, Marie 330
Winkler, Robert 535
Winters, Gloria 647, 674, 696
Winters, Roland 539, 549, 562, 568, 577, 581, 592, 594, 625, 654
Wisbar, Frank Bentick 387
Withers, Grant 133, 158, 170, 174, 181, 187, 191, 195, 205, 210, 218, 220, 227, 235, 249, 446
Withers, Isabel 400
Wolfe, Bill 376, 482
Wolfe, Ian 408, 605
Wolfe, Sammy 546
Wonder, Tommy 161
Wong, Barbara Jean 507, 568
Wong, Bruce 174
Wong, Jean 467, 539
Wong, Victor 249
Wood, Brendan 282
Wood, Charles B. 179
Wood, Douglas 455
Wood, G.D. *see* DeMain, Gordon
Wood, Gloria 648
Wood, Grace 158
Wood, Marjorie 315
Wood, Natalie 710
Wood, Wilson 533
Woodbridge, George 317
Woodbury, Joan 131, 268, 294, 303, 337, 345, 352, 372, 403, 449

Woodell, Barbara 398, 416, 664, 692, 709, 710
Woodell, Woody, and His Riding Rangers 470
Woodford, Helen 569
Woodforth, Jack (Josiah Pitts Woolfolk) 74
Woodruff, Frank 398
Woods, Buck 217
Woods, Craig 390, 397
Woods, Donald 424, 635
Woods, Harry 324, 332, 338, 348, 358, 376, 388, 449, 483
Woodward, Bob 527, 544, 545, 550, 552, 554, 555, 557, 559, 561, 563, 566, 567, 571, 572, 575, 576, 582, 584, 586, 595, 597, 600, 602, 604, 608, 624, 650
Woodworth, Marjorie 422, 486, 496
Woolfolk, Josiah Pitts *see* Woodford, Jack
Woolrich, Cornell 75, 515, 516, 556
Worden, Hank 159, 171, 173, 369, 535, 678
Wormser, Richard 547
Worth, Constance 295, 440, 457, 611
Worth, Harry 132
Worthington, William 112
Wrather, Jack 516, 533, 547
Wray, Fay 170
Wright, Cobina, Sr. 361, 396
Wright, Mack V. 81
Wright, Wen 437
Wrixon, Maris 243, 350, 387, 462, 467
Wyatt, Charlene 154
Wyler, William 529
Wynne, Peggy 517, 684
Wynters, Charlotte 220

Yaconelli, Frank 165, 169, 176, 183, 209, 211, 212, 229, 286, 290, 296, 307, 312, 318, 483, 502, 510
Yaconelli, Lou 286
Yarborough, Barton 283, 468, 501, 528
Yarbrough, Jean 268, 272, 275, 283, 287, 300, 303, 306, 320, 323, 329,

Name Index

336, 341, 350, 585, 598, 609, 614, 620, 626, 631, 633, 634, 641, 643, 668, 670
Yarnell, Sally 441
Yerkow, Charles 708
Yetter, William 614
Yohalem, George 99
Yordan, Philip 377, 407, 427, 440, 484
York, Duke 170, 639, 653, 687, 717
Young, Carleton 148, 160, 168, 221, 223, 241, 257, 301
Young, Carroll 645
Young, Clara Kimball 4
Young, Clarence Upson 510
Young, Ernest F. 99
Young, Frank H. 395, 397, 406, 425, 431, 437, 443, 464, 473, 497, 527, 544
Young, Gerald 101
Young, Harold 328, 361, 364
Young, J. Arthur 273, 275, 278, 344, 345
Young, Lon 116, 129, 133, 141
Young, Mary 678
Young, Nedrick 496, 534, 693
Young, Polly Ann 77, 175, 182, 213, 228, 264
Youngman, Henny 422
Yukl, Joe 659
Yule, Joe 505, 540, 580, 607, 629
Yung, Victor Sen 491, 499, 507, 539, 549, 562, 568, 581

Zaner, Jimmy 389
Zanette, Guy 639, 680
Zaro and D'Lores 670
Zarova, Kalina 269, 434
Zeisler, Alfred 424, 472
Zelnik, Fred 240
Zucco, George 394, 409